GEORGE PELL

Defender of the Faith
Down Under

TESS LIVINGSTONE

GEORGE PELL

Defender of the Faith
Down Under

Foreword by
GEORGE WEIGEL

IGNATIUS PRESS   SAN FRANCISCO

Original edition published in 2002 by Duffy & Snellgrove
Potts Point, New South Wales, Australia
© 2002 by Tess Livingstone

Cover design by Roxanne Mei Lum

American edition © 2004 Ignatius Press, San Francisco
ISBN 0–89870–984–9
Library of Congress Control Number: 2003105168
Printed in the United States of America ∞

Contents

5

APPENDICES

For Jacinta Kate, thirteen, with infinite love

and

with gratitude to Father Tim Norris, P.P., S.T.L.
(Propaganda Fide), a dedicated soldier for
Christ on the front lines as Pastor of
Saint Kevin's, Geebung, since 1959

Foreword

George Pell's appointment as Archbishop of Sydney was a major news story across Australia—one that I could follow in real-time in Washington, D.C., thanks to the Internet. Having been Down Under just five months before Archbishop Pell's March 2001 transfer from Melbourne, I thought I knew at least something about the robust give-and-take of Aussie journalism. But it was difficult to recognize the man I had known for almost thirty-five years in many of the reports I read on his appointment to Sydney.

According to one feature story, a "key" to understanding Pell is his "love of Church trappings. . . . Back home in Melbourne, it is said, his vestments line his hall: gorgeous and theatrical." I do not know who was saying these things, but they obviously had not stayed in Archbishop Pell's home in Melbourne, as I had just done. There was nary a vestment on display in the halls, or anywhere else for that matter.

What I did see were books—books in profusion. The hallways were filled with packed bookcases. The floor behind Archbishop Pell's desk in his study was piled high with new titles in history, philosophy, theology, political theory, social and medical ethics. His sitting room held a year's worth of the back issues of the major opinion journals in the English-speaking world.

There are very few Catholic bishops anywhere who are, in fact, less interested in "Church trappings" than George

Cardinal Pell, whose sartorial style and self-presentation say "footballer" rather more than "metropolitan archbishop". By the same token, there are few who are so intellectually engaged or who read as widely. Inside and outside the Catholic Church today, bishops are usually thought of as managers. Throughout his fifteen years as a bishop, George Pell has lived an earlier model: the bishop as intellectual leader, the model pioneered by such giant figures of Western civilization as Ambrose and Augustine. The press accounts of Pell's Sydney appointment were also replete with charges that Pell is an authoritarian who enjoys imposing his judgments on others; the charges have continued ever since. It is an indictment that misses both the nature of episcopal leadership in the Catholic Church and the personality of George Pell.

The Catholic Church is not simply a voluntary association dedicated to humanitarian causes. It is a community of disciples who measure their fidelity according to an authoritative tradition, not according to their personal opinions. And that authoritative tradition, Catholics believe, binds and frees at the same time.

This is, admittedly, a difficult notion to grasp in cultures in which freedom has become largely synonymous with liberation from any "external" authority—which describes a lot of the Western world, unhappily. The Catholic Church, however, has a different understanding of freedom: like the nineteenth-century English scholar of the history of liberty, Lord Acton, the Catholic Church teaches that freedom is a matter, not of doing what we like, but of having the right to do what we ought. Freedom is not doing things "my way". Freedom is doing the right thing in the right way for the right reason, and as a matter of habit (which is another word for "virtue").

A Catholic bishop, teaching authoritatively, is speaking for the binding-and-liberating tradition of the Church. He is not imposing his personal opinions on the community. When Pope John Paul II teaches that using the natural cycles of fertility is the method of regulating births most consistent with human dignity, he is not teaching the personal moral opinions of Karol Wojtyla; he is proposing the settled teaching of the Catholic Church. Similarly, when Cardinal Pell teaches that homosexual acts are sinful, he is not imposing on others the personal crotchets of George Pell of Ballarat; he is teaching the moral truth that the Catholic Church has taught for two millennia. Bishops are servants, not masters, of the truth the Church carries in the world and proposes to the world. And bishops, if they are true to their episcopal ordination, must be faithful and courageous servants of the truth, even if fidelity involves personal risk—and George Pell has had ample reason to know that it sometimes does.

In understanding the Church's authoritative tradition, of course, the bishop ought to consult broadly with knowledgeable people. Similarly, bishops in a media age ought to take counsel with experienced men and women who can help bishops propose Catholic teaching so that it can be "heard" by others. And that brings us back to George Pell as a man.

During his years as Archbishop of Melbourne, Pell hosted a quarterly "think tank" of local intellectuals and activists in order to exchange ideas over dinner. I was fortunate enough to address one of these sessions in October 2000 and was struck by the diversity of the community of conversation in which George Pell lives. This is clearly not a man who likes his ideas or his intellectuals in one flavor. I was also impressed by the utter frankness of the debate, which Pell clearly relished. An archbishop who takes copious notes of

what others are saying (as I watched Pell do that night) is
a man who understands that teachers must study and learn
before they teach.

When I first met George Pell in 1967, I was struck by
the freshness of his personality and by his lack of clericalism. Those same qualities are manifestly alive in him today.
He combines the rugged good humor (and vocabulary) of a
star athlete with the intellectual edge of an Oxford-trained
historian and the piety of a convinced Christian disciple.
He is at home with lay people and children in a way that is
matched by few other senior Catholic prelates. He attracts
deep loyalties, not because he demands obeisance, but because he is a magnet for friendships that he works hard to
keep green.

That Cardinal Pell is a sign of contradiction in the Catholic Church in Australia and in Australian society, and indeed throughout the English-speaking world, is obvious. But
why? Pell has become a lightning rod, it seems to me, not
because he is the conniving, authoritarian heavy portrayed
by some, but because he has ideas—ideas that challenge the
dominant consensus among Western intellectual and cultural
tastemakers. And that, I suggest, is why the attacks on him
over the years have had a particularly venomous personal
character: as any debater knows, *ad hominem* arguments are
the last refuge of people who have the sneaking, nervous-
making suspicion that they are about to lose an argument
on the merits.

George Pell believes that there are truths embedded in the
world and in us. He is convinced that we can know those
truths and that, in knowing them, we incur certain moral
obligations. He believes that living according to those obligations is liberating, in the deepest sense of human freedom.
Nowadays, these are all profoundly countercultural claims.

Yet the idea that truths are built into the world and into us is one of the building blocks on which democracy was slowly constructed by the English-speaking peoples from Magna Carta on. The same idea undergirds the Universal Declaration of Human Rights.

The College of Cardinals has been strengthened by George Pell's nomination to its ranks; there, he will be an important voice in the highest councils of the universal Church and, one suspects, in the next conclave. As the rest of the world Church gets to know him better, it is not hard to imagine Cardinal Pell becoming one of the leading Anglophone churchmen of our time. At home, Australia is fortunate to have a religious leader who has such a clear-minded view of the moral and cultural foundations of democracy and who is eager to make arguments in such a way that others can engage them. Sydney is lucky to have as its cardinal archbishop a man who is committed to the fullness of Catholic faith and truth and who can defend the Church's settled teaching vigorously.

And if, in doing so, he challenges a few shibboleths, well, there is a typically Australian formulation for that, too: good on him.

GEORGE WEIGEL
Washington, D.C.
January 24, 2004
Memorial of Saint Francis de Sales,
Bishop and Doctor of the Church

Preface

The crimson of a cardinal's attire, Pope John Paul II reminded the thirty new cardinals receiving their birettas from him in Saint Peter's Square, "symbolizes the color of blood and recalls the heroism of the martyrs", a sign of love for Jesus and for His Church that knows no bounds.

It was a sunny, hot autumn morning, October 21, 2003, and the square looked its best, brightened by the red and gold tulips, the red of cardinals, the purple of bishops, and a crowd of faithful people from many races and cultures, who filled the square close to its two hundred thousand capacity. At the center of it all sat a frail old man in gold vestments and gold miter with the pallium, symbol of his authority, around his neck. Unable to stand, walk, or sit straight and struggling to speak and just to breathe, the Holy Father, two days earlier, had beatified Mother Teresa of Calcutta and, a few days before that, had celebrated his silver jubilee as Vicar of Christ. At that point, he was the fourth-longest-serving pope in history behind Saint Peter himself, Pius IX, and Leo XIII.

The thirty new cardinals from twenty-two nations and their tens of thousands of supporters speaking different languages were the perfect illustration of what Bernini's colonnade expresses so beautifully. The basilica, as the Holy Father was to remind the crowd, "opens its arms wide to all humanity, as if to show that the Church is sent to proclaim the Good News to all men and women without exception". The old and the new Church of Christ, he said, "shines out today, assembled round the successor of Peter". Many of the faithful would not have understood the Italian language in which the Pope's address was read out, but even the children present were moved by the old man's courage and mere presence and sensed they were witnessing history.

In the distance, to the left of the square when facing the basilica, stood the proud vista of the Pontifical Urban University and College atop the nearby Janiculum Hill. Remarkably, four of the thirty being elevated to the office of cardinal that day were graduates of that one institution. The twenty-first-century cardinals following in the illustrious footsteps of cardinals like Oliver Plunkett and John Henry Newman were: Stephen Fumio Hamao of Japan from the ordination class of 1957, Australia's George Pell and Nigeria's Anthony Okogie from the class of 1966, and India's Telesphore Toppo from the class of 1969.

"I'd like to say how honored and delighted I am to have been made a cardinal during the pontificate of our present Holy Father", Cardinal Pell told a crowded press conference at the Vatican radio center immediately after the ceremony.

> I'm a great admirer of Pope John Paul II, and, talking about Australia as part of the Western world, I think that his diagnosis is basically correct. And I worked for years to support and implement that.
>
> Certainly in Australia and in most parts of the Western world, those religious communities who preach the message of Christ more faithfully and strongly and have real service and create genuine community, they're going better than those communities who have a much more liberal sort of approach, or radical approach. Many of those are just slipping away and dissolving. Now even if we were preaching Christ

and following Christ and we weren't getting the results that we have now, we'd still be obliged to do so. But we believe that Christ is the Son of God. We believe that His teaching is not just cumulative human wisdom, but a divine revelation, and I don't find it surprising therefore that when we preach it truly, we live it, people are attracted by it today as they have been for two thousand years.

But how would he reconcile such conservatism with the need to attract younger people to the Church, he was asked.

I think it's very difficult for a Catholic or a vital Christian not to be conservative, because our basic teachings come from the great teacher who we believe was the Son of God two thousand years ago, and one of the great tasks of every bishop, and certainly a cardinal, is to preserve the apostolic tradition and to present it in a way that people can understand it. It comes at a cost; we have to take up our cross; but it works, and I think it works much, much better than the neo-pagan mix that is often presented, which is superficially attractive but, over a longer term, has brought considerable suffering to our society.

In Australia, some of the press comment about the new cardinal's promotion remarked on the long distance George Pell had traveled in his sixty-two years from his parents' hotel in the Victorian country town of Ballarat to Saint Peter's Square. Undoubtedly, his story—local, sports-loving country boy from an ordinary family who grew up to be a priest and then a bishop—"would not be untypical of the variety of background of the different new 'princes' of the Church".

Sydney has always been Australia's cardinatial see, but Pell had arrived there only two-and-a-half years earlier, when he was appointed Archbishop of Sydney. That 2001 appointment was unprecedented because at the time, Pell had been Archbishop of Melbourne for five years, a city with a culture and personality as different from Sydney's as Los Angeles is from Boston. Nobody, not even Pell's hero, Irish-born Archbishop Daniel Mannix, who reigned over the Melbourne Church from 1917 to 1963, had made the same transition before.

Pell had been liturgically installed as Archbishop of Sydney in Saint Mary's Cathedral in the city's heart on the evening of May 10, 2001. His reputation had preceded him, and that night, the cathedral, like the city itself, had been abuzz with expectation, some excitement, and some derision as well. Saint Mary's, not surprisingly, was packed out with three thousand people, including Governor-General (Australia's head of state and Queen Elizabeth II's representative) Sir William Deane, the head of government, Prime Minister John Howard, Opposition Leader Kim Beazley, and many onlookers from other denominations and non-Christian religions.

Outside, a children's choir sang with joy, just yards from a vocal group of homosexual-rights and pro-abortion protestors howling, hissing, and waving placards: "George Pell, go to hell." As the mob lurched forward, three were arrested. This was a big story, and the media were out in force. Sydney is one of the world's most racy, secular cities, home of the annual gay Mardi Gras. As Pell said in his homily that night, "One or two local writers seem to think sin is a recent Sydney invention."

Most of the laity in the pews were delighted. So were many of the three hundred priests, although a few agreed with the disgruntled Church bureaucrat who had grumbled to the press: "Melbourne's gain is Sydney's loss." Most of the nuns, hard to pick out in ordinary clothes with no religious insignia, were wary, although those few sisters dressed in any semblance of habits were extremely happy. Seated around the altar, the faces of the fifty Australian bishops present were inscrutable, although one or two could barely hide their hostility. Certainly, more than half would have preferred to see somebody else taking on the role, either a Church liberal or an innocuous functionary who would not rock any boats. Pell was neither.

At almost six feet three inches tall, with an athletic strength that matched his height, and a formidable intellect and personality, Pell was respected throughout the universal Church. Pope John Paul II regarded him as one of the leading English-speaking bishops of the world. Nobody doubted the story circulating that Pope John Paul II, looking at a list of three other names provided to him to fill the vacancy in Sydney, said: "I want Pell." He was also a highly controversial figure, recognized by many Australians, few of whom were short of an opinion about him. Pell's ideological enemies, those determined that secular humanism would have the last word in Australian public life, recognized in him a formidable, credible opponent—a caliber of Church leader not seen in Australia for half a century.

As well as five years behind him as an archbishop in Melbourne, Pell, then fifty-nine, had nine years experience as an auxiliary bishop, three years as a seminary rector, eleven years at the helm of Aquinas College, a tertiary (higher education) college in Ballarat, and plenty of pastoral experience working in parishes. He had just completed ten years as a member of the Vatican's Congregation for the Doctrine of the Faith in Rome, where he had been ordained thirty-five years earlier before going on to achieve an Oxford doctorate in history.

Already he had come through some enormous battles— and, although nobody realized it that evening, a few more horrendous ones lay just over the horizon, the kinds of battles that remind Catholics very sharply that Christ reserves some of his heaviest crosses for his closest friends.

For a few minutes before his installation Mass began, George Pell summoned his reserves of interior silence, shut out the atmosphere around him, and faced his Lord in the Blessed Sacrament, asking for the grace he needed to undertake the job. Only a handful of priests, seated in the front pews beside the back of the main altar, saw the tall, impressive figure at close quarters as he knelt down in his soutane and faced the tabernacle. One priest watching later recalled: "For those few minutes it was just George and God, alone. The cathedral might as well have been empty; he was oblivious to it all. He was so intent on praying to our Lord, so still . . ."

Only a few of those in Saint Mary's that night, and even fewer watching the Consistory in Saint Peter's Square in October 2003—George Pell's family and close friends—knew what a very reluctant starter he had been originally for a life in the Church. At eighteen, a professional football contract followed by a lucrative career in law or medicine had been his for the taking. The only way to understand why George Pell took the road less traveled, a path that in many ways is anomalous in modern-day Australia, is to return to the start.

Chapter 1

Child of the Trinity

George Pell was born in Ballarat, Victoria, on June 8, 1941, Trinity Sunday, the day that marks one of the central doctrines and mysteries of the Church. The baby's father, George Arthur Pell, manager of the Gordon Gold Mine outside Ballarat, was thirty-four, and his mother, Margaret Lillian Burke, was thirty-seven. They had met in Ballarat in 1938 and were married in April 1939, in Saint Alipius Church, Ballarat East. George Arthur was a nominal member of the Church of England, while Margaret was a devoted Catholic. In those pre-ecumenical days, mixed marriages were not contracted in front of the altar but in the sacristy. Margaret and George Arthur were strong, interesting characters. Like most of their contemporaries, neither had the chance to finish secondary school. From all accounts, they were very well suited.

George Arthur's ancestors were from Leicestershire in England. He was one of six children and grew up in Western Australia. He worked in Kalgoorlie's gold mines and came east in 1936 for the Melbourne Cup, Australia's biggest annual horse race, and stayed. George Arthur was an excellent athlete—captain of Perth City Surf Life Saving Club, Western Australian heavyweight boxing champion, and at one stage a leading contender for the heavyweight boxing championship of the British Empire. He boxed under the name "Bell" because his mother did not approve. Whether she eventually found out is still a matter of family conjecture.

Margaret Lillian, known as Lil, was of Irish descent and the fifth of twelve children of Paddy and Catherine Burke. Within the family, she was regarded as a born leader. Staunch piety was a Burke family trait. One of the Cardinal's aunts was christened with the second name of "Mannix" in honor of the long-serving Melbourne archbishop, Doctor Daniel Mannix, whose portrait hung on the wall of the Pell home. Pell later recalled some of the family's Lenten observances: "One of my great-grandmothers, a strong Irish Australian Catholic, used to fast on black tea with bread and dripping on every Friday in Lent." The less heroic, he admitted, might only give up chocolates. "I can remember sitting poised, with a box of chocolates on my knees, waiting for the fast to end at midday on Holy Saturday."

Baby George was not his parents' first child. Twins, a boy and a girl, had been born and died the year before, in 1940, so it is hardly surprising that George received considerable affection. He was graced with only one Christian name because his mother thought one so very English name was quite enough. The second or third name he would have been given—Berkeley—was also quintessentially English, after his paternal great-great-grandmother, formerly Miss Elizabeth Berkeley. Miss Berkeley, the daughter of a Protestant doctor, Thomas Berkeley, from Skibbereen in Ireland, married Joseph Thompson in Saint James' Anglican Church, Sydney, in November 1840. "My paternal grandmother was pressuring my mother that I should be George-something-Berkeley Pell, and Mother felt that George was enough for that tradition, so they couldn't agree on other names, so they just left it at George."

When George was born, Irish-born Doctor Daniel Mannix was twenty-four years into his reign as Archbishop of Melbourne, which extended from 1917 to his death in 1963 at the age of ninety-nine. Across the world, Karol Wojtyla, twenty-one, was a forced laborer shoveling limestone in a quarry in Nazi-occupied Poland. In Rome, the ascetic Eugenio Pacelli was in his second year as Pope Pius XII.

The Pell family home at 66 Rowe Street was a solid, weatherboard house with an iron roof and attractive, intricate iron lace decorating the front. Paddy Burke, the Cardinal's grandfather, who worked in the local railways, had built the house, adding some rooms on in stages. He called it Innisfail, an affectionate name the Irish sometimes use for their homeland. The Pells shared the home with Margaret's sister, Molly Burke. The house stands on a large corner block, then as now an average home in an average part of town, not poor but not palatial, either. During the war, George Arthur was in the Construction Corps of the Australian Defence Force, using his expertise with explosives and mining. When his daughter, Margaret, was born, he was underwater in Williamstown, Melbourne, blowing up a sunken steamship, the *SS Kakarriki*.

Margaret and her children were always Sunday Mass-goers and said the rosary at home every day. They attended the Novena to Our Lady of Perpetual Help every Wednesday night at the Ballarat Cathedral, led by Monsignor Fiscalini, when the cathedral would often be packed. On Saturday afternoons, at least once a month when they were old enough, the Pell children would ride their bikes to the local church for confession.

At one side of the house at Rowe Street, a small opening leads down to a cool area that the Pells called "the cellar". On hot summer Sundays, after Mass, the Pells would gather here with friends and relatives for a "Catholic" hour. This was nothing to do with religion. It meant hot scones and butter, with beer for the adults, and lots of lively conversation before the traditional Sunday roast lunch.

The Pell and Burke families were always very close. George Pell remembers his Uncle Harry Burke as "a real mentor", an old boy of Saint Patrick's Christian Brothers College who worked all his life in the office of the railways in Ballarat. A great reader deeply interested in politics, he used to write to the *Ballarat Courier* under the pseudonym of "Demos". In the days before professional spin-doctors, Uncle Harry was part of Liberal Premier Tom Holloway's campaign team and wrote many of his speeches. "He was a most lovely man," Pell recalls, "and for years and years I used to go up and talk politics with him and listen to him."

The Cardinal's father was a supporter of the Liberal Party, which had been founded by Robert Menzies in 1944 as an anti-socialist, pro-private enterprise party. Initially, his mother was inclined to lean to the old Labor Party, but like many Catholics of the time, she sided strongly with the Democratic Labor Party after the mid-1950s split.

This split, which shaped the course of Australian politics for decades to come, came about primarily because of the concerns of the brilliant Melbourne Catholic lawyer B. A. Santamaria and his supporters over the rising tide of Communist influence in the trade union movement and, through it, the Labor Party in Australia in the 1950s.

Santamaria and his supporters, who formed what was known as "The Movement", precipitated a major split in the Australian Labor Party in the mid-1950s, which led to the formation of the Democratic Labor Party, a small, influential party in several Australian states that packed the Liberal government in the Senate, Australia's upper house.

This split is credited with keeping the Labor Party out of office nationally until 1972. The Democratic Labor Party was also able to use its leverage in the Senate to lobby successfully for measures such as government assistance for Catholic schools.

George Pell recalls that his parents regarded Santamaria as someone who "had style and wit and was somebody to be admired". Like many "mixed marriage" couples, the Pells found that the Labor split brought them closer together politically.

By today's standards, children in country Australia in the 1940s and 1950s lived blissfully carefree lives. In Ballarat, George and Margaret and their friends rolled down Black Hill behind their home in a billycart, paddled in Yarrawee Creek, rode their bikes around town, and explored far and wide. They played games with their cousins, their neighbors, and their schoolmates, with Paddy, the family's collie/heeler tagging along. Television did not arrive until George was fifteen. For entertainment, his mother, who had an excellent singing voice, used to lead sing-alongs around the family piano.

George's first school was Loreto Convent, Ballarat, where he made his First Communion in 1948. Unlike most future priests of his generation, he was never an altar boy, because of a childhood illness that at one point became so severe his parents feared for his life. He had an abscess or growth in his throat and was quite ill for a number of years.

His sister remembers that over the space of several years he underwent the ordeal of twenty-four operations—several of them major ones—to remove the growth, which kept recurring. The boy was taken to every available specialist. Margaret remembers her mother praying to Saint Blaise, the patron saint of sore throats: "He is lucky to be alive. When he was seven, eight, and nine he had to wear a poultice tied around his head so it was pressed up against his throat. I would fight his battles for him when kids would sling off and laugh at him." Perhaps this is where his hide, which friends and foes claim is "several rhinoceroses thick"—probably erroneously—first developed. The intense loyalty and solidarity between Margaret and George, evident then, has lasted half a century. Margaret recalls: "Finally, a Doctor Greening did the last operation and took out what looked like a little plant with roots, and he recovered and never had any problems again." Doctors attributed the problem to the filling of a rotten baby tooth that should have been left alone. Instead, something poisonous from the filling had apparently seeped down into the gum and throat. The condition never recurred. Despite missing a lot of school, George had no problem with the work. During his illness he became an avid reader and has read voraciously ever since.

Shortly after George recovered from his illness, his brother, David, was born in 1951. A major share crash in 1949/1950 had compelled George Arthur to leave the mining industry. The family ventured into the hotel business, left Rowe Street, and moved, first, to the Cattleyards Inn and, later, to the Royal Oak Hotel. George by now was embarking on a vital stage of his life, as a student at the school that has produced more Catholic priests than any other in Australia, Saint Patrick's Christian Brothers College, Ballarat.

One of the classmates who started with him in grade five was Michael Mason, now Father Michael Mason C.Ss.R. (a Redemptorist priest) with a Ph.D. in sociology. Mason remembers the ten-year-old George as big for his age, a good scholar, and prominent because of his prowess at running and football. The two were playmates. George was a responsible kind of boy and, unlike many of his friends, not a troublemaker. "Neither parent would have been very tolerant of mischief", was Mason's impression.

In the Pell family, it was taken for granted that Margaret would have exactly the same educational opportunities as her brothers. Their mother was keen for her children to learn music. George studied piano and sang in competitions, and Margaret learned both piano and violin, with a talent that was to take her, at a very young age, to the top of her field in the first violin section of the Melbourne Symphony Orchestra, where she stayed for thirty years. After completing year twelve at Sacred Heart Girls' College, she went on to Melbourne University to complete a bachelor's degree in Music.

When Michael Mason first knew George, the family ran the Cattleyards Inn, opposite the Ballarat saleyards: "They were very hard-working, really, that's what struck you. I never encountered the Pells sitting around. It was the nature of the work; it was from morning to late at night. They were always bustling; there were always a lot of things to do around the place." He remembers the primary-school-aged George helping out at the bar on Saturdays. "I remember going in there, and he'd be serving people, and I remember thinking, 'Crikey, this would be a pretty scary place to work.' The Cattleyards was a very old pub, right opposite the saleyards. There'd be farmers and people like that."

Later, the Royal Oak in Raglin Street South was close to an area where most people worked in the woollen mills. "It was definitely very working class", Mason recalls. "George was obviously very well accepted, and later when Marg was a bit older they used to help out many times. I'd go down there to play chess. He'd be allowed to come out, and we'd go out on our bikes and muck around." For the children, part of pub life was knowing who drank what, who had had too much and would not be served, and what to do about it. Such experiences gave Pell an ease at mixing with people.

Saint Patrick's, set in extensive, leafy grounds in Sturt Street on the western edge of Ballarat, was opened in 1893, and since that time more than 310 graduates of the college have been ordained priests. It is the alma mater of three bishops—Pell, his predecessor as Archbishop of Melbourne, Sir Frank Little, who was college dux in 1942, and Brisbane's Bishop Brian Finnigan. While Saint Patrick's was always an intensely sports-oriented school, the yearbooks from the 1950s show that the principal of the time, Brother John Lynch, also put strong emphasis on academic laurels, public speaking, cultural events, and music appreciation. Gilbert and Sullivan operettas were favorites. The 1958 Saint Patrick's production of *The Mikado* featured George Pell in the role of Pooh Bah.

While the vigorous masculinity of Saint Patrick's might have crushed more timid or indifferent students, it suited Pell perfectly, as the honor boards around the school demonstrate: College Captain 1959 . . . Rev. Br. D. G. Purton Oratory Award 1958 & 1959 . . . Cadet Corps Under Officer. . . . In a highly competitive school, Pell was sprint champion from his under-twelve year through to under-sixteen, when pulled muscles took their toll. He made the athletics team every year and was a good long-jumper and shot-putter. He also played cricket and rowed, but he felt a bit awkward as an oarsman. Later, he became a good tennis player and swimmer.

But the only real game in Sturt Street, and in George's schoolboy heart, was football, of the Australian rules variety, a fast-paced game with eighteen players a side in which points are scored for kicking goals rather than for scoring tries as in rugby. An outsider can perhaps begin to understand what the sport meant at Saint Pat's from Gerard Ryan's book, *Ecka Dora*, the history of the 1st XVIII at the school. The book talks about "the aura of the 1st XVIII" as small boys stood at the front of the assembly watching the senior students being presented with their 1st XVIII jumpers and listening to the headmaster speak about "the responsibility these young men have in upholding the tradition of the College". No student, Ryan contends, could have gone through Saint Patrick's without being "imbued with some of the spirit of the 1st XVIII".[1] In 1956, when he was in year ten, George joined the 1st XVIII. In photos on the college walls, he stands in the center of the back row of the team photograph from that year—as tall and strong as the older boys, but with a younger face than the rest of the team. In a legendary football school at a legendary time, George Pell played as ruckman in Saint Patrick's 1st XVIII for four years, from 1956 to 1959. Part of his work in the game was to punch the ball out. A former fellow pupil, Paul Bongiorno, now Network Ten's political editor, remembers that George could punch the ball out "as far as some people could kick it". Brother William Theodore O'Malley coached the team for twenty years, including the time George was on it. In a newspaper tribute to O'Malley in 2000, Pell wrote:

> His teams were full of confidence, fight and spirit, and he was capable of eloquent flights of oratory in tight matches, which frequently called on the memories of past victories and the need for heroism and sacrifice. In retrospect, many of us took it a bit too seriously, but it was a marvellous experience. We learnt to win, believe in ourselves and in the romance of tradition. I would not have missed it. Barry Richardson, the Richmond champion of the 1960s and 1970s,

---

[1] Gerard Ryan, *Ecka Dora*, p. 3.

found the spirit at Richmond an anti-climax, something less, after St Pat's College football.[2]

Old Bill, as O'Malley was known out of earshot, kept a firm hand on his players. Catching the ball with one hand was strictly forbidden—which is exactly what George Pell did one day at practice. Old Bill angrily marched him off the field for the rest of the session, lecturing him all the way to the sidelines. "I think old Bill thought George was being a bit of lair, showing off a bit, but the catch was freakish", one onlooker remembered. Up to 1954, when it lost in the finals to neighboring Ballarat College, Saint Patrick's had not lost even a game in the Ballarat public schools premiership competition for forty-nine years. The team was back on top the following year and remained there during George Pell's playing days.

George later played Aussie rules at the seminary at Werribee, as a student and subsequently as rector. As rector, his students and colleagues (both supporters and detractors) were struck by how fast and strongly he played.

A large glass cabinet packed with football memorabilia has pride of place in Saint Patrick's foyer today. It contains a football or two, mementos of vital games through the years, and a large photograph of Brother O'Malley and his list of the "best twenty players" from his time as football master, 1928 to 1959. Along with names of subsequent professionals like Frank Hickey (Fitzroy), John James (Carlton), Frank Drum (Richmond), Less Mogg (North Melbourne), Kevin Hogan (Richmond), Brian Molony (Saint Kilda), Bill Drake (Footscray), Brian Gleeson (Saint Kilda), and Jack Cunningham (Hawthorn) are several who became priests, including George Pell. "Some say being named in such a team was a

---

[2] *The Age*, Friday, December 29, 2000.

boost to my priesthood. Others, more unkindly, said being a priest helped my chance of being named in the team", Pell says today. Two of the players listed—John James and Brian Gleeson from the class of 1952—later won Brownlow medals.

In 1959, George Pell was offered a professional contract by Richmond, which he signed. Not surprisingly, his father was ecstatic. At that point, George was completing year twelve for the second time, this time living at the school as a boarder. The first time around, excellent academic results, especially in French, Latin, history, and English, meant he had been offered a scholarship to study law at Melbourne University. But he decided to repeat year twelve and do physics and chemistry with a view to becoming a doctor. Repeating year twelve, or matriculation, was not unusual at that time, when as many as a quarter of the students, uncertain of what tertiary courses to pursue, did the same thing. Under the public exam system, different books were set for English each year, and George, being attached to school and sport, found "doing a second year of school quite convenient". But he found he did not enjoy studying science at all.

The school's yearbooks from the late 1950s show that scholastic results in public exams "were the best for some time". One of Saint Patrick's Latin teachers, Brother Lou Williams, nicknamed "Chesty", was regarded as a genius by his students for the way he encouraged students to piece together their own translations of the set Latin texts rather than learning off translations written by others. By the time the exam came around, students were proficient and excelled in the subject. This was to stand Pell in good stead a few years later in Rome, grappling with textbooks and lectures in Latin.

In George's day, Saint Patrick's had few academic failures. Brother O'Malley, for example, taught year ten Intermediate A, comprising students taking Latin and French, and prided himself on his class' success in the government-supervised external exams. Pell's recollections of O'Malley are a clear insight into his schooldays:

> Classes began about 8:15 or 8:30 A.M., with an oral test in the section of a Latin author to be learnt overnight. Julius Caesar's *Gallic Wars* was one such. One miss and you were sent to the line, and a second miss meant one cut with the strap [something Pell admits he, like all his classmates, received "many time"]. Although Brother Bill mellowed with the years, he remained in charge until his last year of teaching, as [Victorian Labor] Premier Steve Bracks reminded me a little ruefully. (He was in Inter A in that year.)
>
> Old Bill was nearly always just, although he could be fierce when provoked to righteous indignation. Ronald Conway, writer and psychologist, has claimed that fifteen-year-old boys are half angel and half orangutan. This underestimated our animality, but we knew where we stood, we knew that he liked us, wanted what was good for us, and we had no problem with discipline justly enforced. There were no drugs then to distort perceptions, less family breakdown, little psychologising, and students, like the teachers, did not wear their hearts on their sleeves. There were many worse ways of producing men.
>
> There was an examination in all subjects once a month, and the class was graded into places on the results. The front row was the prime minister and cabinet [George's classmates recall he usually made it into the cabinet, if not into the prime minister's seat] from the dux in descending order to those in the back bench on the last row. I never heard anyone in the last row complaining of damage to their self-esteem, probably because they were confident in Brother Bill's ability to get

them a pass. And, for better or for worse, we thought it was something of an honour even to be in Inter A. Competition within the rules was taken for granted, and we were taught that there was honour in victory or defeat, provided these were accepted graciously after we had given our best efforts. We were punished for cheating or whingeing.[3]

By the end of year twelve, with a football contract in the bag, the future was full of promise. Decisions, decisions—law, medicine, or professional sport: choices most young men would dream about.

Staying at school gave him time to think, to weigh up the options. Life in Ballarat was good, and he and his Saint Patrick's friends went to school dances and enjoyed mixing with the girls from the city's Catholic secondary colleges, Loreto Convent and Sacred Heart. One brother even instituted dancing classes and encouraged the boys to organize socials with the girls. These, the headmaster wrote in one of his annual reports, were "smart without sophistication, elegant without ostentation, decorous without stiffness, carefree and friendly without boisterousness". The young ladies' grace and charm, he said, brightened "so considerably, if only temporarily, the somewhat severe masculine atmosphere of St Patrick's". It was an age of innocence for many, of happiness and growing prosperity. Like his classmates, George enjoyed the girls' company, but there were no serious romances. In fact he was feeling dissatisfied and unsettled, despite all that was happening to him and around him. The time had come to deal with what he describes today as "a small cloud" that had been "on the horizon for some time".

~

[3] Ibid.

"I was waiting for you to come along. I thought you might have come along earlier", said Father John Molony, part-time chaplain at Saint Patrick's College in 1959. George had come along, reluctantly, to ask him whether, perhaps, he should try to become a priest. Michael Mason had already begun his first year as a Redemptorist seminarian in Wendouree near Ballarat, and while that had some significance as George pondered his own future, he was far from sure. "I think I would have been quite relieved if Father Molony had said 'No, you're not suited.' It wasn't as though I was brimfull of enthusiasm to become a priest", he recalls.

He later admitted that: "To put it crudely, I feared and suspected and eventually became convinced that God wanted me to do His work, and I was never able to successfully escape that conviction. I fought against it for a long time and made the decision to be a priest in my final year of schooling. I still marvel that I made that leap of being interested in it and thinking about it to saying 'I'll have a go.'"[4]

Molony had been educated at the Pontifical Urban University in Rome. Later, he was to leave the priesthood, marry, and become Manning Clark Professor of History at the Australian National University and a professor at the Australian Studies Centre in Dublin.

Today he has very clear memories of the eighteen-year-old George Pell coming to him—a highly gifted student academically and at sport, active in the school sodalities. "Most of all, I remember his determination. As a young man, once he knew the direction he wanted his life to take he followed that direction with real determination."

Pell recalls: "He was a very good friend and a powerful influence on me. He used to lecture us for an hour or so a

---

[4] Interview with Bryan Patterson, Sunday, September 21, 1997.

week, and that was probably the first time that I had been introduced to anything like theology or to an intellectually stimulating presentation of debate, and I found him a most interesting teacher."

Michael Mason agreed.

> John had a heck of an impact on us. He came in our last year. The thing about him was that he was a great scholar, a real intellectual. He'd read stuff and studied stuff, and it was allright to ask him questions, and this was kind of new. It was wonderful to actually say: "Well, what's wrong with Communism actually?" and "What is dialectical materialism?"
>
> I can remember the enthusiasm he generated. For the first time we could let loose our curiosity and our intellectual rationality. There had to be reasons for things, and we were bursting to know all that. This door opened which showed there was a lot of thinking about these things that we hadn't been exposed to.

The intellectual, emotional, and spiritual factors behind any man's vocation to the priesthood are extremely complex. Essentially, it requires a sense of the transcendent and a willingness to continue the saving work of Jesus Christ. Accepting the mission of Christ is often difficult, for it means struggling with faith and trusting in the unseen and unfathomable God. As Saint Paul says, we "see these things darkly". Even Pell admits he has "moments of difficulty" but "not serious doubt, no".

The loss of loved ones often sparks an interest in the final things—death, judgment, heaven, and hell—especially in the young, and George Pell was no exception. In his last year at school there were three deaths in his immediate circle within a few months. His teacher of English literature, Brother J. B. Ulmer, a man whom he had admired and who had helped instill a deep love of the subject in

George, died suddenly of a heart attack. Two of his uncles, to whom he had also been close, also died of sudden heart attacks. The young man's outlook turned more serious, his thoughts wandering occasionally to the mysteries of the next life. The foundations for responding to Christ's call to the priesthood were already there—strong faith from his mother and a thorough grounding in the Catholic faith at school, to which Brother O'Malley contributed. "My greatest debt to Brother Bill is a religious one", says Pell. "Fifteen-year-old boys are often looking for a cause to follow or leader to admire. In him, many of us found an admirable man of faith and integrity, who prayed without embarrassment and urged us to pray outside formal prayer times, to repeat often what he called aspirations and what we might now call mantras." O'Malley's favorite was "Lord, I believe; help my unbelief."

O'Malley's exhortations did not go unheeded. The college chapel was the center of life at Saint Patrick's, with students frequently attending Mass and Benediction and dropping in for a few minutes of private prayer. In 1949, George Pell's first year at the college, the college newspaper highlighted the tradition: "Big and small drop in for a few moments to converse with the Prisoner of Love in the Tabernacle. This beautiful custom has existed in the College for many years. Our fathers did as we do in the matter. College boys have their God very near them."

In Victoria in those days, the Christian Brothers and their old boys and students and their families were the core of Mannix' support. As a senior student in 1959, Pell attended the opening of the Christian Brothers teacher training college. Mannix, then ninety-five, gave what Pell recalls as "the finest speech of the day", receiving "a tumultuous reception".

As the decision about his own future crystallized in his mind, George had to tell his family. He knew his mother would be overjoyed, but he dreaded telling his father he wanted to be a priest, so he dithered and put it off. The priest in charge of the cathedral, Monsignor Leo Fiscalini, was a great friend of Pell's mother, and he said that if Pell was going ahead he should tell his father quickly, so he did.

George Arthur thought it was a waste of time. He had high ambitions for his son both sports-wise and intellectually, and he was disappointed. In fact, his father lamented to Sister Ann Forbes, a good friend of the family, that as George was joining the Church he might just as well have been "a bloody dill.[5] But you probably don't want dills, do you?"

However, George Arthur told his son that when he was young he had followed his own path, and, Pell remembers, "he would let me follow mine. I suppose it was only many years later that I realised just how broad-minded, how magnanimous, that was."

[5] A dill is Australian slang for a person who is not especially bright or clever.

Chapter 2

Corpus Christi

George Pell first met Denis Hart and Gerry Diamond on March 1, 1960, the day they all entered Corpus Christi Seminary, Werribee, in outer suburban Melbourne. Corpus Christi was the seminary for Melbourne, rural Victoria, and Tasmania. The three students were part of a class of thirty-two newcomers—of whom around twenty are functioning as priests today. Denis and Gerry were students for the Archdiocese of Melbourne under Archbishop Daniel Mannix, while George belonged to the Diocese of Ballarat, under Bishop Sir James Patrick O'Collins. George's cousin Henry Nolan, who later became Vicar-General of the Diocese of Ballarat, accompanied him to Werribee.

Denis Hart, a Xavier boy from Hawthorn, was always very efficient, even in the seminary. Pell recalls: "We had a study group of people of mixed abilities. Denis's role was always to type up the notes from the tutorials. He was always a wonderfully efficient, competent administrator who would have been a magnificent businessman." As for Gerry, he was "even then, slightly eccentric, but an extremely brilliant man with an encyclopaedic memory. We did speed reading courses in the seminary, and they were supervised by Father Syd Lennon, S.J., an Irish Jesuit, a brusque, direct sort of man. I think Gerry Diamond was reading six thousand words a minute. Syd Lennon refused to believe that anybody could do that and was rather aggressive towards him. But the thing was, Gerry got about 95 percent right in all his comprehension tests."

Today, Denis Hart is Archbishop of Melbourne and recalls that, as a seminarian, George Pell was "a very complete kind of leader, not only academic but sporty. He was well-read, he had a great intellectual curiosity, even at a young age, and a great interest in literature. In a way he was probably the most well-rounded member of our year." Diamond was struck by Pell's height and by his awesome football reputation "from the wilds of Ballarat". Before long, he was also impressed by the young man's interest in writers like G. K. Chesterton and Hilaire Belloc and by his skill with words, a talent honed by years of copious reading and school debating.

Diamond regularly topped the class in nearly everything, with Pell outshining him in English and coming close to the top in other subjects. However, it was no two-horse race. Four of those in the class who were not ordained excelled elsewhere—one as an international maritime engineer, two as senior Melbourne academics in philosophy, while another became Victoria's state architect.

Aside from the fact that two future archbishops joined the seminary, March 1, 1960, was notable for another reason. Until that year, students for the priesthood had completed all eight years of their training at Werribee, but by the beginning of the 1960s the number of students was so large that overcrowding was a major problem. A second seminary, at Glen Waverley, was built for students completing the second half of their training, four years of theology. Werribee was to cater for the first year class and the second, third, and fourth-year students, who formed first, second, and third philosophy.

The seminary in Werribee Park looked like a gracious sandstone country manor. It was set in extensive grounds, conducive to study, prayer, and contemplation. It was staffed by Jesuits, renowned for their rigorous academic standards and for encouraging young men to study and learn independently. From 1923 to 1973, when it was closed and the students transferred to a modern but rather soul-less center at Clayton near Monash University, Werribee turned out more than 760 priests.

The routine of the seminary, like most seminaries around the world at that time, was designed to foster growth in faith and in moral virtue. It included daily Mass, meditation, spiritual reading, and a daily examination of conscience, as well as weekly confession and Benediction. Seminarians were also expected to continue their daily spiritual life over the holidays and were warned against placing themselves in imprudent social situations that could serve as occasions of sin.

Sceptics sometimes claim that men entering seminaries do so to shy away from the real world, from relationships with women, or from earning a living and climbing the career ladder. But to meet some of the group who started at Werribee in 1960 (and many other equally impressive priests) is to realize they could have excelled in life outside the Church.

For many people caught up in the secular world, it is not easy to understand why such men would opt for the priesthood, putting the spiritual side of life ahead of considerations like professional or business careers and love and marriage. Being religious cranks or fanatics has nothing to do with it. In fact, anybody so inclined inevitably fails in a vocation. Rather, those called to the priesthood and who succeed at it tend to be normal men, grounded in the faith of the universal Church, with a strong desire to help others come to the knowledge and love of God. The commitment needs far more depth than wanting to be some kind of social worker with a touch of religion thrown in. Good priests understand and appreciate how much the faith has to offer the world. If what the Church teaches is true, it is hardly surprising that the Lord would call people of talent (including men of the intellectual caliber of John Henry Newman, Fulton Sheen, and Karol Wojtyla) to the priesthood.

The Werribee group who came together in 1960 bonded strongly with a greater sense of "year consciousness" than many other classes. Each year the students traditionally put on a play, an event they referred to as the Werribee Wintergarden. In 1960, the first years performed the light comedy *Arsenic and Old Lace*, with George Pell playing the lead, Mortimer Brewster.

More than half the class who came together in March 1960 are today functioning as priests, a very successful group overall. Periodically, they get together for reunions, and Gerry Diamond attributes the success of the class partly to its close bonding in the seminary "because by and large, the characters who have left tended to have cut themselves off long before".

After 1960, a few other students from interstate and overseas joined the class, bringing the total number to thirty-eight. In second year, when the class was in first philosophy, they made their mark by fielding not one but two football teams in the seminary competition. They managed this by having the nineteenth and twentieth men from the firsts (Denis Hart and Ted Teal, now pastor of Oakleigh in Melbourne) play for the seconds. Not surprisingly, George Pell, who could have been wearing the black and gold for Richmond at the MCG, was a key man in the firsts. "The couple of years ahead of us were football mad, and here were

these upstarts in first philosophy, second years, actually taking on the rest of the house, actually the best of the rest
of the house, and winning", Gerry Diamond recalls. The
team's motif was "play the man", a mischievous twist of the
"play the ball, not the man" motto.

Not everybody, however, was amused, either by George
Pell's dominance on the field, by the way he went about his
duties as a prefect in his later years at Werribee, or by his
high spirits.

While established to train secular priests (that is, most
parish priests) Corpus Christi was, as already noted, run
by the Society of Jesus, or Jesuits, an order with one of the
strongest intellectual traditions in the Church. Their method
of running the seminary provided excellent training to students in authority and responsibility. Basically, teachers were
scarcely seen outside of classes, so seminary life was organized by the students themselves.

A head prefect from the senior class coordinated the whole
place, and another prefect was in charge of the first years.
There was a music prefect (Denis Hart held that job in his
time), a kitchen prefect (who liaised with the nuns over
meals and who organized the provisions for days off), a
press prefect (in charge of stationery), and numerous others. In his second year, George Pell was the class prefect
during the class' spiritual semester, a six-month intensive
period of prayer, a role he carried out with no fuss.

In the second half of his third year at Werribee, however,
Pell was appointed first-year prefect. It was an important
job. There was a priest who was Dean of Discipline, who
worked from something of a remove, but for those in the
first year the prefect was responsible for the implementation
of the discipline. Pell found the role straightforward and had
no trouble at all exercising authority when appropriate. He

continued in the job in the first half of his fourth year. In the atmosphere of intellectual upheaval and social experimentation that began permeating the Church during the Second Vatican Council, some of those in the first year did not take kindly to his style and, even today, do not hesitate to say so.

Father Martin Dixon, now pastor of Saint Simon's Rowville in Melbourne's southeast was in that first-year class. His assessment of his old prefect was: "George has always been a big bully on and off the field; he's a tall, strong man, and he loves a fight and will do anything to get his own way." Dixon said Pell came as something of a shock after Sean O'Connell (who now works in the social justice arm of the Church in Victoria), the prefect who saw them through their first six months at the seminary. "Sean would not tell us what to do; he would allow us to make our own mind up. George was supposed to be looking after and guiding the first-year class, helping us settle in, but he was quite authoritarian." Others from that first-year class backed up Dixon's assessment but were not as brave in saying so publicly.

However, another member of the rhetoric class, Paul Bongiorno, had no problems with his old schoolmate's style and got on well with him. "He was dominant but very fair, and I guess I was pretty compliant", he said. "George thought men had to be men and that pansies belonged in the garden, and no matter whether individuals wanted to play football or basketball at the prescribed times he'd push them out. But that was his job."

Gerry Diamond said that before Pell was made their prefect, that first-year class had enjoyed "four months of running riot". Pell, Diamond insisted, was merely bringing those in the first year into line with the standards prevailing at the time, insisting that they kept silent at the prescribed times, turned up for prayer dressed correctly, and kept the rules generally. Diamond had a sense of real generational change taking place, as not only the inferences drawn from the Second Vatican Council but also the moral and social rebellions of the swinging 1960s made their presence felt even behind seminary walls. "That particular group was anti-anything all the way through. It was particularly noticeable when they arrived at Glen Waverley (the senior seminary), on March 1, 1966. In the late sixties there were endless, lengthy discussions that finished up with some sort of minor change, buzzers instead of bells; there was no real sense of the background of things. With that particular grouping it wasn't simply a matter of George, it was anything." Diamond is correct in his judgment that George Pell's time as a prefect at Werribee did color some slightly younger priests' views of him for the future.

Several priests who were seminary contemporaries of Pell have never forgotten their encounters with him on the football field. "There were better footballers, more talented players, but he was effective and would play in a certain way, the way the Brothers drilled fellows to play", Father Leo Saleeba, now pastor of Geelong East said. "He was very strong, and his arms tended to fly out; he was a bit awkward." Another priest found: "You tended to get a headache after playing against him."

Several priests, including Dixon, mentioned the antics of Pell and his friends on seminary outings, where they would roll up newspapers and whack others with them. "George was usually the initiator", Dixon insisted. He cited the incident as an example of the "bully" side of George Pell. Asked to provide more examples, Dixon mentioned his former boss' style of play at football and also an incident decades later when, as Archbishop of Melbourne, Pell stopped a group of priests at an official archdiocesan priests' gathering from spending time watching the film *Jesus of Montreal*. Pell's friends remember the newspaper "bashings" as "healthy high spiritedness". "He enjoyed it and gave as good as he got; it was part of the fun", Diamond says.

Others still take it all more seriously. Doctor Paul Connell, pastor of Pascoe Vale, who began at Werribee in 1964, the year after Pell had left for Rome, said the Pell legend and folklore lived on at Werribee after him. "Dunking, bullying people, forceful, outgoing to the point of riding roughshod . . . he was a legend in those days if one was talking about an over-bearing bully." Thirty years later when Pell was appointed Archbishop of Melbourne, Connell was seminary rector.

In his fourth year at Werribee, Pell was summoned by the seminary rector, who broke some news that was to shape his future career. From September that year, 1963, he would be continuing his studies at the Pontifical Urban University in Rome. It would take some time to get used to the Latin of the lecturers, he was warned, but he would love the experience. At a time when the dynamism of the Second Vatican Council had gripped Rome, this opportunity for an outward-looking student in his early twenties from provincial Australia was more than a dream come true. Pell had good reason to be heartily grateful to his mentor, Bishop O'Collins. A late vocation to the priesthood after working as a plumber, O'Collins prided himself on his ability to spot up-and-coming talent in the ranks of the Church and encouraged his priests to pursue university studies.

Before leaving Melbourne, Pell and two other seminarians, as was the custom for students going to Rome, put on their best black suits and ventured out to *Raheen*, a stately home on Studley Park Road, Kew, to pay their respects to Archbishop Mannix, then ninety-nine years old and a few months from death. In 2004, in a foreword to Australian author Michael Gilchrist's biography of Mannix, Pell recalled that the old Archbishop "rather deflated our self-importance by asking if we had been working in the garden!" The seminarians each kissed the Archbishop's ring—Pell little realizing that he himself would one day wear the same one. He would even sit in the same chair, which Mannix willed to his close confidant B. A. Santamaria, who in turn left it to George Pell. Pell remembers the visit: "Mannix had a rug over his knees and an Irish theological journal on a table next to him. He wondered who we were—we told him we were going to Rome to study, and he courteously wished us well. There was certainly no sign of any confusion."

Shortly after that memorable visit, George, twenty-two, sailed from Melbourne on the final voyage of the *Stratheden*. By this time, Margaret was a music student at Melbourne University, and David, twelve, was at Saint Patrick's College in Ballarat. Before air travel took over, ocean liner departures were quite an event. Hundreds of well-wishers gathered, holding streamers thrown from the ship by the European immigrants returning to their old countries for a visit and the young Australians embarking on the big trip to London and Europe. Clutching streamers thrown by Pell from the deck, all his family and a number of his friends were there to wish him bon voyage. His father fell silent, and Margaret's and his mother's tears flowed as the ocean liner drew out from the dock to sail from mid-winter Melbourne, via Suez, to Naples in the European summer of 1963.

Chapter 3

"Euntes docete omnes gentes"
[*Go Teach All Nations*]

Few visitors to Rome see Saint Peter's Basilica and its square from a vantage point as panoramic or as close as the grounds of the Pontificia Universitas Urbaniana de Propaganda Fide, or, in English, the Pontifical Urban University for the Propagation of the Faith. The university and its residential college stand on the Gianicolo (the Janiculum Hill) just behind the Vatican. In any light, the basilica's dome—Michelangelo's magnum opus—and the colonnade around Saint Peter's Square—designed by Bernini to suggest the welcoming arms of Mother Church—are strikingly beautiful. Viewed from the Gianicolo on misty mornings or at sunset, these architectural wonders take on an awe-inspiring, even ethereal quality.

The Vatican's proximity, less than half a mile downhill, puts the university and college, referred to as Propaganda or "Prop" by its graduates, at the very heart of the Church. Strictly speaking, the college is on Vatican territory, not Italian land, which partly explains why Jews were sheltered safely within its solid walls during the Nazi occupation of Rome. Entering the Propaganda grounds, it is impossible to miss the prominent lettering across the top of the main university building: "Euntes docete omnes gentes" (Go teach all nations), drawn from Christ's instruction to His apostles.

That, in a nutshell, is what the Pontifical Urban University and College is all about.

Dating back to 1627, the university and college were named after their founder, Pope Urban VIII. The college coat of arms includes the papal crown and keys (to the kingdom of heaven) and three bees that were part of the personal crest of Urban VIII. It was Urban's predecessor, Gregory XV, who established a new Vatican department, the Congregatio de Propaganda Fide, to spread or propagate the Catholic faith to all corners of the world. Urban extended Gregory's initiative by creating the missionary seminary.

Urban VIII also commissioned the papal summer residence outside Rome, at Castel Gandolfo—about ninety minutes drive from Rome, overlooking Lake Albano. In the 1960s, Propaganda College had its own villa near the Castel, where Pell and his classmates spent most of their summers. Pope Paul VI would invite them into his villa once every summer for afternoon tea. Like all popes, Paul VI was presented with an extraordinary array of mementos and gifts, and these he would often give away to the students he met at the Castel. Pell received a statue of John the Baptist baptizing Christ, which had stood on Paul VI's desk for years. (The Pope's baptismal name was John Baptist Montini.) Unlike his more austere predecessor, Pius XII, who rarely mixed, even in Rome, Paul VI also visited each ordination class at Propaganda Fide.

Senior students were allowed to venture farther afield during their summer holidays, and one year Pell won a scholarship from the French government and did a summer French language course at the Sorbonne. Bernie Mahoney (now Father Mahoney in the Diocese of Sale in Victoria) and he spent an idyllic summer in Paris, living in a youth hostel. Unlike many others in the same time and place, summer romances were out of the question. "We told people who we were, and that provided some sort of protection. And also, it was still then, even in Paris, with mainly Americans, it still was a different world to what it is today. The sexual revolution hadn't run on to the extent it has now", Pell recalls.

Now as in the 1960s, the college draws its students from all nations, especially the countries of Africa and Asia. They mix socially in small groups of about fifteen, known as cameratas, drawn from different years and countries, speaking in Italian. The language serves as an effective leveler. In Pell's time, the English-speaking students got together once a week —on Sundays after lunch—and the Australians gathered for special events like the annual Australia Day picnic and Anzac Day Mass and commemoration.

This extraordinary spiritual oasis was George Pell's home from 1963 to 1967, some of his most formative years and also the most formative years of the modern Catholic Church. When he arrived in time for the start of the academic year in September, Pell was disappointed by his first sight of Saint Peter's. "In my Australian prudishness I thought it looked very dirty from the outside." Most of the Australian students reacted the same way and felt rather shocked that the main church in Christendom was not better maintained. (Saint Peter's has since been cleaned extensively and is now flood-lit at night.) Much of Pell's time in Rome coincided with the sessions of the Second Vatican Council. Many of the two thousand bishops there for the Council were Propaganda Fide alumni and would visit the students at the college and say Mass in the chapel. The lecturers would talk in detail about the Council, enthusing about or occasionally berating its decisions. From the college gardens, the students could see long lines of all the bishops coming and going to and from the sessions, carrying documents in their briefcases. The 1960s was a time of ferment, great expectations, excitement, and tension in the Church. Those times set the stage for vast, positive reforms and also upheavals, uncertainties, and unforeseen conflicts for decades.

Propaganda's English-speaking students had a Newman Society, which produced an annual journal, *Loquitur* (taken from the motto of English Cardinal John Henry Newman, *Cor ad cor loquitur*—heart speaks to heart). The journal comprised articles and poems by the students on theological and contemporary questions or issues related to their own countries. Most volumes of the journal were produced with plain covers. In contrast, the 1964/1965 volume, which saluted the memories of Pope John XXIII and President John F. Kennedy, pictured those men on the cover, with the domes of Saint Peter's Basilica and the Capitol. It was edited by two second-year students, George Pell and New Zealander Neil Darragh. After the straitjacket world of Pius XII and Dwight Eisenhower's 1950s, it is understandable that Kennedy's and John XXIII's brief, tumultuous times on the world stage caught the imagination of young people in the 1960s. Most Catholics expected Pope John, elected pope in 1958 at the age of 76, to be a short-term stopgap who would make little impression on the Church. These expectations could not have been more wrong. In calling the Second Vatican Council, Pope John left an indelible impression that continues to unfold decades after his death.

The Pell/Darragh editorial, written, as they put it, to "catch the spirit of our times", paid tribute to the two Johns as "men of men, these men of God" who "presaged the return of the Church to the centre of Western life". The edition included articles on black saints, African so-

cialism, the Church in West Irian, Buddhist-Christian dialogue, an adaptation of Mark Antony's speech entitled "On
Calvary's Top", and a prayer for the canonization of Cardinal Newman. George Pell contributed two pieces—a poem
and a spirited attack on Australia's White Australia policy
(a stance that would have been controversial at home at
the time). With shades of arguments to come thirty-five
years later in the debate over Pauline Hanson's One Nation, Pell branded the policy unjust and outdated: "Eleven
million whites in an empty land surrounded by 1,500 million coloured Asians might have been a going concern when
the Dutch, the French, and 'Mother England' held most of
Asia under 'protective custody'. Today it looks suspiciously
like an anachronism." Australia would pay a price for "preferring third-class Europeans to first-class Asians". As Australia was completely unprepared to replace the annual intake of 100,000 Europeans with 100,000 Asians, he argued,
"it would be best to start with a much smaller number,
perhaps 10,000 a year, followed by consistent increases as
the newcomers assimilated. The great unknown is the dark
silent stream of prejudice, buried beneath the topsoil of Australian public life, born from cultural superiority and colonial achievement and strangely nourished by ignorance, fear,
and a superiority complex; yet slowly and certainly losing
itself in an ocean of changed conditions."

In the following year's journal, Pell wrote a critique of
one of the most controversial plays in the world at the time
—*The Deputy*, by German playwright Rolf Hochhuth—
which suggested that Pope Pius XII could have prevented
Hitler's Jewish persecution. As he reported: "At the Basle
première people rioted. In London, Evelyn Waugh sailed
into the fray claiming bad theatre and worse history, while

in America (where else, except perhaps Australia?) a prominent churchman condemned the drama and then admitted he hadn't read it." The critique concluded that while the play held together as drama, the character of Pope Pius as depicted bore no resemblance to the real person.

> The play's whole thesis rests on the naive assumption that Pius could have prevented Hitler's Jewish persecutions. This is incorrect. Pope Paul, then assistant secretary of state, along with most others involved, insists the situation could have been worsened. A protest of Dutch bishops had this effect, other Catholic protests were more effective. No-one could truthfully have predicted a successful intervention; and here lies the real issue. Was Pius, because of the enormity of the crimes, as a Vicar of Christ and father of all people and despite the menace of an unequalled barbarianism; was he yet obliged to bear a prophetic witness to the truth that might have been successful, or more probably have sent most of Catholic Europe back to the catacombs?

Propaganda has a rich history of colorful characters. Saint Oliver Plunkett, the Primate of Ireland and Archbishop of Armagh who was martyred at London's Tyburn tree in 1681, studied and was ordained in Propaganda and was its theology professor from 1657 to 1669. Cardinal John Henry Newman, the former Oxford don and convert from the Anglican clergy, also studied at Propaganda. In true Propaganda spirit, he went on to found the London and Birmingham Oratories, modeled on Saint Philip Neri's Roman Oratory, and to create the Catholic University of Ireland. In Newman's time, Propaganda was located near Rome's Spanish Steps (it was later moved to the Janiculum Hill), but the altar where Newman said his first Mass is still in use in the college today.

Vast numbers of Propaganda graduates have become cardinals, archbishops, seminary heads, pastors, and also martyrs. "Be faithful unto death, and I will give you the crown of life", one of the inscriptions in the college chapel reminds students at daily Mass. Even in the twenty-first century, Propaganda students from countries like Angola know they face dangerous lives, possible imprisonment, or eventual death when they return home, but most approach the future with a missionary zeal equal to that of any student from the college's 375-year history. Propaganda is highly influential in the rapidly growing Church in the developing world, from where most of its students are drawn. The university's library has 11,000 volumes in 530 non-European languages alone, including 270 African languages.

Australia is no longer classed as a "missionary country" entitled to free college places. However, several Australian bishops value the college so highly that they pay for some of their best students to attend. In George Pell's time, all university textbooks were in Latin, as were the lectures (officially), although the lecturers sometimes broke into Italian. Like most new students, Pell took several months to become used to the accents and idioms of the teachers. "Everyone had enormous trouble at first, but at least we had immediate access to the textbooks." (And sufficient grasp of the Latin needed to read them.) Pell and his fellow Australian students had done a little Italian study before they left for Rome and had a few lessons in the language at the college, but basically they picked up Italian themselves.

Many of the university professors were the international leaders in their fields. They taught from their own textbooks, among many other sources, books used in seminaries throughout the world.

The university was just over twenty yards from the college, across the driveway. It was also attended by students who lived in other colleges throughout the city. Many of the Italian seminarians belonged to religious orders and were training to work in foreign missions abroad. They attended classes in their full religious habits. Lectures were held in large theaters, including the Great Hall (*Aula magna*), a steep, five hundred-seat semicircular amphitheater.

One of the unforgettable teachers of George Pell's time (and for decades of students before him) was Monsignor Anthony Piolanti, a lecturer at both the Pontifical Urban and Lateran Universities in Rome. Piolanti, "Pio" out of earshot, was a tall, solidly built man who taught Christology. He wore a long, black soutane and a Roman hat on his bald head. When he arrived for classes, he would toss the hat on the desk, say the customary opening prayer, and pick up where he had left off the last time with "Ut dicebamus" (as we were saying).

Blessed with phenomenal recall, Piolanti lived for his subjects and rarely, if ever, referred to a note or textbook. In his lectures, he quoted the early Church Fathers and Church scholars through the ages, both those he admired and those he despised, with perfect accuracy and at length. His highest accolades were reserved for Saint Thomas Aquinas, whom he revered: "Saint Thomas Aquinas says and *we* say. . . ." It was clear what he expected in exams. Delving deeper and deeper into his subject, he would occasionally tell the students "Pro doctioribus inter vos . . ." (for the more learned among you). Piolanti fascinated generations of students, including Pell.

A centralist at heart, Piolanti was aghast at moves by the Vatican Council to give individual bishops more authority in their dioceses. On one memorable occasion, he made an impassioned speech about the "one, holy, catholic and Roman, apostolic Church". When a Spanish student dared to ask why he inserted "Roman" into this line from the Creed, he thundered "Because to say Roman is to say apostolic."

In later years, Piolanti became something of a recluse. Before his death in 2002, he spent considerable time studying the life and work of Pius IX, a fact that would surprise none of his former students. Pius IX, who died in 1878 after a reign of thirty-two years, was one of the Church's strongest, most traditional popes. Among other things, in 1854 he defined the dogma of the Immaculate Conception. He called the First Vatican Council in 1870, which defined the doctrine of papal infallibility. Upon his death, his Masonic enemies attempted to toss his body into the Tiber.

Delivering a paper at Boston University in 1991, Pell was to recall how amazed he had been to learn that the reign of Pius IX "coincided with steady, and sometimes spectacular, spiritual regeneration in many places, and especially in the English-speaking world. This is a fact that I, as a young priest ordained immediately after the Second Vatican Council and deeply committed to its liberal reforms, found puzzling and indeed somewhat shocking. How could such intransigence have coincided with and helped to bring about such a genuine revival?"[1] These days, with far more experience, Pell is no longer surprised by Pius IX's effectiveness. Over time, the liberal outlook of his student days has given way to a more pragmatic conservatism.

---

[1] George Pell, *Rerum Novarum: One Hundred Years Later* (Boston: Boston University, 1992).

Far more enthusiastic about Vatican II than Piolanti was a Slav lecturer, Vodopevic, an accredited expert consultant to the Council, who played an important role in drafting one of its main documents, *Lumen Gentium*, a decree about the Church herself. George Pell recalls Vodopevic as "a very good lecturer on ecclesiology (the study of the Church herself)", with an enthusiasm for the Council that was contagious among the students.

Another lecturer Pell respected for being "thorough and quite influential" was Father Roberto Masi, who taught sacramental theology. Such was the turmoil of the time that Masi brought out an important document defending the Real Presence against some of the Dutch theologians who were already, with the Council barely closed, attempting to undermine that basic tenet of the faith. It was a foretaste of things to come. The Dutch Church, once one of the strongest in Europe, with more vocations per head of population than any other European country, including Ireland, would be all but a wreck by the end of the twentieth century, with hardly any priests, religious, or parishes to speak of after relentless and ruthless internal upheavals.

However, the Dutch Redemptorist Father Jan Visser, who taught Pell moral theology in Rome, was anything but a heretic. In the 1960s, Visser was a member of Pope Paul VI's commission of inquiry into the birth control pill—one of the minority on that commission who opposed it.

A young Italian, Father Carlo Molari, who taught dogmatic theology, was Monsignor Piolanti's assistant and a real Pell favorite: "He was a very exciting lecturer; I certainly liked his enthusiasm and ambition to speak to contemporary people." Dogma, canon law, Scripture, the Psalms, and patristics made up the remainder of the heavy academic program. An elderly, bearded Lebanese archbishop, Sfair, struggled to teach the students Hebrew.[2]

Propaganda's *Aula magna* was also the scene of some lively theatrical performances by the students, including a production of *The Mikado* in November 1965, when, as Father Peter Brock recalls in his account of life at Propaganda, *Home Rome Home*: "A big footballer from Ballarat played Pooh Bah while Katisha and Koko were a tall New Zealander and a diminutive Ceylonese. At the end of their final duet Katisha swept poor little Koko up in her arms and carried him off the stage like a baby. It brought the house down. It had all the best of amateur theatre—energy, much hard work (sometimes unfocused and undisciplined) and results that formed and consolidated friendships."[3]

Students from Japan, India, and Senegal played the three little maids. Several performances were staged, with about five hundred people attending each one, including nuns and students from Propaganda and other English-speaking colleges (such as the English, Irish, Scots, and North American colleges). Many Australian bishops, in Rome for the Second Vatican Council (including Bishop O'Collins from Ballarat), came along to watch. Brock, who was in charge of the music, recalls in his book: "We turned on a smashing finale and the audience clapped for nearly five minutes. After it, [Sydney's] Cardinal Gilroy got up and said a few words, complimenting us on the 'feat we had accomplished', and then came into the dressing room to congratulate the

[2] The descriptions of the Propaganda lecturers are drawn from conversations with Cardinal Pell, other Propaganda students of various generations, and from Peter Brock's illuminating work *Home Rome Home* (Victoria, Australia: Spectrum Publications, 2001).

[3] *Home Rome Home*, p. 101.

fellows—who were in petticoats, underwear, etc.—much to everyone's amusement."[4]

A few days later, on December 8, 1965, the feast of the Immaculate Conception, Propaganda students crowded into Saint Peter's Square with tens of thousands of other onlookers for the historic closing ceremony of Vatican II. Such interludes were a welcome break from the rigorous timetable of the college. The students' days began at 5:30 A.M. (6:00 A.M. Sundays), with prayer, meditation, and Mass before breakfast. Classes were held in the mornings, followed by lunch (the main meal of the day). After lunch there were times for a *siesta* (part of Roman life), recreation and sport, study, evening prayer, supper at 8:00 P.M., more study, and a Great Silence from 10:30 P.M.

Always a keen sportsman, George Pell was an enthusiastic player on the college basketball team. Much to his disgust, the old soccer field was much reduced due to a car park underneath, but basketball courts remained. His contemporaries say he played basketball with power and "sheer physicality" and had a "strong presence" both on and off the court. In general, he was somebody whom the other students expected to make a significant mark, perhaps as a writer for academic and theological journals. Paul Bongiorno, whom George met at the boat at Naples when he arrived for the 1966–1967 academic year at Propaganda, remembers him as "an imposing figure with a real personality and an enormous intellectual capacity".

Pell kept in close touch by letter with his friends at Corpus Christi Seminary in Werribee. "He wrote to me regularly, and I got the impression of broadening interests during the Second Vatican Council in Rome", Denis Hart says. On

---

[4] Ibid., p. 100.

Thursday and Sunday afternoons, the Propaganda students were allowed out to explore the city of Rome but were expected back at the college in time for the evening meal at 8:00 P.M. Much to her brother's delight, Margaret Pell had completed her bachelor of music degree at the University of Melbourne in December 1965, and in June 1966 she sailed for Europe on the *Oriana*. Margaret studied the violin in Rome with Angelo Stephanato and, later, under the famous Remi Principe. Her playing secured her a place in the prestigious Santa Cecilia academy chamber orchestra. Margaret supported herself by working as an *au pair* for a Norwegian family and later lived in an international student hostel.

Margaret and George, always close, met up on Thursday and Sunday afternoons and explored the city together. They traveled, in the summer of 1966, to East Germany and Czechoslovakia, staying in youth hostels where even toilet paper was rationed, with four or five flimsy sheets doled out to each guest every day. They found life behind the Iron Curtain dull, gray, and heavily policed, with some of the trams dating back to the Austro-Hungarian empire. However, they were fascinated by the experience, especially George. His secondary schooling coincided with a time when the Communist menace loomed large across the world. As a teenager keen to look up to strong leaders, some of his great heroes were the Catholic bishops and cardinals of the Eastern bloc who kept their people's faith alive in the face of brutal repression. These included Cardinals Wyszyński of Poland, Beran in Czechoslovakia, Stepinac in Croatia, and Mindszenty in Hungary, imprisoned for many years under Communism. This first-hand experience of Communist countries brought home to him some of the heroic and political aspects of Catholicism that were not so evident back in Australia.

Chapter 4

You Are a Priest Forever

Friday morning, December 16, 1966, dawned a cold day in wintry Rome. Like most of his fifty classmates, who had spent three and a half years in Propaganda College, George Pell was surprised by how tense and churned-up he felt. Aged twenty-five, he was about to give his life to Christ as a priest: ordination day was the end point of many years of thought and study.

A few months earlier, when they became subdeacons on August 15, Pell and his classmates had been given the breviary to read every day for the rest of their lives and the Roman collar to wear. They had also taken vows of lifelong celibacy. The sacrifice demanded by such a vow inevitably provokes soul-searching and even fear, and George Pell was no exception. His sister, Margaret, recalls her brother pouring out his anxieties about that vow one afternoon during a long walk over some of the bridges that cross the Tiber.

On their ordination morning, the class of 1966 walked together down the narrow footpaths and winding, cobbled laneways of the Janiculum Hill to Saint Peter's Basilica, watching, as always, for the odd speeding car or Vespa. They wore their spectacular Propaganda College uniforms, dating from the 1600s, black soutanes with red buttons, red piping, and red waistbands. A black Roman hat—a dome with a broad, flat brim—completed the uniform, much to the chagrin of some of the students, who felt silly in it. They were very proud of the distinctive soutane, however, as are today's Propaganda students, who relate the legend that its designer was Michelangelo.

After a ten-minute walk, they turned a corner, and in front of them was the largest church in Christendom. Inside, they headed for the Altar of the Chair, at the very top of the basilica, underneath the sole stained-glass window in Saint Peter's, which depicts the Holy Spirit in the form of a white dove against a yellow and orange background.

One by one, dressed in white, the fifty young deacons from five continents were ordained priests by Cardinal Agagianian, an Armenian who had come to Rome as a student at the age of thirteen and stayed for a lifetime. He was head of the Vatican Congregation for the Propagation of the Faith (now known as the Congregation for the Evangelization of Peoples). The Cardinal anointed each deacon's hands with oil and then wound fine white cloths around them.

Among the congregation were Pell's mother from Ballarat, his sister, Margaret, and their young brother, David, then aged fifteen, who was rapidly catching up to his brother in height, all reunited after four years. His father, though fully reconciled to the idea of his son being a priest, had to remain at home in Ballarat to manage the hotel. For a mother with a very strong faith, like Margaret Pell, the strength of feeling she experienced as she watched her beloved son being ordained a priest is difficult to describe. Some have reported being overwhelmed with love, pride, gratitude to God, humility, faith, and wonder. Margaret Pell remembers a lump in her throat during the ceremony and shedding some tears, knowing how hard George had worked and how well he was suited for the difficult vocation to which God had called him.

A sung, Latin rendition of "Thou art a priest forever according to the order of Melchizedek" swirled around the basilica, reinforcing the solemnity of the moment. Peter Brock, a Propaganda student two years younger than the class ordained that day, reveled in the rare privilege of playing the basilica organ. Among other pieces, he played Bach's triumphant *Fantasia in G*. Brock recalls the moving ceremony: "It was a little unbelievable to see them walking back, their hands anointed and joined in front of them, wearing their long, white vestments, looking like priests in every way except that their faces were exactly the same as they had always been."[1]

The white cloths put around George Pell's hands that day would be wound around the hands of his mother after she died and be buried with her. The same has happened or will happen to the cloths of every other man ordained that day —a special honor the Church affords the women who give birth to future priests.

George junior remembers Praglia's *Tu es sacerdos* being played that day. But for him and many others, the music that evokes the strongest memories of Rome is Wagner's "Pilgrim's Chorus" from *Tannhauser*, sung by the Propaganda choir on special occasions. Its stirring words greeted the ordination class of 1966 as they returned to the college from Saint Peter's for lunch and celebrations.

The day after his ordination, Father Pell, surrounded by his family, friends, and passers-by, chose the Roman Church of the Christian Brothers as the venue for his first Mass. The Mass was in the Tridentine Rite, in Latin, with the celebrant facing the altar. Shortly, Pell, along with his contemporaries,

---

[1] Peter Brock, *Home Rome Home* (Victoria, Australia: Spectrum Publications, 2001), p. 186.

would be facing his congregations and praying in the vernacular in an attempt to implement the reform of the liturgy
desired by the Second Vatican Council.

Within the Propaganda family, the ordination class of
1966 stands out for an important reason—the vast majority of its members stayed on as priests. The significance of
this is evident when comparing the class to others in the
years immediately before and afterward. Of those classes,
only about 10 percent of the men from some countries, including Australia, are still functioning as priests. Either they
were not ordained or they left afterward. Perhaps the class
of 1966 had the best of both worlds—a solid grounding in
the certainties and intensity of the preconciliar Church com-
bined with the new springtime that flowered as the Council
progressed.

After a family Christmas in Rome in 1966, life at Prop for
George Pell went on its rigorous way. The ordination class
still had its most important six months of study ahead, to
complete the much sought-after licentiate in theology. Pell
preached, heard confessions, and did some work at churches
around Rome in his first six months after ordination, and
he said daily Mass at one of the many altars in the college
chapel. He spent his first Easter as a priest at Notaresco in the
Abruzzi mountains, helping out in the local parish. Study,
however, was a priority. The licentiate was a stiff, searching
exam, oral and written, covering 120 topics from four years
of the course.

The previous year, as part of the course, each student had
produced a written dissertation. Pell's dissertation delved
into the controversial work of the French Jesuit Pierre Teilhard de Chardin. Hero or heretic, genius or muddled fraud
. . . opinions among Catholics are sharply divided about this
extraordinary priest, geologist, and palaeontologist who was

a volunteer stretcher-bearer on the Western front in World War I.

Teilhard de Chardin attempted to reconcile certain modern positivistic theories, such as evolution, with Catholic theology. But his writing was fraught with difficult and obscure passages, some of which seemed to contradict the Church's unchanging teaching regarding the natures of both God and man. Thus he met with constraints imposed by Church authorities, and, in 1957, the Holy Office issued a *monitum*, a warning, against his posthumously published works.

In his dissertation, Pell lamented the Church's not allowing de Chardin to publish freely during his lifetime and thus develop and refine his work under the stimulus of the criticism it would have attracted. "Those of us who know something of the priest-scientist's private life will not be surprised that he regarded much of his work as tentative . . . yet another reason for sympathetic judgement."[2]

While critical of aspects of his subject's writings, the young student concluded that Teilhard de Chardin's work was intended, not to compete with divine revelation, but rather to enrich its perspectives and to penetrate farther into its mysteries. "The frightening upsurge of secularism and the separation of the Church from so much of what is good in modern life show the need for something deeper than a scrupulous intellectual 'orthodoxy' and adherence to traditional formulas", Pell wrote. "We cannot expect that his answers be perfect. They are not. However, without slurring over his deficiencies, and without failing to warn if nec-

[2] George Pell, *A Bird's-Eye View of Teilhard de Chardin in Christology*, third-year dissertation written under the direction of Rev. Father C. Molari, May 1966.

essary, there is no doubt that the new Church coming to birth after Vatican II will regard him as one of our greatest prophets, accepting him as he is, with his prejudices and failings, and despite his slightly garbled message. A voice crying in the wilderness, condemned to wandering amidst a primitive people."[3]

Three and a half decades on, a more experienced Pell regards Teilhard de Chardin, no longer as "one of our greatest prophets", but as "an interesting writer who tried to reestablish the traditional alliance between science and Catholicism" and who made an important contribution to the Christian discussion on evolution.

The Teilhard debate will undoubtedly rage for decades more: George Pell, who read the works in their original French, could not have chosen a livelier topic to pursue en route to his licentiate.

Most priests who have studied in Rome regard the licentiate as their academic highpoint, much harder to earn than a doctorate, which comes later if the student stays on. Decades after leaving Rome, some priests still dream about facing up to Piolanti, Visser, and the other Propaganda examiners. Pell was deeply absorbed by the lectures and the subjects and worked very hard, but he was largely untroubled by the course once he adjusted to the Latin (and sometimes Italian) spoken by the lecturers.

Of the fifty Propaganda College classmates who sat the licentiate, Pell came out fifth, his degree awarded *magna cum laude*, the second highest of the five grades. Among those ahead of him was Father Bartholomeo Adoukonou, who went on to be secretary of the West African Bishops' Conference and a member of the International Theological

[3] Ibid.

Commission. To date, the Propaganda class of 1966 has produced two Cardinal Archbishops (Pell and Archbishop Felix Job of Ibadan) and one Archbishop, Anthony Okogie of Lagos, Nigeria, as well as numerous bishops, seminary rectors, academics, and pastors. To the best of Pell's knowledge, there are no martyrs. Because such a fate was not unknown to graduates of the college returning to countries like Vietnam, Korea, and parts of Africa and the Middle East, and because many of the priests would probably not meet again after living and working so closely together for three years, their final farewells after the licentiate in the summer of 1967 were very moving.

While many of his classmates prepared to face up to the difficulties of ministering amid Third World poverty, George Pell, temporarily, tasted life at the opposite end of the mission. That summer after ordination, Pell took the opportunity to spend three months working in Baltimore in the United States, where it was a tradition to bring young English-speaking priests to help out while the local priests took holidays.

At the wealthy cathedral parish of Mary Our Queen in the northern part of the city of Baltimore, the people were very friendly, and Pell found it a wonderful introduction to parish life. While there, he made lifelong friends with a Catholic family called Weigel, who had two sons—John, who became a doctor, and George, still in high school at the time, who became an academic and writer, specializing in Catholic social teaching, religion and democracy, religious freedom, and the just-war tradition. George Weigel is known today as the author of the definitive biography of Pope John Paul II, *Witness to Hope*.

George Weigel recalls:

We first met Father Pell in the summer of 1967. If memory serves, he was third in an apostolic succession of young Australian priests coming to the Cathedral of Mary Our Queen for the summer. I was about to enter my junior year of high school.

My family was very involved in the cathedral parish; among many other things, my brother and I used to answer the phones in the evening, so we got to know the priests well. Father Pell became a friend of the family and even came to the Georgia shore with us for a few days that summer.

We stayed in touch over the years, although my contact with him has been much more intense in the past ten years, as our work has intersected at many points. I think everyone who met Father Pell in 1967, shortly after his ordination, was impressed by his freshness, openness, and candor—qualities we often associate with Australia.

Like many Propaganda students, Pell was keen to pursue a doctorate, but he was determined not to stay on in Rome for a doctorate in canon law. He had his sights set on Oxford and a doctorate in history. It was his good fortune that Bishop O'Collins supported the idea wholeheartedly. As is the case in secular universities, the leading academics in Catholic universities and seminaries are expected to hold doctorates in their fields, and Pell at that stage seemed destined for a life as a Church academic. Apart from all other considerations, Bishop O'Collins hoped Pell's years at Oxford would give the Australian Church someone who could beat the then-prominent liberal Catholic commentator Max Charlesworth at his own game. Some of Australia's bishops had long considered the articulate, controversial Charlesworth a thorn in their sides and were becoming increasingly aware that the Church needed to educate young priests like Pell to take the Church's message to the people through the mass media.

Chapter 5

Campion Hall, Oxford

Pell arrived in Oxford in 1967 for the Michaelmas term, which starts in September and extends to Christmas. For four years his home was Campion Hall, operated by the Jesuits. The Hall was originally opened in 1896 in the Saint Giles area of Oxford, and the present sandstone building, with quadrangle garden at its center, was built in 1935. It has a dignified, scholarly atmosphere, and its walls are decorated with religious art. Most of its residents were Jesuit students from around the world, along with priests and seminarians from other religious congregations and some diocesan priests like Pell. The Hall is tucked away in Brewer Street, a quiet lane opposite Christ Church Cathedral. A blue plaque on the house next door commemorates writer and scholar Dorothy Sayers, who was born there in 1893 when her father was headmaster of the cathedral school.

Scholars were lecturing in Oxford on theology and canon law before 1150. By 1180, a large group of scholars were resident in the town, with the earliest schools growing up around the monastery of Saint Frideswide, where Christ Church now stands. From 1220, the new Catholic orders —the Dominicans and Franciscans—began teaching in Oxford. More established orders like the Benedictines and Carmelites also moved in, setting up what were the forerunners of some of today's colleges.

In 1571, during the reign of Elizabeth I, the thirty-nine articles of the Church of England were imposed on the university, excluding Catholics. Among those who conformed initially was Edmund Campion, then a much-feted Oxford scholar, who deeply impressed the Queen when she visited Oxford in 1566. Campion, however, began having second thoughts about the Reformation, thoughts that soon turned into anguish. He fled to Ireland, Douai, and later Rome, where he joined the Jesuits. After his ordination in Prague, Campion risked his life returning to Britain in 1578. For three years he traveled through Britain, preaching, writing, and reconverting many to the Church, before being captured in Berkshire in 1581. He was paraded through London with a label "seditious Jesuit" stuck to his hat en route to the Tower of London, where he was tortured on a rack. Brought before Elizabeth herself, Campion was given a final chance to denounce the papacy in exchange for his freedom, but his loyalty to the Holy See proved too strong, and he was hung, drawn, and quartered at Tyburn on December 1, 1581. He is known as "the Pope's champion", and his portrait adorns the foyer of Campion Hall.

While well-spoken Oxford tour guides often stand before the Anglican Bishops' memorial and lament the burning at the stake of the Church of England martyrs Bishops Ridley, Cranmer, and Latimer during Queen Mary's counterattacks on Protestantism, they rarely mention the fate that befell Campion and others who were executed for their fidelity to the Catholic Church, nor do they mention much of the history of Catholic Oxford.

Pell's time in Oxford coincided with the canonization of Edmund Campion by Pope Paul VI, on the initiative of Cardinal John Heenan of Westminster. At the time, Cardinal Heenan was deeply worried that the Catholic Church was in danger of losing her identity in Britain in the rush toward ecumenism after Vatican II. To restore a sense of perspective, he decided to put forward the forty English martyrs, including Blessed Edmund Campion, for canonization.[1]

Initially, in Oxford, Pell was interested in studying the life and times of Saint Augustine of Hippo. He was advised, however, that in order to study Augustine, it was essential to study the period before his life, when much of the Church's structure of authority was being formed. Pell was steered toward an eminent Anglican academic, Canon Greenslade, the Regius Professor of Ecclesiastical History, who was to supervise his thesis. The topic settled upon was "The Exercise of Authority in Early Christianity from about 170 to about 270". In hindsight, a thesis dealing with authority in the Church was a perspicuous choice for someone destined to wield authority as the archbishop of Australia's two largest cities and to serve on important Vatican bodies like the Congregation for the Doctrine of the Faith.

The work involved years of poring over early Church documents in Latin and Greek and meticulous note-taking, as well as reading and analyzing scholarly works already produced in the field, many of them in French and German. Oxford's Bodleian Library became his second home (and his sister, Margaret's, as well, when she visited him and helped copy out copious pages of Latin and Greek). With the help of some tuition in German, Pell delved deeper and deeper into the world of the early Fathers of the Church's formative years—Cyprian, Irenaeus, Origen, Clement of Alexandria, and Tertullian.

His research brought him face to face with the extraor-

---

[1] Cardinal Heenan of Westminster told this personally to Father Tim Norris and his cousin, the late Bishop Patrick Casey of Brentwood.

dinarily influential Gnostic heresies of the early Church—theories, breakaway groups, and upheavals as ubiquitous and fundamentally anti-Christian in their time as today's New Age movement (and just as hard to pin down and categorize). While the events he studied happened more than seventeen hundred years ago, it is hard to think of a more useful academic background for a modern Church leader facing challenges to Catholicism from within the Church and from outside her. The early Fathers' handling of the Gnostics puts today's problems firmly in context as nothing particularly new. Pell's intimate knowledge of such a sensitive period in Church history has stood him in good stead in defending the Church and her structures against those desperate to see them changed radically.

The Master of Campion Hall in Pell's time as a student was Father Edward Yarnold, S.J., whose academic background is in classics and theology. Yarnold died in July 2002, six months after he was interviewed for this biography in a nursing home on the outskirts of Cheltenham, an hour's drive through the Cotswolds from Oxford, where he was recovering from a knee operation. His recollections of George Pell as a student were crystal clear: "An imposing presence, he had leadership qualities, initiative, and a great sense of humor. He was a bit of a scholar, certainly a hard worker, and he had a strong ecumenical interest."

Yarnold said George Pell stood out at Campion for the amount of priestly work he undertook in the Oxford district. Although his parish experience to date extended only to helping out occasionally in Rome and over a summer in Baltimore, the pastoral instincts of a good parish priest were already apparent. Apart from concelebrating Mass with his fellow students and the staff in the Campion Hall chapel every day, Pell also at different stages of his four-year stay:

served as a chaplain for the Catholic boys at Eton College, where he said the first Catholic Mass since the Reformation, said Masses and heard confessions for the Catholic boys at Summerfields, a privileged, selective school north of Oxford, once attended by Ronald Knox and Harold Macmillan; taught catechism to Catholic primary school children at the request of the Notre Dame sisters in Oxford, said Mass at Notre Dame Girls High School, and coached the prep school soccer team where the girls helped make up the numbers; frequently said Mass for the students at the Oxford University chaplaincy; and regularly helped out his friend Father Cyril Murtagh in the nearby parish of Hinksey with Sunday Masses.

Yarnold also remembers Pell standing out for daring to argue one evening with one of the most prominent and controversial Catholic theologians of the twentieth century, Father Edward Schillebeeckx, a Dutch Dominican and teacher of the history of theology at the University of the Netherlands. One of Oxford's great strengths was and is the way graduates and undergraduates are encouraged to speak up every day in lively, informed academic debate with regular and visiting professors.

Great excitement was afoot at Campion Hall when Schillebeeckx accepted an invitation to lecture and stay. Yarnold recalls that Schillebeeckx, in his talk, touched on several points that Pell was examining as part of his thesis: "Everyone else just asked questions, but I remember George argued with him on one or two points."

Father Michael Tate, the former Australian federal Attorney General, who left politics and became a priest, was an Oxford (Worcester College) contemporary of George Pell. Verbal dexterity, Tate explained, is part of the Oxford game. Tate, who also attended the Schillebeeckx lecture, recalls that

Pell was "not belligerent, but not deferential either" on that occasion.

This is a telling episode for what it says about the assurance of a young priest who dared to argue with one of the world's most renowned theologians in front of his college Master, senior fellows and fellow students, at a time when Schillebeeckx was hailed as the voice of the future. Three decades on, Schillebeeckx is still revered by those who believe "relevance to the world" can improve on "divine revelation"—in other words, he is a favorite son of the radical left of the Church. Catholics well-grounded in tradition, however, recoil especially from Schillebeeckx' fiddling with terms like "transignification" (Consecration achieves a change of meaning) and "transfinalization" (Consecration changes the purpose of the elements) to replace "transubstantiation" (Consecration turns the elements into the actual, physical Body and Blood of Christ). Aside from these serious issues in Schillebeeckx' work, and his influence on the fate of the Church in Holland, Pell regards Schillebeeckx as a "very substantial theologian" and especially admires his early work *Christ, the Sacrament of the Encounter with God*.

It was under the influence of theologians like Schillebeeckx that the Church in Holland was to embrace radical theological change more ruthlessly than any other in the world in the 1970s. The roles of priests and laity were blurred to the point that they were often indistinguishable. Much of the Church's traditional sacramental theology and supernatural mystique was abandoned in the name of "relevance".

Pell, too, was touched by the tumultuous time the Church went through in the late 1960s and the 1970s, when many of his contemporaries were leaving. "As a young priest at Oxford once or twice I wondered whether I was in the right line of business", Pell admits. But his fleeting doubts about his choice of career were not a significant crisis. He persisted with his study and priestly work and found things calmer going within a year or two, but many others did not. Perhaps his time at Propaganda had given him a more solid grasp of fundamentals than some other priests had acquired, perhaps he was endowed with a deeper faith; or perhaps he and the majority who survived just tried harder than those who left or took their ordination promises more seriously.

Up to fifty thousand Catholic priests were laicized (released from their priestly vows) during the pontificate of Pope Paul VI as uncertainty took hold of both younger and older priests and the Vatican adopted a liberal approach to releasing them. Contrary to popular misconception, celibacy was not the central issue in many such cases. As Pell observed among some of his contemporaries, it was more a question of a weakening of faith, a loss of the supernatural dimension of religion and a loss of sight of the call to follow Christ. For many such men, meeting a potential partner or wanting to carve out a different career might trigger the decision to leave the priesthood but was not the root cause.

Oxford, as Evelyn Waugh observed decades ago, retains a touch of the arcane. One or two of the elderly Jesuits at Campion, for example, claimed to be "amazed" that some bishops would send their students to Rome before Oxford —and pointed out with some glee that baths and time out of the college were in short supply in Rome compared with Oxford. Father Vincent Bywater, S.J., now in his eighties, was a senior fellow of Campion Hall in Pell's day, teaching geography, and he lives there still. His brand of charm would not be out of place around a luncheon table in the 1930s with Charles Ryder, Sebastian Flyte, and their friends. True Oxford students, Bywater contends, "live the life and pick up their degree on the way out". Chaps do not talk about what they are reading—"it just isn't done." Bywater says he advises new lay students to "hunt in packs" and not let their energies be drained by one-on-one relationships (very wise advice given how distracting romance and subsequent broken hearts can be). The old priest's first impression of Pell was that he "looked like a Rugby player". Wrong code, correct sentiment. In fact, at Oxford, Pell did play Rugby, for Corpus Christi College in the "cuppers" competition. He also played tennis in a joint team for Campion Hall and Saint Benet's, the residential hall of the Benedictine Order. And he traveled regularly by train to London's Paddington Station to catch the tube around to the opera at Covent Garden and occasionally drove to nearby Stratford-on-Avon to see the Royal Shakespeare Company perform. It was there, after a performance of *Othello* in 1968, that he met Father Eric D'Arcy, a philosophy lecturer from the Archdiocese of Melbourne for the first time. They became lifelong friends.

More important, in Bywater's scale of values, is the belief that Catholic bishops "should all have their blade". Pell passes muster on this score. For a sportsman, rowing on the beautiful Cherwell and Isis with their weeping-willow banks in summer twilight is an experience to treasure. Pell thinks he was an awkward rower, not well taught, and that he lacked some of the balance needed to excel at the sport. He rates himself a "much better rowing coach", which he was several years after returning from Oxford, when he coached teams at his old school at Ballarat. In Oxford, he rowed for Corpus Christi College in what he refers to as a "fat boys' team" (Campion Hall, with only about fifty students, did not have a team). The boat was apparently dubbed "Don't Feed the Vicar". Legend, and Bywater, suggest he is a little modest about his prowess on the water. The eight did so well in the university competition that they "won their blades" by achieving four "bumps"—overtaking four boats in front of them—over four days of racing. Along with his treasured D.Phil., the Corpus Oar (dark blue with two red stripes) came home to Australia with Pell, checked onto the plane. It now graces Margaret's home in Melbourne.

Bywater remembered little, if anything, about Pell's studies, but he did recall the effectiveness of his work with the Catholic boys at Eton and Summerfields and how the boys responded well to the positive influence of the athletic young priest: "The boys looked up to him; he was a kind of hero. The wrong priest in that role could have been a negative influence."

One night, in his first term in Oxford in 1967, Pell attended an Australian dinner at Rhodes House, center of the Rhodes scholarship scheme. There he met a theological student for the Anglican priesthood from Melbourne. Peter Elliott already held two degrees in history from Melbourne University and was reading theology. He was part of Oxford's strong Anglo-Catholic subculture, which had flourished from the time of Newman 120 years earlier. Pell invited Elliott back to Campion Hall for dinner. Elliott recalls:

> What struck me, I remember, the first time I visited him was his devotion to the Holy Father, Pope Paul VI. He proudly showed me his beautiful bronze, the baptism of Christ by John the Baptist, that the Pope had personally given to George in his last year at Propaganda.
>
> He was also very deeply immersed in the Second Vatican Council. I think some people today would be surprised, because he's been so bitterly criticized as a conservative. He was a great dining companion and told stories about Propaganda College and all the different ethnic groups and characters there and was very entertaining. What struck me also

was his common sense and very broad intellect. He was not just focused on the early Christian centuries, which are his specialty, but his view of British history was intensely broad. Anyone who looks at his library can see this. He has got at his fingertips the basic sources of British constitutional, political, and social history.

Pell and Elliott became close friends, dining together regularly until Elliott did not call for a few weeks. One night, in October 1967, Elliott, who had been ill, sought out his friend: "I went to spill the beans to him. I said 'I've been through a crisis the last few weeks, I haven't been at all well, and what's come to a head is the fact that I've got to be honest with myself, I've got to seek instruction in the Catholic religion.'"

Pell's first comment was: "I'm not surprised." His second comment was: "I'll stand by you." He also promised: "When the day comes, I will offer to be your sponsor." Those words, at one of the most important junctures of his life, still have a moving effect on Elliott when he thinks of them today. A former Vatican official in the Congregation for the Family, Vicar for Religious Education for the Catholic Archdiocese of Melbourne, and head of Pell's religious-education-texts-for-schools project, Monsignor Elliott is now pastor of Malvern East in Melbourne.

Not surprisingly, as the son of an Anglican clergyman and as someone living in a high Anglican theological college, Peter Elliott's conversion was a lengthy process of seven or eight months.

> It had to be done at my own pace. George was there as the kind of person that I could go to when I was blue, and I often was. He could send you up, and be a bit silly if need be, but he was very gracious. He never pushed me; he never put pressure on me. George has a sense of freedom and great

belief in the autonomy of persons to make their own decisions. His critics know nothing of that. George helped me
have a sense of humour about it all. Through his father, he
had a respect and a curiosity about Anglicanism, and that was
a learning curve for him those years in Oxford.

Although they had never crossed paths in Australia, Elliott
and Pell shared a strong abhorrence of Communism and considerable respect for B. A. Santamaria's "Movement". Both
Elliott and his father supported Catholic social doctrine and
the DLP, although many people did not realize that Angli-
cans were involved in the Movement. In the late 1960s,
Marxist Catholics were active and vocal in Oxford, centered on Blackfriars, a residential hall operated by the Dominican order. This angered Pell and Elliott, who made a
point of attending their public meetings and using their historical knowledge to ask pointed, awkward questions about
the incompatibility of Marxism and Catholicism. Not surprisingly, being prickled and needled in public angered the
hosts of the meetings, accustomed as they were to adula-
tion from their followers. But there was little they could do
about the pair they dubbed "the big Australian bastard" and
"the little Australian bastard".

While still an outsider to Catholicism, Elliott, in late 1967,
could sense the tensions building up within the Catholic
Church. In his words, these "exploded" the following year,
July 1968, when, against the expectations of the many liberals who regarded him as one of their own, Pope Paul VI
issued *Humanae Vitae*.

On June 24, 1968, Pell stood behind his friend and put
his hand on his shoulder as his sponsor as he was received
into the Catholic Church. He teased Elliott about "going
to Rome over Folly Bridge" after he had moved out of his
Anglican College to live in a small, medieval flat over Folly

Bridge. On December 8, 1968, the feast of the Immaculate Conception, Pell again stood behind Elliott as his Confirmation sponsor at Corpus Christi Church, Headington Quarry, outside Oxford. Elliott has vivid memories of the evening—for the wrong reasons. "I said to George, 'How are we getting up to Headington?' and he insisted 'We'll go up on my bike.'"

The 50cc motorbike was no larger than a Roman motor scooter, a Vespa, and small for the six-foot-three-inch Pell alone, let alone with a passenger. Following the ceremony, the Irish pastor put on a splendid dinner, after which the two Australians got back on the bike to return to Oxford.

> I was feeling elated, but as George hit the starter my foot slipped, and my heel went into the spokes of the wheel as it spun. It ripped the back off my shoe and the back of my heel, so I let out a loud expletive—very good after Confirmation—and was carried into the presbytery by George, with blood pouring out of me and my face pale. George was looking very embarrassed and the pastor was reminding me I needed to have fortitude (one of the seven gifts of the Holy Spirit conferred at Confirmation). The scar's still there to remind me of my Confirmation and its indelible character, and George drove me back very gingerly, all bound up, to Saint Benet's Hall where I was living by then.

His doctoral research going well, Pell took time out at Christmas 1969 to visit New York and Baltimore to see the Weigels. His old schoolmate Father Michael Mason was studying for a master of theology at Union Seminary at the time, a Protestant seminary in New York. The year at Union was a preparation for his doctorate in sociology at Columbia University, which he began the following year. They were turbulent times, not just for the Church. The United States was in the grip of the Vietnam War, the draft, student strikes, and turmoil generally. In contrast, Christmas had a touch of magic when the two old boys from Saint Pat's met up again. New York was especially cold and with half a dozen Union students, male and female, Mason and Pell caught the subway and startled and entertained commuters by singing Christmas carols. As Mason remembers: "It was to contribute a bit of Christmas spirit. We were always having to move on when we saw any subway cops, because busking wasn't allowed at that time, and they probably couldn't comprehend that we weren't collecting money. We took the subway all the way from Union to Battery Park and then went across to Staten Island. People were looking at us as though we were weird."

It was Christmas Eve, and after the concelebrated midnight Mass in the parish on Forty-third Street, where Mason lived and worked, Pell and he went out for dinner. "To cap it off perfectly, we walked out onto Second Avenue, and it was snowing thickly. There wasn't anything moving on Second Avenue, and for both of us, it was the first time we'd seen snow at Christmas. It was really magic. So we ran down Second Avenue like idiots, throwing snowballs at each other."

Pell's thesis for his doctor of philosophy degree at Oxford University was due to be presented at Easter 1971. In the centuries immediately after the death of Christ and his apostles, how did the Church as we know her continue to take shape? Pell's thesis paints a picture of the theology of the succession of bishops following in the footsteps of the apostles in the early Church.

The thesis' bibliography lists among its principal ancient sources the extensive writings of the early Church Fathers, including Clement of Alexandria's *Paedagogus*, *Opera Omnia* of Saint Cyprian, Hippolytus' *The Apostolic Tradition*, Saint

Irenaeus' *Adversus Haereses*, Origen's homilies and commentaries, and Tertullian's *Opera*.

"There's no doubt that reading the basic sources so extensively at that period, they shape your way of thinking semi-consciously", Pell observes. The period examined in the thesis begins as the Church is emerging from a crisis inflicted by the loose, heretical Gnostic movement. Many of the writings of the early Church Fathers were directed against Gnosticism, and the discovery of more than seven hundred pages of Gnostic writings in 1945 in Egypt vindicated the reliability of the Church Fathers' descriptions of the movement.[2] Irenaeus, Bishop of Lyons from about 178, was impatient with the Gnostics, declaring caustically "Are not there as many heresies as philosophies?" While most heretics were condemned to a life of searching and never finding, others, he said, "claim to discover a new doctrine a day, while others went one better than even the Apostles and discovered another God!" For Irenaeus, teaching one and the same faith, drawn from Scripture and tradition, united the Church in her many places.

At a richer and deeper level, the Church's unity is rooted in the Holy Spirit and so transcends history as well as participating in it: "Where the Church is, there also is the Spirit of God, and where there is the Spirit of God, there is the Church and every grace", Irenaeus wrote.[3]

Saint Cyprian, Bishop of Carthage from 248 or 249 until his martyrdom in 258, was a pivotal factor in Pell's Oxford studies. Judging from the thesis, Cyprian was a stable, self-assured character, capable of reducing complex arguments

---

[2] George Pell, *The Exercise of Authority in Early Christianity from about 170 to about 270* (D.Phil. dissertation, Oxford University, 1971), p. 10.

[3] Ibid., p. 37.

to a few basic points and then defending his position with force and clarity—a natural leader and a good writer. He articulated the loyalty Christians felt for the Church, which he repeatedly referred to as "Mother" or "Mother Church", a term still widely used today. Mother Church, he taught, weeps over her lost children or rejoices "to welcome back the glorious confessors [people who had suffered for their faith by jail or other punishments but who were not martyred]".[4]

Cyprian's main preoccupations were promoting loyalty, a sense of duty, and unity within Mother Church—a mystical unity founded on the activity of the Holy Spirit, a unity of doctrine and in organizational cooperation. Pell noted: "On many of the intellectual problems then confronting interested Christians (like the literalist interpretation of Scripture), he [Cyprian] was deeply insensitive; a quality which he sometimes used to advantage in the struggles of his episcopate."[5]

As the Pell thesis put it: "Cyprian's concern for unity is closely connected with his equally firm conviction about the unicity of the visible Church. God himself ordained that there be one Church, so that there is one God, one Christ, one Church and one (teaching) chair founded by Our Lord on Saint Peter."[6]

Cyprian was intransigent on matters of doctrine. At the same time, he was sensitive to the political subtleties of the many difficult situations that confronted him and pastorally had a great deal of common sense. In 250, he was the first bishop of his time to permit the deathbed reconciliation of

[4] Ibid., p. 305.
[5] Ibid., p. 290.
[6] Ibid., p. 309.

repentant *lapsi*, those who had left the Church. This magnanimous, compassionate gesture flew in the face of the traditions of the time and, as the thesis explains, "is the first recorded and certain example of a Christian bishop acting alone in a monarchical fashion to resolve a new and significant problem".[7]

In October 1970, toward the end of Pell's research and writing, Father Gerry Diamond arrived in Oxford to pursue his own M.A. studies. He found that he and "certain other characters had to put some pressure on to make sure deadlines [for the Pell thesis] were met". It was due to be submitted on the Thursday before Easter (Holy Thursday) in April 1971, and if not submitted by then, Pell would have had to wait another two months. Diamond was in the thick of the last-minute flurry, helping with proofreading along with Pat Bearsley, a New Zealand Marist, and taking the thesis back and forth to the typist at Wallingford (outside Oxford) for last-minute corrections. Pell then rushed it to the bookbinder and presented it by the deadline.

The Melbourne Symphony Orchestra happened to be in New York, so Margaret Pell flew to England to spend Easter with her brother. The Pells and Gerry Diamond visited Canterbury that weekend, and Pell defended his thesis successfully on Easter Tuesday. (In 1975, when he had saved up the fare, Pell would return to Oxford for the presentation of his doctorate in the Sheldonian Theatre, wearing the blue and scarlet gown of an Oxford Doctor of Philosophy.) On the Wednesday after Easter, Doctor George Pell, S.T.L., D.Phil (Oxon) left for Australia via a two-week holiday in the Holy Land and India, where he caught up with old friends from Propaganda Fide.

[7] Ibid., p. 324.

Only those who have been there and been awarded an Oxford degree fully understand the tremendous self-confidence the process and achievement bestows—the knowledge that you have mixed it with the best. People tend to forget, or never knew, that Pell holds an Oxford doctorate. Challenged once on Australian television about his qualifications to speak on matters of Church history, he pointed out the qualification.

Back in Ballarat, Pell's mentor, Bishop O'Collins, had retired, and Bishop Ronald Mulkearns had succeeded him. In Oxford, Pell and Diamond had a standing joke that he could look forward to being appointed curate at Manangatan, one of the most remote outposts of the diocese. In the event, Manangatan did not have a curate, but Pell was appointed curate to the next parish, Swan Hill on the Murray River. After eight years in Europe, it was time for some pastoral experience in the bush.

Chapter 6

Country Curate, Editor,
and the Battle for Aquinas

"This could only happen in Communist China", Paul Bongiorno, himself a Ballarat priest by 1971, remembers his old friend Pell fuming about his appointment to Swan Hill. At the outset of their careers, young people with a lot to give are generally in a hurry to put their training and education to good use. George Pell was no exception, although, in hindsight, he concedes that his pastoral experience at Swan Hill was "one of the best things that ever happened to me".

He accepted that life would be very different after returning from Europe, and he was, after all, reasonably familiar with country Victoria. So after getting out a map to pinpoint Swan Hill's exact location, Pell put his reservations to one side, packed up his books, and drove north, ready to get stuck into his first full-time job.

Ballarat is a large diocese, covering the western third of the state of Victoria. It stretches from the South Australian border in the west to the Murray River in the north and Bass Strait in the south. Swan Hill is about five hours' drive from Melbourne and four from Ballarat. It is a service center for the surrounding Mallee wheat-growing area. Dried fruits, vegetables, some wine, and forestry are among the district's other industries.

Working in remote locations is the norm in country dioceses, but it can be something of a culture shock for newcomers. To people accustomed to cities or to more fertile areas, even the drive up to Swan Hill is a mental challenge—hour after hour of barren, monotonous terrain that makes staying awake at the wheel a real effort. While the town itself, on the Murray River, is well appointed and reasonably prosperous, most of Pell's work was in centers up to an hour's drive from the town center.

However, country Australians are hospitable, and the people of the district gave their new curate a great welcome. He took to them immediately and quickly became absorbed in the pastoral work of the Church—saying Mass, preaching, hearing confessions, anointing and visiting the sick, conducting Baptisms, weddings, and funerals, and helping with religion in the schools. "You're confronted with all sorts of personal situations and personal sufferings", he recalls. "That was a very good time. I was very lucky. My parish priest [pastor], Father Bill Melican, was a good parish priest, very good company, a good talker and raconteur, and a good host. It was a very lively parish with a couple of out stations, and I looked after one end of the parish (Nyah West)." He also worked in Piangil (current population 190) nearby.

Father Pell was the best-educated priest in his diocese and one of the best educated in Australia. However, applying that knowledge to practical pastoral situations was something he could only learn on the job: "It wasn't just that you were confronted with the personal consequences of Church teaching, but in a certain sense I had to relearn all my theology, or reformulate it, so that I could make it accessible and understandable to people."

Like many before and after him, Pell found it surprisingly hard work. "I didn't write nearly as fast then as I do now under pressure, and a background difficulty was that I had done my theology in Rome, and the Roman world of theological formulation, at least as it was taught then, was very much a Continental world. It was quite different from the patterns of thought in the English-speaking world. To some extent my four years in England had helped me to start that transition, but nonetheless it was solid work to get together a decent sermon."

He need not have worried unduly. Numerous Swan Hill parishioners still speak highly of his early sermons and all aspects of his work. They pride themselves on being his first parishioners and believe that grass roots experience is essential to any bishop. They also found him a lot of fun. "He loved swimming in the local pool with the youngsters; he loved kicking around a football with the boys. And he loved food—the cakes at parish socials always went down well—and he was sincere and very approachable", Claire Betts remembers. Margaret Jirik, a mother of five, including three sons who attended Saint Patrick's College Ballarat, says Pell was "spot on and is still spot on".[1] He had a few meals with the family, and Margaret remembers him urging her son, John, to aim high, even suggesting he try for a Rhodes scholarship. Audrey Walsh, who served on the newly formed parish council with the young curate, found him "most unassuming; he threw himself into parish life— I felt the parish had a real buzz while he was with us."

At a time of upheaval following the Second Vatican Council, when parishioners were confused and a little apprehensive about the radical changes taking place, Pell organized a series of speakers to talk on the issues of the day. One of them was his old friend from Oxford, Peter Elliott, by this

---

[1] "Spot on" is Australian slang for exactly right.

time a Catholic seminarian in Melbourne. Pell invited him
up to give the people of Swan Hill and Nyah West a kind
of teaching mission on successive nights. Elliott was not yet
ordained a deacon, but he accepted the invitation and flew
up on a "flibbity-jib plane from Essendon" and spoke. The
people turned out in good numbers and rated the mission
a success.

The people Pell served in the Murray region showed no
signs of being impressed about his being an Oxford graduate: Margaret Jirik thinks many people probably never even
knew he was really Doctor Pell. "He was never high and
mighty; he was always very easy to communicate with. He
came back for a funeral a few years ago, and he came and had
a cup of tea with us, and he was just the same. If he had got
too big for his boots one of the women in the parish with
twelve children would have had something to say. That lady
treated him like one of her own children, anyway." Some
people in the parish were more impressed when they learned
that he had ventured behind the Iron Curtain.

It was in Swan Hill that Pell wrote his first published
book, an account of the fifty years' work of the Sisters of
Saint Joseph in the district from 1922 to 1972. The folksy,
close-up portrait of the Church's fledgling days in the Mallee
district captured the spirit of the pioneering Church in general and the tireless work of the sisters in particular. The order was founded by Mother Mary MacKillop, who was "far
ahead of her time in her conviction that the same educational
opportunities should be available to all classes of people."
From the beginning the sisters opted out of educating the
richer classes and concentrated their efforts on the poor, and
especially the many thousands of Australian children living
on farms and settlements throughout the bush, tens of miles
and sometimes hundreds of miles from a large town. "Not

only were these children to be given an education at least
equal to that of the State system, but they were to be prepared for the wider dimensions of life through instruction
in their faith. . . . It was above all the Sisters who converted
the largely ignorant and somewhat indifferent religious sentiment of last century into the robust and articulate commitment of so many of our 'over-thirties' today." The sisters, the book recalls, battled harsh conditions in their early
years, including dust storms in the 1920s that were so fierce
that visibility was limited to a few feet and flying sand cut
the skin. On such occasions, they learned to keep the children overnight at school and after one storm removed sixty
pounds of sand from the convent when the storm settled.

As a tribute to the sisters, Pell ended the book with an
appropriate verse from priest/poet John O'Brien:

> Your name in dust is hid,
> No thought or word has earned you immortality;
> Immortal only are the kindly things you did—
> Amen I say, you did them unto me.

In 1973, Pell's second appointment as a curate brought
him home to Saint Alipius in Ballarat East. The church is
an impressive bluestone Ballarat landmark, on the left-hand
side of the wide, main street driving in from Melbourne.
George and Margaret Pell senior, now well into their sixties, were still working as hard as ever in the Royal Oak
Hotel. Margaret junior was living in Melbourne, playing in
the orchestra, and David was an accountant. Pell's mother,
who had been unwell for some time, suffered a heart attack
at her youngest son's wedding in 1972. She recovered but
suffered subsequent bouts of ill health.

Pell's pastoral work continued much as it had in Swan
Hill. Ballarat East was a busy parish with four priests and

five schools. In March, Bishop Mulkearns appointed Pell his Episcopal Vicar of Education, a non-executive part-time position representing the bishop on education matters. The main task was to chair the diocesan education board, an advisory group on policy.

Pell's time as a curate at Saint Alipius overlapped for twelve months with that of another curate in the presbytery, Gerald Ridsdale. Ridsdale's hidden, fiendish behavior at that time, as well as before and after it in a string of parishes—Apollo Bay, Ballarat, Edenhope, Inglewood, Mortlake, and Swan Hill from 1961 to 1982—eventually led to his jailing as one of Australia's most notorious pedophile priests. In 1994, Ridsdale (Pope John Paul II had stripped him of his clerical faculties the year before) received a record eighteen-year jail sentence in Warrnambool County Court. He pleaded guilty to forty-six charges, including thirty-six counts of indecent assault, five of committing unlawful sexual intercourse, four of gross indecency, and one of attempting unlawful sexual intercourse, against twenty-one children, aged nine to fifteen, between 1961 and 1982. The previous year, 1993, he had been jailed for three months on similar charges.

The court heard that Ridsdale had assaulted victims in toilet blocks, showers, bed, and in the confessional. He had allegedly carried a jar of Vaseline in his car and once rewarded an altar boy with sacramental bread after twice molesting him while driving home from Mass. Another victim underwent anal surgery after being sodomized by the priest. The court also heard that Ridsdale indecently assaulted a girl, aged ten, after officiating at her father's funeral. Ridsdale, the judge said, "heartlessly abused his power" by committing "wicked and appalling acts of debauchery". During his time at Saint Alipius, Ridsdale was the chaplain at the nearby Saint Alipius Christian Brothers primary school. The court heard that Ridsdale sodomized one boy in Saint Alipius' bike shed after he came to him for help after being molested by a Saint Alipius' Christian Brother.

During the time he lived in the same presbytery as Ridsdale, George Pell had absolutely no inkling of his colleague's real nature. Other priests, and former priests, who shared presbyteries with Ridsdale say the same thing. So do many parishioners from various parishes where he served. It was two decades later that the dark truth emerged. Such clerical abuse had been going on for decades in many countries of the world, with few people—parents, teachers, or fellow priests—suspecting anything. Those who had tried to draw Church authorities' notice to the problem were generally swept aside, probably due to a mixture of disbelief, indifference, and incompetence, by those authorities.

Pell was not around the Saint Alipius parish a great deal at the time Ridsdale was in residence. He spent more and more of his time working for the Catholic Teachers College in Ballarat, where he was appointed principal in November 1973, a job that took him to Melbourne one or two days most weeks.

In 1973, with Pell looking on, Peter Elliott was ordained a Catholic priest during the Eucharistic Congress in Melbourne. The following year, Gerry Diamond returned from his studies abroad with a licentiate in Scripture from Rome as well as his Oxford M.A. He, George Pell, and Denis Hart, who had been working as a priest in Melbourne, had dinner together for the first time since George had left the seminary at Werribee in 1963. His friends were in the same financial straitjacket as Pell himself, so when they wanted to meet up, as they did several times a year, dining at a good Italian restaurant like Melbourne's Florentino meant saving up for weeks beforehand. However, having lived in Europe they appreciated good food and wine, and it was worth the effort. Peter Elliott was also part of this close circle, referred to by some as "the gang of four". This camaraderie was important to them all at a time of upheaval and uncertainty in the Church. To the deep sadness of those who remained, large numbers of priests were leaving the mission around that time, including Paul Bongiorno, who remembers Pell lending him a sympathetic ear and shedding a few tears when he went to tell him the news. Such a loss of talent was something the Church could ill afford.

~

Despite years of service as archbishop of Australia's two largest cities, George Pell rates "saving Aquinas College, Ballarat, as one of the best things I have done"—an indication of the priority he affords Catholic education, especially tertiary education. The college, now the Aquinas Campus of the Australian Catholic University (which also has campuses in Sydney, Melbourne, Brisbane, and Canberra), is located at 1200 Mair Street near the center of Ballarat. It is a leafy campus with a striking focal point, a Guy Boyd sculpture of the Madonna and Child, commissioned by Pell. The campus' newer buildings are in sympathy with the stately Victorian home, Manifold House (circa 1881), with its wide, iron lace verandas, at the heart of the campus.

Catholic teacher training began in Ballarat as early as 1884, when the Loreto Sisters operated a training college until 1906, when they transferred to Melbourne. Shortly after, the Sisters of Mercy stepped in, opening Aquin College in 1909, with some students sent as far afield as Melbourne University for academic studies and even overseas for expert music tuition. Aquin College soon became known as the Sacred Heart Training College, because it operated in the same group of buildings as the secondary college of that name. Initially, the average number of graduates per year was around thirteen, rising by 1971 to thirty-seven. By that time, eighty-six students were enrolled in total, and numbers began to increase dramatically. This was due to several factors—the opening up of new Catholic parishes and schools, the advent of smaller class sizes, which meant the need for more teachers, and the exodus of nuns, brothers, and priests from teaching, which created new opportunities for lay teachers.

In 1972, Bishop Mulkearns and the Sisters of Mercy agreed that, to facilitate the necessary expansion, the Diocese of Ballarat would assume financial responsibility for the college, which the sisters would continue to administer. By 1973, it was evident that the college could not accommodate the 180 students who wanted to enroll in 1974 and that it should increase its numbers to a level that would attract further government funding. An urgent meeting was called by Sister Clare Forbes, the acting principal of Sacred Heart, on July 5, 1973. Pell, as Ballarat's Vicar for Education, chaired the meeting, which was attended by other priests, lay officials of the diocese, and the Sisters of Mercy. At the meeting it was agreed to rename the institution Aquinas College and to lease 1200 Mair Street. The property was once the stately home of businessman and mining engineer Cyrus Bath Retallack, who came to Ballarat from Cornwall in the middle of the nineteenth century and who had surrounded his mansion with a tennis court, croquet lawn, an orchard, and stables. It later served as Queens Anglican Girls Grammar School, but it had been bought earlier in 1973 by the Saint John of God Sisters, whose hospital was adjacent. Numerous meetings followed, and a deputation, including

Pell, was sent to discuss the future of the college with the education minister in Victoria's Hamer Liberal Government, Lindsay Thompson. Later in the year, Pell was offered the position of director of the college and accepted it for three years beginning November 5, 1973. New lay staff were selected to start at Aquinas in 1974, and a crest for the new college was designed around the motto chosen by Pell—*Umbram Fugat Veritas* (Truth puts shadow to flight). Its crest included the many-pointed star symbolizing the patronage of Saint Thomas Aquinas.

Putting the interests of Aquinas ahead of her own, Sister Clare Forbes, who had been acting principal, was happy to stand aside to allow Pell to take the position, as she knew he had better academic qualifications for the job. Pell appointed her as his deputy, and they forged a powerful partnership, earning the nicknames George and the Dragon. "Clare was one of my closest friends, and I think even our strongest enemies would concede we made a formidable pair", he says.

Forbes, from Bungaree just outside Ballarat, had entered the Sisters of Mercy in 1943, the year her only brother died at age ten. Two of her four sisters were also Mercy nuns. In 1977–1978, when she finally had the chance to pursue postgraduate study, she completed a master of education degree at the Jesuit university Boston College, where she was inducted as a member of the *Alpha Sigma Nu* society, a Jesuit honor society reserved to those who made an outstanding contribution to the university. As Pell recalled at her funeral in Saint Alipius in 1992 (she died, aged sixty-seven, from a brain tumor), Clare was energetic, vigorous in argument, and passionate about her causes as only those with Celtic blood can be: "Speaking personally, words cannot express how much I owed her as friend and supporter, tactical adviser and spiritual mentor. She reinforced, as no-one else did except my mother, my own devotion to Our Lady. She was born on the feast of Our Lady of Perpetual Succour and believed it significant that she received the news the cancer had spread to her brain on the feast of Our Lady of Guadalupe, to whom she had a special devotion."

While it could have been mere coincidence that Forbes received the news on that day, many Catholics with devotion to a particular saint or to the Blessed Virgin Mary have noticed that major milestones in their lives, both positive and sad, occur on related days in the Church calendar. This is interpreted by the faithful as a sign, as the poet Tennyson wrote, "that more things are wrought by prayer than this world dreams".

In the 1970s, the principal and his deputy faced two long-running and interrelated battles, the outcomes of which were vital to the survival of Aquinas. These battles involved, first, having the college admitted to the State College of Victoria, essential for its courses and diplomas to be given official recognition and accreditation and for its graduates to be qualified to work as teachers outside the Catholic system if they wished; and, second, waging a continuing and vigorous campaign to secure full federal government funding for Aquinas, to put it on a par with similar but larger institutions, both secular and religious.

In 1973, Victoria's Catholic teachers' colleges, Aquinas and three Melbourne colleges, Christ College (Oakleigh), Mercy College (Ascot Vale), and Christian Brothers College (Box Hill), formed themselves into a single entity—the Institute of Catholic Education—with the intention of being recognized, as soon as possible, as a multi-campus, single college of advanced education, funded by the government but retaining the necessary autonomy to train teachers specifically for the Catholic education system. On February 6, 1974, Cardinal Archbishop of Melbourne James Knox appointed Bernard Callinan—a war hero, engineer, and later to be president of the Melbourne Club and Melbourne Cricket Club—as chancellor of the Institute. His vice-chancellor was the Very Rev. Eric D'Arcy, the Archepiscopal Vicar for Tertiary Education in Melbourne and a lecturer in philosophy at Melbourne University. As head of Aquinas College, George Pell was one of the Institute of Catholic Education Council members. At Bernard Callinan's instigation, he also joined the Melbourne Club.

The Institute faced formidable opposition in its quest to join the State College of Victoria (SCV). Two of the state's most powerful education bureaucrats—the Director General of Education, Doctor Laurie Shears, and Doug McDonnell, head of the Melbourne Teachers College—adhered strongly to the notion that education should be free, compulsory, and secular and that the Catholic Church had no place in teacher training. Both made their views known loudly and clearly in education and government circles.

In February 1974, the State College of Victoria replied to Cardinal Knox' request for the Institute's admission to the SCV, offering to admit the Institute's member colleges, *providing* "in the selection of students such a college should select its intake irrespective of vocational destination of graduates".

Clearly, the SCV was saying to the Catholics, secularize your college *or else*. The battle lines were drawn for protracted wrangling, meetings, and negotiations in which Bernard Callinan, D'Arcy, and Pell played leading roles. With five sons, major business commitments, and many other interests, Callinan had accepted the job as chairman of the Institute on a promise from Cardinal Knox that it would involve only a few meetings a year. Such were the struggles of the time that it was more like a *few dozen* meetings a year.

Aside from the battle for recognition at state level, Aquinas College was facing another desperate problem on its own. The Australian Commission on Advanced Education had decided not to recommend federal assistance for Aquinas in 1974 or 1975—although the main Melbourne Catholic teachers' colleges, Mercy College and Christ College, did secure funding. Despite its special clientele and its unique role in training almost all of Victoria's Catholic teachers who worked outside Melbourne, the federal authorities were pushing for Aquinas to merge or affiliate with the Ballarat College of Advanced Education. While the two signed an agreement to work closely together for their mutual benefit, and did so (with Pell even serving on the board of the Ballarat CAE), Aquinas and its staff insisted on retaining their separate status.

As the long and protracted negotiations continued at state level, different parties mooted different options, many of them unthinkable to those dedicated to Catholic teacher training. Some state bureaucrats suggested that the Catholics abandon their teachers' colleges altogether and seek teachers for Catholic schools from the state college. One possible deal unofficially mooted would have involved the Catholic Church withdrawing from teacher education but offering some religious education in state colleges. As a quid pro quo for being so compliant, the Church, it was suggested, would have received extra money for Catholic schools. Cardinal Knox, D'Arcy, Pell, and Callinan, however, would have no part of any such deal.

At one stage, some of the Catholics associated with the Institute of Catholic Education's efforts to join the SCV even began talking among themselves of a compromise that would have also meant the demise of Aquinas. This proposal would have seen Mercy College and Christ College admitted to the SCV, while Aquinas would have been merged with the Ballarat Institute of Advanced Education. Understandably, such an idea was anathema to George Pell and Sister Clare Forbes, who found they could not have had a stauncher ally than Bernard Callinan. In June 1974, in a letter to Angus Jones, president of the State College of Victoria, Callinan argued that the proposed compromise was "unacceptable in principle and impossible in practice" as "any attempt to separate off elements of the Institute as being suggested would entail the complete reopening of settled Catholic policy on teacher education in Victoria."

The exchange of letters, as well as meeting after meeting, continued through July, August, and September 1974. As one problem was ironed out, another, even sharper snag would emerge. At one stage, the state government insisted it should be free to appoint the chairman of the council of the Institute of Catholic Education. Cardinal Knox argued that, as "it was essential that its students be imbued with the [Catholic ethos]", he should appoint the chairman. Again it fell to Pell and Callinan to argue the case for the Church.

At one point, in order to break the deadlock at the state level after numerous letters to the government from himself and Callinan had proved fruitless, Cardinal Knox, a Propaganda graduate and former Vatican diplomat in Japan and east Africa, ventured over to State Parliament in Spring Street. He ensconced himself in the main hall and sent word to Premier Dick Hamer that he was there and would not leave until he had been seen. When he was, he insisted that the government keep earlier promises made and admit the Institute of Catholic Education (comprising the four colleges) to the State College of Victoria.

The pace of negotiations accelerated during October and

November 1974, and the breakthrough was made with an Order-in-Council on December 24, 1974, incorporating the Institute into the State College of Victoria. As head of Aquinas, Pell served on the State College of Victoria's academic board and as a member of its local governing council in Ballarat.

This left just one, even greater, hurdle to overcome—federal funding. As promised, the two largest colleges in the Institute of Catholic Education—Christ College and Mercy College in Melbourne—began to receive full government funding from 1974 onward. This, however, was not extended to the Christian Brothers College at Box Hill or Aquinas College, even after all four colleges joined the SCV at the end of 1974. Articulate, forthright pleas to the Whitlam government, including its Education Minister Kim Beazley senior, fell on deaf ears. Commonwealth funding made up about a third of Aquinas' recurrent costs, with the remainder funded by the Catholics of the Victorian dioceses of the Catholic Church, who benefited from the services of the one hundred or more Aquinas graduates who emerged from the college every year to teach children from Melbourne to the Riverina, Bendigo to Horsham.

Regardless of the financial straitjacket in which he operated, George Pell looks back on Aquinas in the 1970s and the early 1980s as a "most happy" tertiary institution, where the staff and students reveled in the casual, egalitarian atmosphere he encouraged. As in some of the smaller liberal arts colleges in the United States, the thirty or forty staff and the students mixed freely—not just the academic staff, but the administrative and support staff as well. Attendance at the fortnightly college Mass was voluntary, but around 70 percent of students were generally present. By 1975, the number of students had grown to four hundred.

As director, Pell, always more of a night owl than an early

bird, started at the college about 9:00 A.M. and often continued through until 9:00 or 10:00 P.M. At the height of the accreditation and funding battles, he was usually in Melbourne several days each week and often traveled to Canberra to put Aquinas' case to the federal government.

Michael Gilchrist, editor of *AD2000*, the Melbourne-based journal of religious opinion, taught at Aquinas while Pell was in charge. Gilchrist said his boss' style was "rugged Australian without excess authoritarianism. His staff meetings were a delight—he did not allow waffle; he kept things to the point and kept it moving. Once a month or so he would give the students a pep talk, commenting on any reports of serious misbehaviour, chiding them that excessive drinking or rowdy partying 'was not what we expect of future Catholic teachers'." Despite being only in his thirties, Pell was something of a father figure to the students and got on well with them, Gilchrist said, despite never being able to come to grips with what he termed their "barbarian music".

The atmosphere of Aquinas drew positive comment from one surprising source, Doug McDonnell, the head of the Melbourne Teachers College, who had vigorously opposed Aquinas in its battle for accreditation and entry into the SCV. When McDonnell was retiring, he took Pell aside. "I want to tell you something", he said. "I have never encountered an atmosphere as good as what you have in your college in Ballarat and the Mercy Campus in Melbourne."

As well as running Aquinas, Pell taught moral education at the college. In 1979, to deepen his own understanding of the subject, Pell took four months' leave to begin researching the writings and influence of American psychologist Lawrence Kohlberg, whose theories dominated the discussion of moral education in the English-speaking world for many years up to the time of his suicide, at the age of sixty, in 1987.

A former professor of education and psychology at Harvard University, Kohlberg was best known for his work in the development of moral reasoning in children and adolescents. Pell's research led to a 234-page scholarly evaluation of Kohlberg, with a ten-page bibliography of sources as diverse as Aristotle and Kant. While acknowledging that Kohlberg "was not entirely wrong" and praising him for resisting moral relativism, Pell concluded that he was:

> inconsistent and deficient in his treatment of morality and religion. . . . Despite his insistence on the separation of morality and religion, his highest form of moral reasoning requires and demands a post-conventional religious orientation, because the "why" of moral living is not resolvable on purely logical grounds. The fact that the religion he espouses involves a cosmic or pantheist type of divinity does not exonerate him from the flight from rationality into some religious orientation. The morally autonomous person cannot be religious, yet must be religious!

The thesis earned Pell a Master of Education from Monash University in 1982. He chose to focus on Kohlberg because he was well aware of Kohlberg's subtle but pervasive influence on teacher formation throughout the Western world, especially in relation to how people viewed issues of morality and religion in the broad curriculum. Taken too far, Kohlberg's approach was, in Pell's view, incompatible with some of the principles of Catholic education and therefore needed to be analyzed and understood thoroughly.

Throughout 1975, 1976, and 1977 Aquinas staff and some Institute board members, including Bernard Callinan, frequently lobbied parliamentarians and produced newspaper articles to argue for full recurrent funding for the college.

The breakthrough came on July 6, 1977, when the education minister in the Fraser coalition government, Senator John Carrick, announced that Aquinas College would receive full federal recurrent funding from January 1, 1978.

In making the announcement, he said: "The Government recognized that the distinctive character of non-government schools depends on the availability of teachers committed to the ethic on which the schools are founded."[2]

Pell also had to lobby for capital grants for buildings to accommodate the increasing numbers of students. This exhaustive effort met with only limited success, with Aquinas receiving minor works grants of Au$24,000 in 1978 (about US$18,500), Au$43,000 in 1979, and Au$30,000 in 1980. At the same time, he managed to have a new library built, raising funds from a variety of sources, mainly non-government, and being frugal with day-to-day spending. The substantial salary to which Pell had been entitled since the beginning of 1974, which he did not accept (as one of his Aquinas colleagues revealed to me) but rather plowed back into the cash-strapped college, also helped. The Callinan Library, named in honor of the Institute chairman, opened in 1980 and was expanded with a Au$165,000 grant in 1982. A new administrative block, and the Forbes Student Centre, named after Sister Clare, soon followed, built in a style in keeping with the traditional beauty of the college's main buildings.

In naming the library after his great friend, Pell was honoring an outstanding Australian. Knighted in 1977, Bernard Callinan, born in Moonee Ponds in 1913, qualified as an

---

[2] Information on government funding for Aquinas and the formation of the Institute of Catholic Education and its entry into the State College of Victoria was drawn partly from *Institute of Catholic Education—an Overview of Its Formative Years*, by J. N. Kellett, completed in June 1987.

engineer in the 1930s and volunteered for duty at the start of World War II. As one of the commandos in the ill-fated Sparrow Force that landed on Timor, Callinan and his three hundred comrades withdrew to the hills to fight on against odds that saw them outnumbered eventually by one hundred to one. The commandos, whom Callinan eventually commanded, did much to immobilize thirty thousand Japanese troops on Timor. As Nevil Shute wrote of them: "Few soldiers in history can claim to have done more than that."

As Auxiliary Bishop of Melbourne in 1995, Pell preached his friend's eulogy in Saint Patrick's Cathedral:

> Bernard Callinan led a small band of heroes, whose exploits will pass into Australian legend as the only Allied troops in 1942 between India and Eastern Papua who had not surrendered to the Japanese. . . . In that campaign he was awarded the Military Cross and mentioned in dispatches. . . . Sir Bernard served Australia with distinction in six years of war; he served it with equal distinction in peace for almost sixty years . . . his leadership roles in the construction of the new Parliament House (Canberra) and La Trobe University. . . . His Catholicism, among the best of its type and generation, was the informing principle of his life . . . he was devoted to the Mass, the sacraments, and the daily rosary. He recognised and accepted the clear lines of religious authority . . . and accepted, without hesitation, the proper religious authority of pope and archbishop.

During his time at Aquinas, Pell produced two booklets on Catholic education. *Are Our Secondary Schools Catholic?* and *Bread, Stones or Fairy Floss* were published by the Australian Catholic Truth Society. These thirty-page booklets, which sold for twenty-five cents and were well received interstate, were significant in that they first drew the attention of Catholics outside Victoria to Pell. In a straightforward way, the booklets set out what Catholic education should be about—or rather, what Catholic parents assume it is about. It is interesting to note that these booklets, which from to-day's perspective are middle of the road, helped establish George Pell's reputation as an up-and-coming conservative in the Church. This was perhaps a reflection of the radical "new church" direction that was being taken in the late 1970s and 1980s.

As Peter Elliott points out, although *Bread, Stones or Fairy Floss* was very popular among conservatives, it put Pell into a middle position on catechetics. "He didn't fall for the old conservative line of 'just teach them the catechism and everything will be solved', which is impossible", Elliott explains. "That's what he meant by the stones. The fairy floss was the light situation ethics and sugar Catechetics of the 1970s, and the bread was a good balance in doctrine and life and Scripture."

Under the heading "Fairy Floss" Pell argued: "Many of those graduating from our secondary schools are good people and good Catholics, but most of them are theologically illiterate. . . . Youngsters are encouraged to spend too much time talking about themselves and too little time talking about Christ and the gospel message." Catholic schools were not turning out enough people interested in God and religion, as distinct from those "with a vague interest in humanity and the fashionable concerns of the moment".

He also called for greater professionalism and better education for teachers of religion: "There can be no viable answer in the simplicities in the past." However, while the Church had changed many things, such as the language of the Mass, "we should never imagine that she can abandon her claims to some absolute truths or turn away from her basic strengths." One religion was not as good as another, however soothing it might be to believe otherwise. "Ecumenism is not indifferentism."

In *Are Our Secondary Schools Catholic?* (1979), Pell wrote:

The ideal of a liberal education, formerly limited to the ruling elites, is now regarded as appropriate for the big numbers of pupils attending secondary schools in advanced Western society. Such an ideal requires not only a developed capacity for abstract thinking, and an acquaintance with and reverence for the achievements of the past, but a cultivated understanding of what is central and important. "A great intellect", says Cardinal Newman, "possesses the knowledge not only of things, but of their mutual and true relations; knowledge, not merely considered as acquirement, but as philosophy."

This probably seems a far cry from the concerns of those pimply creatures consigned to our care in lower secondary, obsessed with sport and barbarian music, but even then we can be developing an admiration for excellence and rationality (by demanding it), and helping to cultivate an absolute distaste for bigotry and ignorance.[3]

Each generation, he argued, gets the generation of young people it deserves.

Adolescence is our last best chance to influence people, to tap the idealism which is present in most cases, to provide models of leadership and service so that intellectually and politically, as well as religiously, we shall have people at a local and national level who will stand up and be counted. Many of our Catholic students can be interested in things higher than parties, money-making and being president of the local race club.

[3] George Pell, *Are Our Secondary Schools Catholic?* (Catholic Truth Society, 1979), p. 16.

More than 20 years ago, Ronald Conway wrote in a beautiful article on the role of the teacher: "The age from fourteen to eighteen years can be the time of true Christian romanticism—an age when a boy can be led to any goal if only he can find a leader worthy of his loyalty and admiration." Each generation (not each individual teacher or parent) gets the generation of young people it deserves.[4]

These booklets attracted attention because they supported the notion that Catholic school students ought to be taught the fundamental theology of the Catholic religion and inculcated with an understanding of absolute truth. That was a far cry from the situation in most Catholic schools in the 1970s, where Catholic doctrine was barely taught at all. Students at that time might find themselves spending religion classes sitting in circles on the floor discussing the environment or the evils of capitalism or lying on their backs with their eyes closed listening to relaxing music as they "discovered their inner selves". In rare instances where issues like the priesthood or *Humanae Vitae* were raised, students were generally treated to diatribes in favor of women's ordination and contraception. Pell might not have fully realized it at the time, but in penning those two booklets, he was taking the first steps in a much wider battle for the minds and hearts of Catholics and the future direction of religious education and much else in the Church.

In April 1980, Pell put on the vestments in the sacristy of Saint Alipius for one of the hardest tasks of his fourteen-year priesthood—saying the Requiem Mass for his mother, who had died after a long struggle with heart disease and breathing difficulties. He paid tribute to his mother as a woman

[4] Ibid., p. 28.

of great strength and faith, a faith very typical of the west of Ireland in its certainties and its impatience with theological subtleties. "She knew as well as Saint Paul and any of the Gospel writers that any human achievement meant hard work, struggle and sometimes sorrow. She and Dad worked enormously hard that their children would have opportunities not open to themselves. Mum was very proud that her children, through the grace of God, and luck and strong management direction from her and Dad, to some extent availed themselves of their opportunities."

One consequence of a fairly long illness, Pell noted, is that it enables the family of the sick and dying to come to terms with what is happening.

> In fits and starts, slowly at first but inevitably, they come to realise that the time for birth, for planting and healing has passed, that now we are at the time for parting and for death.
>
> For Christians this cannot be just an occasion of sadness, or grief without hope. Just last night one of our parishioners from the East told me that it was hard to give condolences to a priest; with the clear implication that priests above all must take seriously the promise of eternal life. Wouldn't we all be delighted, he added, if our mother was to meet the Queen or the Pope—and of course the dead have gone to meet Someone much more important . . . a God who loves us and is interested in us, and who has a task for each one of us.
>
> This is true of course because we are sons and daughters of God, not slaves dominated by fear, but it is only one side of the coin. We are still waiting for the final revelation; we are still limited (probably a happier way of describing our lot than Saint Paul's references to our decadence!); groaning in one great act of giving birth as we wait for our bodies to be set free.

I ask you then to pray in the Mass a prayer of thanksgiving for the good she accomplished; to pray in the hope of the resurrection that she may be loosed from her sins.

By that time, the Catholic Church, with the charismatic Pope John Paul II at the helm, had become newsworthy in a way she had not been for decades. This period coincides with the beginning of Pell's journalistic career. In December 1979, Bishop Ronald Mulkearns appointed him editor of *Light*, the Ballarat Catholic news journal. During Pell's five-year editorship, it was published at first every two months and eventually ten times a year. In his first editorial, in March 1980, Pell summed up where the Catholic Church stood at the beginning of the new pontificate:

The Second Vatican Council was the most important event in the Catholic Church since the Reformation. It shook the Church out of her immobility, and headed her into the next millennium. There have been wonderful and new developments, but these have been purchased at a considerable price. In retrospect, some who appealed to the "spirit of the Council" and justified their claims under this head are now seen to have been following aberrations. Just as surely some refused to accept any changes, or accepted them reluctantly or with bad grace.

To some extent the Church was polarised. . . . We must work and pray that the worst doubts and divisions are behind us.

Most regional religious newspapers are as parochial and gossipy as they are amateurish, but *Light* under Pell was notable for its broad world view of the Church, the range of subjects it tackled in depth, and its book reviews (everything from detective thrillers and biographies to religious books). Such diverse characters as Malcolm Muggeridge, Caroline

Chisholm, Mother Catherine McAuley, Mary MacKillop, Mary Ward, and Saint Thomas More were profiled.

The journal's regular contributors included Aquinas teacher Michael Gilchrist, now editor of *AD2000*, who wrote a column on public life, and Babette Francis. Her organization, Women Who Want to Be Women, was the *bête noire* of feminists at the time and something of a joke to most modern-thinking female journalists. However, more than two decades later, it is interesting to note that her early health warnings in regard to the birth control pill, the IUD, and abortion have since became part of mainstream news.

Most issues of the journal carried a special theme— teenagers, Australian rules football, television, saints and heroes, life after death, abortion, prayer, the Eucharist, Christ, Lent, Education, Justice and Peace, and our Lady, with stimulating and substantial articles that have stood the test of time. The journal's editorials also give a clear insight into Pell's view of the world and the Church, as she was emerging in his late thirties and early forties.

His editorial of August 1981 was about the spectacular wedding ceremony of the Prince and Princess of Wales, with its "marvellous ritual and pageantry, organised to perfection with that mixture of dignity and showmanship that only the English can achieve". Pell went on, then, to predict that

> an increasing percentage of Australians will see the British monarchy not simply as irrelevant, but also as not being in the best interests of Australia.
>
> Australia will become a Republic, although whether it will be sooner or later cannot be predicted. The issue is not important enough to justify major bitterness in the Australian community. Much better will be a pattern of evolution.
>
> An Australian Republic does not necessarily mean a change of flag, nor a withdrawal from the British Commonwealth;

not even an increase of our fashionable anti-British sentiment. We owe most of our public institutions, and much of
the basic stability of our Australian way of life, to the contribution that the British made to our country. We should
be grateful for this.

However, our eyes should be towards the future. It would
be ironic if the Catholics in a diocese which saw the Eureka
Rebellion[5] and which was proud to be regarded as Mannix
territory should now become, or at least be seen as, stalwart
defenders of the British monarchy.[6]

Later that year, Pell set out the role he believed the pope,
bishops, and priests should take in speaking out about moral
and political issues—a foretaste of his approach as a bishop.
Clerics, he said, have an obligation to speak out on moral
issues in public life.

In a democratic country like Australia, they also have a democratic right to express their political views without necessarily
implicating their congregation; a point Archbishop Mannix
made on many occasions. The pulpit is never the place for
partisan politics, although it can occasionally be used to discuss public moral issues. . . . In the long run, the separation
of Church and State is good for both parties. . . . There is
no single Catholic political ideal, no single model of Christian social life, anymore than there is a single model for a
Catholic school or parish. Some models of Government are,
of course, clearly incompatible with basic Christianity; such
regimes would be dictatorships of the left or right, who sys-
tematically violate human rights. Politics is for lay people.
Clericalism in politics is wrong in principle and wrong in
practice.[7]

[5] On Sunday, December 3, 1854, Ballarat gold miners took up arms
against the corruption and unfairness of goldfield authorities in a battle
regarded as the birth of true democracy in Australia.

[6] *Light*, August 1981.

[7] Ibid., December 1981.

In a special supplement, *1984 in Australia*, published in June that year and built around the Orwell novel, Pell lamented that:

> Many Australians, and certainly many Australian Catholics, are proudly and persistently anti-intellectual, and this often takes the form of an hostility to education and schooling. In the world of tomorrow, the children of today could pay a bitter price for this stupidity. . . . No group of schools anywhere has a better record than our Catholic schools in educating children of parents who were not highly educated themselves and often not at all prosperous. We must do even better with this generation and the next, especially in country areas and for the children of our migrants.[8]

As he observed, however, while larger numbers of students were staying in formal education for longer periods, "it is doubtful whether people are reading more, especially material of a more serious nature."

Pell's sense of history and literature were often to the fore in *Light*'s editorials. For Anzac Day[9] 1984, he quoted Wilfred Owen:

> Behold,
> A ram, caught in the thicket by its horns;
> Offer the Ram of Pride instead of him.

[8] Ibid., June 1984.

[9] Anzac Day, commemorated in Australia and New Zealand every year, marks the landing of the Australian and New Zealand Army Corps (Anzacs) at Gallipoli in the Dardenelles on April 25, 1915, during World War I. Over the years it has acquired a deep symbolism and reverence in Australia and is a day when all those who perished in war are remembered and prayed for at dawn services, Masses, and memorial ceremonies around the nation. George Pell, a keen student of the war poets of the Great War, quoted English poet Wilfred Owen, whose words capture eloquently the human cost of World War I, a war in which sixty thousand young Australians died.

But the old man would not do so, but slew his son,
And half the seed of Europe, one by one.

The editorial observed that World War I produced the
greatest war poetry in the English language but little else
that was good. Churchill, he noted, the main advocate of
the Gallipoli landing, at least learned from the defeat and
made doubly sure of Allied superiority before he allowed the
Normandy landing in World War II. He also noted that despite Archbishop Mannix' opposition to conscription during World War I, no less than fourteen Victoria Cross winners, in uniform and riding gray chargers, and ten thousand
soldiers in uniform marched with him in the 1920 Saint
Patrick's Day procession in Melbourne.

In November 1983, to mark the centenary of Karl Marx'
death, his editorial lamented "We are all influenced, often
unknowingly, by Marxist theory, and yet there would not be
six Catholic secondary schools in Australia that teach about
Marx!"

For most of the 1970s, Pell continued to live at Saint Alipius with several other priests and to work as assistant priest
in the parish. He was often on hand when his eldest niece,
Sarah, (now in her late twenties and a Ph.D. student) would
knock on the presbytery door after coming out of school for
the day. Sarah, then aged six or seven, would ask whether
"Georgie" was at home, and if he was, the curate and his
little "Princess", as he called her, would have afternoon tea
together or go for a walk. A few years later, Sarah's younger
brother, Nicholas, would often visit his uncle when he was
administering the quiet Bungaree parish outside Ballarat.

Family holidays were spent in January at Torquay, a small
town with a superb surfing beach on the Victorian south
coast, in a three-bedroom house the Pell family had bought.

Denis Hart spent the summer holiday of 1975 there with Margaret and George and returned every year for the next twenty-five years to "flop around" in the surf they all enjoyed so much. The house was regularly full of Pell family members—brother David, his son and daughters and their friends, extended family and parishioners. Hart remembers it as a "constant flow of people—a complete kaleidoscope —what you'd describe as the ordinary parish people, people with whom he had an academic contact, many of the families of the young men and women he lectured at Aquinas College. He seemed to strike a chord both at the highest intellectual level and at the most common human family-friend level. He had to have a group of people around—he wasn't keen on it being quiet."

Hart remembers his friend encouraging the young students who came in their careers and their faith. He also encouraged a literary interest. Sometimes, the guests included one or two of the Saint Patrick's students Pell knew through coaching rowing at the school, including Peter Tellefson, principal of Saint Kevin's Junior School at Toorak, Tim O'Leary, a Melbourne businessman, and Michael Casey (now his private secretary and author of the philosophical work *Meaninglessness*). "I'm sure Casey's interest in philosophy and logic came from the way Pell nurtured him and gave him books to read", says Hart.

For years in summer, Torquay Catholics became accustomed to the two priests saying Mass together each weekday morning at 10:30 A.M. in the local church. On Sundays, they said a private Mass.

One of Pell's earliest and most important mentors in the Church was Sir James Patrick O'Collins, Bishop of Ballarat from 1941 to his retirement in 1971, who lived on after his retirement in what was known in Ballarat as the old Bishop's

Palace, a large, grand old home with extensive grounds. Pell is happy to acknowledge that O'Collins was "a father and friend, source of strength and confidence and practical wisdom" to him. The Bishop, who initially completed only primary school, worked at South Melbourne gasworks and as a plumber before completing his secondary education at night and studying for the priesthood. O'Collins was highly intelligent but dyslexic. Nevertheless, while he was in Rome, he managed to master Italian, and when Pell read O'Collins's diaries years later, he was struck by the excellent Italian as well as the man's deep spirituality.

In 1981, when O'Collins was nearing ninety, Pell left the presbytery at Ballarat East and moved into the Old Palace with him to give him company and to be on hand to look after the old man, along with his loyal housekeeper, Nancy Nugent. It was a household with a bizarre mixture of formality (a gong was rung to announce that meals were served) and eccentricity, with the Bishop, even in the freezing winter, insisting on sleeping on the outside veranda. This was probably partially penance and partially because he believed it was good for his health.

After the limitations of preparing soft, chopped-up food for the elderly Bishop, Nancy relished the chance to cook for the young priest and his friends. As a daily outing, Nancy and the Bishop drove Pell's sandwiches for lunch over to him at Aquinas College, Mair Street, in the Bishop's Mercedes-Benz.

Fathers Elliott, Diamond, and Hart made the trip up from Melbourne several times a year for a roast lunch at the Palace. Elliott recalls those times with affection, including the day the three Melbourne priests, all dressed in black for the benefit of the old Bishop, were stranded on the highway with a flat tire. "The only practical one of the three of us was

Denis Hart, who knew the basics of changing a tire. Gerry knew the theory, and I did the rhetorical encouragement, with people driving by laughing at the three hapless priests."

These dinners in the Bishop's Palace were relaxing and, at times, sad. Occasionally, the Bishop's mind wandered back through the years, deciding one day that the Melbourne visitors were all from Rome and it was about 1922. He began inquiring about Cardinal Fumasoni Biondi (the former head of the Propagation of the Faith in Rome) and other well-known characters from six decades earlier. Sad but also amused in an embarrassed kind of way, the four young priests did the only thing that seemed reasonable in the circumstances—they played along, reassuring him that those he asked after were exceedingly well.

After Bishop O'Collins died in November 1983, aged ninety-one, Pell moved again—this time to the small rural parish of Bungaree, just outside Ballarat, as administrator, a less permanent and less authoritative role than that of pastor. He took Nancy and her culinary skills with him as housekeeper. He ministered to the people of the parish and continued editing *Light* and running Aquinas College.

As director of Aquinas, Pell was responsible for the training of almost one thousand Catholic teachers. At graduation ceremonies, he stressed to the teachers the importance of their role, not just in education, but also within the Church. At one of the first such ceremonies during his tenure he said:

> The Australian temptation is to tame Christ, not to crucify him, to trivialise his life and mission, not to grant them significance by an act of repudiation. . . . The whole drift of our society is pressuring the Church to abandon her claims to any kind of exclusive connection with revealed truth.
>
> The religion we profess is not a general "do-goodism" or a

gentle humanism, but one which makes difficult and particular moral demands and requires specific beliefs. [This was]
as alien to the people of today as to the Jews and pagans of
Christ's time.[10]

He asked the female graduates (the large majority of students) to consider their role in terms of the "revolutionary
change" that the role of women in Australia was undergo-
ing. "The Church will be relying on you as teachers, and
generally as wives and mothers, to accept the strengths of
the women's movement, to resist its pagan excesses and occasional silliness, above all to adapt and retain the strength
of Catholic family life."

Pell relished life as head of a tertiary institution and over
the years became increasingly proud of Aquinas, its students,
academic standards, spirituality, and environment. He says
he had no further ambitions at the time, although his influence on Catholic teacher training in Victoria was further
extended in 1980 when he began a three-year stint as principal of the Institute of Catholic Education. In that role he
had overall responsibility for the Victorian Catholic teachers' colleges, which by that time were well established and
on a firm footing. As well as overseeing the Institute, Pell
continued running Aquinas on a day-to-day basis. In later
years, courses in nursing and business were introduced by
these Catholic colleges, which became part of the multi-
campus Australian Catholic University.

In his decade at Aquinas, Pell took time out twice to
recharge his own intellectual batteries—firstly as a visiting scholar at his former Oxford college, Campion Hall,
in 1979, and then again at Saint Edmund's College, Cambridge, in the Michaelmas term of 1983. In both places he

[10] *Light*, March 1980.

caught up on reading, did a little writing, heard lectures, and participated generally in university and college life. At Cambridge, he attended lectures by the controversial Anglican clergyman Edward Norman and particularly enjoyed a series of lectures on Aristotle by Catholic philosopher Elizabeth Anscombe, whose scholarship contributed to a revival of interest in Aristotle's definitions of virtue and of the good life. Anscombe, an eccentric genius and passionate Catholic, studied and taught at both Oxford and Cambridge and in 1970 was appointed to the chair once held by her former teacher, Ludwig Wittgenstein.

When Anscombe died in January 2001 at age eighty-one, Pell, by that time in his fifth year as Archbishop of Melbourne, paid tribute to her in the magazine *Kairos* as "a giant in the world of twentieth-century philosophy" and the mother of seven children.

"Anscombe became a convert to the Church in 1940, allegedly after reading G. K. Chesterton's Father Brown detective stories. I have nowhere encountered a more formidable exponent. This was seen dramatically in 1968 as she defended Pope Paul VI's teaching against artificial contraception. Always dressed in slacks, often with a Kimono-type top, she wore a monocle and often carried a small brown paper bag for her cigars."

In 1984, preparing an editorial for *Light* on Pope John Paul II's encyclical *Salvifici Doloris* (the Christian meaning of human suffering), a tragedy in one of the small country communities Pell was serving, near Bungaree, meant the encyclical hit home extra hard. As he told *Light* readers: "A young mother and two of her three beautiful young children were killed in a car accident. A few weeks ago a schoolmate of the young mother had also died tragically on the road. These brute facts, which none of us can completely escape, added a new dimension to this small article. The families involved and all the local community were again confronted with one of life's great mysteries." The young woman also lost the unborn child she was carrying. Recalling the Requiem Mass he celebrated for her and for her children, Pell wrote later that the task was

> as difficult as burying my parents. . . . Like other helpers priests regularly have to confront suffering and evil, and try to help people to cope. This is not easy. Presence and support are important and few words are far better than too many words. Human suffering is a mystery and the suffering of good people is a greater mystery still. For those without faith, suffering is a brute fact, without meaning, which many bear stoically and with dignity. For those people with faith in a personal God, who is good and has endowed life with pattern and purpose, suffering can seem to contradict the Good News.
>
> A sudden and unexpected death, or a massive injustice, can shake and test a faith lived out and supported by many years of prayer and good behaviour. . . . It is natural in the first shock to see little but our loss. . . . Christ's teaching repeatedly ruled out any necessary connection between suffering and personal or family guilt. The instinct of many people when stricken with misfortune to ask why God is punishing them is mistaken. The Old Testament book of Job wrestled with the fact that the innocent often suffer. . . .
>
> But it is no coincidence that the cross or a crucifix is the most powerful Christian symbol. It helps us when in trouble to know that the Son of God suffered too. Suffering can poison us, harden our hearts, confirm us in our obsession with self. But Christians believe that suffering can purify, spark unexpected growth humanly and spiritually.
>
> We also believe that the scales of justice balance out in eternity, just as surely as this does not always happen in this life. Those who suffer more than their share will have redress.

This is part of what Jesus meant when he said "Blessed are those who mourn, they shall be comforted."

In mid-1984, Peter Elliott came to stay with Pell while attending a conference in Ballarat. Elliott, who was secretary to Bishop John Kelly, Melbourne's auxiliary bishop, found his normally gregarious friend "a bit blue . . . unusually quiet". Elliott suspected that his friend had the same thing on his mind that he did—that was, who would be appointed the new rector of Corpus Christ Seminary in Melbourne. Elliott, as a bishop's secretary, was privy to some of the intrigue surrounding the post. "But I kept my mouth shut, of course." As the seminary served the whole of Victoria, the rector did not have to be a Melbourne priest but could come from provincial or country Victoria. In fact, a large number of Ballarat students had recently dropped out of Corpus Christi, something that worried and annoyed Bishop Mulkearns of Ballarat and his priests, who were keen to have one of their own priests at the helm for a change. There was no doubt that Pell had the academic and administrative experience. While he would have been content to remain in academia for the rest of his working life, it was probably time to move onward if he were ever to do so.

Bishop Kelly was deeply concerned about the liberal, free-and-easy direction the seminary was taking. With the post of rector falling vacant, the wily Kelly, who was known in Melbourne as John A., was determined to see Pell promoted to the position. Kelly also knew that his first choice would never be accepted by Archbishop Sir Frank Little and those around him, so he apparently drew up a short list of three names, with Pell as number three. Those in spots one and two were older, more conservative priests, whom Kelly supposed, correctly, that Archbishop Little and his colleagues would reject in favor of the "third way". "By the time they got down to number three they were ready to stop arguing and go home", was how one Melbourne priest, who was a seminarian at the time, relates the story.

Elliott remembers that Kelly was working flat out to get Pell into the job: "The place was obviously falling apart; they needed a strong rector. Bishop Kelly knew George was a strong man who would inspire and discipline, but he also had the academic background. One night at Bungaree George said, 'Well, who is going to be the new rector, there are all these rumours?' and I just looked at him, and I don't think I said anything. I just pointed at him, and he said 'Oh'."

And sure enough, it happened. At age forty-three, with eleven years at Aquinas behind him, as well as almost five years as editor of *Light*, Pell prepared to leave Ballarat, to become rector of his Melbourne alma mater, Corpus Christi Seminary. Pell's father, for one, did not think the move was a promotion, with his son moving from running an institution with two thousand students to one with fifty students. On the other hand, seminary rectors, with the responsibility for training future priests, are entrusted in a very special way with shaping the future of the Church, and the job is considered a very important position. It was not a job Pell sought out. "I took the position because I was asked", he said.

At the seminary, on June 28, 1984, Archbishop Frank Little gathered the students together and announced that from the following year, Doctor George Pell, director of Aquinas College, Ballarat, would be their new rector.

"That'll give you all something to talk about," the Archbishop added.

It did. They are still talking about it two decades later.

Chapter 7

"A Few Small Changes"

The tall, dark-haired rector sat alone, facing his staff and students in a semicircle at Corpus Christi College in June 1985. The hostility in the room was palpable—almost all of those he was addressing were opposed to the changes to life at the seminary he was announcing. The meeting was a follow-up to the memo he had posted on the notice board earlier, headed "A few small changes". Despite the angst surrounding him, Pell looked utterly relaxed and in control, long legs stretched out comfortably in front of him. At this and other such meetings, one or two of the seminarians burst into tears.

A small minority of the students, who regarded the "few small changes" as long overdue to transform what had become a rather miserable student hostel into a house of prayer, were on the rector's side and aghast at some of their classmates' reactions. Fed up with the institution, one of those who supported the rector privately referred to the seminary as "the house of horrors". This small group knew it was high time someone tackled the malaise sapping life and strength from the Church around them in general and the seminary in particular. Now ten to fifteen years into their careers as priests, the small group who favored what the new rector was trying to do are, interestingly, among the most successful

priests of their generation so far. But as students they were
in a tiny minority. While many students sat on the fence and
kept their views to themselves, a sizeable group were openly
hostile. Father Charles Portelli, pastor of Keilor Downs in
outer suburban Melbourne, recalled: "George was really in
the bear pit; none of his staff gave him any support in front
of the students; he was sitting there out on his own, but he
was not intimidated, not in the slightest."

Ordinary Catholics in the pews, the Mass-goers of Victoria and Tasmania whose generosity maintained the seminary, would undoubtedly have been shocked to discover that
the "few small changes" causing such a fuss included the
introduction of a daily rosary for the seminary community,
an extra community weekday Mass, and prayers before the
Blessed Sacrament. Students were also to attend one of the
daily Masses said at different times at the college. Most lay
people would have assumed that daily Mass was a routine
part of life in the seminary and been incredulous to learn that
the new rector was facing such opposition as he tried to restore the practice. In the training of a priest, could anything
else be more important than the Sacrifice of the Mass? What
sort of priests would these students make? How would they
cope in parishes with at least three weekend Masses as well
as weddings and Baptisms, daily Masses on weekdays, devotions, visiting the sick, and working with different parish
groups and parishioners? Another "small change" meant that
Sunday lunch was to be a more formal meal, preceded by
drinks, with grace to be said.

Up to the mid-1980s, the ever-increasing chasm between
the traditional and liberal factions in the Catholic Church
had been fairly peripheral to George Pell's own work as a
priest. If pressed, the people he had served as a curate in
Swan Hill and Ballarat would have characterized him as a

modern priest, in tune with the young in an ever-changing world. The atmosphere at Aquinas had been egalitarian and liberal, and since his student days in Rome and in Oxford, Pell had been an ardent advocate of the reforms of the Second Vatican Council.

By the 1980s, however, it was clear that in the name of the "spirit" rather than substance of the Vatican Council, many in influential positions were determined to alter the very essence of Catholicism by impugning its traditions and even some of its most important doctrines. At Corpus Christi, this split was evident long before Pell's arrival as rector. Several students, for instance, said they felt persecuted and "left out of the loop" because they preferred to receive Holy Communion on the tongue rather than in the hand. The Church afforded everyone that choice after the Council, yet at Corpus Christi and elsewhere, those opting for the traditional method had been ostracized and even abused verbally for their choice. Likewise, students who objected to theology lecturers criticizing the Church's opposition to artificial birth control felt powerless to deal with the derision this earned them from those in charge. As rector, Pell saw firsthand how and why the Church was heading for a serious crisis of faith.

Students who had felt persecuted up to that time welcomed his arrival. A few never accepted him but most of these opted out of seminary training altogether. After a few months, most of the students got on well with him, but, in the words of one, were "gobsmacked" (figuratively, not literally) when he took to the football field with them for a kick around. "He used to hit, push in the back with a real force and was still incredibly fast even though he was twenty-five years older", one student remembered. "He never meant to hurt you playing football, but he played tough, and if

he wanted the ball and you had it . . . well, that was how
Brother O'Malley had taught him to play." In Pell's view,
the seminary teams of the early 1960s, drawn from a much
larger group of students, would have flattened those of the
1980s easily. "There were less of the muscular Christianity
types coming through", Pell recalls. "When I was rector,
one of the cultural shocks—it was a foolish, frivolous example, but nonetheless it did jolt me—was the low standard of
the football. It was largely a function of numbers. In a large
seminary of several hundred, it is not difficult to get thirty-
six decent players." The encounters with his seminarians
generally cost the rector two days of bandaged knees and
painful genuflections, but to him it was worth it.

When the new students for 1985 entered Corpus Christi
on March 1, the college in which their new rector found
himself was vastly different from the one he had entered as a
first-year student twenty-five years earlier. The old seminary,
at Werribee, had looked something like an English stately
home—after extensive refurbishment, it is now a luxury hotel. The new seminary, near Monash University at Clayton,
was modern in every way—from the gray concrete blocks
of its buildings to the outlook of most of its staff and students. Peter Joseph, one of fifteen new students entering
the college for the first time in 1985, thought it looked
like an army barracks. Architecturally, and in more significant ways, the institution was not to the new rector's taste.
Pell recalls an instructor from the Royal Melbourne Institute of Architects threatening to bring students to the college, because "he would tell his students you can see more
building defects in a confined space here than in most other
places."

Pell was responsible for the spiritual formation of the
seminary students, who were training to be priests in Mel-

bourne, Tasmania, and in Victoria's regional dioceses—
Ballarat, Sale, and Sandhurst. He was not responsible for
their academic program, which was undertaken by the Catholic Theological College. Pell regarded this program as "academically pretty solid, though it didn't have enough philosophy studies". Among other issues, he had to come to grips
with the latest thinking in matters like psychosexual development, which were relevant to the training of young men
for lives of celibacy.

Charles Portelli was one of twelve men ordained from
Corpus Christi College in Pell's first year as rector. Portelli
remembers Pell's determined battle to have an appropriate
image of our Lady installed in the seminary chapel dissolv-
ing into high farce with the antics of one of the liturgists on
the seminary staff. The rector, concerned by the absence of
any image of our Lady in the chapel, had decided to have
an image of Mary at the foot of her Son's crucifix carved by
the wife of the man who had carved the crucifix itself. The
statue duly arrived, but some on the college staff wanted it
mounted on the wall or in some other location well away
from the crucifix. Portelli recalls standing at the chapel door,
watching as one of the seminary staff gestured and pointed
at the unfortunate student holding the statue, ordering him
to move it farther and farther back from the cross. Just as
the hapless student would do so, Pell would order "No, no
—closer, closer", and back it would come until the other
staff member gestured for it to be moved in the opposite
direction. Pell's wish prevailed—eventually—until he left
as rector. The statue disappeared shortly afterward.

Professionally and personally, 1985 was one of the hardest years of George Pell's life. By the time he began work at
the seminary, his father was dying, spending time in hospital and at Margaret's home in Melbourne, where she cared

for him with love and devotion, despite his protests to his family to "Be on your way; don't be wasting too much of your time on me; I'm alright." He died on April 24, 1985, five years exactly since his wife, Margaret's, funeral. Like her, George senior was buried from Saint Alipius in Ballarat East, where his son preached the eulogy, recalling his father's colorful career and personality. This time his sermon was more expansive than the very moving one he gave at his mother's funeral Mass. Family members say he was slightly closer to his mother and so cut up over her death that he felt unable to speak for very long. By 1985, he also had more experience of coping with sad occasions in the pulpit, and to some extent he was able to take his cue from his father, who "would not want us to be too troubled, too disturbed at this time. Recently he repeated many times that he had had a good innings [a cricket term meaning 'a long life'], had enjoyed a good life. . . ."

For twenty-five years in the Royal Oak Hotel, Pell said, his father

dispensed hospitality, administered justice, kept the peace and incidentally built and maintained a sense of community which was as good as that in many of our parishes. . . . All who met him agreed that he was a great character, who regularly expressed himself colourfully and eloquently, sometimes with a pungent humour. I think he was a remarkable man. Dad was devoted to his family. Like most Australian men of his generation, he did not wear his heart on his sleeve (and was none the worse for this), but his devotion to his family was complete. I only realised fully how lucky I was in my parents as I grew older and saw a bit more of the world. Often in talks or sermons on the family I have told people that as a child and an adult it never once crossed my mind that my parents did not love me; I never doubted for a moment that they would do anything they could to help us.

If every adult could say this honestly about his parents our world would be a much better place. It is this quality of love which enables us to be sure that good people in their dying pass from death to life.

For the funeral, Pell chose scriptural readings that suited his father's life and outlook. "To the extent that he understood and accepted our teaching on life after death, he would have agreed that either there were many mansions in the Father's house or there were none at all."

He recalled his father as a strong man, physically and personally, who told it as he saw it and who had high principles and kept to them.

I know that he would have approved the second reading where Christ, in the Holy City, the new Jerusalem, is giving "water from the well of life free to anybody who is thirsty". He would have been pleased for another reason. Like most of us, he too affected to being anti-British, at least in unimportant matters like cricket matches; when it was a matter of importance, for example, war, things were different. In fact, he was very proud of his origins, of the people and tradition to which he belonged. It is this scriptural passage, of course, which Blake used as one starting point for his marvellous poem on the New Jerusalem, which English people now sing just as we sing 'Waltzing Matilda'. Dad would have been pleased with this reading and thought it only right and proper. . . . It is a privilege as his son and as a priest, with faith and full confidence, to commend his soul to the care of our loving God.

A large group of senior students from Corpus Christi traveled to Ballarat for the funeral, en route to a "weekend of reflection" at the beach. Lunch was organized especially for them at a private home, but after the Mass only four of around thirty of them opted to stay behind—each one of them appalled and deeply embarrassed at their classmates' insensitivity.

Pell's family and close friends were also shocked by the attitudes of some of the seminary staff. At one seminary dinner, for instance, the priests organizing it seated the rector in a part of the room distant from the main action, with his back to those who had to speak. "It was unbelievably rude and hurtful", said someone who was there.

Why such open hostility? How much of it, if any, did Pell deserve, and if so, why? The basic problem was a deep clash of ideas. One of the priests on the seminary staff who was part of the earlier regime and admired it said Pell's "few small changes" amounted to "George's wish list" and that they had about as much intellectual sophistication as "the man of straw" from *The Wizard of Oz*. He and others resented the rector's determination to bring in the changes and believed his methods amounted to "bullying" and claimed he had a romantic notion of trying to recreate the Church of yesteryear.

The other side of the argument is that, for the sake of the students and their future parishioners, Pell was gently but firmly attempting to redress a slackness and lack of direction that had crept into the seminary, He believed that the first step in training priests is to focus them on their own personal relationship with God, ensuring it has the strength to endure whatever tests and tribulations lie ahead. Mass and devotion to the Real Presence of Christ in the Eucharist and to the Blessed Virgin Mary are central to the Catholic faith, and if young priests leave the seminary without a firm grasp of these building blocks, their faith and that of their people will suffer.

Weighty tomes have been produced on these very questions and undoubtedly the debate will continue, but the experience of the past twenty years suggests that the slackness of the 1970s and 1980s, so evident in seminaries, was an aberration that is being corrected in many parts of the world. Those who resent this view claim that Pell and his ilk are conservatives "stuck in the 1950s". His supporters would reject this wholeheartedly and paste the "conservative" label on his critics "for being stuck in the 1970s" rather than moving onward.

Doctor Peter Cross, now pastor of Melbourne's bayside suburb of Brighton, was dean of studies at the seminary when Pell was rector. He was also moderator of one of the groupings of students within the seminary. Like Pell, Cross had attended Campion Hall, Oxford, and had completed his Ph.D. in Rome. Cross said Pell's appointment as rector was "an initial shock for the seminary staff. I don't think anybody expected it." He was four years behind Pell in their student days and had been a member of the first-year rhetoric class that had sometimes clashed with Pell when he was their prefect. However, unlike some from that class, Cross did not nurse any grudges.

Cross said that as rector, Pell "could be fairly confronting" but that he had a "great way with the students", and he "impressed me greatly for talking so openly with them about issues concerning the college." He said staff and students "always knew where they stood with Pell" and also exactly what he wanted and expected. Accustomed to the Oxford culture of students speaking up and arguing with their lecturers, Pell never resented the Corpus Christi students speaking their minds. Staff meetings, too, were sometimes fiery.

While Pell's "few small changes" were highly controversial, Cross agreed that they were basically that—small changes, even symbolic ones. "I was not opposed to them", he said. "As dean of studies I was also concerned that the students should be doing a bit more work." Cross said that the few students not attending daily Mass had also been of concern to previous rectors. These, apparently, had not tackled the problem as directly as Pell, who stunned the students by scheduling Mass at around 7:00 A.M. a couple of mornings a week (the students had been accustomed to attending Mass later in the day).

According to Cross, some of the students resented Pell because they believed he was accusing them of not praying. "I don't believe he was ever trying to say that, but he hurt a lot of them by insisting on prayer in the chapel", Cross said. As a spiritual director to some of the students, Cross said they were meditating regularly in their rooms, yet Pell wanted prayers in the chapel that could be "measured" by what could be seen publicly. He said some of the students also found some of the military imagery invoked by Pell in his talks to them too provocative. Such phrases as "soldiers for Christ" and "We're fighting a battle", used by Pell to provoke discussion, put the students off, Cross found.

Doctor Frank O'Loughlin, now pastor of Melbourne's bayside suburb of Sandringham, served on the seminary staff from 1977 to 1990. He had graduated from Propaganda Fide three years after Pell and also completed his doctorate at the Pontifical Urban University. O'Loughlin taught the seminarians sacramental theology and was a moderator for a group of eight or nine students. He and his colleagues found Pell "great fun socially", and there was an atmosphere of "good bonhomie among the staff having a drink at night". But when it got down to serious matters, he and Pell were usually diametrically opposed about what direction the seminary should be taking. Unlike Peter Cross, O'Loughlin did not view the "few small changes" as minor. "On the surface they looked minuscule, but in fact they meant a change of spirit that was quite significant", O'Loughlin said. "They took backwards a formation system that was trying to give a much more thorough formation."

O'Loughlin said with Masses at different times of the day, it was hard to know if and when students were attending. But to the best of his recollection, most of the students were daily Mass-goers, but many of those who were not were probably in the process of making up their minds that the priesthood might not be for them. O'Loughlin said one of the difficulties he had with Pell was the rector's insistence on "what the eye sees and what the ear hears" in terms of community prayer for the students.

Father Peter Joseph is now Chancellor of the Maronite Diocese of Australia. He wrote the updated version of the definitive Catholic reference book *Sheehan's Apologetics* during his time as vice-rector and theology teacher at Vianney College, the seminary for the Diocese of Wagga Wagga in New South Wales. In 1985, from his perspective as a first-year student at Corpus Christi, the meetings were extremely open and frank, with some students rude and presumptuous. Joseph looks back on his time under Pell with real affection. He is fond of claiming, in jest: "I was taught by George Pell, and I've got the scars to prove it." At the famous "few small changes" meeting, Joseph remembers one student complaining bitterly to Pell about the fact that one compulsory morning Mass would be held on a weekday, to be attended by the entire student body.

"I was hurt when I saw that notice", the student protested.

Pell replied: "You have got to ask yourself why you were hurt."

Even with eleven years' experience of running a tertiary institution behind him, Pell found the job as rector challenging because a seminary is quite different from a teachers' college. But the experience was to have a major impact on the future training of priests in Victoria and Tasmania when he became Archbishop of Melbourne twelve years later.

As rector, he was unsure of whether he would be able to secure the backing of the trustees of the seminary (the bishops of Victoria and Tasmania) for all the changes he wanted to make. His political skills, honed through eleven years of doing battle with politicians on behalf of Aquinas College, came to the fore. He was determined to "win" on major issues like daily Mass attendance by the students (only a few diehards held out, and they later left without being ordained). But Joseph observed that Pell picked his battles carefully.

For example, Pell had also discovered almost no devotions in the college, although the students did meditate and did read the morning and evening prayers of the Church individually. In Pell's own student days, Benediction had been held once a week and, at certain times of the liturgical year, once a day. At Clayton, despite trenchant opposition from some quarters, his efforts to encourage the students to pray the rosary every day bore fruit, with half to two-thirds of the students joining in.

"And I did manage, eventually, to put on Benediction once", Pell recalls.

When asked, "Was that once a week or once a month?"

He replied, "Once in three years."

In time, Pell won over many of the students' trust and confidence. Most of them enjoyed the Church history that he taught them, and while many of them shied away from the "muscular Christianity" of the football field, they liked matching it with the rector on the tennis court, where sometimes they were able to beat him. Peter Elliott said that after a few rocky patches, the students accepted Pell because they saw him as a man, and there was nothing devious about him. The packaging told you the product. You knew where you stood. He'd tell you off if you were wrong, and he was usually right, but he'd do it in a straight way without being too aggressive. He'd just let you know, and he'd also have options and advice for you. He'd never leave you up in the air. I don't believe the staff ever accepted him, they resented him.

The problem was, he couldn't change the staff, and there weren't enough bishops who could help him on that one. He had a couple of bishops supporting him, but not all. It slipped back after he left, of course, because the staff were still there.

It would be a mistake to assume that the problems of Corpus Christi were significantly different from any other Australian seminary at the time. In Sydney, for example, at Saint Patrick's Seminary, three senior seminarians were discovered to be active homosexuals and left shortly before they were due to be ordained. Church sources say their "secret" was discovered one day when they were having a bitter argument in the refectory.

In Melbourne, Pell said the homosexual subculture at Corpus Christi "was not manifest" during his time as rector, although "a number of students who left quickly moved into gay life-styles, which was a surprise." Two former students of the seminary died of AIDS.

The numerical decline in seminarians was also a major worry in Melbourne, as elsewhere. In 1973, the Clayton seminary opened with 144 students. Each subsequent year saw a steady decline of around 7 to 10 percent. By 1984, when Archbishop Little announced Pell's appointment as rector, student numbers had more than halved to sixty-three students. A larger than average intake of fifteen in 1985 saw an increase to sixty-eight. Pell's final year as rector, 1987, was another good year with sixteen students starting. Only eight newcomers, however, arrived in 1988. From that point, the downward trend accelerated, with just four students starting at the beginning of 1996, the year George Pell became Archbishop of Melbourne, bringing the college total to twenty-one. Slow but steady increases in enrollments, and a much lower rate of attrition, have since seen that number almost double to forty-one.

"It was more than just ugly; it held no happy memories", one man said. "No wonder nobody complained when it was closed down and the seminary moved to Carlton [when George Pell became archbishop in 1996]." Another priest turned down the chance to undertake university studies while he was a seminarian at Clayton "because it would have meant I had to spend an extra two or three years there." This priest gives Pell full credit for his being ordained, "because if it had not changed I could not have stuck it out a moment longer".

Several former students claimed that before Pell, staff members encouraged students to spy on each other, reporting their classmates for anything negative they said about the prevailing regime. After Pell arrived, staff members who disliked him accused students who did like him of sneaking off "like Nicodemus by night" to tell tales of them.

Portelli remembers having a room on the "shady side" of one block of the seminary. Of the seven students on the opposite "sunny" side of the block, every single one left shortly before he was due to be ordained priest or deacon. Portelli says it is nonsense to blame the upheavals of the now long-ago Vatican Council for the situation in the 1980s. Rather, the policies and practices of the day in seminary training were simply a failure, and students lost confidence in the place and also, sadly, in many cases, in the ideal of the priesthood itself. "Seminary formation imploded. The transcendent, sacramental side of the priesthood was not emphasized at all." Nor were the students particularly directed toward the social welfare aspects of the work of a priest. Against such a backdrop, it took extraordinary faith and determination for students to persevere, and those who did have generally emerged as outstanding.

Father Greg Pritchard, pastor of Ringwood on Melbourne's east side, said "group night" in the seminary was a "sacred cow". "You could be excused from Mass, but not from group night." On one occasion he remembers, group night consisted of ten students and a staff member whining and complaining about how hurt and pained they felt by Pell. When it came to his turn, Pritchard said that he did not feel he had anything to complain about, and the staff member made it clear he was out of line. One group even devoted an entire "recollection weekend" at the beach to discussing, in largely negative terms, "the effect of Father Pell in my life".

Other students, however, simply did not trust the old regime. One man said that before Pell's time, he had even stopped going to confession to any of the staff because "I felt I couldn't trust them and didn't want to pour my heart out to them."

Even after a decade or more as priests, some former students today cannot bear to return to Clayton to stay overnight (it is now a Catholic conference center). Another survivor from the era said: "I'm not sure what our training was about." The most committed students helped each other, talking over problems and offering plenty of tea and sympathy when the need arose. In one case, this peer group assistance extended to a few friends encouraging a young man, who had given up seminary studies in disgust, to return. Their instincts that he had a strong and genuine vocation proved correct. He was duly ordained and is now a pastor in Melbourne, with the talent to be a future bishop.

Cross acknowledged that many of the former staff did not realize until years later just how deeply the students he described as "more conservative" hated their days at Clayton, but he said he thought their perceptions were not entirely fair.

Coming from Wagga Wagga in New South Wales, Peter Joseph would normally have studied in Sydney, but he had asked his bishop, William Brennan, to allow him to study in Melbourne under George Pell. Joseph said he had not been keen to study at the Sydney seminary because at that time Sydney students were subject to what was known as the Ira Progoff "intensive journal method" of Jungian psychology, which involved making copious daily notes about their personal feelings. Also, he had happened upon Pell's booklets *Bread, Stones or Fairy Floss* and *Are Our Schools Catholic?* "I thought the booklets were intelligent and orthodox", Joseph recalls. "I hadn't heard of George Pell when I bought the booklets, but I read them and thought, 'He knows much more than he's saying'." Peter Joseph spent eighteen months at Corpus Christi before Pell called him in one evening in mid-1986. "Have I done something wrong?" the younger man inquired. "Nothing you need confess," the rector reassured him. The news was, from September, he would be studying in Rome, at Propaganda Fide. "You'll find it very difficult at first, but you'll love it", was the advice Pell proffered, similar to that offered to him by his rector two decades earlier.

Early the following year, 1987, Pell received some news of his own. After just two years and a few months at the helm of Corpus Christi, he had received a letter from the Apostolic Nuncio (Vatican ambassador) in Canberra, informing him that the Holy Father wished to appoint him an auxiliary bishop of Melbourne and asking if he would accept. He did. It was a major promotion. Pell says he was "partly surprised" at the promotion, "because my views were certainly not the flavour of the month" in Australian episcopal and theological circles at the time. "It was a shock of course. It's one thing to have this sort of thing talked about; it's quite different to have it happen", he said. "I had mixed feelings. Certainly I hadn't had long enough to do what I wanted to do at the seminary. But the other thing was that I was pleased to be out of the seminary because it was a difficult assignment. The majority of the staff and a goodly percentage of the students felt that I was heading in the wrong direction."

Several of his more cynical friends even suggested that he was "kicked upstairs" because he was having too much influence on the seminary. Others tell a different story, claiming that the archbishop of the day, Sir Frank Little, asked Rome if he could appoint two auxiliary bishops, Hilton Deakin and Peter Connors, and Rome replied, through the nuncio, that yes, he could have two new auxiliaries, provided one of them was George Pell. Several priests mentioned that when he was in Melbourne in 1986, Pope John Paul II made a point of visiting the ailing Bishop Kelly at the hospice where he was living. It was not impossible that Kelly, an admirer of Pell, offered His Holiness a little advice. One of Pell's colleagues on the seminary staff has long believed he was destined to be a bishop while running Aquinas and was sent to the seminary to broaden his experience before entering the episcopate. Asked now why he selected Pell as one of his auxiliary bishops, Archbishop Little merely says: "Others do the choosing."

The announcement, made at noon Rome time, was broadcast on Melbourne radio at 9:00 P.M. Pell rang his friend Peter Elliott and asked him over to the seminary staff room for a drink. "I remember coming into the staff room and everyone sitting there and having a beer, but they all looked like stunned mullets, and you could read that they were trying to weigh up whether it was better to have him as their rector or auxiliary bishop", Elliott recalls. While Pell's "few small changes" at the seminary had been nowhere near as comprehensive as he believed necessary, he had learned some invaluable lessons: "I learned how things should not be done in future." But most of all, he realized that a seminary could only be reformed with leadership from the very top of the Church—the archbishops or bishops at the head of the dioceses that owned it.

He was consecrated a bishop at only forty-five years of age in Saint Patrick's Cathedral on May 21, 1987. It was reasonable to think, as many did, that his time in charge of a regional Victorian diocese—or perhaps even the Archdiocese of Melbourne—would come one day. If and when it did, seminary reform would be one of his top priorities.

Chapter 8

"In many places no birds sing"

"Evil is nearly as deep a mystery as saintliness, as heroic goodness, and much more of a problem. But in Cambodia nature did register a protest. Under Pol Pot, the misery and hunger were so great that the people, in their battle against famine, ate all the wild birds. More than ten years later there are very few birds in Cambodia; in many places no birds sing."

So wrote Bishop George Pell in December 1989. His visit to Cambodia, as chairman of Australian Catholic Relief (ACR)—the overseas aid agency of the Catholic Church in Australia, now known as Caritas—was one of many working visits to lands torn apart by war, tyranny, natural disasters, or sheer poverty. His job was to ensure that the donations of Catholics to ACR were put to the wisest possible uses in countries where so many urgent demands were pressing . . . for food, water, shelter, infrastructure, medical supplies, education, and sustainable enterprises that, hopefully, could help people survive in the future. Cambodia was a different world, where at that time trains on one of the few remaining railway lines traveled with two carriages ahead of the engine, in which passengers traveled free because of the ever-present risks of land mines.

Shortly after his consecration as a bishop in May 1987,

Pell's fellow bishops had elected him to the post of ACR chairman, a job that took at least a day a week. It was a major part of Pell's life for his nine years as an auxiliary bishop, although by no means the only part. Other aspects of his work during this period will be covered in the chapters following this one.

ACR/Caritas, affiliated with its counterparts in other countries throughout the world, is funded from the donations of Mass-goers, who are encouraged by their priests to give generously, especially during Lent, when even many children do their bit for the six-week Project Compassion appeal. The chairman's job is strenuous and demanding, with frequent visits to the world's trouble spots and poorest areas. In 1987 it was a potential quagmire and a stern test for any new bishop. The Church's justice, peace, and humanitarian aid efforts were under a darkening cloud. For several years beforehand, sections of the secular media, and Bob Santamaria's National Civic Council, had been asking pertinent and pointed questions about monies donated in good faith being diverted to Communist organizations in the Philippines. The Australian Bishops' Catholic Committee for Justice and Peace had become extraordinarily anti-American, issuing a discussion paper for schools and parishes, *Work for a Just Peace: Reflections on Peacemaking in an Armed World*, calling for Australia to reappraise its military relationship with the United States, suggesting that the latter's lease on the northwest cape military installation should not be renewed. The publication drew a sharp written protest from the United States embassy in Canberra. As Santamaria observed: "The gulf between the Catholic bishops and the great majority of their people on this question is obvious."

Economic times were hard. In October 1987, a major plunge saw 20 percent slashed from the value of Wall Street's

Dow Jones index, and the Australian Stock Exchange followed suit. Despite such problems, in 1988, Pell's first full year in the job, Catholics donated just over Au$3 million to the Project Compassion appeal, allowing ACR to direct more than Au$4.7 million toward relief and development projects in Asia, Latin America, Africa, and the Pacific. In Pell's last full year as chairman, 1996, the Project Compassion appeal raised almost Au$4.5 million. Extra donations and government contributions allowed Au$6.8 million to be distributed to the world's greatest areas of need.

As chairman, Pell devoted the greater part of nine years to the poorest people on earth—some of them Christian, but the vast majority not—ravaged by starvation, natural disasters, and brutal regimes. Frequently, he flew to Sydney from Melbourne for a day or two a week to work at the organization headquarters in North Sydney. Frequent travel to the places where ACR was working in partnership with local Catholic agencies was an exhausting and emotionally draining part of the job. In his nine years at the helm, Pell visited India (three times—once immediately after a deadly cyclone), Cambodia (three times as it was rebuilt from the human rubble of Pol Pot's "Killing Fields"), Zambia, Thailand, Vietnam, Indonesia, and the Philippines. On such journeys, the Bishop kept detailed diaries. He also attended meetings in Rome and Hong Kong of Caritas Internationalis, the worldwide federation of Catholic aid agencies.

In an article written after his first visit to Cambodia in 1989, Pell recalled:

> American bomb craters are still visible on the approaches to the Phnom Penh airport, and the huge modern bridge over the Tuleg Sap river has three spans missing. . . . The American bombing of Cambodia produced a climate of hate, which helped the Pol Pot cancer to spread. Pol Pot himself

was Western educated in France where he had been heavily
influenced by French Stalinists. The Western tradition of revolutionary tyranny stemming from the Jacobins of the French
Revolution of 1879, through Marx himself and then Lenin
all contributed to making Pol Pot what he was, and is. . . .

Pol Pot drove all the population of Phnom Penh into the
countryside to be "re-educated". Today there are still a few
rusting hulks of cars, abandoned by the side of the roads,
without petrol, in this exodus. Evidence of higher education
was often a death warrant. Some responsible estimates assert
that one or two million Cambodians died or fled, out of a
population of eight million. Today 90 percent of the population of Phnom Penh are newcomers.

Six of the seven Catholic churches in the capital were completely destroyed, stone by stone, while the Khmers (Cambodians) who returned from France to join Pol Pot's revolution had to demonstrate their loyalty by working on the
destruction of the Catholic cathedral. This site is now occupied by a telecommunications centre. The visit certainly
affected me. I rarely dream, or, as the medical people tell us
more accurately, I am one of those who do not remember
dreaming. But I dreamt every night in Cambodia.

His diaries, penned in haste on planes and at the end
of long days travelling by road and boat, describe ACR-
sponsored projects and pinpoint local needs for future projects. The Mass, prayers, and the Church feature prominently. Occasionally, the diaries mention the books Pell
happened to be reading. At the end of a long day in Vietnam
in 1993, staying in a Communist-run guesthouse, he took
out Saint Gregory of Nyssa's *Life of Moses*, published in the
fourth century, and Le Carré's *Night Manager*; during a long
delay at the Bombay airport later the same year it was Owen
Chadwick's *From Bossuet to Newman*.

On December 12, 1989, Pell visited Site 2, a camp on the

Thai/Cambodian border that was home to 150,000 Cambodians, half of them under the age of fifteen and about one in
five under the age of three. His guide was French-speaking
Bishop Yves Ramousse, Cambodia's only surviving Catholic
bishop still working in the region at that time. Pell recorded
in his diary:

> Father Pierre, missionary in Asia for 50 years and history
> written on his brown, weather-beaten face, told me, as a
> child clutched his hands, that the children are God's blessing
> on the place!
>
> Camp divided into squares surrounded by ditches with
> bamboo shacks. Three rooms: kitchen with open fire, living
> space with table and benches and bedroom. Everything in
> bamboo, even sliding doors. Quite clean, and many attempts
> to plant flowers and trees. Visited 2 Catholic churches in
> north and south of camp. In northern church, Stations of
> the Cross on wall, picture of Holy Family. Building topped
> outside by white crucifix. Gaggle of small children ran to
> Bishop Ramousse and some of the women came forward
> too, straggling in for choir practice for Christmas. 100 Bap-
> tised Catholics in the group with 200 catechumens. The in-
> struction is done by the people themselves, sometimes by the
> newly baptized. Preparation takes two years . . . the rebirth
> of the Cambodian church!
>
> Two Khmer bishops and 14 priests martyred for the faith
> under Pol Pot. At his house R. [Ramousse] told me this and
> his usual jollity fell away to reveal immense sadness and some-
> one near to tears. Other bishops including R. expelled. R.
> now responsible for Cambodian Church. Children friendly
> and many of the adults friendly, too. Every type represented
> in community of 150,000 including gangsters and war lords.
> Difficult to imagine such pleasant people being such mur-
> derers!

From Site 2, Bishop Pell travelled through Thailand and Vietnam to catch a plane for Cambodia—

14/12/89: By Russian plane from Ho Chi Minh City to Phnom Penh. 30+ passengers, tiny seats, front 5 or 6 rows full of luggage inc. cases of whiskey and beefeater gin. Noisy, no air vents, clouds of vapour from air-conditioner spewing up front. Jolted landing, drab, drab, drab.

16/12/89: Anniversary of my ordination. Spent morning visiting local fine arts institute (or school) and saw the youngsters practising Khmer dancing—older teachers, one with large stick which she beat upon the floor, were from former Royal Ballet. . . . Visited hospital, 50 km away. Many malaria patients and amputees, some of them 18 to 22, one or two looked about 15. One amputee friendly, others less so, not taking my hand when I offered it.

In afternoon visited former high school, which was jail and extermination camp for Pol Pot. Instruments of torture there. Enormity of crimes too much to take in. Barbed wire entanglements still on perimeter of school and some on verandas in one of buildings, where prisoners were confined in brick cells constructed in class rooms. Saw cell where Foreign Minister of Pol Pot executed, saw statues of Pol Pot. There has to be a heaven for those who died here, whatever their earlier faults, and the idea of hell for those who led and organised this barbarity has a certain logic. To what extent did the American bombing prompt this hate? 20,000 exterminated at camp.

In evening met with Maryknoll Fathers (USA) now working in Cambodia. . . . Earlier in evening, home Mass at Dario's house in suburbs. Only European there and protected by locals, Gregorian chant in background for Christmas. . . . Soldier on guard during night outside our hotel.

18–19/12/89: Choeung Ek is quiet and beautiful, near a lake, not too far from Phnom Penh, the capital of Cambodia. Nearby the peasants work the fields pretty much as they have always done since the jungle was cleared. The Cambodian countryside is still like the Garden of Eden, but the serpents of evil have swarmed there.

Choeung Ek is also the site of the killing fields, the mass graves where thousands of victims of the government of Pol Pot (1976–1979) were taken for extermination. 8985 corpses found, not all mass graves disinterred—perhaps 89 out of 139. Splendid Khmer monument to the dead, with layer upon layer of human skulls. Mythology tells us that Saint Patrick drove all the snakes from Ireland and Pol Pot drove the birds of the air from Cambodia. I remembered this as I marvelled how so much evil and suffering could have occurred in such a setting of peace and beauty. Surely nature must have objected. Surely the wind or the trees must have murmured in protest at the outrages, at the barbarism.

Stayed overnight at two-storey Pol Pot residence at Takeo —in middle of lake, accessible only by narrow footbridge and now by a road for cars. Was home of Democ, provincial Pol Pot governor, known as "the butcher". Slept like a log under mosquito net. . . . Visited Chief Buddhist Monk in Cambodia, Venerable Thep Bong in large hall with photo of Pope at one end. He did not support recognition of Catholics or freedom to worship, said time was not ripe. Ven prayed for us and we prayed the prayer of Saint Francis.

20/12/89: Met with Chem Snguon vice-minister for Justice. Had been ambassador recalled for briefing by Pol Pot and then locked up on edge of Phnom Penh with other ambassadors to till soil. Said that there was not much improvement in last 2 years in administration of justice!

Some of the diary entries capture a sense of the Catholic Church's centuries-old missionary effort in southeast Asia and the high price it sometimes extracted:

Samray [one of the Catholic Relief workers] just out of hospital after a bad traffic accident. Scars on face and some brain damage affecting concentration. Quietly spoke in French, expressed his determination to request recognition of Catholics again and again from government until it is given! He used to travel to Vietnam to bring back the Blessed Sacrament. His wife and children fled (to camps?). . . . Has there ever been an age in which so many Catholics have suffered and died for their faith?

Visited Teachers' College at Takeo where ACR are building a dormitory which we saw incomplete. . . . In afternoon crossed Tuleg Sap by boat and visited former Carmelite nuns' monastery, now used as an orphanage with 100 orphans. Received by management at a long table in the derelict chapel —all religious symbolism removed but portraits of the President (20 years younger than he is actually!), Marx and Lenin. Statue of Sacred Heart, with no arms, had been replaced in room behind chapel within former cloister. Brought back after Pol Pot threw it out. Convent built in 1911 and bell of 1922 restored and used to summon children. Prayed at tombs of sisters at rear of convent. Immense niche in wall for crucifix had not been removed, so form still visible and derelict building still topped by cross visible from river.

Pell and ACR were satisfied that Cambodia's government in 1989, while Marxist and therefore far from perfect, was an immense improvement on the past, with sufficient basic food, limited small business, schools open, and infrastructure slowly being replaced.

Cambodia is like a chessboard and the players are ruthless [Pell wrote after the trip]. But the signs of hope were strong. Children are everywhere and children are a sign of hope, a reaction to the slaughter. Some locals claim that Cambodia now has the highest birth rate in the world, except for the Cambodian refugee camps on the Thai border! Religious freedom has been restored to the Buddhists and the small

Moslem minority, and the small Christian communities hope
they too will receive similar recognition.

ACR, with the support of the Australian Government, has
worked in Cambodia for nearly 10 years, not because we approved of the government, but because we wanted to answer
human need, to lessen human suffering.

The Catholic Church's relief efforts in Cambodia reached
out to the people in general, with no special concentration
on the small Catholic minority, in the provision of relief
and development aid. Religious freedom for Christians was
finally granted by the Cambodian government in May 1990
—a step for which Australian Catholic Relief and George
Pell can share a little of the credit.

In 1992, Pell returned to Cambodia, accompanying Cardinal Edward Clancy, for the opening of a rural development center in Takeo province, supported by ACR to assist
agricultural, health, water, and reforestation projects. ACR's
efforts in working with and equipping local people to repair
over 260 feet of a vital retaining wall, which had been swept
away by floods the previous year, had saved much of the
area's water supply. By doing this, fifty to sixty thousand
people were fed with rice for a year.

The three years since his last visit had made a real difference. Pell's diary entry dated February 29 records: "Airport
much changed with small terminal thronged with people . . .
big advertising bill boards outside airport on road to Phnom
Penh. Four or five times as much traffic as in December '89;
cars, motorbikes and pushbikes. Many more houses, shops,
etc., restored; great activity business-wise, around streets.
Smell of hope in the air. . . . Mass with Maryknollers, quite
public (unlike celebration for Christmas in Dario's room
in '89)."

On March 1, he was mobbed by an "immense throng of Vietnamese" Catholics in Cambodia, eager for blessings and to kiss his ring. He also met Sister Matilda "who was the solitary religious working in the whole of Cambodia in the late 80s". On March 5, Pell and Clancy were received by Prince Sihanouk in his beautifully restored palace.

> "Sihanouk protected by 20 or 30 North Korean guards in grey tropical uniforms—about 30 years old, fit, strong, vigilant and like something from James Bond. Incidentally Onesta's number plate was 007 [Onesta Carpene was the woman in charge of ACR's operations in Cambodia]. Sihanouk beautifully dressed in Western suit, smooth and voluble. Allowed Cardinal to sit on couch with him as Cardinal ranks as a prince!
>
> Like many of the leaders we met, he spoke quietly, excellent English interspersed with a few French phrases. . . . Sihanouk spoke of the genius of the great and noble Catholic religion; of the pivotal role of Polish Catholics in overthrowing communism. . . . He spoke of Khmer Rouge deriving inspiration from the French Revolution and especially Robespierre and from the Chinese Cultural Revolution. . . . Stressed importance of justice and peace for long-term future. Acknowledged role of ACR and Christian work in helping the unfortunate.

The ACR-backed Agricultural Centre in Takeo had forged even farther ahead when Bishop Pell returned for a third visit on November 25, 1993. This time, the journey from Phnom Penh took ninety minutes on a good road, rather than three and a half hours on a goat track. After a 7:00 A.M. start from Phnom Penh, now clogged with traffic, he arrived at Takeo to find: "Enormous change in Agricultural Centre even from official opening 18 months ago. Gum trees much higher, banana trees now too, deep moat around field next

to centre and variety of veggies, fruit growing. Locals now
have three crops a year of rice and significant improvement
in yields achieved. Attended meeting of team with 20 local
leaders in afternoon . . . very proud of work being done for
health in the six local primary schools."

Most Australian Catholics in the pews, who faithfully
contribute to Project Compassion year-in, year-out, have
never heard of Takeo, but their contributions helped turn
around the lives of a community that, a decade earlier, had
been as desperate as any people have ever been in human history. The day after he visited Takeo, Pell met Kom Sam Ol,
Minister for Agriculture, who wanted to make the Takeo
Project a model for all southeast Cambodia as a means of
spreading prosperity among the farmers, many of whom
were still very poor.

Pell's third visit coincided with Cambodia's colorful, joy-
ous Water Festival and boat races. He found: "Shops re-
opened, all sorts of food available including fresh fruit and
vegetables. Two Western supermarkets open—including
'Le Shop' managed by an Aussie! Children cheeky—many
bright-coloured and western clothes about. The United Nations Transitional Authority in Cambodia forces—22,000
military and civilian personnel—had just left unlamented,
with the tragic but accurate nickname of 'United Nations
Transmission of AIDS Commission'."

Even nature, given time, had healed itself. Overhead, one
day, Pell spotted something that brought the killing fields
to mind—three or four V-shaped flights of birds. Even the
beautiful ibises had returned. Slowly but surely, life and hope
were triumphing over death.

When Caritas commits itself to particular areas and projects, it is generally in for the long haul, maintaining involvement until local Church agencies (which themselves often

need years of rebuilding after traumatic wars and oppressions) are able to manage on their own, with financial assistance where necessary. By 1996, when George Pell was Archbishop of Melbourne, he told supporters in his final letter as Caritas chairman:

> The most significant change during 1996 in Caritas Australia's global development and relief work was the reorganisation of the programme in Cambodia. In the 17 years since the end of the devastating Pol Pot regime, Cambodian society has been slowly rebuilt.
>
> During that period, Caritas Australia has invested more than [Au]$14 million into rehabilitation programmes, the building of infrastructure and the training of Cambodian people in agriculture. In the past few years in particular, many local non-government organisations have been formed by Cambodian people to tackle social issues in their own society. Caritas Australia maintains a small programme of its own in Cambodia but is putting its emphasis on building partnerships with local organisations.

On the other side of the world, however, new challenges for Caritas were opening up. Pell also reported in 1996 that Caritas had committed itself to long-term housing reconstruction in Zaire, Rwanda, and Tanzania, after more than 1.5 million refugees began returning. The project not only helped provide homes, it taught invaluable carpentry skills to local men and secondary schoolboys. Other projects undertaken were also one-offs (one of a kind), but they were lasting in their impact. In Peru in 1996, a small grant of US$6,000 helped the community of Tucucucho in Huancaveliaca build a sheep dip. "Sheep are the major source of income for these families, and the dip will increase their income by reducing animal loss from parasites and disease", Pell wrote in his annual Caritas report.

The organization was also at the forefront of social justice campaigns. In 1994 Pell joined sixteen other Australian Catholic representatives as part of an ecumenical election-monitoring team during South Africa's first all-race elections, where he found the people's joy and spirit of optimism overwhelming. The following year Caritas drew together thirty-three Church agencies to promote awareness of the appalling death and injury toll and upheaval caused by the use of anti-personnel land mines. In seven weeks, the campaign collected two hundred thousand signatures for a petition to the Senate, forcing political leaders to take the issue seriously. Pell was one of a delegation of Australian bishops to the Ukraine, led by Cardinal Clancy, to establish a practical working partnership with Caritas Ukraine, as the Catholic Church in Eastern Europe reestablished her social mission after official exclusion from all humanitarian work during the decades of Communist rule.

As chairman, Pell sometimes worked at the "front line" in major emergencies, such as the Indian earthquake of 1993, one of the worst ever on the subcontinent. Before dawn on September 30, 1993, a series of earthquakes struck southwestern India, about 250 miles southeast of Bombay, razing towns and villages to rubble. The official death toll from the quakes and aftershocks was thirty thousand but aid workers on the ground estimated the true figure at between fifty and sixty thousand. While most of the victims were at home in bed, many were in the streets before dawn celebrating the festival of Ganesh and immersing idols of the elephant-faced "god" in water.

The effects were most severe in two villages—Killari and Umarga Taluk. Homes with walls up to a foot and a half thick —large granite stones pasted with mud—tumbled down, killing those inside. Pell, along with representatives from

Caritas France and Caritas Germany, was at the scene within two weeks, by which time not even half the dead bodies had been buried. Trauma and shock abounded. "We gave comfort 'being with' not with things," he wrote. "When people come out of shock then they can eat." He assisted, not only with Caritas relief efforts, but in long-term planning for rebuilding twelve hundred homes and infrastructure like schools and health centers and water systems. Church personnel from the local Catholic diocese of Aurangabad and Mother Teresa's sisters, the Missionaries of Charity, played leading roles in the effort.

It was clear to Pell that the survivors would need food and medical supplies for the next six months and that local workers would be able to play a major role in rebuilding homes. At that point, daily rain, unusual for October, was hampering the burning of corpses and made life even harder for the survivors, some of whom insisted on sleeping out of doors in tents for fear of more aftershocks. Catholic relief workers had been among the first on the scene, with Mother Teresa's nuns allowed through the roadblocks before others. The Catholic teams concentrated on the isolated villages, as these were being largely ignored in the general relief effort that concentrated on villages easily accessible by road.

Pell's diary entry of October 15, 1993, began:

> Mass for chapel full of nuns—Salesians, Fatima sisters and Missionaries of Charity. Preached briefly on *In your word is faith and life*, i.e., interdependence of faith and service. Travelled 90 km from Latur to Killari, richest village in the area, reduced to immense piles of rubble 15 feet high. Some of homes 200 or 300 years old—walls 18 inches or more thick with two feet of mud on roof to keep houses cool. Immense irregular granite stones held together simply by mud. Village

reduced to a few doorways. In Killari, probably 12,000 died out of 22,000. . . .

Met middle-aged man on top of his rubble, who had lost six or eight of his extended family in large house. Apparently a young girl found alive unconscious after being buried for five days—was under an iron cot. . . .

Wondered how God allowed earthquakes (perhaps God not all powerful, even cosmologically—because of original sin and allowed scheme and potential of suffering). But God does leave room for us to act!!! May God help victims and my weak faith.

Destruction at Mangloor worse than Killari—not a stone upon a stone. In Mangloor 5500 died out of 6,000. Especially at Killari, sightseers and thieves ransacked village for gold buried in homes or on the victims. Soldiers now in charge in villages and on the approach roads.

At Nandunga met old grandma in green sari weeping because she had lost eight family members. Salesian sisters told how women flocked to talk with them because so few women among first visitors, e.g., soldiers, police relief workers. One brother told me he was battling for the untouchables. Spent 6:00 P.M. to 7:30 P.M. in rosary and then holy hour with nuns before Blessed Sacrament. Power off intermittently and news threatened another major quake between 7:00 P.M. and midnight. So far (9:50 P.M.) so good!

Bishop Pell traveled home via Bombay and Madras, with a detour to Wattala, outside Colombo in Sri Lanka, for Caritas meetings. In the 1980s and early 1990s, Caritas Australia contributed more than Au$1.5 million for relief and rehabilitation programs for victims of the civil war. In his Madras stopover, Pell hired a car and visited Saint Thomas Cathedral, where the tomb of Doubting Thomas the apostle is believed to be located. "Of greater interest was an altar before which Saint Francis Xavier prayed. Prayed there that Jesuits be given another Ignatius and Xavier. They need them."

The ACR/Caritas annual reports from 1987 to 1996 show that administrative expenses were kept to a minimum— around 4 to 8 percent of expenditure a year. In such an organization, allocating millions of dollars a year donated by practicing Catholics in good faith, a vital part of the chairman's job is to ensure the money is well spent. Even before he took over stewardship of ACR, Pell was well aware that a few administrative land mines needed diffusing. Throughout the early 1980s, several commentators had raised serious concerns that some ACR funding allocated for humanitarian work in the Philippines was finding its way to violent Communist-infiltrated organizations. At that point in history, Communism remained a force in Asia, including the Philippines. As commentator Michael Barnard wrote in the *Age* in June 1989: "The controversy over whether the Australian Church and other aid agencies and 'solidarity' groups have been—directly or indirectly, knowingly or unknowingly—aiding violent communist revolutionaries in the Philippines has been bitter and unrelenting."[1] The evidence, Barnard said, was "overwhelming". Such concerns were taken seriously both by the head of the Catholic Church in the Philippines, Cardinal Sin, and by Pell, who was determined to get to the bottom of the matter and ensure that Australian Catholic aid money was not sidetracked. Following the money trail proved a complex, time-consuming, and expensive task, but it was essential to restore ACR's credibility, which was in dire danger of being compromised very seriously in the minds of donors.

[1] Michael Barnard, *Age*, June 20, 1989, p. 13.

In 1988, Cardinal Sin admitted that the Church's National Secretariat for Social Action in the Philippines had been "infiltrated, highly infiltrated", and that overseas funds had been diverted "to buy weapons and strengthen and develop" the Communist New People's Army (NPA). The NPA, founded in 1969, was the armed wing of the new Communist Party of the Philippines (CPP) established in 1968 under Jose Maria Sison in opposition to the corrupt United States-backed regime of Ferdinand Marcos. The CPP's aim was to rebuild the party securely on the revolutionary heritage of the teachings of Marx, Lenin, and Mao Tse Tung.

When Sison visited Australia in 1986, he was sponsored, incredibly, by the Catholic Commission for Justice and Peace, the Australian Council of Churches (a Protestant organization in those days), and teachers' unions, among others. In the Philippines, the CPP's front organization, the so-called National Democratic Front (NDF), was charged with the task of harnessing moral and financial support from the West, and, handily for the Communists, its international representative was a former Roman and German-educated Catholic priest, Luis Jalandoni, who had left the priesthood to marry a former nun. Reports furnished to Pell in the second half of 1988 showed that Jalandoni, while still a priest, had channeled Church funds to the CPP/NPA when he was social action director in the Diocese of Bacolod, under Bishop Antonio Fortich.

In the 1970s, Jalandoni and his wife based themselves in Utrecht, Holland, to muster support from across Europe, boasting that by the end of that decade he had fifteen "solidarity" committees established in different countries from Ireland to Sweden, Greece to Austria. The CPP had numerous other off-shoot organizations, including the KMU, a far-left Filipino trade union, and these, too, set up support organizations in Europe. The NDF's European base remained in the Netherlands, with a range of non-government organizations and Catholic aid agencies from the Dutch Church providing generous assistance to a complex web of far-left Filipino organizations. Significantly, this process continued for years after the fall of the Marcos government and the accession of Cory Aquino as Filipino President in February 1986, threatening the emergence of the Philippines' then-fledgling democracy and free economy.

In Belgium it was found that much of the Catholic Lenten appeal was benefiting left-wing militant organizations in the Philippines including the KMU, the KMP (militant peasant organization), and Gabriela (a Marxist/feminist women's group)—all strong sympathizers with the CPP and Jose Maria Sison. Similar patterns arose in the distribution of German, French, British, Italian, Irish, and Scandinavian Catholic aid. In a nutshell, years of work by Jalandoni and the now European-wide web of related organizations had succeeded in strongly influencing the churches, the media, and aid bodies. Both the Catholic and Protestant Churches were implicated, with the World Council of Churches financing a trip to Europe by Sison in 1987.

Australian aid agencies, including ACR, were also enmeshed in the mess. The ACR annual report for 1987 showed that Au$816,000 was given to the Asia Partnership for Human Development (APHD), with another Au$422,000 given in 1988. APHD, funded by Catholic aid agencies in twenty-one countries, including Australia, was founded in 1973 to coordinate projects across Asia. By 1988 it was funding five hundred projects, including dozens in the Philippines, some of which attracted strong criticism in Australia, from B. A. Santamaria and others, for their pro-NDF bias. KMU (the pro-Communist trade union organization) was one of the beneficiaries of some of this money.

Within the Catholic community at the time, both in Australia and overseas where the criticisms were noted, the comments from the right inflamed some on the left and vice versa. As Pell observed in an article in Melbourne's *Advocate* Catholic newspaper: "Catholics are deeply resentful when priests and religious working for social reform are automatically dubbed as communists. They find it equally objectionable when those opposed to communism are presumed to be uninterested in social justice and fuelling the violence of the civil war."

Shortly after the Tiananmen Square massacre in June 1989 in Beijing, Michael Barnard blew the whistle on the KMU in the *Age*. He reported:

> A group of Australian hard-left unions have always insisted that the KMU is just an innocent federation motivated by only social justice and democratic ideals. Any such image was surely shattered last week. Even as the communist masters of Beijing were still mopping up the blood from the massacre of Tiananmen Square . . . the KMU, would-be representative of downtrodden workers, peasants and out-of-work residents in the Philippines, was declaring its faith in the Chinese party leadership.
>
> "The KMU," announced chairman Crispin Beltran in Manila, "expresses its full support to the Chinese people under the able leadership of the Chinese Communist Party in their struggle to build a progressive socialist society." And all those frightful scenes of party-ordered repression we followed in the media here? Why, the KMU assures us, that's

just "aggressive media hype", part of a plot by the US and Britain to "sabotage and derail" the Chinese "socialist system".[2]

However, as Pell discovered when he visited the Philippines, Tiananmen proved a major blow to the Communists among the ordinary people, as it showed the Communists, and the KMU/KMP in a more realistic light.

A month after Tiananmen, Pell kept a note of a telephone conversation he had with Bishop Claver, head of the Church's National Secretariat for Social Action (NASSA) in the Philippines at 11:45 A.M. on July 16, 1989: "Told him money to KMU and KMP is an embarrassment to us. He replied (1) no new grants—only continuing grants already promised. (2) no grants to these *national* bodies. Sometimes local branches are not too bad and local bishop approves."

To see the situation firsthand, Pell, accompanied by Father Sam Dimittina, a Melbourne priest and a member of the ACR national committee, had paid an exhausting nine-day visit to the Philippines in December 1988, traveling to Manila and north through the center of the island of Luzon to Vigan, and south to Bacolod on the island of Negros. On his first night in Manila, the quiet was broken by occasional rifle and pistol shots. "Unemployment rate in Manila would be doubled if population law-abiding—reduction in no. of armed guards", he quipped in his diary. The following day, he found Cardinal Sin "expansive, humorous [like he'd] kissed the Blarney Stone!" In Manila they visited Smoky Mountain, a vast rubbish dump, home for thousands of families in makeshift shacks, "where the rats and the stench would knock you over. . . . It gave me

[2] Ibid.

a jolt to visit some of the people who live on the suburban railway network in Manila and are helped by the St James Foundation, a joint venture of the Australian government and ACR. Tens of thousands of squatters live in shacks along the railway lines, with their main entrances often three or four metres from the passing trains."

On the island of Negros, Pell and Dimittina concelebrated Mass with Bishop Antonio Fortich, a "gnarled, fearless old lion" who spoke his mind as he smoked his pipe after the Mass. His flock, the poorest of the poor—sugar workers earning US$1.50 a day—followed him with devotion and trust akin to that afforded Archbishop Mannix by Melbourne Catholics during World War I. "How much is he in control of underlings? How much is he used?" Bishop Pell wondered in his diary. "[Fortich] asked about B. A. Santamaria; when told he is anti-communist, but pro-justice, 'How can that be?' I told him B.A.S. worked for 30 years with Mannix, a great champion of the poor."

In the cooler north of the country, in the diocese of Nueva Segovia, founded by the Spanish in 1594 or 1595—the area from which Ferdinand Marcos came—Pell found a huge cathedral built in Italian Renaissance style in 1612 by forced labor under the Spanish. A few days before his visit, the priest editing the diocesan paper had had five bullets pumped into his air conditioner after campaigning against lottery gambling. Pell met the local archbishop, Orlando Quevedo, who was dissatisfied with almost a third of APHD's 1987 projects for the Philippines and determined to improve the system for the future. He had a file of "problem" projects an inch thick. Now archbishop of Mindanao in the south of the archipelago, Archbishop Quevedo and Bishop Claver, a Jesuit, were strongly committed to social justice but anti-Communist and worked conscientiously for years afterward to make the best use of incoming Church aid, including that from Australia—a process that was to keep them in close touch with Pell.

As Pell and Dimittina traveled around, every bishop they spoke with admitted that some aid money had gone to the Communists, though the problem should not be exaggerated and other projects financed were worthwhile. They found that the Filipino bishops were effectively remedying the situation, replacing more than 75 percent of NASSA staff and refocusing the organization from its previous ideological/political outlook to an evangelical Christian one in tackling the practical problems of poverty and underdevelopment. All aid spending for future projects had to be endorsed by local bishops—a stance that drew strong opposition from the Dutch aid agency but which was a relief for Pell as it ensured Church involvement in development work and greater control and accountability.

To ensure further that money donated by Australian Catholics was used for the purposes it was intended, Pell decided that, in future, ACR money given to the Asian Partnership for Human Development would be for non-Philippine projects only. Instead, ACR would make a grant of Au$400,000 a year for the next two years directly to the revamped NASSA for development work. This settled the situation down and satisfied the Church's sternest critics on the matter in Australia, including Bob Santamaria.

Pell's visit to the Philippines convinced him more strongly than ever that Australian Catholics had an important role to play in assisting the country, 85 percent of which is Catholic. He told readers of Melbourne's Catholic *Advocate* after his visit: "Those of us who accept Christ's teaching about our obligations to the poor, who support the struggle for justice, who believe in democracy as the best form of government, who believe communism is an evil—we have a special regional and religious obligation to increase our help to this Christian nation."

In his *Advocate* article, Pell noted that the Catholic Church was the one institution in the Philippines that had grown in respect and standing during ten tumultuous years. "We have seen priests and religious in the Philippines, sometimes people we know, branded as communists when this was clearly false, and we have been tempted to dismiss the communist menace entirely as a figment of right-wing imagination. This is an elementary mistake. . . . In 1987, for instance, communist urban guerrilla 'sparrow units' killed more than 100 people, soldiers and civilians in Manila alone."

Right-wing fanatics were just as deadly both in Manila and the countryside. Pell's article was accompanied by a photograph of a Filipino nun, Sister Gemma Silveria, negotiating in the mountains of eastern Samar with female Communist rebels, members of the New People's Army, over their possible surrender to the government of President Aquino. The four rebels, handkerchiefs covering the lower halves of their faces, are listening carefully—and one is pointing a revolver directly at Sister Gemma's heart.

In Vietnam, working with the Communist authorities was all part of a day's work for Pell and ACR (Cardinal Edward Clancy and he stayed in the guesthouse of the central committee of the Communist Party in Hanoi in 1993). It was a vast cultural leap for the former Ballarat boy from a DLP background. But those assisted by ACR/Caritas were grateful that the Catholic Church cared enough about them to make such an effort with humanitarian aid, irrespective of the religious beliefs or non-beliefs of the recipients. In Hanoi in August 1993, Pell and Michael Whitely, ACR's national director for eighteen years, visited the Blind Association. "Somewhat unnerving at first because the president and vice presidents are all blind! Both VPs in army-type uniforms with impenetrable dark glasses. Impossible not to be impressed by the enormity of their task. We help Blind Society with talking books programme. Were told story of blind woman whom the family had never heard laugh until she heard a talking book! And when she laughed then her family cried!"

Driving along Highway 1 outside Hanoi, Pell observed an exotic landscape, with many fine Catholic churches left over from the French colonial days. Some were being repaired. The surrounding countryside was "flat, fertile, irrigated land ablaze with recently planted green rice". The flatness was interspersed with "sheer outcrops of layered granite—à la Hanging Rock—but craggy, not smooth". In Ho Chi Minh City (Saigon) the Cardinal and Pell visited Archbishop Paul Binh in Thong Nhat Hospital, which formerly belonged to President Thieu and until a couple of years earlier had been reserved for the Communist hierarchy. The old archbishop, a Propagandist from 1933 to 1938, had suffered a stroke but was clear in his mind, dignified, and shrewd. He was able to assure the visitors that the Church was intact, with three thousand converts a year. "He was very touched by our visit. Govt. was atheist, but we must co-operate, help all, Catholics and non-Catholics."

The following day, Pell visited an orphanage for 250 street kids in the Go Vap district of Saigon. "Boys and girls, lively, cheeky uninhibited, from 8 yrs. to 15 yrs. Short of affection, as they came around us without hesitation. Clean but very poor, but seemed well run. 40,000 dong given for food monthly for child—120,000 needed."

Later in the day, the vicar-general of the Saigon diocese

arranged for Pell to say a public Mass at 5:00 P.M. in the Cathedral of Our Lady, Saigon. "Striking and moving to see large statue of Our Lady still in place dominating large square in front of red brick cathedral. Sixty or more people present; a range of ages but many elderly. Applauded loudly at beginning and end, I preached in French. . . ." Speaking French was invaluable for the ACR chairman both in Vietnam and Cambodia. Invaluable, too, was his background at Propaganda College, Rome, in providing a network of contacts in many parts of the developing world.

From the killing fields in Cambodia to the Ukraine, where people were beginning to regroup after decades of oppression, from the orphanages of Vietnam to the rubble of southwest Indian villages after a severe earthquake, Pell's nine years of running Caritas were absorbing, at times exhausting, and rewarding. As he sees it: "I think things [like Caritas] are intrinsically worthwhile. It sounds a bit lofty, but my friend Michael Mason says that even when we make mistakes, what we are doing is of 'ultimate significance'."

By the time Pell relinquished the position of chairman of Caritas in April 1997 he had explored corners of the world, far from the beaten tourist tracks, that most people can only wonder about. Those visits underlined his appreciation of Australia. "I never returned home from one of those visits without thanking God for the type of quality of life we have here in Australia, and I would often resolve to tell people of that and point out what an obligation we have to keep it good and to make it better."

Chapter 9

Preparing for the Second Spring

George Pell's nine years as auxiliary bishop to Archbishop Sir Frank Little in Melbourne were a time of contradictions, both for him personally and for the wider Church. He was often exceedingly busy, usually working seven days a week from early morning to late into the evening. His experiences with Caritas have already been covered, and he was also overseeing the creation of the Australian Catholic University (and spending five years as its foundation pro-chancellor), serving as a member of two important Vatican organizations, traveling, lecturing, attending meetings, visiting parishes, and conducting Confirmation ceremonies in the southern region of the Melbourne archdiocese. His home was a house in the southern bayside parish of Mentone, where nominally he was the pastor, although the day-to-day work of running the parish was done by successive administrators, Fathers Ted Teal, John Murphy, and John Walshe.

Despite the sometimes frenetic schedule, the role of auxiliary bishop is strangely devoid of heavy responsibilities, prompting Pell to say to one of his friends: "The only decision I have to make every day is which side of bed to get out on." Tongue-in-cheek, but an accurate reflection of the power of any auxiliary bishop. In many ways, auxiliary bishops have less autonomy canonically and in practice than pastors, who are directly in charge of their parishes. Auxiliary bishops have no control over archdiocesan policy or finances and are subject to their archbishop, who may or may not delegate significant responsibilities to them. The archbishop, however, is the ultimate boss.

Archbishop Little, who now lives in retirement at Camberwell in a house Pell bought for him on behalf of the Church after succeeding him as archbishop, was uncomfortable with the description of himself as the "boss".

"I liked to think of it as a team," he said.

And did he and Bishop Pell make a good team? "Not as good as I had hoped", Archbishop Little admitted—and he did not just mean that they were at odds when Pell's beloved Tigers were up against Sir Frank's team, the Essendon Bombers.

"Well, we never discussed theology—history was his area", Sir Frank said.

It was no secret that the two men, both graduates of Saint Patrick's Ballarat and Propaganda Fide, were often at odds over the Church's direction, especially in relation to issues like seminary formation, school catechetics, and devolution of some of the traditional roles of pastors to lay administrators and nuns as paid pastoral associates.

"I suppose that I found George ever ready to share his point of view quite strongly, and that is what I would want", Sir Frank reflected.

However, Pell's forceful arguments were presented to his boss behind closed doors, and once specific decisions had been made, Sir Frank said, Pell supported them in public, regardless of how much he might have argued against them in private.

"One of the things for which I remain grateful was that

he was ready to take on the tough assignments", Sir Frank said.

Pell describes his relationship with Sir Frank from 1987 to 1996 as "cordial and correct". "I was loyal to Frank." Their differences, he says, were never personal but related to their different views on the best way forward for the Church.

Denis Hart, at that point a priest in Melbourne, said that as Pell worked around the southern region of Melbourne, he became increasingly concerned about the serious laxity in religious education at the time and at the inroads secularism and feminism were making into the life of the Church. "As auxiliary bishop he couldn't do a great deal about it, but he was a rock of strength to people who were troubled by what was happening."

Peter Elliott, who began work in the Vatican on May 1, 1987, a few weeks before Pell's consecration, said Pell "would not even confide in his friends about some of the anguish he went through when he had to at least tolerate things going on which he knew were wrong or that would not enhance the growth of the Church."

In the 1970s, 1980s, and 1990s, the majority of Australia's Catholic bishops, including the senior archbishops—Little in Melbourne, Leonard Faulkner in Adelaide, Francis Rush in Brisbane, and Edward Clancy in Sydney—while very different characters, were in broad agreement about the direction of the Church. They tended to give their Church bureaucrats, liturgical "experts", and Catholic education offices and seminary formation staff considerable rein in terms of experimentation and new ideas, and in turn, these people pushed the boundaries of liberalism well beyond what those archbishops would have approved of themselves.

For example, in many parts of Australia, the first rite of Penance, or individual confession, was replaced by the less demanding "general absolution", or third rite, where a large congregation of several hundred were absolved of their sins en masse without confessing them individually. It was rarely, if ever, mentioned that the Church reserved general absolution for genuine emergency situations (such as an army going into battle) and that penitents were obliged to confess serious sins individually as soon as possible afterward. Priest meetings openly lauded some bishops for "turning a blind eye" in the face of opposition from Rome.

In classrooms, Catholic teachers openly defied Catholic doctrine on matters such as purgatory and the virginity of our Lady, some priests and nuns claimed it was not a grave matter to miss Mass on Sundays, traditional furnishings and statues disappeared as many churches came to resemble lifeless assembly halls, and, in regard to the Mass, the emphasis in some places shifted from Christ's Sacrifice on Calvary to the mere commemoration of a "meal", albeit a special one. The ripping out of high altars reminded some of one of the edicts of the English Reformation, under Edward VI: "All the altars in every church taken down, and in lieu of them a table set up." In some cases, people attending Masses were encouraged to stand around the altar holding hands—when some people objected, they were branded "snobs" and "conservatives". Many who wished to continue to receive Communion on the tongue rather than in the hand were shunned, as were those who wished to kneel. Some priests abandoned large chunks of the official Roman Missal and improvised parts of the Mass. Serious-minded Mass-goers cringed as the traditional, familiar introductory rite—"The grace of our Lord Jesus Christ, and the love of God and the fellowship of the Holy Spirit be with you all" gave way in many places to banal openings like "Hi everyone, nippy morning for getting up, wasn't it?" or "G'Day . . . 'ow are

y'all?" The mumbled responses of those gathered were usually followed by the priest urging them to turn around and
have a chat with those nearby. Seminarians socialized more
than ever before, and some took part-time jobs in hotels during the term. Vocations and Mass attendances plummeted.

Pell's ascendancy in Melbourne and later Sydney helped
put the brakes on avant garde liturgical trends before they
reached the levels of absurdity—admittedly unusual—that
have been witnessed elsewhere in Australia, including children chomping into cream cakes near the altar after First
Communion, priests "sitting out" most of the Mass and allowing laity to do everything until the Consecration, vast
and important sections of the Mass left out, and poems and
other works substituted for scriptural readings.

By the mid- to late 1980s, when it was clear that Pope
John Paul intended to fight the encroaching malaise head on,
many observers, including George Pell, felt that the Church
in Australia was digging herself deeper and deeper into a
1960s and 1970s rut and was being left behind the dynamic
resurgence in spirituality evident overseas. In parts of the
United States, including New York, where the Dunwoodie
Seminary was filling up once again under Cardinal John
O'Connor after some lean years, this revival was known as
"the second spring".

While heavily constrained by the limitations of his position as an auxiliary bishop, Pell still managed to lead the
way in putting important issues of the time on the Catholic agenda in Australia. The forum he used effectively was
AD2000, a glossy journal of religious opinion launched by
B. A. Santamaria and the National Civic Council in 1988.
Bob Santamaria was regarded as politically incorrect, but
he was one of the few Catholics in Australia who had the
capacity intellectually and organizationally to launch such

a project. While ALP supporters and many Liberals, too
—especially those who understood the benefits of economic rationalism—rubbished Santamaria's socioeconomic
outpourings against free trade and globalization, many of
those same people came to appreciate his magazine. In many
parishes, however, the publication was outlawed as contra-
band, with a few priests even brandishing it in their pulpits
as they condemned it as the "rag of the devil". Sir Frank
Little hated it, as did almost all of Australia's bishops, with
the exception of Pell and one or two others. In a letter to
the *Age* in 1993, responding to a column by commentator
Michael Barnard, Little attacked what he called a small minority "who seek to set themselves up as the sole or the
true and final arbiters of orthodoxy". He went on: "Theirs
is the style of 'dissent' which has characterised the method-
ology of a minority group of 'traditionalists' who continue
to alienate themselves from the Church. It is the style of in-
nuendo, guilt by association, near slander and near character
assassination which one finds paraded in fringe publications
such as *AD2000* and the misnamed *Fidelity* [another traditionalist Catholic periodical]."

Santamaria, an old friend of Pell's earlier mentors, Bishop
O'Collins in Ballarat and Bishop Kelly in Melbourne, had
become close friends with Pell during his time as seminary
rector, when Santamaria wholeheartedly approved of Pell's
"few small changes". As rector and more often as auxiliary
bishop, Pell often lunched at Santamaria's NCC headquarters in North Melbourne and regarded the older man as
something of a father figure.

While Pell agreed with the broad thrust of many of Santamaria's economic and social views (such as bolstering the traditional family), he was far more of a political agnostic than
Santamaria and did not share his entire critique of economic

rationalism. The two men shared a love of history and a deep admiration for Doctor Mannix (who had been Santamaria's mentor) and enjoyed lively intellectual exchanges. Pell also enjoyed mixing with Santamaria's large, bright family. The glue that bound their friendship, however, was a deep concern about the direction of the Catholic Church in Australia.

From the outset of *AD2000*'s publication, readers noticed the contributions of George Pell, whom most Catholics outside Melbourne had not heard of before. His photograph suggested he was a generation removed from the older Church hierarchy, and, while more conservative than that hierarchy on many issues, he appeared more in tune with the vision of Pope John Paul II, then at the height of his pontificate.

AD2000 readers also soon became familiar with the writings and initiatives of Archbishop Barry Hickey in Perth and the success of Bishop William Brennan in attracting students for the priesthood and launching Vianney College, a successful new seminary in the small rural diocese of Wagga. Pell, Brennan, and Hickey, though very different in their pastoral styles, were soon identified by Catholics across Australia—supporters and opponents—as offering a vision different from that generally prevailing at the time. In January 1995, Pell wrote an article praising Wagga for taking the lead in Australia in producing a 530-page religious education syllabus, *We Belong to the Lord*, soon after the publication of the English-language edition of the new *Catechism of the Catholic Church*. The *Catechism* was one of the important initiatives of Pope John Paul II's papacy.

In *AD2000*'s first few years, Pell contributed more than half a dozen pieces, including condensed speeches. These struck a chord with those Catholics who were looking askance at the blatantly left-wing, anti-American stance of the Catholic Commission for Justice and Peace (the body set up by the Australian bishops to research and teach about such issues to Catholics) and at emerging liturgical and theological trends and falling Mass attendance. In some parishes, liturgical dancing and even "clowning" had become part of Mass.

Overseas, especially in the United States, the battle lines were drawn sharply and the fight-back of the center/right was well underway, especially through the books and magazines published by organizations like Ignatius Press, California, and through the cable TV programs of Mother Angelica's EWTN (Eternal Word Television Network). "Does Saint Bozo's Parish no longer amuse you?" asked one of the friskier advertisements, accompanied by a picture of a circus clown, for the orthodox publication *New Oxford Review*. Such a statement would have meant nothing in earlier decades, but it struck the right chord with Catholics irritated by the increasingly outlandish liturgy pushed at them on Sundays, as most priests and bishops stood idly by, apparently helpless and hapless.

Church teachings on marriage, contraception, and the all-male priesthood were increasingly ridiculed from within the Church's own ranks. More seriously, aspersions were even cast in some clerical quarters about fundamental tenets of the Catholic faith like the bodily Resurrection of Christ, His divinity and the Virgin Birth. Many Catholics felt bishops needed to take a stronger line in stamping out such heresies and restoring certainty. In Sydney, a young Rhodes scholar and seminarian by the name of Tony Abbott, who was later elected to Parliament and became Australia's Health Minister, abandoned his studies and wrote about the Church's internal disarray in an article in *The Bulletin*.

A trend was emerging in many parts of Australia to

differentiate the local community or church from the "official Church" and to question the need for a ministerial priesthood as distinct from the priesthood of all the baptized. As the lines between the ministerial priesthood and the so-called priesthood of the laity became increasingly blurred, elements within various dioceses and even some bishops seemed to want to move toward a congregationalist-style or communitarian Church, led at the local level by middle-order functionaries rather than traditional parish priests. In Melbourne, for instance, in 1996, Sir Frank Little hired a layman, Terry Curtin—a former public servant and the father of four children and the grandfather of three—on a Au$40,000 package to run the parish of Aspendale.[1]

Ostensibly, such moves were made to meet future shortages of clergy. But they also signaled a move toward a different kind of lay-led Church, and one in which the vocations slide was unlikely to be reversed. While far more restrained in his comments than most proponents on the right of the debate, Pell's articles in *AD2000* opened up important issues for discussion. He knew his stance on various issues would attract attention:

> I was certainly aware that I was offering something somewhat different. I don't think those articles were provocative—they didn't look for trouble—but yes, I had consciously decided that I should say something—in a prudent, unfolding sort of a way. I suppose my ideas developed as the years went along too. I think *AD2000* made an enormous contribution because it created a network of orthodox Catholics throughout the country. It gave them information, it gave them ideas and theology to support the Holy Father. I think it was one of Bob Santamaria's biggest achievements.

[1] Referred to in Pell's Crusade (a newspaper feature) in *Age*, November 10, 1997.

As for his senior episcopal colleagues: "They weren't commendatory, as you can imagine. But nobody rebuked me." They were hardly going to, given the fact that the themes of the articles were, to use George Pell's phrase, "four square" behind the Pope.

Some of the underlying tensions boiled over in public in October 1993 when *Four Corners* televised a studio debate, with audience participation, to discuss the recently released papal encyclical *Veritatis Splendor* (The splendor of truth). Pell was in the hot seat, defending the encyclical's reassertion that there exists a set of fundamental moral truths that are binding on the conscience of Catholics and that personal conscience may not override. The encyclical also called on bishops to defend those basic moral truths inherent in the Catholic faith and to ensure that those whom the bishops appoint to teaching positions will be men and women who can be trusted to proclaim and defend them. Bishops were being told by the Pope, Pell said, to "get out and correct rampant misapprehensions" about Catholic moral teaching.

The studio audience was sharply divided, with the debate one of the most fiery on a religious theme seen on Australian television. In defending the encyclical, Pell not only clashed with Australian philosopher Professor Peter Singer but was opposed by prominent Catholic priests including Father Bill Uren, then the head of the Jesuits in Australia, Uren's colleague Father Michael Kelly, and Sister Veronica Brady, I.B.V.M. Uren admitted that a number of people "may be disappointed" with the encyclical if they had been hoping for an alteration of the Church's position on contraception, artificial reproduction, and women priests. While the language was diplomatic, commentator Andrew Olle was perceptive in his quip: "It sounds like theological civil war."

In stark contrast to the passionate theological arguments of the time, the process of establishing the Australian Catholic University was harmonious, if laborious. In 1988, the education minister in the Hawke government, John Dawkins, announced a new direction for tertiary education in Australia, promising extra funding to institutions that joined a unified national system and had at least two thousand equivalent full-time students—a process that resulted in amalgamations of colleges of advanced education under the umbrella of existing universities and in the creation of new ones, around the nation. The eight Catholic colleges in the eastern states—three in Victoria, three in New South Wales, one in Canberra, and one in Queensland—decided quickly that in the interests of retaining their identities, they would prefer to merge with each other rather than with other local colleges in their areas.

With eleven years experience as a tertiary administrator at Aquinas, Pell was appointed by the Australian bishops to chair the Amalgamation Implementation Committee, which included his old friend and fellow warrior from Aquinas days Sir Bernard Callinan and representatives from each state/territory involved. Representatives of the colleges had first met with Dawkins in August 1988 to tell him of their plans to form a single institution, with one chief executive officer and a single governing body, a single academic board, and one set of academic awards. Such an undertaking was a vast challenge, with some 1250 miles separating the eight campuses involved. These were McAuley College in Brisbane; Signadou College in Canberra; Victoria's Institute of Catholic Education Campuses at Ballarat (Aquinas), Oakleigh (Christ Campus), and Ascot Vale (Mercy Campus) in Melbourne; and the three campuses of the Catholic College of

Education Sydney—Castle Hill, MacKillop Campus, North Sydney, and Mount Saint Mary Campus, Strathfield.

In October 1989, after winning federal government approval to create one new body with the status of a university, the Catholic archbishops of Sydney, Melbourne, Canberra, and Brisbane announced that the Australian Catholic University would begin operating in the 1991 academic year. The Implementation Committee had to oversee asset and liability transfers, staffing structures and appointments, admissions procedures, communications infrastructure, libraries, administrative arrangements, and most importantly, the academic organization. Six faculties were established: education, nursing and health sciences, arts and science, business and administration, social science, and theology, with both undergraduate and postgraduate degrees offered as well as diplomas.

The university opened on schedule at the beginning of 1991, with 5,668 students, including 2,303 first-year enrollments. Cardinal Clancy was the inaugural chancellor, while Bishop Pell was appointed pro-chancellor, retaining a close interest in the running of the university and its direction for five years.

Aside from working to form ACU, Pell was frequently invited to speak at university conferences both in Australia and overseas. His paper to La Trobe University's Seminar on the Sociology of Culture in May 1988 was published as a booklet, entitled *Catholicism in Australia: Immortal Diamond on a Darkling Plain*. Not inappropriately, as he was speaking in Melbourne, Pell opened with a sporting analogy, comparing the Catholic Church with a game of Australian rules football in which the Church was kicking against the wind:

In this scenario we are only approaching quarter-time in the match. The wind is against us and conditions are muddy and difficult. We are a few goals behind, but there have been patches of good play, although some of the veteran players are rattled and another group inclined to play their own game.

The captain-coach (Pope), a player of extraordinary strength and skill, is performing well but has not yet succeeded in imposing a coherent game plan on his team. Fewer supporters come to the home and away games, although there are big crowds for the finals at Christmas and Easter. As always, many of these supporters, some only interested spectators, give contradictory, often useless and occasionally damaging advice. But active support is vital even from those supporters. . . .

Due to retirements and recruiting difficulties we are battling to field a good first 18, we do not have as many under-age teams, although there are a number of youngsters coming through who are keen to have a go in the big time. Other teams from the same district are still in the competition, with many attractive, clever stylists, but they are not physically strong and the crowds at their games have fallen steadily.

The Catholic team's opponents now play a different type of game, no longer applying heavy physical pressure, but moving the ball around freely and unexpectedly. Some Catholic key position players lack mobility, being better suited to the older, tougher, more direct type of encounter. However, the Catholic side has no alternative except to utilise its strengths. The match is not lost, although the team has to regain confidence in its ability to play in its traditional style. Our opponents too are finding conditions harsher, their easy confidence shaken by developments elsewhere.

In other words, the Catholic team has to slow the game down and close up play. We should start a few fights. This tight defensive play will give us time to see which of our young forwards adapt best to the new conditions. As they grow in confidence, we will be better placed to take advantage of the wind change (which shall come certainly at some stage), to take more risks and regularly run the ball out of defence. The remainder of the first quarter should be quite exciting!

At a time when the pursuit of unity between Christian denominations seemed paramount to most Catholic bishops, Pell threw a healthy dose of realism onto the subject, calling for "abandonment of the mirage of imminent church union". He made it clear that the ordination of women by other Churches lessened the likelihood of Catholic participation in local church unions but advocated greater emphasis on practical and sometimes political cooperation between the Churches.

Nor did he mince words on the importance of the priesthood, insisting that a resurgence of vocations "is even more important than the continued expansion of lay activism for the future of the Church". The pope and bishops, he said, were the servants and defenders of a precious, two thousand-year-old tradition, which they were not at liberty to dismantle.

> Certainly core doctrines, for example the divinity of Jesus, the central position of the Pope and important moral teaching on for example the indissolubility of the family, the defence of life and human dignity through social justice, cannot be jettisoned to gain adherents.
>
> In other words, Catholics need a style which is a mite more confrontational and certainly much less conciliatory towards secular values. The Cross is a sign of contradiction. The doctrine of the primacy of conscience should be quietly ditched, at least in our schools, or comprehensively restated, because too many Catholic youngsters have concluded that

values are personal inventions, that we can paint our moral
pictures any way we choose. This devastating illusion is one
of the causes of the AIDS epidemic.[2]

At the time the paper was given, Pell was one of Australia's most junior bishops, although he spoke as if he knew
he would be guiding the Church in the future. While he
could not guarantee that Catholicism would prove an effective long-term opponent to the "forces of disarray and dark-
ness", he did promise that "the leadership of the Church
will dedicate its best efforts to this end." There were, he
acknowledged, "other approaches to Catholic life, with a
different diagnosis and different prescriptions from mine",
and he professed "no ambition to coerce independent parties to my point of view, only an ambition to do what I feel
the Church needs". It will be Christ, he said, "who is the
immortal and transforming diamond".

Three years later, in a speech on the centenary of Melbourne's Gardenvale Parish, he further developed those
themes. "It is often stated that we must not go back to
the fifties, and there can be no such refuge in an impossible
return to the past; doubly so in this case because the Church
is irrevocably committed to the teachings of the Second Vatican Council. However what is acknowledged far less frequently seems to me to be equally true; many of the priorities and policies of the Church of the sixties are quite
inappropriate to the changed situation of the nineties."[3]

In terms of the battle inside the Church at the time for
the hearts and minds of Catholics, Pell's strongest comments
came in an *AD2000* article in August 1994 entitled provoca-

---

[2] *Conversazione*, Seminar on the Sociology of Culture, La Trobe University, 1988.

[3] *AD2000*, October 1991.

tively *How Dissent Operates in the Church*. No organization, he insisted, could survive "Alice-in-Wonderland individualism" but would dissolve and disappear within a generation. The Catholic Church was not "a free-thinking group of do-gooders" and should declare which beliefs and practices are Catholic. "Those who cannot maintain cabinet solidarity leave the cabinet", he said. "Bishops cannot remain silent when writers seek to build a consensus against official teachings, against the Pope, and teach regularly and publicly that Catholics can write their own tickets, can decide themselves the tenets of their Church." Rejecting the often trotted-out argument that "women are invisible" in the Catholic Church, he asked: "What about the many saintly and powerful women in Church history, ranging from Mary, Mother of God, to Mary MacKillop?"

The validity of Christ's teaching has never depended on popular approval—He was crucified for His opinions. The fundamental Catholic appeal is to the truth of Christ's teaching; this norm cannot be set aside by changing fashions. Dissent, he wrote, was being disguised or dressed up with various ruses worthy of Orwell's "double-speak":

— Attack the Pope and then call yourself conservative and middle-of-the-road, redefining the "centre" in a heterodox fashion. The American priest Father Richard McBrien (author of *Catholicism*) is an old hand at this, but the line has been run in Australia.

— Claim that the Pope is divisive (or the *Catechism* is) when traditional truths are restated.

— Claim that the Church is "authoritarian", as month in and month out you attack her while remaining safely in your position of leadership and responsibility.

— Claim that freedom of conscience enables you to choose
  your faith and morality, to contradict Christ and the
  Pope, yet claim to be as good a Catholic as the Pope.
  (The Church has never taught that conscience is supreme.
  Conscience is at the service of truth.)

— Claim that the Church at the Second Vatican Council
  recovered a proper historical understanding of truth and
  escaped from the static, neo-Platonic world-view which
  dominated during the Counter-Reformation. Then go
  further and imply, rather than state, that fundamental dog-
  mas and sacraments are liable to further change and development, and imply, rather than state, that fixed points
  of belief and practice are only for "fundamentalists".

However, he warned, the party is over. "The Pope has
now delivered three massive blows against the forces of dis-
solution in the Church: *Veritatis Splendor, Ordinatio Sacerdo-
talis*, and the *Catechism of the Catholic Church*. As a result, it is
no longer possible to claim that basic Catholic positions are
unclear. It is the opponents of Catholic teaching within the
Church who now have the problems: Do they accommodate
themselves to these restated teachings inside the Church—
or outside her?"[4]

By November 1995, Pell had broadened his battlefront
and took his own advice about "starting a few fights"
when he targeted controversial philosopher Peter Singer.
In a speech reproduced in *AD2000*, he told a seminar at
Sydney University on the recently released papal encyclical
Evangelium Vitae (The gospel of life) that there was

> only one serious candidate for the role of King Herod's pro-
> paganda chief in Australia, our most notorious messenger of

[4] Ibid., August 1994.

death. Peter Singer,[5] who for twenty years has never ceased to advocate abortion, euthanasia and infanticide. Appointed Professor of Philosophy at Monash University, Melbourne, at the age of 31, he is a prolific writer and determined propagandist. His zeal for dispatching "sub-standard" humans is accompanied by great enthusiasm for animals, especially apes, while his 1975 book *Animal Liberation* is sometimes described as the bible of the animal liberation movement.

Singer, Pell acknowledged, was "our best known philosopher overseas, author of the entry on ethics in *Encyclopaedia Britannica*, a regular contributor to quality journals such as the *New York Review of Books*." On some issues, the bishop said, Singer was clear-headed; on others he was muddled. "He admits that the foetus is a living human being and therefore claims that he and the Pope 'at least share the virtue of seeing clearly what is at stake in the debate' on abortion."

"However, he puts the human foetus at a level much lower than a chimpanzee, even lower than a dog, with no right to life simply because it is human. It is self-awareness, in his view, which grounds a right to life. In 1988 his colleague at the Monash Centre for Human Bioethics, Helga Kuhse, compared the human embryo to a lettuce leaf."

Australia's moral decline, the bishop observed, "would need to slip a few more notches" for Singer's views on newborn children to be acceptable to public opinion, "even in the Northern Territory". The Catholic Church, Pell argued, had to be at the forefront in the struggle for public opinion, "for there is no other non-government organization with our Church's capacity for influence. We have many religious allies: a potentially huge number of fellow travellers

---

[5] In 1998, Peter Singer was appointed the DeCamp Professor of Bioethics at the University Center for Human Values, Princeton University.

among nominal Christians and the recently unchurched, but unfortunately no Australian parallel to the strength of Protestantism in the USA, especially in the southern states. We bear a heavy responsibility for the defence and extension of Judeo-Christian influence in our public life."

For decades, the Church in Australia had drawn apathy rather than either passionate approval or disapproval. That was rapidly changing, as Pell took to the role of social commentator with a vengeance, telling the Sydney seminar:

> The "modern" spirit is deeply subjectivist and relativist, at least in the realm of general moral theory, although this is often married, in the same individuals, with fierce moral convictions on particular issues. It is not only traditionalist or orthodox moralists who are tempted to intolerance. *Webster's Dictionary* defines political correctness as 'marked by or adhering to a typical progressive orthodoxy on issues involving especially race, gender, sexual affinity or ecology. . . .
>
> Earlier this year, a New York writer, George Sim Johnston, claimed that in our dreary decade of Clinton and Yeltsin the present Pope was the only world leader with the stature of Churchill and De Gaulle. Certainly his role, with Ronald Reagan, in the collapse of communism dwarfs the efforts of Pope Leo the Great and then Pope Gregory the Great in the fifth and sixth centuries to defend Rome and the remnants of the Roman Empire in the West from the depredations of the barbarians. Most of Eastern Europe today is still far from the promised land, economically and politically, but they are free. It is not surprising that one magazine I saw spoke of the Pope as a second Moses!

But John Paul II, Pell argued, had set himself an even more difficult task: to help strengthen and revive the moral and religious sensibility of the Western world, setting in place much of the intellectual groundwork with the new Code of Canon Law, the *Catechism*, and his many encyclicals. To date, the fruits in the West had been scarce.

Pell told the seminar:

> In *Gospel of Life*, the Pope has not just spelt out his intellectual arguments on the sanctity of life. I also believe that in his attack on the 'culture of death', the soft nihilism which has settled over Western Europe and the English-speaking world, he has also struck a popular chord. His is a message, not just for the Catholic community, but for all society. . . . It is our task to exploit these opportunities and for this we shall need the media—print, radio and television. It is one of the Holy Father's most important writings, an eloquent and passionate appeal to respect, protect, love and serve life, every human life!

Why was the encyclical so well received? A couple of reasons come to mind. In all societies influenced by the great religions there are huge reservoirs of respect for life, selective and imperfect as these enthusiasms always are. There are oceans of basic human decency, ripe for development and refinement, especially through the media, by Christians and all lovers of life. The encyclical taps into a rich vein of human conviction and sentiment in favour of life, even among weak and sinful people who might no longer be regular church-goers, but whose moral imagination and even subconscious stirrings move to a rhythm established by generations of Christian liturgy and learning.

Those who have laboured mightily to overturn community sensibilities on abortion and euthanasia, usually under the banner of personal autonomy and moral relativism, are well aware of this inconvenient moral bedrock. The enemies of life do not like their deeds to be brought into the spotlight. Always the supporters of abortion will be among the most vocal opponents of any public showing of films which demonstrate what actually happens in the womb when life is extinguished.[6]

---

[6] Ibid., November 1995.

However divisive such forthrightness made him seem to some in Australia, Pell's arguments were noticed internationally. In 1990, Pope John Paul II appointed him to the Rome-based Pontifical Council for Justice and Peace, an international body of bishops and priests who advise him on matters related to social justice, international relations, and global conflict resolution. The Pope also appointed Pell as a participant in the synod of bishops in Rome on the preparation of priests, where he was a synod spokesman and part of the committee that prepared the final synod message and set the course for priestly training for decades to come. His approach might not have been popular at Clayton, but the Vatican's Congregation for the Evangelization of Peoples appointed him to inspect the national seminaries of New Zealand (1994), Papua New Guinea and the Solomon Islands (1995), the Pacific (1996), and Irian Jaya and Sulawesi (1998).

In 1990, just two and a half years after his consecration, the biggest surprise of his life arrived out of the blue from the Secretary of State in Rome, informing him that the Holy Father wished him to join the Congregation for the Doctrine of the Faith—the most influential body in the Church in terms of faith and morals. It is hard to imagine any bishop declining such an honor, and so certain was the Vatican of Pell's acceptance that his appointment was announced from Rome even before he had had time to reply to the letter. As the first Australian appointed to the organization, Bishop Pell, at forty-nine, was clearly an up-and-coming figure in the universal Church.

Chapter 10

The Universal Church

The Palace of the Holy Inquisition (Palazzo della Sacra Inquisizione) was built by Saint Pius V when he was pope in 1571 to house the Sacred Congregation of the Universal Inquisition, which was founded in 1542 to defend the Church from heresy. This it did primarily through intellectual and legal endeavors. In its early days, the Sacred Congregation, in keeping with the times, imprisoned and tortured serious offenders and occasionally referred others to civil authorities for burning at the stake before the Church abandoned execution for heretics in the 1640s. Such ruthlessness was part of the rule of law in European life. In England, for example, Catholics suffered from imprisonment, torture, and execution under both King Henry VIII and his daughter Elizabeth I, who was excommunicated by Saint Pius V. A strict and dedicated Dominican friar, Pius V was a key figure in the post-Reformation Church—implementing the decisions of the Council of Trent; forbidding the sale of indulgences; introducing a new catechism, breviary, and missal; reemphasizing the works of Saint Thomas Aquinas; and forming the Holy League with Spain and Venice, which defeated the Islamic Turks at the Battle of Lepanto.

In 1908, Pope Pius X discarded the term Inquisition and renamed the body the Sacred Congregation of the Holy

Office. It was renamed the Congregation for the Doctrine of the Faith in 1965. Currently, its official duty, as defined by Pope John Paul II in 1988, is to "promote and safeguard the doctrine of the faith and morals throughout the Catholic world: for this reason everything which in any way touches such matter falls within its competence."[1] It is charged with the responsibility of spreading sound doctrine and defending points of Christian tradition that appear to be in danger. Since 1981, the Congregation's prefect has been Cardinal Joseph Ratzinger, formerly the Cardinal Archbishop of Munich.

The first Australian ever appointed to the twenty-three-member Congregation, George Pell attended his first meeting in 1990. Proceedings began with a concelebrated Mass in Pius V's ornate chapel. At the Mass, another one of the younger officials of the Congregation preached the sermon —a Dominican friar by the name of Christoph Schönborn from Austria, who was secretary of the committee that drafted the new *Catechism of the Catholic Church* and who is now the Cardinal Archbishop of Vienna. The Congregation for the Doctrine of the Faith is regarded as the most influential of the Vatican's congregations, and membership is a rare honor. While the Vatican attempts to include bishops from different parts of the world, members are selected primarily on the basis of their intellectual and theological stature.

The Congregation was housed on the site of its original palace, which was vastly enlarged in 1930. The sturdy stone building with the smoky blue window shutters is almost beside Saint Peter's Basilica—a two-minute walk through the left-hand columns of the square. The top floor contains

[1] Congregation for the Doctrine of the Faith.

apartments of curial officials—Australia's Cardinal Edward Cassidy, now retired, lived in one when he headed the Council for Christian Unity. A portion of the Congregation's secret archives, a treasure trove of history dating back to the Middle Ages, was opened to scholars in 1998.

As a Congregation member for ten years, Bishop Pell was required to attend plenary sessions at least every eighteen months. Before such meetings, hundreds of pages of documents relating to different matters under investigation would arrive so each member could study them in depth, consult his theology books, and prepare his judgments on the matters to be decided. Cardinal Ratzinger chairs the Congregation meetings so that every member has the floor in turn, to expound his views once. Most speak in Italian—as did Pell. The Cardinal then sums up the situation concisely, demonstrating a rare breadth of knowledge and an enormous capacity to synthesize and analyze expert opinion.

Matters discussed by the Congregation are strictly confidential, although some final judgments, outlining why a particular book or enterprise has been found not to have the Church's approval, are published. Pell regards Ratzinger, a courteous, reserved man, as one of the most formidable intellectuals he has ever encountered. "His working relationship with the Holy Father has been one of the high points of papal history", he said. "The Church of John Paul II owes Ratzinger an enormous debt; his contribution has been invaluable, and the abuse heaped upon him is totally unjustified."

A significant portion of the hostility toward the silver-haired German comes from bishops inside the Catholic Church as well as from outsiders. In June 2002, for example, Canberra's auxiliary bishop, Patrick Power, branded the CDF's 2000 document *Dominus Jesus* (Lord Jesus) as "a deliberate regression from the teaching and spirit of Vatican II".[2]

From Galileo to Hans Küng, from Teilhard de Chardin to the seven women involved in the mock "ordination" on a moored boat on the Danube in July 2002, hundreds of scholars, clerics, religious, and lay people, including a number of Australian priests, have faced the intellectual might of the Congregation's examinations. Diocesan bishops and archbishops visit it, often somewhat nervously, on their regular five-yearly *ad limina* reports to the Vatican. The Congregation is the Church's final intellectual and moral arbiter in matters of faith and morals, the body that draws the disciplinary line between what is acceptable teaching/writing/behavior within the universal Church and what is not. Some issues are clear-cut, others are complex and involve years of close examination.

In Rome, Congregation officials meet regularly with their local consulters (priests with relevant expertise), and Ratzinger meets the Pope at least once a week. In the past two decades, the Congregation has issued many of the most important and controversial documents and decisions of the current papacy. In 1995, for example, after several years of argument and debate in the United States, Australia, and other countries, the Congregation issued a definitive ruling, approved by the Pope, that the Church's claim that she had no authority to ordain women to the priesthood was "to be held always, everywhere, and by all, as belonging to the deposit of the faith". In Australia, Pell had already set out the Church's teaching on the matter in a pamphlet of which seventy thousand copies were distributed. That pamphlet was later incorporated into his 1996 book for upper

[2] *AD2000*, June 2002, p. 4.

secondary students, *Issues of Faith and Morals* (Oxford University Press and Ignatius Press).

As well as being appointed to the CDF in 1990, Pell also was appointed for five years to the Vatican's Pontifical Council for Justice and Peace, a body comprising twenty-five men and women, lay and religious, that included bishops, social workers, a former South American president, academics, a priest who described himself as an old friend of the Communists, a specialist in the arms trade, and the vice president of a United States bank. The Council's work, in which Pope John Paul II takes a close, personal interest, is to promote and develop the Church's work for social justice, of which the campaign to relieve Third World countries of much of their crippling international debt was a prime example. Pell's time on the Council coincided with the centenary of the Church's landmark encyclical on social teaching, *Rerum Novarum* (On the new situation), promulgated by Pope Leo XIII in 1891. The centenary occurred at a momentous time in world history—shortly after the collapse of European Communism and the disintegration of the Soviet empire, which originally had been committed to ridding the world of religion. To mark the centenary, Pope John Paul II issued a commemorative letter, *Centesimus Annus*, in which he wrote about the collapse of Communism, insisting that the causes were far deeper and more complex than economic inefficiency.

The centenary of *Rerum Novarum* was considered significant enough by three universities—Oxford, Boston, and Melbourne—to warrant a major paper at an international conference on the *Worth of Nations* held at Boston University in February 1992. As a member of the Pontifical Council for Justice and Peace, George Pell delivered one of the major papers in Boston, setting out the history of Catholic social teaching. He outlined how and why, at the age of eighty, Leo XIII, the author of eighty-six encyclicals—the most important contribution to papal teaching since the Middle Ages—gave qualified approval in *Rerum Novarum* to democracy and the modern age and urged Catholics to become involved in political life for the common good of the people.

The encyclical, Pell said, had been written largely in response to the social situation of Catholics, many of whom belonged to the working classes. Leo set out to address the problem of the condition of workers, in order to find remedies quickly, such as a just wage and regulated working conditions, "for the misery and wretchedness pressing so heavily and unjustly" on most working people. These remedies would depend more on Church social teaching appealing to individual responsibility and conscience than on government intervention. While condemning greed and defending the rights of workers to form trade unions, the encyclical also defended the right of individuals to own private property and rejected socialism and government ownership of the means of production. "Leo XIII's sanctioning of trade unions was a decisive factor in their becoming an integral part of Western society", Pell said. "The success of trade unions was, in turn, an important reason behind the failure of Marx's prediction about the increasing misery of the working class in capitalist society."

Switching his attention to the current world, Pell reiterated the Pope's resolute opposition, expressed in *Centesimus Annus*, to the Marxist version of Christianity, liberation theology. Looking at the then-recent revolutions in Eastern Europe and the burgeoning of freedom in the former Soviet republics, he found deeper reasons for the collapse of Communism than the rejection of Marxist philosophy and economics or the triumph of the human spirit. Rather, the collapse of Soviet communism was "the penultimate blow to the whole Enlightenment project" that had extolled the perfectibility of mankind and led to the "radical secularisation of the European mind".

Bishop Pell argued:

> The connection with the French Revolution is immediately apparent. More problematic is the connection of the Enlightenment with the darker side of that revolution and some of its terrible progeny in recent history—for instance the revolutionary violence of Lenin and Stalin, the Maoist crimes of the Great Leap Forward and the legacy of the Parisian Stalinists who trained Pol Pot for the Cambodian Genocide.
>
> The communist collapse has been a massive blow to the Enlightenment myth that progress is inevitable . . . that traditions can be ignored, or should be denied, and that human reason is all powerful. It is also another proof that without religious belief, it is difficult, perhaps impossible, for altruism to flourish and persist, and curb the selfishness and weakness of human beings. These would appear to be impossible attainments in the absence of belief in an intelligent and benign Supreme Being ready to reward and to punish and somehow to atone for and redress the worst human sufferings. If the collapse of communism is the denouement of the French Revolution, the beginning of that end may well have been marked by the issuance of *Rerum Novarum* in 1891.

Pell acknowledged that following Vatican II, the Church's efforts to cooperate with people of goodwill in different regimes, including those behind the Iron Curtain, had brought mixed blessings for the Church. "Before his death in 1978, even Pope Paul VI spoke of 'the smoke of Satan in the Church'," he said. "There has been no resurgence of faith and practice throughout the West. Indeed, the Church has virtually collapsed in some countries such as Holland and has been severely damaged in parts of French-speaking Canada." This had been offset by rapid growth in central and Eastern Europe, in parts of Asia, like Korea, and in Africa (although the growth there was slower than the Muslim expansion).

While Australia's public debate on euthanasia was still some years away when he was speaking at Boston University in 1992, Pell cited the views of his friend Cardinal John O'Connor of New York as to what lay ahead: "I predict that the 'right to die' will dwarf the abortion phenomenon in magnitude, in numbers, in horror. As mothers have become legalized agents of the deaths of their children, so children will become legalized agents of the deaths of their mothers—and fathers. Fathers will have no more legal right to defend themselves than they currently have to defend their unborn babies."

Social justice programs in the English-speaking world, he argued, should involve constructive efforts to enhance and strengthen family life. "No civilized society can afford to be complacent about the evident growth of an underclass, riddled with gang warfare and broken families, single parents, uncontrollable children, alcoholism and drug abuse."

In a pluralist, secular, and liberal society, the Catholic Church was a continuing source of authority and tradition, able to provide hope, inspire service, and encourage self-restraint. On that point, Pell told the conference delegates, he was happy to leave the last word to a London journalist, not a Catholic himself, who had written of *Centesimus Annus* in the *Financial Times* that, ". . . the absence of all religion, as envisaged by the late Mr John Lennon, is a terrifying prospect. It would return humanity to the jungle, armed to the teeth. We all need the pope, and his encyclicals. If there were no such thing it would be necessary to invent him."[3]

The Boston conference was one in an annual series of diverse gatherings from the worlds of science, philosophy, academia, business, and (occasionally) religion organized by Professor Claudio Veliz, a good friend of Pell's. Veliz, a prolific author and former economics history professor in Chile, came to Melbourne in 1972 when he was awarded the chair of sociology at La Trobe University. After La Trobe, Veliz was university professor and professor of history at Boston University until mid-2002. Veliz met Pell early in his time as an auxiliary bishop, and he became close friends with Veliz and his wife, Maria Isabelle, who had a holiday home at Lorne on the Victorian south coast, not far from Pell's former holiday home. Veliz, who has a Calvinist background, said he was amazed to find himself "agreeing with nearly everything Pell says" despite their differences in beliefs and backgrounds.

If Pell's work on the Congregation for the Doctrine of the Faith and the Pontifical Council for Justice and Peace put him at the very heart of John Paul II's pontificate, another part of his overseas travels was bringing him face to face with people who understood all too well what Karol Wojtyla had suffered under the Nazis and Soviet Communists in his native Poland.

Pell made three visits to mainland China in the late 1980s and early 1990s. By far his most memorable encounter was in Shanghai, with Father Vincent Hongsheng Zhu, a gentle Jesuit in his mid-seventies and part of China's persecuted,

[3] George Pell, *Rerum Novarum 100 Years Later*, at Boston University, 1991, quoting Joe Rogaly, *Financial Times*, May 3, 1991.

underground Church. When Father Vincent wanted to kiss the bishop's ring as a sign of respect, Pell found it one of the most humbling moments of his life. It was 1989—just after the Tiananmen Square massacre—and Vincent had been released the previous year from seven years' imprisonment by the Communist authorities: still his every move was monitored. But after enduring pain and suffering as punishment for his faith for much of his life, Father Vincent had no fear left. "The Communists can't touch me—they know —because I'm not frightened of dying and I'm not frightened to go back to jail", he told Pell. Vincent had also been imprisoned and tortured from 1960 to 1978, surviving day and night for some years in a tiny cell submerged in eighteen inches of filthy, freezing water—his "crime" was refusing to renounce the authority of the pope as the Vicar of Christ on earth.

Meeting Bishop Pell, the old priest was overwhelmed . . . he had given his all, including his freedom and comfort for Christ, and this was the first time since his imprisonment that he had met one of the successors of His apostles from the West. It was one of the highlights of the old man's life —and one of the most unforgettable encounters of Pell's life as well. Father Vincent, who in his youth had studied in France, Ireland, and the United States, impressed Pell with his excellent English: "He was a marvellous man, full of life, quoting Thomas More and Cardinal Newman. He will be a saint—canonized—a man of outstanding piety, most impressive and absolutely fearless." Father Vincent, who has since died, was one of forty priests and bishops mentioned in a 1994 United Nations Commission on Human Rights report on religious freedom.

Pell's journeys to China were in no way connected to his ACR/Caritas work and were not funded by that organization. But as chairman of ACR, and through his other work, he had become known internationally and was asked to visit China, which was a major concern for Church authorities. Before 1997, such visits were often organized by secular and religious-order missionary priests working out of Hong Kong. Hong Kong's reverting to China has made such activity riskier, and arrests are not infrequent.

Pell kept his customary diaries on his China trips, with vast slabs written in Italian for a little extra protection in case he was detained and the diaries confiscated. Like other Catholic visitors, he brought moral and practical support to Chinese Catholics, including theology books on the post-Vatican II Church, which was yet to take shape in China. On one occasion, Pell entered China with US$20,000 strapped in his money belt, money provided by support organizations in the West to help the Church in China. On another occasion, some of Pell's contacts in China were involved in setting up a factory in Wuhan, a riverside city of four million southwest of Shanghai, and he sent in sewing machines to assist. Had the authorities examined the machines more closely to find out why they were so heavy, they would have found them packed tightly with Catholic theology books.

While Pell and Father Sam Dimittina traveled to China "incognito" (their papers showed that they were teachers), the Chinese authorities knew they were Catholic priests. This was easily worked out from the people and places they visited in Beijing, Shanghai, Wuhan, and smaller centers in the far west of the country, close to the border with Tibet. To understand the significance, complexity, and danger of these visits, it is essential to understand some of the bloody and brutal persecutions suffered by Catholics in China, which continue up to the present time. Two "Catholic" Churches operate in China—the underground Church

(of Vincent and hundreds of others like him) in full communion with Rome but illegal in her own country, and the
Patriotic Church, established by the State in 1957 as a kind
of substitute for Catholicism. The Patriotic Association operates with state approval and uses the buildings left behind
from pre-Communist days and confiscated from the underground Church.

Strictly speaking, the Patriotic Church is not Catholic because it is not in full communion with Rome: it does not
recognize the authority of the Supreme Pontiff, and, officially, Rome does not recognize it. On October 1, 2000
(China's national day), Pope John Paul II canonized 120
Chinese martyrs—eighty-seven of them Chinese, as well
as thirty-three missionaries—killed in China from 1648 to
1930. The Patriotic Association "bishops" protested that
the canonizations were "an insult" and "a distortion of history". Whether their protests were genuine or intended to
appease Communist officials, however, is not clear.

In practice, the lines between the Catholic Church and the
Patriotic Association are blurred, and on the ground there is
considerable overlap. Much to the chagrin of some suffering
in the underground Church and bodies like the American-
based Cardinal Kung Foundation, which supports the underground Church from abroad, some in the Vatican, including
the former head of the Congregation for the Evangelization
of Peoples, Cardinal Tomko, appeared to put out the hand
of friendship to the Patriotic Association in the 1980s. This
was done in the hope of restoring religious freedom for all
Chinese Catholics and normalizing relations between the
Chinese Church and the Vatican. Several American seminaries have even gone so far as to take in students from the
Patriotic Association for training, all expenses paid.

Because the Church in China was still isolated from Vatican II in the late 1980s and early 1990s, the Latin Tridentine

Mass was still said, and many of the Patriotic "bishops" and "priests" prayed for the Pope under their breath—one of the tests of their loyalty to the Holy See. Pell conducted many of his conversations with Chinese churchmen in Latin, as it was the only language he and they had in common, and he attended Mass at the old cathedral, now run by the Patriotic Association, in Shanghai, complete with tabernacle and altar, stations of the cross and statues.

The Cardinal Kung Foundation estimates that the Patriotic Association has four million members in China, while about eight million remain loyal to the underground Church. However their differences are resolved in the future, Pell believes that China is the next great frontier for the Catholic Church for evangelization: "In some parts of China there are double the number of Catholics now than when the communists took power. Red Guards destroyed a lot of the moral and intellectual framework so there is a great void amongst the middle classes and young people to be filled. Nobody believes in communist theory any more. In Shanghai a taxi driver refused to take me to [former Chinese Premier] Chou en Lai's house. He said there is no point in going there."

Christianity, Pell said, is spreading in China in much the same way as it did in the pagan Roman Empire, and "the whole Confucian ethos is not wildly incompatible with Christianity, despite a healthy agnostic tradition in Chinese upper-class life." Pope John Paul II has taken a close interest in China, making Bishop Ignatius Kung, the underground bishop of Shanghai, a cardinal of the Catholic Church in secret in 1979. Kung, along with several hundred priests and Church leaders, was arrested and imprisoned in one swift raid on the Shanghai diocese on September 8, 1955, as were hundreds of lay Catholics, including members of the Legion of Mary society, who were sentenced to ten to twenty

years hard labor and "reeducation" at special camps as punishment for their evangelizing work. One woman, Margaret
Chu, spent twenty-three years in various prisons, including
one hundred hideous days in handcuffs, during which she
was made to work in 95°F heat in the fields of a labor camp,
not even allowed to wear a hat or change clothes or take off
the handcuffs at night. Not surprisingly, she prayed for the
gift of death.

While many priests and lay Catholics succumbed to the
pressures and tortures inflicted upon them and agreed to renounce the pope of the time, Pius XII, and rolled over into
the Communist-sanctioned Patriotic Association, many, like
Bishop Kung and Father Vincent Zhu, did not and, despite
imprisonment and "reeducation", managed to maintain contact—the beginnings of the underground Church.

Among those who did acquiesce to the authorities, however, two months after the "round up" of September 1955,
was Father Aloysius Jin, S.J., the rector of the Shanghai seminary, who made a tape recording, played in many prisons,
urging Catholics to support the Communist Government.
For that effort, his sentence was lessened from life to eighteen years (including several in a forced labor camp). In
1985, he became the Patriotic Association bishop of Shanghai. Bishop Pell and Father Dimittina met him in 1989—
a small, gentle man, an eighth generation Chinese Catholic
who was ordained a Jesuit in 1945 after studies in Europe.
For his part Bishop Jin insists there is no division between
the Patriotic and underground Churches. "There is only
one Church in China—the Roman Catholic Church. Both
are very loyal to the Pope. Every day, I pray for the Pope."[4]

His predecessor in Shanghai, Bishop Kung, was finally

---

[4] *Cardinal Kung Foundation Newsletter*, Easter 2002. Father Dimittina also
said Bishop Jin told him that he prays for the Pope every day.

released under house arrest in Shanghai in 1985 at the age of eighty-four. That year, watched closely by the Chinese government and members of the Patriotic Association, he was allowed to meet Cardinal Sin of the Philippines, who had traveled to China to see him. While not allowed to converse in private, Kung got his message of loyalty to the pope out to the world by singing a song in Latin across the banquet table, "Tu es Petrus et super hanc petram aedificabo Ecclesiam meam" (You are Peter and upon this rock I will build my Church). In 1986, Kung traveled to the United States to settle in Stamford, Connecticut. Within a year he was well enough to travel to Rome to receive his cardinal's hat from Pope John Paul II, followed by an unprecedented seven-minute standing ovation from the crowd gathered in Saint Peter's as he returned to his wheelchair.

At the same time, the Vatican has shown a willingness to reconcile some of the Patriotic Association bishops, especially those trained and ordained before the persecutions began, with the Church as a whole. Understandably, this distresses some in the underground Church and those who support her, who felt betrayed by those who joined the Patriotic Association. The only eventual way forward, Pell said, is for both groups to be allowed to practice their faith openly, as a united Church, in communion with Rome and free from domestic persecutions. That goal remains a distant one, with underground bishops arrested and spirited away as recently as March 2002. While Pope John Paul II has been unable to succeed in his wish to visit China and celebrate Mass there, Pell said he is certain that the world's most heavily populated country will be an even greater priority for the next and subsequent popes.

In the early 1990s Pell found that Chinese authorities had hijacked a Christian image to promote the controversial one-child policy—enforced not only with forced

contraception, abortion, and economic sanctions, but also
with infanticide at times. Walking around Shanghai, Pell
noticed large posters of the Madonna and Child, which, he
was told, were being used to promote the one-child policy.
"Such a clever adaptation of a traditional motherly image
for perverse purposes."

In contrast to the concealed piety of the Church in China,
Catholics in Scala, the historic cathedral town behind Amalfi
on one of the most beautiful strips of Italian coastline, gave
George Pell a rapturous welcome when he accepted the
mayor's invitation to visit in 1988. Because they do not
have a diocese of their own, it is a tradition in the Catholic
Church for auxiliary bishops and bishops working in the
Roman bureaucracy to be given *titular* dioceses—old dioceses that have been suppressed or merged into other, larger
dioceses. Under a quaint, antiquated rule in the old Code
of Canon Law, bishops were never permitted to set foot
in their titular dioceses, but this was relaxed in Pope John
Paul II's new Code, issued in 1983. Pell's titular diocese was
home to various noble families of the Mediterranean coast
and was the local bishop's seat from 987 to 1818. By 1988,
Scala was a quiet village surrounded by chestnut and oak
woods, with its 130 churches for thirty-five thousand inhab-
itants a reminder of more bustling, prosperous centuries.

Visiting Rome on Church business, Pell was staying with
his old friend Peter Elliott, who was by then working in the
Vatican curia and living in a 1930s monastery about a mile
and a quarter away. They borrowed a car and drove south
through Naples and along to the glorious Amalfi coast. Peter
Elliott will never forget their day:

> In the morning, it was all strictly arranged, and George had
> to wear his cassock and his cap, and as we drove into town
> there were signs up all over the place—"*Welcome Monsignor
> Pel*" (Italians tend to chop off double letters). He was ushered

into the cathedral, then the mayor greeted him with a florid speech, and then they sat him on the throne and took photographs. It was the first time a bishop who was a real bishop of Scala had sat on the throne for almost two hundred years. The bishop of the area knew about it and let it all go ahead.

Then we went off to the sacristy and all dressed up for solemn Mass, and they gave George the most valuable mitre in Italy—parts of it dated back to the eleventh or twelfth century. It was remade about twenty times, and he came out wearing that and carrying a fifteenth-century crosier looking a million dollars, and the Mass proceeded (in Italian). At the exact moment of the elevation of the host, they exploded a bomb outside the cathedral to celebrate the sacred moment. It made a lot of noise—an unusual form of liturgy.

The celebrations after the Mass made for an extraordinary day. Pell and his party enjoyed a banquet inside the cloister of an enclosed order of nuns in the town, with the nuns performing eighteenth-century dances for the visitors —a tradition at recreation time in the convent for hundreds of years. "Then we were led out after going to visit the old sisters, I mean those who'd gone to God in the cemetery, to throw holy water over them, then we went out and the huge iron gates closed behind us."

The visitors were then escorted from one place to another, plied with coffee and cakes, and, late in the day, left town loaded with gifts and feeling as though they had caffeine poisoning.

Eight years later, when George Pell was promoted to be Archbishop of Melbourne, he had to relinquish his *titular* diocese. But when he moved into the large, comfortable archbishop's residence in a leafy street in Kew, one of Melbourne's eastern suburbs, he found that the house lacked a name, so he had a nameplate made. He called the house Scala.

Chapter 11

Be Not Afraid

Important announcements from the Vatican generally come at noon sharp Rome time, 9:00 P.M. or 10:00 P.M. in eastern Australia. On the evening of Tuesday, July 16, 1996, morning newspapers scurried to get a major story into their first editions. "Archbishop in shock resignation", the *Australian* reported:

> The Archbishop of Melbourne, the Most Reverend Frank Little, last night shocked the Catholic Church when he announced his resignation for health reasons. Archbishop Little, 70, who had served in the position since July 1974, is understood to have only informed colleagues of his decision early yesterday.
>
> The Catholic Church said last night that His Holiness Pope John Paul II had appointed the Most Rev George Pell, currently an Auxiliary Bishop in the Archdiocese of Melbourne, to replace Archbishop Little.

The *Australian* said Archbishop Little was "unavailable for comment last night but had scheduled a press conference where he was expected to elaborate on his reasons for resigning".

The next day, Wednesday, July 17, the outgoing archbishop told that press conference: "Will I start with the ingrown toenails? It's a little bit of everything." While expressing "a great sense of relief to be departing from the high-pressure job", Sir Frank also admitted that: "I also have a sense of sadness and no doubt will feel a sense of grieving. That will be something that I'll have to work through."

Was the quick-witted Sir Frank, who was five years younger than the retiring age for bishops, sending up the "health reasons" cited for his abrupt departure? Did the in-grown toenails line mean the explanation should be taken with a grain of salt? When bishops and archbishops retire, their dioceses are generally left vacant for weeks, months, or more than a year in some cases, but the concurrent announcement of George Pell's appointment showed Pope John Paul II's determination to see him in a senior leadership position as soon as possible. The Vicar of Christ is not bound to consult anyone, but some highly confidential consultation had taken place beforehand, although not as extensive as some would have liked. Father Bill Uren, then the provincial superior of the Jesuits in Melbourne, said he would have expected extensive consultation before such an appointment.

Sir Frank Little said: "I don't know whether George was the logical choice, I knew he would be a very strong contender, he had shown qualities of leadership." *Australian* columnist James Murray was spot on when he suggested that Little and Pell's was a "civil rather than warm" relationship, "though public disagreement never surfaced".

Regardless of their differences, Pell and Little kept up appearances during the changeover, being photographed together in a show of unity, with Sir Frank leaving gracefully, his dignity intact. Pell wished his predecessor "many years of peaceful retirement" and paid tribute to him as a man "admired and respected both within and outside the bounds of the Catholic Church". Sir Frank says Pell was "very kind and thoughtful to me after I left, and I'll always be grateful."

Not surprisingly, Denis Hart, the master of ceremonies

for the Archdiocese of Melbourne, was delighted by his best friend's appointment: "I think that a sense of purpose had been lost; people were doing their best, but we had been overtaken by the scourge of professional misconduct; public confidence was down, and it needed drastic action. It also needed a prominent public figure, and Archbishop Pell dealt with the media with confidence. Often you need a great leader to come in and get the impetus. George had a clear vision and the ability and readiness to carry it through."

From the outset, Hart said, Pell had a clear set of priorities for his episcopate: priests, including the role of priests as leaders in parishes, seminary education, and encouraging vocations to the priesthood; proper formation in religious education, including better religious textbooks for schools; fostering the link between Melbourne and the universal Church, meaning the Holy See. ("I don't mean following what other dioceses think"), and finally an extensive building and restoration project for the areas surrounding Saint Patrick's Cathedral in East Melbourne. Writing in *Eureka Street*, the liberal magazine she edited for the Jesuits, Morag Fraser acknowledged that the morale of the clergy needed a boost but, in an especially shrewd prediction, said that the job ahead for Archbishop Pell "makes heading Coles Myer look like a picnic at Albert Park".

Whatever the maneuvers behind closed doors in Rome that led to Pell's appointment, the problem of clerical pedophilia had, by that time, well and truly reared its ugly head. On May 27, 1996, just seven weeks earlier, the ABC *Four Corners* program had broadcast a damning report by journalist Sally Neighbour, entitled "Twice Betrayed", focusing on clerical sex abuse in the Catholic Church in both Ballarat and Melbourne. The program left viewers shocked, particularly by the evasive and indifferent responses of Ballarat Bishop Ronald Mulkearns and Monsignor Gerald Cudmore, the then-Vicar-General of the Archdiocese of Melbourne, to such serious allegations.

Evidence was presented on the program of rapes and indecent assaults against minors and adults, male and female, of offending priests being moved from parish to parish, of repeated cover-ups, and of a victim's suicide. One interviewee told the program, "This really is Armageddon for the Church."

The matter featured prominently at George Pell's press conference the morning after his appointment had been announced. He admitted that the Church's response to the problem up to that point had been "a bit spotty". "There's no doubt it's been really damaging and perhaps the worst blow to our prestige in the community that we've suffered for quite a while." The media reported the press conference under such headlines as "Clean-up Pledge", "Archbishop Vows Restoration of Public Confidence", "Archbishop Vow on Pedophiles".

Pell officially took over as Archbishop of Melbourne at Mass on a chilly winter's night, August 16, 1996. Because Saint Patrick's Cathedral was in the middle of a major restoration, the Royal Exhibition Building, where Australia's first federal parliament met, was the venue, allowing a congregation of eight thousand people to join Cardinal Cassidy, the Rome-based head of the Council for Ecumenism, fifty bishops, and four hundred priests in welcoming Pell to his new role. Archbishop Little laid his own crosier on the altar after he and the papal nuncio had led Pell to the cathedra. Pell had come with his own crosier, which was a gift from Saint Patrick's College, Ballarat, on his ordination as bishop in 1987.

Preaching in the sonorous voice that was about to become well known across the nation, Pell set the tone for his episcopate, emphasizing the distinctive roles of the laity and ordained priests and stressing the need for more priestly vocations. While Melbourne should be able to provide its own priests, he would also welcome priests from abroad who wished to serve the city. He recalled his boyhood hero, Archbishop Daniel Mannix, consecrating the archdiocese to the Immaculate Heart of Mary in May 1944 at the height of World War II in the Pacific and once again placed the city of Melbourne under our Lady's protection.

It was a confident performance, frequently interrupted by lengthy applause. While his sentiments would have been standard fare for a Catholic archbishop in other times and places, the sermon was groundbreaking in the modern Church in Australia, where many senior clerics were playing down the role of Mary, the Mother of God, as they bent over backward to pander to the perceived sensitivities of the Protestant churches. While reveling in their "liberal" labels, those same clerics were also proving to be anything but liberal on the question of welcoming priests from overseas who wanted to serve in Australia. Unlike Pell, who was well-disposed to newcomers from other races, many of the supposed liberals regarded the "cultural differences" of foreign priests as insurmountable.

Likewise, Pell's determination to tackle the vocations crisis was not mirrored across the Church in Australia. Some senior clerics and Church bureaucrats (who perhaps had a vested career interest in doing so) viewed the looming shortage of clergy as an opportunity to develop a lay ministry or some form of congregationalism. But this was never the desire of the Church. As Pope John Paul II told priests in Rome on Saint Valentine's Day 2002: "We must not be easily satisfied with the explanation which says that the lack of priestly vocations can be compensated by the growth in the apostolic commitment of the laity, or that it is willed by providence to foster the growth of the laity. On the contrary, the more numerous the laity who want to live their own baptismal vocation with generosity, the more necessary is the presence and specific work of the ordained ministers."[1]

Among those in the front row of the congregation was the colorful Victorian premier, Jeff Kennett, a non-Catholic who had become accustomed to receiving Communion from Archbishop Little, a practice that was not in keeping with the Church's teaching. While there was no incident at the Mass, Pell offered to go over to Kennett's office to explain the Church's position, but the premier declined the visit and requested that the explanation be sent to him in writing. Pell wrote and asked Kennett, as a non-Catholic, to refrain from receiving Communion in the Catholic Church. That stance very much annoyed Kennett, who branded it as "silly" and "petty" and announced that he had invited Little to officiate at his funeral if he predeceased the retired archbishop. "If ever he [Pell] was hoping to get a convert, I would have thought that those who enjoyed participating in things Catholic were the first line of potential candidates", Kennett commented.[2] For his part, Pell refused to back down from his decision but said he had not given up hope of converting Kennett.

Pell concluded his first Mass as archbishop by inviting the congregation to "go forward together on the next stage of our journey towards God, who will become all in all, for all of us." His long walk down the aisle of the Exhibition Building with Denis Hart, his master of ceremonies for the occasion, at his side, was accompanied by the triumphant strains of Handel's "Hallelujah Chorus".

[1] Zenit News Service.
[2] Sunday, May 2002.

For the motto on his archbishop's coat of arms, Pell chose, in English, "Be Not Afraid", echoing Christ's words to his followers and reiterating a constant refrain of Pope John Paul II. The coat of arms includes a *Pelican in Her Piety*, a traditional eucharistic emblem, based on the medieval legend that the pelican would feed its young with blood from its own breast, which it would lacerate with its beak—a symbol of Christ feeding us with his own flesh and blood. The pelican is also a traditional emblem of the Pell family. *The Sun in His Splendour* is a traditional emblem of Saint Thomas Aquinas and serves as a reference to Aquinas College Ballarat. It is also a eucharistic emblem. The monogram MR, with the coronet, is a traditional symbol of the Blessed Virgin Mary and is in the coat of arms of Pope John Paul II.

Pell took up the reins of the Melbourne archdiocese the day after his liturgical reception, but the final, formal part of his accession was not completed until June 29 the following year—the feast day of Saints Peter and Paul—when he received the pallium from Pope John Paul II in Rome. A tradition dating back to the fourth century, the pallium is a circular cloth band, about two inches wide, worn by the pope and archbishops over their chasubles at Mass. It has two pendants, one hanging down in front and one behind, each about two inches wide and twelve inches long, weighted down with small pieces of lead covered with black silk. The pallium is made of white wool, part of which is supplied by two lambs presented annually to the pope. Decorated by six black crosses and a gold pin set with a precious gem, it symbolizes the archbishop's communion with and participation in the office of the pope.

Forty people journeyed with George Pell to see him receive the pallium—Margaret, his sister, David, his brother, David's daughter, Sarah, his cousin Mary, his friends Fathers

Diamond and Hart and Monsignor Elliott, some younger Melbourne priests, and several dozen friends. Twenty-nine archbishops received the pallium that day from the Pope, from archdioceses as far afield as Kenya, Canada, Ireland, and Mexico. Two of the best-known men there were Archbishops Charles Chaput of Denver, Colorado, and Francis George of Chicago, two of the most prominent Church leaders in the United States in the vanguard of John Paul II's Catholic revival.

But long before he received the pallium, Pell had been forced to act on the issue of pedophilia. "It was mentioned in my first discussions with the premier, Jeffrey Kennett, and he made it very clear to me that he wanted to get something in place to deal with it", Pell recalls eight years later.

> And just before that at a fund-raising luncheon I was sitting next to the governor, Richard McGarvie, a former Supreme Court judge who had been a friend of mine for years, and I have always been very, very grateful to him for his advice. Now he said: "You are going to have to deal with this problem resolutely because if you don't it will bleed you dry for years—emotionally, and more importantly than that, it will bleed away the good standing of the Church. And of course, your first priority needs to be the victims of genuine attacks." So he said, "Why don't you set up something akin to a royal commission, with a commissioner, and give him the power to deal with it?" I had an absolutely top flight body of senior lawyers and other professionals from around Melbourne, and we put a procedure into place.

Two months after his appointment, in October 1996, Archbishop Pell announced the establishment of the Independent Commission into Sexual Abuse, to be headed by Peter O'Callaghan, Q.C., with another independent legal panel assessing compensation payouts for victims, up to a

capped figure of Au$50,000. This figure was arrived at be-
cause it matched the amount paid by the State at the time
for crime compensation. At the same time, the Catholic
Church nationally was establishing a national program, Towards Healing. While Melbourne was in touch with the
Towards Healing program, Pell decided not to join it because he was satisfied that the urgency of the problem in
Melbourne was being addressed by the comprehensive program of assessment, compensation, and counseling he had
set up. "I was surprised later at the resentment which was
generated amongst some of these other people [officials in
other Catholic dioceses and religious orders], not because
we didn't deal with the problem, but because we dealt with
it another way. I've got no regrets about that at all because
the proof of the pudding is in the eating. It has brought
people to justice, provided counseling, and provided very
substantial compensation to a whole lot of people."

The Broken Rites organization, established in 1993 to assist clerical abuse victims and which has fielded more than
three thousand complaints, branded the Melbourne scheme
as "the best of a bad lot". The backlog of cases facing
O'Callaghan when his commission began was such that in
its first six years, 126 victims received compensation from
the Melbourne archdiocese. In the vast majority of cases,
the payouts were made after the victims' assailants had been
arrested, charged, convicted, and jailed. The process has cost
the archdiocese more than Au$3 million in compensation
and almost Au$2 million for counseling, with victims enti-
tled to counseling for as long as needed. Among the many
disgraceful and heartbreaking cases that came across Pell's
desk in Melbourne as a result of the commission's work was
one in which a woman had borne a Down Syndrome child

to a priest, who later deserted them. The woman finally accepted a payout of less than Au$25,000.[3]

Pell's predecessor, Daniel Mannix, and Mannix' Brisbane counterpart, Sir James Duhig, were nicknamed, in their heyday, "Daniel the politician" and "James the builder". George Pell's time as Archbishop of Melbourne probably entitled him to both those nicknames, and more besides. As it happened, his enemies were delighted to suggest a few—"Pell Pot" (ironic in light of his Caritas work in Cambodia after the killing fields) and the "bully bishop from central casting" among them. Melbournians had from August 16, 1996, to May 10, 2001, to make up their minds about George Pell. An overview of his contribution to the city includes:

— boosting the number of seminarians studying for the priesthood for Melbourne from a paltry twelve to a healthier twenty-six (but still with a long way to go) and ordaining a dozen new priests during that time;

— reforming the seminary's spiritual life in accordance with Pope John Paul II's blueprint, *I Will Give You Shepherds*;

— overseeing the production of *To Know, Worship and Love*, a high-quality set of religious education school textbooks from kindergarten to senior secondary school, to redress the paucity of such materials not only in Australia but across the English-speaking world;

— establishing a new tertiary institution in the heart of Melbourne, the John Paul II Institute for Marriage and the Family, headed by internationally respected moral theologian and bioethicist Professor Anthony Fisher, O.P., and

[3] *Inside the Vatican*, January 1999.

allied to the Pontifical Lateran University in Rome, offering bachelor's and higher degrees to the doctoral level;

— creating a Catholic precinct in the heart of Melbourne, around Saint Patrick's Cathedral, by moving Corpus Christi Seminary and the Australian Catholic University into the area, opening Goold House as the administration center for the archdiocese, with the John Paul II Institute and Mannix Library next door, and restoring and rebuilding the old parish buildings and church at nearby Carlton as a residence and chapel for the seminarians;

— appointing the distinguished philosopher Hayden Ramsay, a former lecturer in philosophy at the Universities of Edinburgh, Stirling, and Melbourne, as an adviser on his personal staff to produce scholarly articles, to teach in the seminary and John Paul II Institute, and, most of all, to "give the archdiocese some philosophical backbone";

— creating a sculpture garden and pilgrim path with cascading water around Saint Patrick's Cathedral and installing two striking tributes to indigenous people in and around the cathedral;

— being only one of three bishops in the world known to have issued a pastoral letter to his people to mark the thirtieth anniversary of the most controversial papal encyclical of all time, *Humanae Vitae*;

— speaking out publicly on a wide range of issues, including Victoria's gambling culture and the One Nation political party, and rallying other churches behind his opposition to the exhibition of the controversial "art work" *Piss Christ* at the National Gallery of Victoria in 1997;

— buying and restoring the site of Mary MacKillop's birth-place in Brunswick Street, Fitzroy, for use as a support center for the families of drug addicts;

— leading four hundred young people to the Holy Land and Rome for a pilgrimage to mark the Jubilee Year 2000.

George Pell secured the appointment of Denis Hart, the man he regards as "probably my closest friend", as his aux-iliary bishop and vicar-general in Melbourne. Under Little, Hart had been a parish priest and master of ceremonies in the archdiocese. He had also been responsible for organiz-ing the liturgy for Pope John Paul II's Australian odyssey in 1986. In his role as auxiliary bishop, Hart described him-self as Archbishop Pell's "enforcer", and his former boss "wouldn't dissent" from the description.

Pell's friendship with Father Gerry Diamond had also sur-vived and strengthened through the years, despite various long periods apart. Gerry Diamond, who completed a licen-tiate in Scripture in Rome and an M.A. in Scripture in Ox-ford and a doctorate at the Melbourne College of Divinity, is pastor of Saint Anthony's, Glenhuntly, in suburban Mel-bourne, where he is known as much for his kindness as for his memory. Much of Diamond's presbytery is wall-to-wall books, all of which he can discuss in fascinating detail. His history collection is even more extensive than that of Pell, whose library ranges over a wider spectrum.

Pell says of Diamond:

> He's a very good parish priest and has some very good support from the people. He's such a clever man but he's a humble man, too. At one stage, he'd prepare his sermons and give them out to one or two people so they could comment on

214   *George Pell*

what was clear and unclear. Not everyone would be prepared
to do that.

I remember as auxiliary bishop I asked him to give me the
evidence on priestesses in the different cultures round the
Mediterranean in the time of our Lord. Within half a day he
had come back with fifty photocopied pages from books he
had read, and he was able to recall in which book he read
what and also more or less the chapters. Prodigious recall.

Diamond noticed a considerable improvement in morale
among Catholics after Pell took over the archdiocese, believing they responded well to the Archbishop taking his message to the wider community through the media and also to
his preparedness to take hard decisions when required and
stick to them. Remembering Pell's Oxford thesis, Diamond
chuckled at the idea that Pell bears a passing resemblance to
Cyprian, one of his heroes among the early Church Fathers:
"The interesting thing is that where Cyprian can get what
he perceives to be desirable through a conciliatory process,
he goes through the process. When he considers that may
not be possible, he goes for it directly."

Another friend Pell worked closely with in Melbourne
was Steve Lawrence, a former Hawthorn AFL player, who
was director of Melbourne's youth ministry in the early years
of Pell's time in Melbourne. Lawrence and his wife, Annie,
named their daughter Georgia, after Pell. The Lawrences
later lived and worked in Rome before returning to Sydney. At age four, Pell's namesake was giggling at the Australian accent she detected in his fluent Italian. Georgia
Lawrence is the second girl named after Pell. The first is his
niece Georgina Pell, now sixteen, who took up the wine
and water with her sister, Rebecca, at her uncle's Mass of
Reception as archbishop. Georgina Pell was a premature
baby, only 5 lb. 2 oz. in size, and looked even more fragile

when her uncle held her for the first time. It was one of the rare occasions Margaret and David Pell saw tears in his eyes.

Once a week as archbishop, Pell made a point of hearing confessions in Saint Patrick's Cathedral—not a routine practice for many modern bishops, some of whom have been known to have trouble remembering the words for absolving penitents. True to his promise to support priests, Pell set aside Thursday afternoons to be spent alone in the cathedral presbytery, giving any priests who wanted to see him informally the chance to speak to him without an appointment. He also initiated a series of clergy dinners, working through Melbourne's long list of priests alphabetically. These were held at his home in Kew and brought together priests of a variety of ages, backgrounds, and viewpoints. At one such occasion, Father Martin Dixon livened up his usual outfit with a single, conspicuously large clip-on earring, worn to tease Monsignor Peter Elliott, sitting across the table, who had recently spoken out publicly against grunge fashion and body piercing among young people.

Dixon, pastor of Rowville in Melbourne's southeast, disagreed with many of Archbishop Pell's decisions in Melbourne and, to his credit, is prepared to put his name to his criticisms, which reflect views held by quite a few of his colleagues. Dixon said Pell was "quite authoritarian" and "dictatorial" and that under his regime, consultation days with priests became more of a matter of "this is what we are going to do." He said authority was largely centralized in the archdiocese during that time and some of the younger priests who strongly supported Pell "wanted to believe in a 'bells and smells' Church of the forties and fifties that had gone by that time." Dixon also disagreed with the Archbishop's transferring the Australian Catholic University campus into the East Melbourne "Catholic precinct" near the cathedral because, he said, it disadvantaged students from the outer southeastern suburbs who had to spend twice as long each day traveling (although it was closer for those in the poorer western and northern suburbs).

Dixon did, however, have a few positive things to say about his old boss. "I would love to say George was a bastard, but he wasn't. He is an enigma. He's very pastoral-hearted, very good with people; he's sociable and likes a drink, and he was generous with priests. He never wanted priests to have to worry about money, and we were most appreciative. He was also loyal to his priests in front of the laity. If one of them complained to him about you when he was visiting your parish, he backed you up."

After his own rough ride as rector of Corpus Christi seminary a decade earlier, Pell wasted little time in moving to alter that institution, agreeing, as he did, with Pope John Paul's assessment that seminaries must be the *pupilla oculi* (apple of his eye) of every bishop. He was determined to press ahead with a new seminary regime from the beginning of 1997, rather than let everyone find his feet in the new episcopate and postpone any real action at the seminary until the beginning of 1998.

Pell had been at the helm exactly four months when, on November 17, 1996, Melbourne's Sunday *Herald Sun* newspaper broke this story on its front page: "The entire teaching staff of Australia's largest Catholic seminary has quit over suggested changes to the training of priests. The mass resignations at Corpus Christi [misspelled by the paper as Christie] were announced at a meeting of staff with Melbourne Archbishop George Pell, who is pushing reforms to make priests conform to stricter regimes." The brief page-one article pointed to a longer piece on page three, headed "Pell's Priests Quit—Staff Walk out over Archbishop's Plans"—which was very close to the mark:

> The head of Australia's biggest Catholic seminary and his entire teaching staff have resigned in protest at planned changes to the training of priests by Melbourne Archbishop George Pell. The five senior staff, including the rector, Father Paul Connell, announced their resignations at a meeting of staff and students attended by the archbishop on Thursday. It is believed to be the first mass resignation of staff at an Australian Catholic seminary. Corpus Christi, which takes in dioceses in Victoria and Tasmania, is Australia's biggest seminary.

According to the article, the resignations were sparked by reforms the Archbishop wished to implement, including changes to daily devotions. "Also being planned is the relocation of the theology college from Clayton to Cathedral College in Victoria Pde, East Melbourne", the article revealed.

One of the departing staff members told the Sunday *Herald Sun* that the reforms were a "subtle vote of no confidence" in the seminary and that the Archbishop's stricter and more regulatory regime was not welcomed by the staff. The paper quoted Pell as saying that the planned reforms were approved unanimously by the seminary's trustees, who included the Catholic bishops in Victoria and Tasmania, and that they were based on Pope John Paul II's pastoral letter dealing with the formation of seminarians.

"I want them to be able to pray better, to celebrate the sacraments more devoutly and pray the word of God more devoutly, especially by example", the article quoted the Archbishop as saying. "They [the staff] are good people who have done a good job, but they have a different vision of seminary formation [the non-academic preparation of priests]. These changes are being made with the intention of strengthening the spiritual environment in the seminary."

Father Connell told the *Herald Sun* that the trustees of the seminary had invited the staff to continue running the seminary in the new style that the Archbishop wanted. "We considered it and decided we weren't willing to do that, and we resigned", he told the paper. "The decision was taken very seriously and after considerable thought."

The others who resigned were Dean of Studies Father Peter Howard, Spiritual Director Father Bill Attard, Director of Pastoral Formation Father Martin Ashe and Sister Maria Bongiorno, I.B.V.M. Another staff member, Father Steve Bohan, the director of first-year formation, had recently come to the end of his term of appointment.

Declining vocations had seen the closure of both Werribee and the senior seminary at Glen Waverley and the opening of Clayton in 1973. Now Pell was determined to move the students closer into town to the new Catholic precinct around the cathedral.

Opponents of the Pell style of seminary formation tend to portray the former staff as intellectual martyrs sacrificed in a reactionary push to return to a 1950s style of priestly training. At the opposite end of the spectrum, others applauded the resignations, claiming the seminary had dropped its standards both intellectually and spiritually before the Archbishop stepped in to reform it.

On balance, it came down to a clash of priorities as to what mattered most in priestly formation—and the Archbishop, who held ultimate responsibility for seminary formation, prevailed. Interestingly, some of those who resigned from the seminary stayed on at the Catholic Theological College (where both seminarians and lay theology students studied) in part-time teaching positions, including the former rector, Doctor Paul Connell. The fact that he remained in a teaching position tends to confirm that the clash of visions between the seminary staff and Pell was more to do with the spiritual formation of the students than with their academic studies (which they undertook at a separate institution).

Connell, who had begun his own studies for the priesthood at Werribee in 1964 (by which time George Pell had left for Rome) is now pastor of Pascoe Vale in Melbourne, appointed there by Pell. While he agrees that he and the other staff did resign, he and others involved insist that "it was absolutely not as simple as that." Connell's former colleague Doctor Peter Howard, who was the seminarians' dean of studies, left the priesthood in 1999. At the time of his resignation, Howard wrote a letter to priests suggesting the staff were sacked:

TO PRIEST FRIENDS, 03-09-99. Yesterday afternoon I met with the Archbishop and advised him of my decision to leave the archdiocese and the priesthood. He accepted my resignation with regret and wished me well in the future. As you will know, my decision has been arrived at after long and deep deliberation, spanning nearly three years. Certainly, while the shock of the dismissal of the seminary staff in November 1996 was the catalyst for the subsequent soul-searching, my decision to depart is not made in bitterness or anger, though, as I told the Archbishop, there are many issues on which he and I would disagree were we to enter into conversation about them. Rather, my resignation stems from a self-knowledge painfully acquired, and a decision to live according to that knowledge. . . .

Connell has prepared a written account of the events of 1996 from his point of view, which he has not yet made public. The account tells a detailed story beginning on Saturday morning, November 9, when the Archbishop met him to set out how he expected the students to have a more regulated daily timetable, including set times for Mass and prayers, and requested a restriction on students keeping cars at the seminary. Connell recalls returning to his seminary colleagues after the meeting and telling them, "We've been sacked." He insists Pell canvassed alternate jobs for the staff with him at that initial meeting.

That, of course, does not mean that the staff were sacked on that day or any other day—and Pell insists that they were not. It is feasible, however, that the Archbishop saw from the outset that Connell and his staff had such a different view of seminary formation that, sooner or later, there would be a parting of the ways. Even five years later, for example, Connell strongly defends the training system in place before Pell's reforms.

Under the system in place up to November 1996, students were divided into small, "moderator" groups, each headed by a "moderator" (a staff member who was a mentor) who interviewed the students regularly and asked them to account for their prayer and spiritual lives, which were basically left up to them. In many ways, it was a rerun of the issues raised in Pell's "Few Small Changes" memo from his own days as rector—compulsory, set prayer times versus voluntary participation at the student's discretion. His reforms, he later told an international religious journal, involved: "the basic sorts of things that most Catholics would already believe were happening in the seminary—daily Mass, morning meditation, morning prayer of the Church, night prayer of the Church, a holy hour once a week in front of the Blessed Sacrament, private recitation of the rosary and devotions to Our Lady in May."[4]

Peter Elliott said that, as he read the situation, the semi-

---

[4] Reported by *Age*, June 4, 2002.

nary staff were trying to give Archbishop Pell an ultimatum
—"Either you don't go ahead with these proposals or we resign." "It was a threat", Elliott said. "He will not take people doing that. You don't threaten George Pell and get away
with it and put ultimatums to him. They made a hideous
mistake, they called his bluff. Another bishop would have
buckled and said 'Please don't go because I can't replace
you.' Actually, that was the risk. They were well-trained
seminary staff; they'd been there for years, which was part
of the problem. It was an ingrained thing."

Connell argues that students can be made to attend Masses
and services at particular times, but that does not guarantee they are praying. His preferred system, he said, while it
appeared more "liberal" in that students could choose their
own times to pray, meant "a long-term interiorisation of the
values that one wants inculcated in preparation for them becoming priests."

Critics of the seminary pre-1996 point to its abysmally
small student numbers and the high rate of young priests
leaving the priesthood in Melbourne as signs that the system
was failing. In both the United States and Australia, it is a
fact that seminaries that have restored some of the discipline
and prayerfulness so evident in seminaries decades ago have
enjoyed a stronger revival in vocations than the more liberal
seminaries. Advocates of this approach insist that young people called by God want the real thing, not a wishy-washy
theology lacking in commitment and discipline, and that
"relevance" to modern values will never match the power
of divine revelation. Those who support Connell's arguments say that while the more traditional seminaries have
seen an increase in student numbers, the type of students
attracted tend to be rigid in outlook and unsuited to dealing
with people in the complex world of the new millennium.

Father Mark Withoos, ordained in 2000, saw both systems

operate at the seminary and preferred the system after the Pell reforms. Even in the more liberal, pre-Pell days, Withoos said he found adjusting to seminary life difficult at first, but he was surprised to find "very, very minimal prayer". "We didn't have adoration [of the Blessed Sacrament] or Benediction", he said. Some staff, Withoos said, were "not necessarily loyal" to Church teachings like *Humanae Vitae*, and he heard "occasional snide remarks about the Pope".

Despite the presence of six staff for twenty-five students, he did not find the system of self-regulated prayer and accountability to a "mentor" satisfactory. "We were required to attend fifteen minutes of morning prayer every day, except Saturday, and I turned up regularly—so regularly that my mentor suggested that I take a second day off a week and sleep in." Mark Withoos felt he had no alternative but to comply.

It was clear that Connell and his team were not the right men to implement Pell's vision of seminary education. Pell was scheduled to visit the seminary on Thursday, November 14 (the last week of the seminary year), to announce the new system of training for 1997. Pell's supporters insist he was most surprised when the staff resigned en masse that day.

Had he intended to sack them if they had not budged? Pell says the issue never arose. He says he was most surprised when the staff resigned, and their timing, in mid-November, left him very little time to get a new team in place for the 1997 academic year. However, since his vision of seminary training and the outgoing staff's were poles apart, it would not seem unreasonable, at least to people who work in the corporate world, for the leader to replace the old team with one in tune with his ideas.

Connell and some of the other staff and their friends insist that as a group, the staff, after lengthy discussion, had decided not to resign just before Pell's November 14 visit but, rather, "let Doctor Pell sack us and wear it". They say it was some of the other Victorian bishops, trustees of Corpus Christi along with Pell, who came up with the idea of the staff resigning to save face all around, both for themselves and for the Archbishop. The staff, Connell said, were reluctant to accept the compromise at first and determined to tough it out, but when the crunch came, they buckled—or blinked—first and resigned. Pell probably was surprised and undoubtedly relieved.

On Saturday, November 30, 1996, the *Age* newspaper reported that Pell was facing a backlash from his clergy over the changes, with "dozens of priests . . . known to have contacted Corpus Christi seminary to express their dismay". The article quoted a nameless "liberal cleric" who said that conservative trainee priests were often misfits. "In four or five years Archbishop Pell might have forty or fifty people in the seminary, but if you gave them a Rorschach test you'd find most of them were at the neurotic end of the scale. You won't get the sort of people who are able to offer leadership in a complex society."

The other side of the argument is that a stronger emphasis on spirituality should help give the priests the strength of character to remain true to their calling when they begin working in the world outside the seminary. At this point in history, the sheer numbers of seminarians in the more conservative United States dioceses show that at least in terms of numbers, the traditionalists are ahead, with some small United States dioceses outnumbering much larger ones by fifty to one.

The argument over seminary formation, while obscure to many, is at the heart of much of the conflict and division within the Catholic Church across the Western world. So deep are the divisions that in one Australian seminary in the 1980s (not Melbourne), students who wanted to say the rosary told friends outside that they had to do so in private, for fear of being dismissed for not being "ecumenical" in outlook.

In subsequent years, Pell boosted the seminary's academic program, enhancing the philosophy component with the help of Doctor Hayden Ramsay. He also resumed the practice of sending occasional students to Propaganda Fide in Rome (which granted scholarships to the Melbourne students even though Australia was no longer a "missionary" country) as well as to other Roman universities.

By the start of the academic year in 2000, the old parish buildings in Drummond Street, Carlton, a short walk from Saint Patrick's Cathedral, had been restored and rebuilt as the new site for Corpus Christi. In March 2000, Doctor Pell opened the new Corpus Christi Chapel—a picturesque bluestone chapel that had started life as a church school in 1855 under Melbourne's first Catholic archbishop, Alipius Goold. Relics of four prominent Catholic figures were installed in the chapel, including two saints—Saint Francis of Assisi and Saint Thomas Aquinas, whose "magnificent theology", Doctor Pell said, "is distilled in the hymns and prayers he wrote for the feast of Corpus Christi. He also wrote the hymn from which the college motto, *De Te Vivere* (To live by You), is taken." At the opening, Pell singled out Thomas Aquinas' faith, piety, intellectual genius, and application as an example to the young seminarians and the staff.

The other relics imbedded in the chapel were of two prominent twentieth-century Catholics—Mother Teresa and Croatian Cardinal Alojzije (Aloysius) Stepinac, who spent fifteen of his twenty-two years of episcopacy in prison and under house arrest and who challenged the totalitarianism of both the Nazis and the Communists and refused to sever the Catholic Church in Croatia from the Holy See. Archbishop Eric D'Arcy, the retired archbishop of Hobart, by then living in Melbourne, said at the opening that the seminary chapel is the most important space in any diocese. "Here the seminarian learns to pray regularly, or at least consolidates his patterns of prayer in good times and bad, in times of enthusiasm and times of dryness."

Ramsay says the change of venue was a masterstroke by the Archbishop. "The Clayton place had to be seen to be believed, the chapel was 1970s concrete—horrible." He said the beautifully restored chapel at the new seminary site in Carlton offered the students the richness of the Church's traditions.

Qualified seminary staff were difficult to find. In the wake of the events at the end of 1996, Monsignor Aldo Rebeschini, a Propaganda Fide graduate and the former secretary to Cardinal James Knox in Melbourne and Rome, took up the position of rector at the start of the 1997 academic year and with it the Herculean task of implementing the Archbishop's desired changes in the face of fierce opposition from some of the older students. In his three years at the helm, Monsignor Rebeschini settled things down and saw a welcome increase in new students. Pell says he did a good job.

The next rector, Father Michael McKenna, returned from a sabbatical at Harvard University and continued building up the seminary. In 2002, nine new students began their studies at Corpus Christi, compared with just one newcomer in 1996. By 2003, the seminary had forty-one students in total—thirty-one of them studying for the Archdiocese of Melbourne, and the others for Hobart, Ballarat, Sandhurst, and Sale.

The seminary crisis behind him, Pell's first Christmas celebrating midnight Mass in Saint Patrick's Cathedral was fast approaching, but festivities that year were tempered by an encounter he had the Thursday before Christmas when he blessed the body of a dead baby, Thomas Walter Joseph Ryan. Thomas had been born the day before in Melbourne's Mercy Hospital. His parents, Clare and Tom Ryan, knew their little boy's life would be brief—an ultrasound scan at eighteen weeks gestation had detected a severe abnormality, anencephaly, and, as expected, the baby's head was incomplete, his fate sealed. The Archbishop's Vicar for Health Care, Doctor Anthony Fisher, a Dominican priest, was helping the couple through their ordeal.

Thomas lived eighteen hours, and as Father Anthony Fisher said at his funeral Mass—"he packed so much into his seventeen or eighteen hours . . . long enough to leave us many memories . . . long enough to give Clare and Tom some time with him, to celebrate little birthdays as he achieved each new hour and especially their private one with him at midnight when against all odds he saw a new day." At the saddest moment in Clare Ryan's life, a tall figure in black came quietly into her hospital room and blessed her dead baby as she cradled him in her arms. Pell said very little, but he was there.

One of Pell's first initiatives as archbishop had been to establish an archdiocesan Respect Life Office. The office offers support, advice, and information to all those caught up in the tragedy of abortion—be it women who have had abortions or those considering one. It provides priests with material to handle the subject effectively and sensitively. For instance, one of its brochures addressed to women who have had an abortion says: "Allow me to speak for every minister of every denomination who has ever failed you: I'm sorry.

Every minister of God tries to faithfully preach both God's law and his mercy. But so often we end up preaching more of one than the other, and the message becomes unbalanced. Please forgive our failings, just as God will surely forgive yours."

Thomas Ryan's story featured prominently in one of the office's newsletters. As Father Fisher noted, Thomas, in his short life,

> made opportunities for his health carers to show their respect and was photographed and delighted in by his parents. Again unconsciously he made a space for care at a time when their profession is under greater and greater pressures to show less and less care and respect. . . . Even while still in the womb Thomas was influencing others, creating opportunities for others, giving his parents a chance to give testimony to the preciousness of human life and to show courage and true love. That they did so with such natural, unaffected heroism is surely the action of grace.

Chapter 12

"Si Monumentum Requiris, Circumspice" [*If You Are Searching for a Monument, Look Around*]

Many thanks for the suggestion that I take a walk around the water gardens of St Patrick's. In early evening Autumn light, they were stunning. I must say that I was deeply moved by the statue of St Catherine of Siena carrying the crown of thorns. She was dutiful and dignified. Then there was the pensive and gentle St Francis of Assisi calmly acknowledging my presence.

Besides the golden lamb in a pool of water with a verse from the Apocalypse, what struck me—apart from the design —was the vision that Archbishop Pell had for Melbourne in this. I mused long on McAuley's words:

> "Incarnate Word,
> in whom all nature lives,
> Cast flame upon the earth:
> raise up contemplatives
> Among us, men who
> walk within the fire
> Of ceaseless prayer
> impetuous desire.
> Set pools of silence
> in this thirsty land."

This is a special place. I will bring my family here. It made me think of the need for children to understand the context of public monuments, religious statues and iconography. Otherwise, they are being denied a rich and extensive cultural heritage. There may be an article in there somewhere.

So wrote Melbourne education consultant Christopher Bantick, a member of the Church of England, after exploring the Pilgrim Path and sculpture garden Archbishop Pell created beside the bluestone cathedral. On a sunny day or even in the gentle drizzle of a dark afternoon, it is an inspiring place to be, with often only the distinctively Melbourne sound of the Collins Street trams rattling past to break the silence.

The Pilgrim Path, opened in the Jubilee Year 2000, has a trail of cascading water, pouring over a selection of quotations cut with gold inlays into bluestone structures. Some are biblical quotations; another is the poem by James McAuley.

I've long had a great admiration for McAuley, [Pell said on ABC Radio after the Path was opened]. I think that's a particularly beautiful Australian piece of poetry. Even the Scripture quotes, I ran them past a whole range of people, learned people, but I also very explicitly ran them past devout Catholics who weren't at all learned, just to see—we had a few others that were possibilities—which ones they preferred. I was always particularly pleased to see so many of the tourists standing looking at McAuley's poetry or looking puzzlingly at the texts.

At the top of the Pilgrim Path are a number of sculptures of saints drawn from some of the ethnic communities that comprise the Catholic Church in Melbourne. Pell himself commissioned the first two statues—fresh, interesting sculptures of the patron saints of Italy, Saint Francis of Assisi (1181–1226) and Saint Catherine of Siena (1347–1380). Sculptor Louis Lauman depicts them identifying with the sufferings of Jesus—Francis with the stigmata of Jesus' wounds, Catherine with the crown of thorns penetrating the palms of her hands.

The statue of Croatian Cardinal Stepinac was commissioned and paid for by Melbourne's Croatian community as a reminder, not just of his heroism and faithfulness, but also of the contribution of the Croatian community to the life and culture of Melbourne. Born in 1898, Aloysius Stepinac was a World War I conscript in the Austro-Hungarian army. He was ordained in Rome in 1930 and became Archbishop of Zagreb in 1937. During the Second World War, Stepinac helped Croatian, Jewish, Serb, and Slovenian refugees and openly criticized the Nazi regime. From July 1943, the BBC and the Voice of America broadcast his sermons to occupied Europe. At the end of the war, however, Stepinac was found guilty of Nazi collaboration at a mock trial staged by Communist Yugoslavia and was sentenced to sixteen years' hard labor in 1946. After five years' jail, Tito released him and confined him to the village of Krasic. Although forbidden to resume his duties, Stepinac was named a cardinal by Pope Pius XII in 1953, and he died in 1960. In tribute, Pius XII stated that "this Croatian cardinal is the most important priest of the Catholic Church." In 1985, his trial prosecutor, Jakov Blazevic, admitted that Cardinal Stepinac's trial was entirely framed and that he was tried only because he refused to sever the thousand-year-old ties between Croatians and the Catholic Church. Pope John Paul II beatified the cardinal in 1998. Other ethnic groups will add further statues to the sculpture garden.

The Irish were already well represented around the cathedral, not just by its name, but with the statue of the "liberator" Daniel O'Connell, the lay parliamentarian responsible for Catholic emancipation in Ireland (and England) in 1829, whose view it was that Irish liberty, while a vitally important cause, was not worth "the shedding of a single drop of blood". In the latter part of Little's time as archbishop, some in Melbourne's Irish community feared that the statue would be moved out of the cathedral grounds. Pell had O'Connell's statue restored and moved to a new spot facing out onto Albert Street, where Irish President Mary McAlese rededicated it. The Archbishop also commissioned another statue—of his Irish-born predecessor, Daniel Mannix, who once wrote of his homeland: "A hundred bonds stronger than steel bound me to the dear old land, from which so many of you, like myself have come."

The ten-foot bronze statue of Mannix, on a bluestone plinth by English sculptor Nigel Boonham, was commissioned for the cathedral forecourt, and those who remember Mannix attest that it is an excellent likeness. The statue exudes a monumental presence over Eastern Hill, much like its subject did for half a century. It was unveiled in March 1999 by the then-governor of Victoria, Sir James Gobbo, who praised Mannix as an intellectual, scholar, man of prayer, international figure, educationist, orator, and wit who dominated the life of Melbourne through his long tenure as archbishop. The Italian-born Gobbo, a scholarship winner educated in the Catholic schools of Mannix' time, is a prime example of the success Mannix wished for the Catholic children of his archdiocese.

Also part of the Pell legacy is the Aboriginal message stick installed in the cathedral on Aboriginal Sunday in July 1998 and an Aboriginal stone inlay in the cathedral forecourt. The stone inlay depicts the Creator Spirit, a continuing source of life in both Aboriginal and Christian spiritual traditions.

Encircled by a border of greenstone and a larger surround of basalt, the design of the stone inlay is based on the conceptual understanding that meaning is multi-layered. Each symbol in the design—the dove, the eagle, the snake, and the water—has dual meaning, and the interpretation of the work depends on the perspective of the viewer.

In Aboriginal culture, the message stick was a means of communicating with other groups. The message stick installed in Saint Patrick's by Pell and various Aboriginal elders and people on Aboriginal Sunday, July 1998, depicts symbols representing each of Australia's Aboriginal Catholic communities. "For too long the indigenous people of this country have been left on the margins of our society, and sadly this has often been true of the Church as well", Pell said at the time. "My intention in encouraging the installation of the message stick and the stone inlay was to acknowledge the wrongs of the past and to highlight the special place that Aboriginal people occupy in the Church."

In her message published to mark the occasion, Wurundjeri Elder Joy Murphy said her people's story was similar to that of Catholics.

> Your story is by your chosen faith, our story is by the Dreaming. We both have creators and we believe in our creators. Ours is Bunjil the Eagle. In the creation story we say we belong to the land, that we are part of the land and the land part of us. Wurundjeri also say that there is a place for everyone and everyone has a place on this land.
>
> Saint Patrick's Cathedral provides a beautiful place and a comfortable environment. We feel happy here too. Today and always we will share this space as the symbol of creation in the lives of all people. We are honoured to form this partnership in respect of your reconciliation of the Aboriginal people and their lives.

Beyond Saint Patrick's Cathedral, the Catholic precinct extends along Victoria Parade, where Pell had the Australian Catholic University's Melbourne campus relocated on the corner of Young Street. On the opposite side of Victoria Parade is Goold House, bought by Archbishop Little and converted by Pell into the archdiocesan and Catholic education offices. The Archbishop's office is on the top floor, with sweeping views across central Melbourne. Near Goold House is the John Paul II Institute building, housing, not only the institute and its chapel, but also the Mannix Library, the Catholic Theological College, where both seminarians and lay people study philosophy and theology at undergraduate level, and the Catholic Pastoral Formation Centre, where non-degree courses are offered in adult education and pastoral care.

Just around the corner at 7 Brunswick Street, Fitzroy, is the Mary of the Cross Centre, housed in a large two-story building on the birthplace of Mother Mary MacKillop. Pell bought the property in July 2000, and it opened in November that year as a center providing ancillary care and support services for the families of drug and alcohol users. Although a staunch opponent of Church involvement in so-called "safe" injecting rooms, Pell was keen for the Church to become more active in responding to Melbourne's drug problem. To explore the different possibilities, he set up an archdiocesan drugs task force in June 1999, which identified the need for a center to help families of drug and alcohol abusers. The Mary of the Cross Centre works with all comers, regardless of religion, race, background, sex, or age, with many of those it helps coming from non-English-speaking backgrounds.

Addressing a joint sitting of the Victorian Parliament about the drug problem in 2001, Pell said heroin deaths were only the tip of an iceberg of misery and depression, much, but not all, of which is caused by other drugs, such as alcohol and marijuana.

He said:

> The Australian youth suicide rate, one of the highest in the world, is a related, overlapping problem. This is not just a problem for the government and the police. Community money as well as government money will be needed. Nor can it be dealt with effectively by handing over the whole load to the schools and churches. The problem is too big. All community organizations, and especially the media and leaders among young people themselves, at school, work and university, will need to combine effectively if we are to change youth attitudes to drug usage, as we have made drinking and driving generally unacceptable.
>
> Knowledge by itself rarely changes behaviour. A spiritual framework (in the broadest terms), a vision, or a system of meaning, perhaps around the Golden Rule (treating others as we wish to be treated ourselves) is needed as the context for information and argumentation, appropriate to the youngster's level of development. This is easily fitted, at a variety of levels, into the ongoing health education units, and units of moral education and religious education when they exist.

Or in other words, education about the devastating health effects of drugs will often be insufficient to steer young people away from them. A solid foundation in religious and moral belief can play a major part in helping prevent young people from becoming drug users or helping those who have become involved to break the habit.

Early in his pontificate, John Paul II created the Pontifical Council for the Family in Rome, an arm of the Vatican designed to promote the traditional family—father, mother, and children—in the world. George Pell is one of a number of international archbishops, bishops, clergy, and lay people who are consulters to the Pontifical Council, and his friend Peter Elliott worked there until he returned to Australia in 1997. As part of the Pontifical Council's efforts, the Pope decided to establish a new "Pontifical Institute for Studies on Marriage and the Family". This was to be announced during his Wednesday audience in Saint Peter's Square on May 13, 1981 (the anniversary of our Lady's first appearance at Fatima, in Portugal, in 1917), but before he could do so that day, the Holy Father was shot by Mehmet Ali Agca. The institute was finally established the following year, entrusted by the Pope to the care of Our Lady of Fatima, to whose intercession he attributed his miraculous survival on the day the institute was to have been born. The institute is a postgraduate academic institute, linked to Rome's Pontifical Lateran University, offering diplomas, master's degrees, licentiates, and doctorates in bioethics, marriage, and family studies. Full branches of the institute have now been established in the Lateran University in the Vatican City State, in Washington, D.C., in Valencia (Spain), and in Mexico City and Guadalajara (Mexico), in Cotonou (Benin), and in Salvador da Bahia (Brazil), with new campuses evolving in India, Austria, and Ireland. In response to the Pope's express wish that the institute be present on all continents, the Archdiocese of Melbourne took up the challenge, and the John Paul II Institute for Marriage and Family opened in July 2001 in Melbourne, with a collaborative arrangement with the University of Notre Dame in Perth.

The Washington John Paul II Institute had begun with nine students. Melbourne's opened with twenty-seven students, and in less than two years the numbers have risen to forty. All candidates already hold undergraduate degrees and, after graduation, can expect to be employed as teachers in seminaries and theological colleges, as leaders in community and church organizations, or as ethicists in the healthcare industry. Academically, it is a rigorous institution. To enroll in the Licentiate in Sacred Theology (Marriage and Family) course, for example, applicants must have achieved an average grade of at least Credit in previous theology degree courses, have a strong background in philosophy, and an adequate reading knowledge of scholastic Latin and/ or biblical Greek and at least one modern European language.

Pell named his protégé and vicar for health care, Father Anthony Fisher, O.P., then forty-one, as director of Melbourne's John Paul II Institute. Now an auxiliary bishop in Sydney, Fisher is one of the Catholic Church's bright young talents and a man whom Pell has gone out of his way to encourage and support. After arts (honors) and law degrees from Sydney University and a first class honors degree in theology from the Melbourne College of Divinity, Fisher completed a doctorate in bioethics at Oxford in 1995. While studying in England, he also worked as adviser to the British bishops on bioethics.

At first glance, Fisher (who wore a full, floor-length religious habit for work in his quaint attic office) could be a medieval Dominican scholar in a monastery. He specializes, however, in the moral theology of the future, in the cutting-edge medical science issues where ordinary Australians are increasingly looking for answers—stem cell research, reproductive technologies, genetic engineering, and cloning. Along with contraception, abortion, and euthanasia, these are the pressing moral issues of today, but it is perhaps contraception that causes the most confusion and division in the Church.

On July 25, 1998—two years into his episcopacy—Pell

boldly took on the issue of contraception by celebrating the thirtieth anniversary of Pope Paul VI's *Humanae Vitae.* Archbishop Pell, Archbishop Hickey of Perth, and Archbishop Charles Chaput of Denver, Colorado, were among only a handful of archbishops in the world who issued pastoral letters to mark the occasion of a document that has been accused of being anti-woman and a contributor to overpopulation and abortion.

But Pell argued that the Church's stand against artificial birth control is, in fact, respectful of women. In a contraceptive culture, women mostly carry the burden of limiting births, often with negative consequences to their health and happiness. Certainly the years since 1968 have revealed that both oral contraceptives and the intra-uterine device (IUD) pose serious risks to women's health. Long-term use of the Pill has been linked to cardiovascular disease as well as breast and cervical cancer. And despite the widespread use of these and other contraceptives, abortion and teenage pregnancy rates have escalated around the world, including in Australia, which has an abortion rate in excess of Great Britain and Holland. At the same time, more and more professional women are speaking openly and honestly about their grief at being unable to conceive after putting off motherhood for too long.

Pell argued the case for *Humanae Vitae* along prudential lines, in tune with today's medical and social concerns. First, he urged Catholics actually to read the encyclical in a spirit of openness. To this end, he made copies freely available at all Catholic churches, pointing out that the document was about far more than contraception and was "probably the most famous and least understood encyclical in history".

The Archbishop admitted that many Catholics honestly believe:

that Pope Paul VI was wrong to reaffirm the traditional Christian teaching against artificial contraception, common to all
Christian churches until early this century. However this may
be argued, the Holy Father was right on two scores: on the
dignity and beauty of married love and on the dire practical
consequences of the contraceptive mentality, of selfishness
at work.

The widespread use of the Pill unlocked the sexual revolution in Australia and the Western World, which brought
an increase in abortions, marriage breakdowns, the number
of single mothers and homeless children. These dark consequences of casual sex are hidden from view, while sexuality itself is debased in films, magazines, and advertising, and
young men and women, their relations often troubled by
a lurking mistrust, are more reluctant than ever to commit
themselves to each other unconditionally for life. Individuals
are asking the Church to legitimise homosexual activity, to
bless single-sex unions. We have now the tragic AIDS epidemic . . . the signs of the times have validated Paul VI's
pessimism about the future, and like the true prophets of
the Old Testament he was derided and denounced for his
predictions.

It is important, Pell argued, to examine the benefits of
faithful married love and natural methods of family planning.

Since 1968 . . . medical scientists have developed the knowledge for couples to manage their fertility without the use of
harmful drugs, surgery or artificial devices. . . . In the past
thirty years, great advances have been made in the area of natural family planning. Sadly, many of our people are unaware
of them and still talk dismissively of what are in fact very
effective techniques. Advances in natural methods of family
planning have . . . empowered women to take a greater role

in decisions about their reproductive health, enhancing self-confidence and self-esteem.

His initiative sparked an enormous debate on family issues in Melbourne's two major newspapers, the *Herald Sun* and the *Age*, with front-page news stories, features, and letters to the editor for and against the statement. In an editorial the *Herald Sun* praised Pell for suggesting that the trappings of the 1990s might have made Australian society materially better off, but in a spiritual and psychological sense life had become much harder for many people.

The editorial read:

> Dr Pell's comments will prick many a conscience. Perhaps it is time to pause and try to balance our obsession for material wealth against the need for spiritual contentment. In a perfect society people would think less of themselves and more about family, friends and those needing help. Dr Pell was right to express concerns about the direction society was heading, that ". . . the general direction in marriage breakdowns, extra-nuptial births, divorces is quite clear and irrefutable."

The same year as his document on *Humanae Vitae*, Pell was put to the test on another question regarding the Church's teaching on marriage—homosexuality. In many people's minds, particularly those unfamiliar with the Church, George Pell's refusing Communion to homosexual activists who protested the Church's teaching by wearing rainbow sashes to his Masses has defined him as a hard-line conservative. Those who better understand Catholic teaching, including clerics and Church bureaucrats who disagree with Pell on other issues, say he had no alternative but to refuse Communion to sash-wearers.

Rainbow Sash protests began in London at Westminster Cathedral in 1997, when a young man in a sash was refused Communion by Cardinal Basil Hume, a gentle, scholarly, Benedictine monk widely regarded as a liberal on many social and moral questions. An Australian homosexual activist and former Franciscan seminarian, Michael Kelly, then helped organize a similar protest at Saint Patrick's in Melbourne, when New York's Cardinal John O'Connor presided as the papal delegate at the reopening of the cathedral that October. Kelly, who lives in Melbourne, said he and his friends regarded O'Connor as "a notorious homophobe". Until his death, O'Connor was one of the most widely respected prelates in the world, well-known for his tough anti-abortion stance and a good friend of Pell, who keeps O'Connor's picture in his Sydney office.

The next protest in Melbourne happened on Pentecost Sunday 1998, when a group of about seventy people attended Mass wearing brightly colored rainbow sashes over their clothes. Pell was the principal celebrant of the Mass, and the group had notified him of their plans in advance. They also notified the local and national media, who turned up in droves, and the story drew international attention. When the time for Holy Communion came, the sash-wearers approached the Archbishop, who refused them the Sacrament unless they took off their sashes. Instead, he proffered a blessing. Michael Kelly told the *Age* newspaper that Pentecost Sunday had been chosen because "that was when the Holy Spirit touched every tribe, nationality and tongue, 'but apparently not gay and lesbian people'."

That Sunday, one of those wearing the sash was Nan McGregor, who, the newspapers reported, was the mother of a gay son. After the Mass McGregor told the press that being denied Communion was "an extremely emotional" experience. "Archbishop Pell said he couldn't give me Holy Communion until I took the sash off. I said I was a heterosexual mother, but he said he couldn't until I took the sash off because the sash indicated I rejected the teachings of the Catholic Church", she said. "I feel sorry for him. I think he is lost in his own bigotry and small-mindedness."

In the next few years, Michael Kelly and others repeated the exercise several times in Melbourne and once in Sydney, with Pell's reactions varying from telling him "repent and believe" to standing silently and not offering a blessing. On one occasion, when Pell was visiting Kelly's local parish, Kelly and his mother wore the sashes and, as chance would have it, came to Communion to a priest standing beside the Archbishop. After some hesitation, the priest gave Kelly Communion. Archbishop Pell says he was unaware of the incident at the time.

A vital point often missed in the debate surrounding the matter is that if Kelly were to approach Pell for Communion without wearing his sash, Pell would likely give him the Sacrament. "Yes, I think I would give Kelly Communion if he came without the sash," says Pell "because I don't know, he might have been to confession. I've never asked anybody when they come up to Communion what they do. If I'm asked what are the Church teachings I will tell them. Receiving the Sacrament is the ultimate expression of our Catholic faith. It's not a question of refusing homosexuals or someone who is homosexually oriented. The rule is basically the same for everyone."

But although Kelly knows that Pell would offer him Holy Communion without the sash, Kelly repeatedly refuses to take it off. So does the sash matter more to him than receiving the Body of Christ? Kelly was surprised by the question. "That's a curious way of putting it", he said. "A lot

of Catholics play the 'don't ask, don't tell' game and go to
Communion regardless of their views on abortion, contraception, women priests. Maybe I could play the game on
some of the issues, but on something as core to who I am as
my own sexual orientation, being actively gay, fudging the
issues would be tantamount to collusion with evil."

Kelly is correct in asserting that many Catholics do wrongly
approach and receive Holy Communion despite using contraception or engaging in extramarital sex or committing any
number of offenses against the moral law of the Church without compunction. However, if such people advertised their
unrepented and unconfessed sins and demanded a change in
Church teaching by a protest at the altar, they, too, would
be refused Communion. Kelly, however, insists that some
issues are too important to be "swept under the carpet". He
was keen to stress that the Rainbow Sash movement was
interested in changing the Church's entire theology of sexuality.

The ordinary people in the pews in Saint Patrick's seemed
firmly on Pell's side on Pentecost Sunday 1998, and they
broke into loud applause when the Archbishop took the
sash-wearers to task at the end of Mass. In contrast, the
crowd at Saint Mary's in Sydney remained silent after a similar speech the first time the protest was staged there.

Despite these varied reactions, among the Australian hierarchy the issue was clear-cut. In Canberra, the liberal auxiliary bishop Patrick Power, while making the protesters welcome for discussions, also refused them Communion. At
the time of the Melbourne protests, the then-Archbishop of
Sydney, Cardinal Edward Clancy, said he also would have
had no choice but to refuse Communion as the protesters
were openly defying long-established teachings. "All Catho-

lics are assumed to know what the necessary dispositions are if they are to receive Holy Communion", Cardinal Clancy said.

Brisbane's Archbishop John Bathersby and Perth's Archbishop Barry Hickey said they would have refused Communion to those wearing the sashes. Bathersby said he was sad that an act of worship was being used to make a political statement. As he pointed out, the Catholic *Catechism* says homosexual acts can be approved "under no circumstances", but "every sign of unjust discrimination" against homosexual people should be avoided and that homosexual people must be received "with respect, compassion and sensitivity. . . ." Hickey said: "I think it is time for the Church to dispel doubts about Church teaching and do what Doctor Pell has done. If a bishop comes out frequently about Church teaching, that does not make [the Church] more conservative. When an issue of public morality comes up one must speak publicly about it. . . . If we have made ourselves unpopular it does not mean we are wrong."

Pell said neither he nor other bishops had the authority to alter Church teaching on the matter. "In wearing the sash, they're trying to get the Church to change the teaching on that subject, which we can't and won't do", he told the *Australian* after yet another demonstration on Pentecost Sunday 2000, when three security guards attended the Mass in case of disruption. "The Church's view on sexuality . . . is clear and unequivocal and derives from natural moral law, which we believe is unchanging."

In Melbourne, the issue of the Church's attitude to homosexuality again flared in December 1999, when gay, lesbian, and AIDS groups attacked Pell over his support for the United States–based group Courage, which he promoted in a pamphlet sent to three hundred Melbourne priests. Courage is a Catholic organization, endorsed by the Vatican's Pontifical Council for the Family, which aims to promote chastity, prayer, frequent reception of the sacraments, and platonic friendships among those with same-sex attractions. Pell says that while Courage does not make any general claim about helping homosexuals toward heterosexuality, a few have been so helped.

Homosexual activists did not find Pell's endorsement of Courage welcome news. In the *Australian*, Michael Kelly argued that Courage believed homosexuality was an illness to be cured and said more people would be driven to "the brink of despair and suicide" by the organization. "It's just a recipe for youth suicide", he said. But Pell held firm. "The great majority of stances I have taken have been reflecting Church views", he said, adding that he was enormously troubled by youth suicides, and if they were connected with homosexuality, it was "another reason to be discouraging people going in that direction".[1]

After the Rainbow Sash protests on Pentecost 1999, Pell noted that homosexual activity posed a much greater health risk than smoking because one sexual encounter can cause AIDS. The epidemic of AIDS around the globe—by late 2000 health authorities estimated that HIV was infecting new victims at the rate of more than one every eight seconds—prompted the National Academics Forum to hold a major symposium on the problem at the National Library of Australia in Canberra on November 29 and 30, 2000. Archbishop Pell was one of the main speakers, along with medical specialists, scientists, and community leaders from the gay community and AIDS support teams.

[1] *Age*, Monday, May 24, 1999.

Given the confusion prompted by the Rainbow Sash controversy, Pell's Canberra speech spelled out the Church's position on homosexuality. At the symposium, he shared the platform with a gay activist, who also made a speech; then they engaged in a dialogue. "I am grateful for the opportunity to discuss the scourge of AIDS; to set out Christian moral teachings, hard as they can appear, as they surround and defend our central claim to the importance of love and compassion; to deny the charge that Christian teaching is homophobic; and deny any suggestion that AIDS is divine retribution", the Archbishop said in the opening remarks of his speech. "God always forgives, humans sometimes forgive. It is nature which is ruthless and never forgives. Against that Christ asked all those who are burdened to come to him and find rest; the yoke is easy and the burden light."

The Church, he told delegates to the forum, had a clear right and duty to comment on public policy. "So often decisions that affect our lives are seen to be merely 'social' and 'economic'; there is clear advantage for everyone in the contributions towards public policy of a group such as the Church whose concern is with moral truth. The Catholic Church proposes; she can no longer impose or prescribe. People accept or reject our truth claims."

In a climate of easy agnosticism among Australian opinion-makers, it was necessary to explain Christian perspectives. He said:

> Catholics believe that Christ is Son of God as well as son of Mary. Because of this divine origin we think our moral and faith teaching has a unique authority, founded as it is on access to truth. We believe these truths are reported to us reliably in the New Testament, written within early Christian communities and authorized by the early Church as an

accurate witness to the lives and preaching of Christ and the apostles.

Christian teaching on the moral legitimacy of sexual behaviour has always been clear, founded on our Judeo-Christian moral framework and proclaimed out of concern for the ultimate happiness and wellbeing of the individual and society. Simply put, sexual activity belongs within the framework of heterosexual marriage and exists for the procreation of children and the mutual love of the couple. Therefore, certain sexual behaviour is considered by Christians to be clearly inappropriate (and if committed with knowledge of the evil involved, sinful). This behaviour includes adultery, pre-marital sex, masturbation and homosexual activity.

No moral blame, he said, attaches to a person simply because he is inclined toward disordered sexual behavior. Personal culpability requires understanding of and consent to the prohibited activity, not just inclination. For Christians, just because a course of activity is regarded as difficult—even almost impossibly difficult—is no reason to reject or abandon the ideal. "We all know some will not—and some can not—live up to good moral standards, but this is not a sufficient reason to abandon the standards. Christians believe in forgiveness and acknowledge human weakness, but Christianity requires the Cross."

The Church's first response to the sick was to love them and care for them, he said.

Everywhere followers of Christ are doing this for AIDS victims. However, we need also to invoke Christ the Teacher for there are difficult lessons to be learned from HIV/AIDS.

Christian teaching on sexual activity is much more difficult for some to live up to than others, but that does not make it false, irrelevant or wildly unrealistic. The social and personal effects of promiscuity, contraception, abortion and marriage breakdown show its relevance and support its truth. Moral standards have an important function even when they are beyond the reach of some, because they point out what should be the direction of our striving.

Catholic teaching, especially sexual teaching, is not arbitrary. It is based on long and careful reflection on what really contributes to human happiness and what really makes a society flourish. Compassion does not proclaim what it knows to be false: that would violate human dignity and add to the tragedy of HIV/AIDS. Instead, it reaffirms the truth and looks for new ways to formulate and communicate it, since we have certainly not done all we could have here.[2]

This did not mean the Church wishes to see homosexual activity made a criminal offense again as it was in the past, he said.

Government has limits to its authority, and there are good common sense reasons too for thinking that legislation and public intervention do not always help (whereas good moral education always will). The Church too, in every society, but especially in a religiously pluralist society, has limits to its authority, e.g., the Church traditionally has not insisted that brothels be closed and does not ask today that homosexual activity be criminalized. Where human motivation is complex the proper public response is a complex issue too and different cases will be best handled in different ways, respecting the separation of Church and state.

Young adults and teenagers deserve to be told the truth about AIDS, he said.

Many youngsters have only the fragments of a framework left over from the "me generation" of their parents; many do

---

[2] National Academics Forum, public symposium on "Every Eight Seconds: AIDS revisited", November 29–30, 2000, Australian National Library.

not even have that. Most appreciate at least hearing about a strong, sound ethical position that claims to be based on ultimate human happiness, presented clearly and charitably. . . .

Secondly, they should be told the truth, the advantages of waiting, the advantages of monogamy. The truth, however, is not a "safe sex" advertisement. The only safe sex is no casual sex. The truth about condoms should be told: they are unreliable, they encourage sterile sex for gratification among the young and they are a public health hazard because of the behaviour they encourage and promote. Sexual addiction is possible and damaging. Twenty-five per cent of sexually transmitted diseases in the USA occur among adolescents.

What Pell did not tell the conference was about his own private hostel visits to AIDS patients. While resolute in his views that rainbow sash wearers should not be offered Communion, Pell rejects any suggestion that he is a "homophobe", pointing out that he has often spoken with people who are openly homosexual and has visited his share of AIDS patients.

Chapter 13

Salt of the Earth, Not Sugar or Artificial Sweetening

In December 1998, George Pell told *Fides*, the Vatican news agency, that Catholic bishops were, as Cardinal Ratzinger had recently told the Australian bishops in Rome, called to be the salt of the earth—not the sugar. Or, he added, "the artificial sweetening".[1] For the benefit of his episcopal colleagues he did not need to repeat the rest of Christ's comment in the Bible—that when salt loses its flavor it should be thrown out and trampled underfoot. After a stressful month in Rome, they were well aware of the warning in Cardinal Ratzinger's words.

From mid-November to mid-December, the entire Australian episcopate had been in Rome, for the Synod of Oceania, along with other bishops from around the South Pacific region, and also in order to pay their regular five-yearly *ad limina* visits to the Pope and the Vatican congregations. *Ad limina* means "to the threshold", and that is exactly where the bishops felt they were. The Australian bishops, some more than others, were admonished for what was viewed in Rome as encroaching liberalism and modernism in the Church in Australia. In his *ad limina* address handed to the

[1] *Courier-Mail*, December 19, 1998, p. 27.

Australian bishops in the form of a letter, Pope John Paul II suggested that the "Australian sense of equality", when taken too far, could be problematic. "While it has many positive elements, tolerance of and openness to all opinions and perspectives on the truth can lead to indifference, to the acceptance of any opinion or activity as long as it does not impact adversely on other people." The worldwide crisis of faith was "manifested in Australia by the rise in the number of people with no religion and the decline in church practice".

At stake were many of the issues George Pell had been addressing for years—and more besides: orthodox seminary training; religious education, particularly in relation to the sacraments in Catholic schools; the importance of maintaining clear distinctions between the roles of priests and laity; nuns returning to their convents and traditional habits and work; and liturgical abuses. These could include priests leaving out important parts of the Mass, or using their own words, or, in extreme cases, encouraging lay people to stand around the altar and say the words of consecration with them, adding in their own bits and pieces as they went along. One Brisbane church even made it a practice to offer chocolates to young children at Communion time. On one occasion, the priest celebrating Mass had to leave the church immediately after the Consecration to bring in the chocolates after a young child missed them and complained. On another occasion, a different priest at the church joked to the congregation about a layman who regularly distributed the chocolates to the children with the phrase "Body of Frog".

At the conclusion of the month-long visit, a twenty-page Statement of Conclusions was signed. It was co-authored by the Australian bishops and curial officials, including Cardinal Ratzinger and the prefects of five other important Vatican congregations: Divine Worship and Discipline of the

Sacraments; Bishops; Clergy; Institutes of Consecrated Life; and Education.

This stormy, controversial visit was reported widely in the Australian media. Newspapers in Europe and North America also covered it. Some of the headlines of the time told the story: "Why Vatican Cuffed Bishop", "Reformists See Papal Rebuke as Setback", "Back to the Old Faith", "How the Papal Hit Squad Brought Priests to Heel" and "Bishops Told to Get Tough".

When they returned to Australia, some bishops vented their spleen in public, admitting they were "hurt, angry and depressed" about the reception they had received at the Vatican and about the letter written to them by the Pope. A few, including Pell, were more accepting, saying that if the Statement of Conclusions and *ad limina* address contained stern words, it was to remind Catholics that the Church was not open to change on central issues. "What [the statement] is saying is these aren't going to change and . . . in a polite sort of way people can't have their cake and eat it", said Pell. "I am not suggesting that anybody who might disagree with the Church on any one or two particular issues, that their membership . . . is called into question. But if you disagree with the Church on a whole raft of things, a legitimate question is to what extent do you remain a Catholic?"[2]

In a written statement, widely distributed in Melbourne along with the lengthy Statement of Conclusions document, Pell spoke of a widespread crisis of faith in society as a whole and a related crisis of Christology among believers. God, he said, was much more than the mighty forces of nature, and only humans are made in God's image. "The Second Person of the Trinity became a man; not an angel or a cabbage."

---

[2] "Why Vatican Cuffed Bishops", *Australian*, December 26, 1998, p. 3.

Problem areas had to be confronted and errors corrected by persuasion and dialogue, not blunt use of authority. The Church in Australia, Pell warned, "must not be like a husband and wife who deny the early signs that their marriage is in trouble; not like a bank manager who will not admit that his Branch is losing money and customers." The decline in worship by Catholics, he said, was significant. "In Melbourne this decline is running at the rate of 1.5 to 2 percent each year. We hope to change this." He branded the trend the "rise of the RCs"—resting, relaxed, or reluctant Catholics.

The truths of Catholicism, he said, were spelled out in the Creeds, "and the possibilities of innocent misunderstandings are legion when we speak of God. This is why home-written creeds are forbidden at Mass, even for home or school masses." Forbidden though such creeds may be, four years after the Statement of Conclusions they are still in use in parts of some dioceses in Australia—but not those run by Pell and like-minded colleagues.

The Statement of Conclusions covered sixty-three issues. Much of the battle, however, centered on one issue in particular—the Sacrament of Penance. In almost every diocese of Australia in the previous decade, including Melbourne, the traditional practice of Catholics confessing their sins individually to priests had been largely overtaken by highly popular "general absolution" ceremonies, generally held at Christmas and Easter. At these liturgies, several hundred people were absolved of their sins at once, after prayers, hymns, a communal examination of conscience, and a communal act of contrition. A communal penance, such as everybody reciting a Hail Mary or two, was usually given. The Church's canon law, however, reserved general absolution (or the third rite) for genuine emergency situations, such as soldiers going into battle or an airplane being hijacked, with the onus on penitents to confess their serious sins individually at the earliest opportunity if possible. Its routine use in parishes, while popular, is illicit under Church law, although the vast majority of those in the pews were unaware that this was the case.

Pope John Paul had reiterated the Church's teaching to the bishops on their 1998 visit: "The personal nature of sin, conversion, forgiveness and reconciliation demands personal confession of sins," he told them.

Pell had always been a strong advocate of the traditional or first rite practice of individual confession. Earlier in his episcopacy, however, he displayed an ambivalence about whether he should ban general absolution in the parishes altogether, although he was leaning toward that course. On May 29, 1998, in a lengthy interview with Geoffrey Barker in the *Australian Financial Review* magazine, Pell was asked: "Will you abolish the Third Rite?"

He replied:

> It is undoubtedly popular. . . . It was introduced as a way of encouraging people back to individual reconciliation and penance. That, I think, has been a spectacular failure. The question is, whether by having the Third Rite we are reinforcing the disappearance of individual confession. That's the crucial issue, and I'm not sure which way we should go on that. . . .
>
> The opinion of church-going Catholics is a very important consideration, but not necessarily the primary consideration. The teaching role . . . is given first of all to the pope and the bishops, and we are very, very much the spokesmen for tradition.[3]

[3] *Australian Financial Review Magazine*, May 29, 1998.

In Sydney, Cardinal Edward Clancy banned general absolution in his parishes at Easter 1998, and in late October that year Pell took the same action, announcing the decision at a gathering of Melbourne priests. Catholics in other cities, however, were assured in the secular media that it would be business as usual with general absolution for Christmas and that nothing would change despite the moves in Sydney and Melbourne. But in Rome a few weeks later, Pope John Paul ordered all Australian diocesan bishops to stop abusing the third rite, declaring that individual confession remained "the only ordinary way for the faithful to reconcile themselves with God and the Church". Most of the bishops complied, albeit some with bad grace, and one or two ignored the edict—at least initially.

Pell sent Denis Hart, the "enforcer", home to Melbourne early from Rome, to ensure that priests adhered to the order. Many Melbourne priests who had never approved of the illicit use of general absolution welcomed the restoration of discipline, although just as many resented it bitterly, and still do, as do many of their parishioners. While many Catholics at both ends of the spectrum praise or blame Pell for what they mistakenly regard as his central role in the matter, he was not one of the main players.

Long before the Australian prelates' *ad limina* visits, groups of concerned Catholics had been monitoring and documenting general absolution ceremonies and reporting their findings to Sydney barrister Paul Brazier, whose Australian Catholics Advocacy Centre had been collating and presenting evidence of liturgical and other abuses in a format consistent with canon law, first to Australian bishops and then, when they appeared not to listen or act, to Rome. The media called the evidence gathering "spying"; and at one point, Pell branded the tactics of those collecting the information "in-

The left-hand side of Pell's shield is the coat of arms of the See of Sydney—
four stars representing the Southern Cross constellation. The tradition of the
Cardinal Archbishops of Sydney using the arms of the see in conjunction
with their personal arms dates back to the time of Cardinal Moran (1884–
1911). *The Pelican in Her Piety* is a traditional eucharistic emblem, based on
the medieval legend that the pelican would feed its young with blood from
its own breast, which it would lacerate with its beak—a symbol of Christ
feeding us with his own flesh and blood. The pelican is also a traditional
emblem of the Pell family. *The Sun in His Splendor* is a traditional emblem of
Saint Thomas Aquinas and refers to Aquinas College, Ballarat, where George
Pell was director from 1974 to 1984. The sun is also a eucharistic emblem.
The monogram MR with the coronet is a traditional representation of Maria
Regina (Mary, the Queen). The motto *Be Not Afraid* echoes our Lord's words
to the disciples in the Gospels of Matthew 14:27, Mark 6:50, and John 6:20,
and also refers to John Paul II's first homily as pope (November 2, 1978).

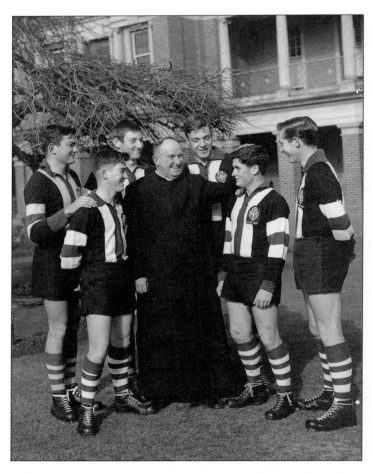

Upholding the traditions of St. Patrick's College, Ballarat. Brother William O'Malley (old Bill) and George Pell (third player from the right) and other members of his championship Australian rules football team of 1959.

Family portrait of 1963 before George sailed for Rome. David, George, and Margaret (top) with their parents, Margaret and George Pell senior and Aunt Molly Burke.

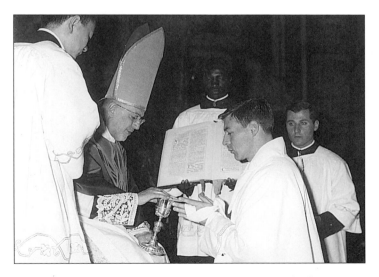

Ordination Day, St. Peter's Basilica, December 16, 1966. Cardinal Agagianian anoints George Pell's hands.

Dr. George Pell, S.T.L., D.Phil. (Oxon) and his sister Margaret in Oxford, Easter 1975. He had to wait and save up for four years to go back for the graduation ceremony.

June 29, 1997. The Archbishop of Melbourne receives the Pallium from Pope John Paul II in St. Peter's Basilica, Rome on the feast day of Saints Peter and Paul.

Archbishop Pell (left), with Cardinal Joseph Ratzinger, Prefect of the Congregation for the Doctrine of the Faith (center), and Pope John Paul II in the late 1990s.

Archbishop Pell addressing the Parliament of New South Wales.

The October 21, 2003 Consistory of 30 Cardinals comprised four graduates of the Pontifical Urban University. From left, Cardinals Fumio Hamao (Japan) ordination class of 1957; classmates Anthony Okogie (Nigeria) and George Pell (Australia) class of 1966 and Telesphore Toppo (India) 1969. Photograph by L'Osservatore Romano.

George Cardinal Pell

Cardinal Pell blesses the Pope John Paul II Building at St Kevin's Primary
School, Geebung, Australia. April 20th 2004. Photograph by Kate Collins.

George Cardinal Pell

trusive" and "un-Australian", although he agreed on ABC's *Four Corners* program that anyone could attend any public Church service.

As Sydney priest Father John Walter wrote in the American theology magazine *Homiletic and Pastoral Review*: "The Vatican had accepted the strong case that Brazier had presented on behalf of orthodox Catholics before the Congregation for Divine Worship and the Discipline of the Sacraments." It was, Walter explained, "water-tight, quality evidence in any court of justice, testimony the Holy See could not and did not ignore. The bishops were greatly embarrassed by the inherent credibility of these sworn eye-witness accounts."[4]

Pell continued to follow up the Statement of Conclusions and urged a return to individual confession by Catholics long after the fuss had died down. Preaching to his priests before Easter 2001, he mentioned the Pope's concern about "a certain dwindling of our enthusiasm and availability" for the demanding work of hearing confessions. "We must always, each week, be regularly available, and we must teach and explain, especially if customers seem to be scarce and every sinner in the parish seems to be over the age of fifty!" he said. "Basic human needs are never cancelled out by crises of culture, much less by passing fashions. The Sacrament of Penance meets the deep human need for forgiveness, and the need for this to be both ritualised and deeply personal."

In more ways than one, 1998 became a turning point for the Church in Australia. In February that year, a Melbourne priest of twenty-eight years standing, Father Michael Morwood, M.S.C. (Missionaries of the Sacred Heart), was summoned to Pell's office and told that his book *Tomorrow's*

---

[4] *Homiletic and Pastoral Review*, April 2001.

Catholic (Spectrum Publications, 1997), which had reportedly sold ten thousand copies, "contains serious errors and is not to be sold, displayed or distributed in any Catholic church or to be used in Catholic schools". The Archbishop also handed him a ten-page critique of the work and asked his reaction before speaking publicly about the matter. A few weeks later, in a public statement, Pell said the work contained, "mistaken teaching on the Son of God, on the divinity of Christ, . . . on the Trinity, . . . on redemption and on original sin"—charges Morwood denied. The priest, for his part, accused the Archbishop of acting hastily as "prosecutor, judge and hangman" and with "an extraordinary lack of judgement". Pell says Morwood never answered, either to him or publicly, the detailed critique of the work.

On Christmas Eve that year, the *Age* reported that Morwood had decided to leave the priesthood and wanted it known that he was leaving, not in anger, but at peace with his decision and looking for new ways to work within the Church.

In March the following year, Melbourne's Catholic Bookshop in Lonsdale Street also withdrew Morwood's earlier book *God Is Near: Understanding a Changing Church*, another Spectrum Publications work that, with fifteen thousand sales, was a religious bestseller and had frequently been used in parish discussion groups.

Although Pell was a member of the Vatican's CDF (Congregation for the Doctrine of the Faith), he did not consult that body about Morwood. He says: "Father Morwood was working in my diocese, the book was published in my diocese; so it was my responsibility to deal with the matter as the chief Catholic teacher in the region."

Morwood hit the headlines about the same time that his then-M.S.C. colleague Father Paul Collins revealed that he had been delated anonymously to the CDF for his book *Papal Power* and that in January his superiors had been informed that a CDF-approved theologian in Rome, who was not named, had discovered several "doctrinal problems" in the work. Collins let it be known that he suspected Pell of turning him in. Asked by a reporter on *A Current Affair* if that was the case, the Archbishop replied: "Paul Collins certainly has a case to answer." Now as then, Pell refuses to discuss any aspect of that or any other matter that came before the CDF during his ten-year term as a member of the congregation. After thirty-three years, Paul Collins left the priesthood in early 2001.

The emergence of these conflicts into the public arena in 1998 stunned many Catholics and non-Catholics alike, most of whom had no idea that theological divisions were running so deep, although the issues at stake had worried Pell and others for years. Preaching at the state funeral for his old friend B. A. Santamaria, in March 1998, Pell elaborated on some of those concerns:

> The Catholic community in Australia owes B. A. Santamaria a great debt for his leadership in the fight against communism in the unions; for his indispensable contribution in obtaining financial justice for all Christian schools from state and federal governments; for his authorship of fifteen of the bishops' statements on social justice; for his brilliant alliance with Archbishop Mannix. . . .
>
> However, some would believe that his greatest religious contribution has been during the last ten or fifteen years as different forces contended for the soul of Catholicism. Here B. A. stood squarely with the Holy Father.

Informing Australian Catholics of the nature of the challenge they faced, he said, was Santamaria's last great struggle, and the conflict is far from over.

There are minority forces in Australian Catholicism who want to subordinate gospel morality to individual conscience. Some want to use this to expand beyond recognition the limits of proper sexual activity. Some reject not only particular papal teachings, but would like to sideline papal authority itself. Others see the ministerial priesthood as one relic of a vanished clerical age.

Even more seriously some do not see Christianity as a revealed religion. So the divinity of Christ is impugned, the Trinity redefined and the worship of the one true God relativised and minimised. It is increasingly hard work to convince our youngsters of the evils of abortion and euthanasia, let alone contraception.

At least now much more of the struggle was out in the open.

Debate and turmoil such as that surrounding the Statement of Conclusions can have positive as well as negative effects. It can heighten interest in spiritual matters and help those keen to join in the discussions develop a deeper understanding of the faith by responding to the arguments of others. For those in authority, such divisions pose the challenge of trying to keep a divided family together, of balancing both the need for charity and the demand for truth. As Pell said in 1998: "Human beings have rights, these have to be respected. So as the Pope said in one of those great moral encyclicals, the individual conscience is a proximate norm, it's indispensable, there's no substitute for sincerity. But it is not the last word, we stand under the truth, and for Christians we stand under the Gospel and the solemn teachings of the Church."

Though he has met with resistance from some members of his own flock, some of Pell's strongest stances have captured widespread popular support from people of different shades of religion. In October 1997, the National Gallery of Victoria decided to stage an exhibition of works by the American artist Andres Serrano, including a photograph named *Piss Christ*, depicting a crucifix immersed in a jar of urine. Pell was outraged: "The National Gallery should be a temple of beauty; not a home for sleaze." Determined to fight back, he organized a coalition of Christian church leaders to object to the blasphemous work. Jewish and Moslem leaders also joined the effort. A phone-in poll in the *Herald Sun* newspaper showed that 93 percent of respondents agreed with the Archbishop's stance. The incident drew international attention and in a speech afterward to the Oxford University Chaplaincy in England, Pell recounted:

> I contacted the gallery and asked them to remove the blasphemous photo to a private gallery. I explained that a publicly funded institution had no right to insult Christians in this way.
>
> The judge ruled against us, but Catholics and other Christians gathered each day outside the gallery, some praying the rosary; some were secondary Catholic students. On the second or third day a man from Sydney pulled the photo from the wall; on the next day a couple of youths attacked the Perspex covering of the photo with a hammer.
>
> There was big press coverage; then unexpectedly the gallery cancelled the entire Serrano exhibition. I am not entirely sure why! I never began the operation thinking we would achieve this result. It was not earth shattering; undoubtedly the result was helped by the mild violence, which did not come from rank-and-file Catholics. But it was a victory for decency. The moral of the story is that we struggle because it is right and proper. Whether we win or lose is secondary; but we can and sometimes will win against the odds.

Just as newsworthy was his outspoken opposition to Pauline Hanson's One Nation Party, which, before it disintegrated, captured 23 percent of the vote in the 1998 Queensland state election. In May that year, the Archbishop condemned One Nation for policies that "set groups of Australians against one another".

"Racist policies are a recipe for strife and for misery", he told a Melbourne gathering. "We commend those political leaders, especially the leaders of the three main political parties in Victoria, who have spoken out clearly against the policies of the 'One Nation' party, who are political opportunists and adventurers."

Many people, he acknowledged, had voted for One Nation, not because they were racist, but because they believed the simple solutions proposed would help them. Governments and others needed to protect Australians from the most drastic consequences of globalization. Hard-line economic policies were chipping away at the social cement built up over generations in Australia and tempting people struggling in life to embrace simple, mistaken solutions and to scapegoat minorities, such as the Aborigines and Australian Asians. All Christian churches, he said, had an obligation to oppose this "demonisation of small groups" and encourage policies that embraced the poorest 20 percent of the nation in both the countryside and the cities.

Pell said:

> All Australians have a right to a "fair go", just as all of us have an obligation to work and contribute. We must resist effectively any set of policies which would take us even some small distance towards the tensions, hate and violence between races that have poisoned Southern Africa and even the southern states of the USA. We should beware. Long journeys often start with small steps. We could find ourselves in

evil situations we now refuse to envisage. Racism, whether it be anti-Aboriginal or anti-Asian, must never be given a respectable face. We have left that behind us in earlier stages of Australian history.

These days, for the record, Archbishop Pell is "a political agnostic", though intensely interested in politics. He has voted Labor, Liberal, and National Party in his time, years ago voted for the DLP, and has friends in all the main parties. "It depends on the issues, but often I am more interested in what I think are the core beliefs and personal attributes of the individuals."

As archbishop he was forceful in his criticisms of the Kennett Liberal government's encouragement of gambling in Victoria (which reports suggested provided as much as 12 percent of State government revenue). He was just as outspoken when the ALP Bracks government began pursuing the idea of "safe" heroin injecting rooms, commenting that Jesus Christ had not gone around "handing out condoms and syringes, literally or metaphorically". Harm minimization, the Archbishop argued, was never right, because a good result could not be achieved by performing an evil action.

Even when the Bracks government moved to ban twenty-four-hour poker machine clubs in country towns and tighten up advertising rules for gambling, Pell wanted it to go much farther and restrict gambling times to twelve to fifteen hours a day and move ATMs well away from pokie venues (casinos and clubs with numerous slot machines). "The more we can get people into the fresh air the better. The more time they have to think about what they are doing the better." The Archbishop himself played the pokies "once or twice", but found them boring: "I put these 20 and 50 cent pieces in the machines, but I'd have just as much fun putting them down the toilet", he said. "Many people get themselves into diabolical trouble. I've seen the results as I travel around parishes. I've spoken to families who have lost houses, and it's not just confined to poorer suburbs. The Catholic Church does not believe that having a bit of a gamble is in itself morally wrong. What is wrong is when it damages you and your family life."

Federally, while many Catholic Church agencies attacked the Howard government's proposals for a goods and services tax that was a major plank in the Liberal Party's 1998 election platform, Pell made the point that the complex tax issue was not one on which the Catholic Church could or should present a single viewpoint. In terms of the Church's concern for social justice, strong arguments could be made for and against the tax.

In 1998, Prime Minister Howard, an avowed constitutional monarchist, appointed Pell as a delegate to the Constitutional Convention to be held at old Parliament House in February the following year. At the convention, he served on the resolutions committee responsible for drafting motions put to the convention and moved the motion in support of the republican model that was finally adopted by the convention. On the eve of the republican referendum in November 1999, Pell issued a statement appealing to "all Australians whatever their religious or politician convictions to vote Yes to a republic to complete our long and peaceful evolution to independence and maturity."

Acknowledging that he was speaking personally and that there was no one Catholic view on the issue, Pell argued:

> The proposed change will preserve all the strengths of the present system, all the present guarantees for our freedom.

It continues the Westminster system of government, with our prime minister accountable to parliament. Those who believe in this system will never have a better chance to preserve it. . . .

An Australian Head of State, shared with no other nation, will be a more effective symbol of sovereignty and unity, and more capable of inspiring a genuine patriotism, loyalty and service across our multicultural society. The monarchy no longer has major support among the people, who are the source of authority in any democracy. The royal symbolism has eroded. The monarchists are relying on apathy, ignorance and those who want a directly elected president. Their argumentation is bankrupt.

By August 1999, Pell had a stronger national profile than any other Church leader in a generation, which prompted a Sydney think tank, the Centre for Independent Studies, to invite him to deliver its inaugural Acton Lecture, named after Lord Acton, an intellectual barred from entering Cambridge in 1850 because of his Catholicism but who was eventually appointed Regius Professor of Modern History at that university in 1894. Acton was a man of immense erudition, best remembered for his aphorism that "all power tends to corrupt and absolute power corrupts absolutely."

The lecture took place on August 4 at the Customs House, and several hundred of Sydney's most influential business leaders, judges, lawyers, academics, and journalists turned up. For George Pell, it was new ground. Many of those there were not Catholic and had previously shown little interest in religious leaders, but they all wanted to hear the Archbishop of Melbourne, who had helped them realize that the Catholic Church had something of value to contribute to contemporary debate.

As a historian, George Pell quickly put Acton in context

for the audience: "In September 1964, as a student in Rome during the third session of the Second Vatican Council, I remember Cardinal Cushing of Boston reminding the council fathers of Acton's claim that 'freedom is the highest political end', a sentiment which the council partly endorsed in its Declaration on Religious Freedom." However, unlike most late twentieth-century Western thinkers, Acton's liberalism was rooted in Christianity.

Turning his attention to the twentieth century, the Archbishop said that by most conservative estimates, ninety million people were killed by Communist governments in the twentieth century. While it was appropriate to regard the Holocaust as the crime of the century, he regretted the silence surrounding the mass murder and torture of various Communist regimes. "Nearly all the twelve-year-olds I speak to know of Hitler; very few have heard of Stalin. I could not even obtain a tax deduction for donations to the descendants of the prisoners of the Gulag, who survive today, millions of them, in Siberia, originally from many different nations."

Catholic intellectual tradition, he said, had an important contribution to make to the debates on freedom and human rights in the contemporary world, especially in the West and in Australia, where 70 percent of the population still call themselves Christian.

"Most Australians would interpret liberty in the classical English sense, following J. S. Mill (unknowingly), as doing our own good in our own way, without hurting others, and without too much government interference, much less imprisonment or other forms of violence", he said.

Such notions, he argued, posed interesting dilemmas: Should a person be free not to wear a seat belt in a car? Should a woman be free to have an abortion? Does the father of the child have any rights here? Does the embryo, fetus, human being, or unborn child however defined have any rights? To what extent should governments be morally neutral or indifferent, leaving the strong to triumph and the poor to go to the wall? Is business constrained by virtue as well as by economic necessity?

From his earliest days as a young philosophy teacher, Pell said, one of Pope John Paul' II's central preoccupations was freedom's connection with truth, particularly the truths expressed in the natural moral law: "The Pope's own view is that there is no true conflict between freedom of choice and moral law. All Christians believe, despite Freud, that each human person has a rational intellect and a free will, rather than being 'a jungle chaos of hidden emotions and inner conflicts with an irrational character'." Human beings are free, Pell said, to build slowly an integrated personality, without gross contradictions. But this is a lifelong spiritual quest. God-given law consists of truths meant to help people make good moral choices, freed from subservience to arbitrary feelings and obsessions in a free choice of the good.

Among the notions that had to be rejected firmly, he said, was the "Donald Duck heresy", which, "rests squarely on the fallacy of overwhelming natural virtue. All you have to do to fulfil yourself is follow your natural impulses. Donald Duck always does this and always gets into trouble. It is a heresy which sanctifies mistakes, provided one is genuine, being oneself."

That intriguing but trivial example, he said, should not blind Australians to the dangers around them, including trends in North America, often replicated in Australia at a later date. Shortly before Pell's lecture, the thirtieth anniversary celebration of Woodstock in America had seen rioting, arson, looting of US$170,000 from a mobile bank, drug-taking and gang rapes. This, Pell said, was an inevitable progression from the first Woodstock love fest and as clear an indication of social disintegration as the Columbine High School massacre.

The participants of both Woodstock gatherings had rejected their parents' values, he said. "This time it was the pacifism of the sixties which was spurned. Either the restraints of thirty years ago were no longer effective; or the self-hatred, anger and alienation of the destructive minority were stronger and were incited, rather than restrained, by the music. The last song of the gathering, as the ambulance sirens wailed through the smoke and the mayhem, boomed out from a group called Cracker. Its chorus summed up the scene, 'Don't f— me up with peace and love.' "[5]

The most controversial and widely reported aspect of the Acton lecture was Pell's contention that Catholic teachers, in the face of the subjectivism and relativism sweeping society, should "quietly ditch" the notion of the primacy of conscience. "This has never been a Catholic doctrine (although this point generally cuts little ice)", he told the audience. "It is a short cut, which often leads the uninitiated to feel even more complacent while 'doing their own thing'."

In today's climate, both inside and outside the Catholic Church, to make such statements definitely is like kicking against the prevailing wind, but the pursuit of popularity was never Pell's *raison d'être*. If Pell polarizes people, so be it: "Christ was crucified for his opinions. It's not as though he was a disciple of Dale Carnegie and set out to massage the population into coming along with him."

Among Mass-goers, however, the Archbishop is more

[5] For the full lecture, see the Centre for Independent Studies website: www.cis.org.au.

widely esteemed. Pell revealed his own assessment of his standing there when he told *Encounters* interviewer Stephen Crittenden: "My job is to do my duty, is to serve the people, to preach the good news, and I'm quite confident (I'm out into two or three parishes a week) that amongst the Mass-goers there's very, very considerable support; no doubt about it in my mind, the majority support me."

There are those few ultratraditionalists who are dissatis-fied with Pell, brand him a "liberal", and complain that he was too gentle in his shake-up of the Melbourne Archdio-cese. Hard-liners who looked forward to a overhaul among Church bureaucrats when Pell took over Melbourne were very disappointed. Professor Anthony Fisher said there was an expectation early on that heads would roll.

> Not a lot of that happened. George had this view that people should not be made unemployed by the Church, so he never pushed anyone out, even the ones who were really shock-ing, and some of them were pretty rotten eggs. He wanted to keep the Church intact. There's a very generous, com-passionate side of him, which I think people should know about. It's softly, softly catchy monkey rather than sack all the people at the top of the bureaucracies and make radical changes immediately. This is a very pastoral father figure, a man of very great charity.

At the other extreme, Pell's "new Church" critics, includ-ing some priests and nuns, label him "a man of the eighteenth century" or "a reactionary trying to recreate the Church of the 1940s or '50s." Pell's response to such charges:

> I fully accept all the major teachings of the Second Vatican Council—collegiality, the great liturgical changes into the vernacular. . . . The doctrine that the State does not have the right to coerce an individual conscience. The other great

advance of the Second Vatican Council in which I have been
an active participant is ecumenism. . . . It's quite impossible
to take the Church back anywhere and it's never entered my
head to take it back into the 1950s, although I think it's a
convenient term of abuse for those who disagree with me.[6]

Philosopher Hayden Ramsay, who worked for Pell in Melbourne, said that, compared with the diffident, media-shy
Church leaders of the past, it was impossible to call Pell
traditional in terms of his pastoral style. Just as priests and
bishops traditionally learned the techniques of good preaching in the pulpit, Pell has been "media trained within an
inch of his life", according to experienced public relations
insiders. Ramsay says: "He has a genuine belief in the media;
he's a very modern man. George's picture, I think, for the
survival and thriving of the Church in the new century is
that it has to be engaged in all the major social issues. It can't
afford to go quiet and disappear into the rubble to become
a remnant of the past, just running parishes and schools. So
he's out there fighting about how we're going to deal with
drugs, he's making statements on divorce which are absolutely provocative."

Ramsay himself plays a low-key role in terms of publicity and prefers to concentrate his writing on scholarly philosophical journals produced for academics rather than the general public. He sensed, when Pell employed him, that the
Archbishop would have enjoyed undertaking such scholarly
work himself and had the requisite academic training but not
the time. As a substitute, he was keen to have someone on
his staff contributing to the cutting edge of philosophical
analysis and writing.

More than a dozen Melbourne priests interviewed dur-

---

[6] *Australian Financial Review Magazine*, interview with Geoffrey Barker.

ing the writing of this book, from the strongest Pell supporters to some of his most vehement critics, agreed that
he was always well received by the vast majority of Catholic people as he visited two or three different parishes a
week in his time as Archbishop. After holding steady for
several years, planned giving receipts (regular contributions
pledged and given by Mass-goers) from Catholics at Sunday
Mass increased 10 percent in Melbourne from 1999 to 2000,
which suggests that most people were contented about the
Church's direction.

Irish-born Father James Staunton, pastor of Blackburn
South, said Pell was "a towering figure intellectually who
lifted the morale of Catholics". Staunton said people in the
pews appreciated the Archbishop's writings and television
appearances in which he presented the Catholic point of
view well and succinctly. Staunton said Pell went out of his
way at clergy dinners and gatherings, as had his predeces-
sors, to show the archdiocese's Irish priests and those from
other overseas countries that he valued their presence and
work. "He was a great priests' man. The worst thing about
his period as archbishop was when he left", Staunton said.
"He was always in charge of the situation, but he had the
brain and brawn to do it well."

Pell forged close links with all of Melbourne's main Catholic communities from overseas—the Italians, the Serbs and
Croatians, the Coptics (from Egypt), the Maltese, and the
Vietnamese. He predicted that "the grandchildren of today
could see the first Vietnamese-Australian Archbishop of Melbourne, and there will be many such ethnic bishops before
then." In 1999, Pope John Paul II appointed Maltese-born
Father Joseph Grech as Pell's auxiliary bishop.

Doctor Frank O'Loughlin, pastor of Sandringham, while
widely regarded as belonging to the Church's liberal wing

and most definitely not in the Pell camp, cited positives and negatives from the Pell legacy in Melbourne. "I think the worst effect was a sense of disenfranchisement among people who didn't share his views, lack of consultation", O'Loughlin said. "George is great fun in a social situation, but when you get down to the serious issues he is an autocrat; yet people expect to be consulted."

However, he praised Pell for acting "firmly and well" early in his term to deal with the scourge of pedophilia. And O'Loughlin believes that Pell had no option but to turn the sash-wearers away from the altar. "It's extremely difficult and conflict is inevitable, but what else can an archbishop do?" O'Loughlin's view on that matter was largely echoed by priests across the spectrum, from the most conservative to the most liberal.

Chapter 14

A Whirling Adventure

Across Australia, Mass-attendance surveys conducted for the Australian Catholic bishops showed a downward trend from 1994 to 2001 to an average attendance rate of 15.9 percent of nominal Catholics, with both Melbourne (17 percent) and Sydney (17.8 percent) doing slightly better than average, and three centers—Hobart, Darwin, and Geraldton— falling below 10 percent.

Even more alarming for priests and bishops in Australia, all too evident in many parish communities every weekend, is the fact that a sizeable proportion of those attending regularly are older people, well into their sixties and beyond.

It is far too simplistic to put the entire blame on rampant materialism, encroaching secularism, or Sunday shopping for these atrocious results. Those factors are probably even more strongly at play in the United States, where Pell says attendance rates are often 50 to 100 percent higher than in Australia.

On one side of the debate in Australia, some argue that turning around the poor attendance rates must involve building better, more welcoming Church communities and offering ever-more modern "relevant" liturgies and upbeat music that "speaks to young people". On the other hand, it is argued, no Church will ever attract and maintain adherents by trying to outdo popular entertainment—substance,

271

rather than style, must be the key. George Pell and others of his ilk see the problem primarily as a deep crisis of faith, one that cannot and will not be solved by gimmickry, peddling counterfeit compassion, or caving in to the prevailing mores of society in a quest for relevance. "Catholic lite has been advertised and sold in some places for years now", Pell says. "It has been a failure. Young Catholics won't buy it. The taste is off."

So off, in fact, that the Church has melted away as a force in the lives of the vast majority of Catholics in their twenties, thirties, and forties, who seem disinclined to return to regular practice. Given the religious education offered in most Catholic schools in the 1970s, 1980s, and 1990s, it is reasonable to assume that many nominal Catholics know very little about the Church, her history, her doctrines and teachings, and have little foundation on which to build any kind of prayer or faith life. While some make a conscious, studied decision to embrace atheism or agnosticism, many more tend to dabble in the various manifestations of New Age spiritualism and/or indifferentism, which expanded exponentially in the 1990s and the early years of the new millennium, suggesting a religious vacuum and a dormant but unsatisfied yearning for deeper meaning in many people.

That many nominal Catholics have opted for this path is hardly surprising. For much of the 1970s and 1980s, Catholic students spent many a religious education class sprawled around the floor listening to profoundly spiritual music like John Denver's "Sunshine", Neil Diamond's "Be", or Simon and Garfunkel's "I Am a Rock". More often, relaxation tapes lulled us to sleep as we "discovered our inner selves" (or snatched a quick catnap to be ready to get on with subjects that mattered later). Annual "retreats" were the ultimate joke in some schools—the chance for an illicit nip of Bacardi and Coke or a cigarette while wandering along the beach "contemplating" at the nuns' or brothers' retreat center. Despite religious faith being heavily reliant upon intellect and will, students were rarely challenged but were subjected to group sessions of psychobabble and touchy-feely waffle about love and fellowship. Paraliturgies (prayer sessions) were usually made up on the spot, usually focused on God made visible in the sun, the stars, and the ocean. The Mass, the Trinity, our Lady, Church tradition and doctrine barely rated a mention, and when many students gave up Mass as a form of teenage rebellion, they had little foundation to which to return.

Evangelizing young Catholics and drawing them directly into the life of the Church has been one of Pope John Paul II's strongest endeavors. As an archbishop, George Pell adopted the same priority, extending his efforts well beyond the normal parish visitations and meetings with Confirmation classes undertaken by every diocesan bishop.

Rebuilding the faith among the young will be a long-term, uphill battle, and Pell acknowledges that there are no easy, quick fixes or guaranteed solutions. From the outset of his episcopacy in Melbourne, he was determined to tackle the problem from the angle of religious education from kindergarten to year twelve by initiating the writing and production of a comprehensive set of religious education textbooks for schoolchildren, one for every year level. Within a few months of Pell's appointment in 1996, he arranged for his old friend Peter Elliott to be released from his duties as an official in the Pontifical Council for the Family in Rome to head the project.

Incredibly, religious education textbooks—especially well-written and well-presented ones—were almost nonexistent, not just in Australia, but also in many places overseas. Most of the primary booklets available were flimsy in content, dull in appearance, and incomplete in many aspects of the faith. Teachers constantly had to supplement them from whatever sources they could. In secondary schools, the situation was even worse, with religious education in many schools devoted to "comparative religion" courses (examining Christianity alongside Islam, Judaism, or Buddhism, for example) to the exclusion of Catholic doctrine classes.

"When people heard the word *textbooks*, they went ballistic, they were horrified", Elliott recalled. "It's not something that many people would have thought of immediately, but George used his pragmatic mind and went straight to a practical solution to a long-term problem."

Elliott was determined to produce lively, colorful texts that were "not some boring old things from the dark ages." The Archbishop was clear about what he wanted in the texts —a mixture of life, doctrine, and Scripture—with good artwork and pictures. After five years' work, half of the series *To Know, Worship and Love* was published in 2001, and the remainder in 2002. The books for each year level came with a detailed instruction guide for teachers, and in-service training in using the materials was provided.

Pell was satisfied that the completed project met almost all of his main specifications. Generally, the works were well received. However, after years of freedom in selecting their own religious education materials almost at will, some teachers, themselves graduates of a much flimsier system of religious instruction, bitterly resented being "dictated to" in terms of what to teach at particular year levels. Such is the divide within the Church that some of the more militant Melbourne teachers threatened to (and for a time actually did) lock the books up in school cupboards and refuse to use them.

Once they were in use, however, many teachers and parents found the books helpful and appealing to children, geared as they were to each stage of their development. The early childhood books, for example, are subtitled "The Good Shepherd Experience" and set the foundations for the child to start building a lifelong intimate relationship with God. Content for the older students is rigorous, detailed, and interesting, exploring, not only religion, but the place of the Church in the world both historically and at the present time. The series is visually appealing, making good use of classic art reproductions, photographs, time lines, Scripture passages, and prayers and lists. As its three-pronged name suggests, *To Know, Worship and Love* combines doctrinal learning with Scripture and prayer and an understanding of the place of religion in the everyday world as an influence for good.

Many priests in favor of the books argue that they would be far more effective if the training of religious education teachers were similarly overhauled within the Australian Catholic University. Pell admits that the university has not lived up to his hopes in terms of training teachers to impart solid Catholic teaching to their students. While determined to encourage improvements in religious education training at the university, the institution's independence means that Pell and other bishops say they can extract the most effective changes through encouragement and persuasion rather than direct pressure.

In addition to producing *To Know, Worship and Love*, Pell took his message directly to schoolchildren of Melbourne in their tens of thousands. On September 5, 2000, he filled the Rod Laver arena at the National Tennis Centre in Melbourne Park with years eleven and twelve students for a special Jubilee Mass. Archbishops rarely have the chance to speak directly and at length to a captive audience of twenty thousand sixteen- and seventeen-year-olds. At a highly impressionable point in their lives, Pell was determined to single out this group for some special attention. "As young Catholics today about to leave school and enter the wider world, the torch is being passed to you", he challenged them.

His sermon that day, different in tone from other homilies, was crafted around some of the themes and ideas of popular teenage culture:

> Many of you will have seen the film *Gladiator* set in the second century under Marcus Aurelius, one of the most enlightened of the pagan Roman Emperors. The brutality of the amphitheatre was mirrored by the brutality of Roman daily life.
>
> My thesis is simple. Christ's teachings were like a river of life-giving water, nourishing and strengthening those who believed in him in this hostile and savage environment. Christian faith, lived out in daily life, produced a movement of cure and renewal responding to the misery, chaos, fear and oppression of daily life in Rome. They came much closer to a civilization of life and love through Christian living. The improvement was a result of Christian faith.

Sexual experimentation, he assured the students with candor, was nothing new. Sexual life in ancient Rome, he said, "was a jungle where the strong oppressed the weak. We know from the mosaics of Pompeii that nothing was off limits; women, men, boys, girls and animals, and all this was portrayed on the walls of the bathhouses before the eyes of even the youngest."

So did the early Christians go with the flow, conform to the fashions of the time because everyone was doing it? "Enough of them, the best of them, refused to do any such thing. With invincible obstinacy they stuck to Christ's teachings; they sometimes fell, as we do, but they persevered", Pell said. Appealing to the students' strong belief in equality of the sexes, he pointed out:

> The Christians taught a new concept of sexuality, not as an escape, not as a recreational right, not as another opportunity for the strong to oppress the weak; but sexuality linked to love; the love between a husband and wife, open to fertility, life and children. Therefore, in a society where the male head of the household had a literal power of life and death over its members, where women were oppressed, almost legally powerless, Christianity required men to love and respect their wives as they respect their own bodies. This was a revolution.
>
> This was a society where men regularly fought each other, or animals, to the death—and hundreds of thousands of spectators delighted in this spectacle. Rome was a city which rarely produced sufficient babies to keep the population stable and relied on regular migrations. These congregated in mutually antagonistic ghettos and race riots were not uncommon. This was a society where abortion was commonplace, as was infanticide, the killing of the newborn, especially if they were girls. There was a significant imbalance of the sexes. Pagan society did not want baby girls.

Then, as now, he illustrated, the Church offered kindness, charity, and a sense of community to even the poorest, loneliest, and most marginalized people:

> To cities filled with the poor and homeless, Christianity offered charity as well as hope. To cities filled with immigrants and strangers, the Christians offered community, friendship. To cities filled with orphans and widows, Christianity offered help and a wider sense of family. To cities torn with ethnic strife and riots, Christianity offered social solidarity. To cities faced with epidemics, fires and earthquakes, Christianity offered effective nursing services. Even Galen, the

most famous ancient physician, fled to his country house away from the plague. The Christians stayed and nursed their sick.

The long struggle of the Cross, with its hundredfold reward even in this life, "is passing into your hand", Pell told the students.

Continue to ponder and pray on the strange life of Jesus Christ, whose jubilee we celebrate. . . . Think on the achievements of the early Christians; of all the good Christians over 2,000 years. Remember always that they, like us, got their strength from this same Christ, the living water, which can bring life and health to any spiritual desert. Continue to drink from this stream, work and pray that it continues to bubble up in your heart too, taking you into eternal life. May you say "Yes" with courage and without hesitation when Christ calls you.

A few weeks later, a special Jubilee Mass for younger schoolchildren at Melbourne's Colonial Stadium broke the previous attendance record of forty-six thousand for an AFL match. Television commentator and Collingwood president Eddie McGuire welcomed the crowd of seventy thousand year four to year ten students on November 15, a warm, sunny day: "It wasn't the Bombers and it wasn't the Magpies that broke the attendance record. It was the Catholics!"

Four choirs and a 150-piece orchestra sounded as though they could raise the stadium's closed roof. Archbishop Pell, wearing gold vestments and magnified on large-screen televisions, concelebrated the Mass with his three auxiliary bishops. Governor General Sir William Deane, Deputy Prime Minister John Anderson, and Victorian Premier Steve Bracks were among the few invited adult guests. The theme of the

Mass was "Who is My Neighbour?" The Archbishop, in his homily, challenged the children to seek to serve rather than to be served and spoke to them about the different "good Samaritans" who had befriended other Australians in the past. Younger children watched the Mass on television back at their schools.

Pell also staged annual get-togethers with vast numbers of children. Every Saint Patrick's Day, the cathedral was packed with children for Mass, which was followed by a picnic lunch in Fitzroy Gardens.

He told the children on March 17, 2001:

> Our country of Australia has been compared to a beautiful patterned carpet of different colours, like a wonderful tapestry. Another comparison is to say Australia is like a happy neighbourhood, many different groups of people, minding their own business, but getting on well together. But one of the most beautiful and colourful pieces of the carpet is our Catholic community, to which we all belong. I hope each and every one of you is proud to be a Catholic; proud to say, "Yes, I believe in the one true God. Yes, I believe in Jesus, who died for us. Yes, I am proud to belong to the Catholic Church, which is led by the Pope and bishops." So today on this Saint Patrick's Day we want you youngsters to join us older people in thanking God for all the good things we have in Australia. I want each one of you to realize, to feel that you belong to a Church which has contributed a lot to Australian history and Australian society, and I want you this morning to decide that you too will do your bit, when you grow up, to keep Australia good and make it a better place.

First-hand encounters with young Catholics have been one of the hallmarks of the long pontificate of John Paul II. World Youth Days were the Pope's idea, drawn partly from his own excursions with young people in Poland when he was a young priest and partly from the enthusiastic reception he received from young people in a Paris park during his visit to the city in 1980. The first World Youth Day in Rome in 1985 attracted 250,000 visitors, and the events—which actually extend over a week—grew from there, being held in a different venue every two years in cities in Europe, South America, North America, and Asia.

From the vigor and strength of his early pontificate to the infirmities of old age and ill health, John Paul II has been the star attraction of each of these gatherings, arriving by popemobile or helicopter to chanting and singing. These unique events, usually held in the Northern Hemisphere summer, are more pilgrimage than holiday and generally involve extreme discomfort—crowds of several hundred thousand, sometimes several million people, blazing heat, long walks to vast outdoor arenas, pelting rain, mud, sleeping outdoors or in church halls, and a mixture of chaos and precise organization. Participants pray together, participate in vast outdoor Masses, sing and dance together, enjoy each other's company across language and cultural barriers, receive catechetical instruction from various bishops from around the world—including George Pell—and explore different parts of the Catholic world. The Pope's closing Mass of the 1995 gathering in Manila attracted what has been estimated as the largest crowd in history—between five and seven million people. As well as being an international celebration of youth and Catholicism, World Youth Day, and the efforts the young people make to raise money to pay their way there, is designed to strengthen and deepen their long-term bonds with the Church. As Pope John Paul explained in a Jubilee newsletter in 1999:

The future of the world and the Church belongs to the *younger generation*, to those who, born in this century, will reach maturity in the next, the first century of the new millennium. *Christ expects great things from young people*, as he did from the young man who asked him: "What good deed must I do, to have eternal life?" Young people, in every situation, in every region of the world, do not cease to put questions to Christ: *they meet him and they keep searching for him in order to question him further*. If they succeed in following the road which he points out to them, they will have the joy of making their own contribution to his presence in the next century and in the centuries to come, until the end of time: "Jesus is the same yesterday, today and for ever."

More than one thousand young Australians were among the two million young people from 120 nations who attended the Jubilee 2000 World Youth Day in Rome. For that event, George Pell, his three auxiliary bishops, and nine young priests from Melbourne led the Melbourne contingent of four hundred, the largest from any Australian diocese. Around 250 members of the group left Australia early for a twelve-day pilgrimage in the footsteps of Christ, from Bethlehem to Golgotha, en route to Rome. Some, including Pell, found it a more powerful and moving experience than the time in Rome afterward. It was a trip that would be impossible to replicate in the near future given hostilities in the region.

In the Holy Land, the group stayed in two places—in Bethlehem, birthplace of Jesus, and at Daganya Kibbutz in the north of Israel near the Sea of Galilee. Each day began with a prayer and Scripture readings about the places being visited, and daily Mass was celebrated at one of the many sacred sites that figured in the life of Jesus. The group traveled around on four buses, with the priests and bishops assisting the tour guides. They visited the Incarnation Grotto inside the Nazareth Basilica, the place where Mary learned she was to bear a son she would name Jesus; Christ's birthplace—the Church of the Nativity in Bethlehem; Mount Tabor, site of Christ's Transfiguration before three of his Apostles; Cana—site of Christ's miracle with the wine at a wedding feast and where the married pilgrims renewed their wedding vows; Qumran, where the Dead Sea scrolls were discovered; Caesarea—where Christ founded His Church "upon this rock" and where the Greeks believed their pagan god Pan was born deep in a cave; the mount of the Beatitudes; the Dead Sea, where they had a swim; the old city of Jerusalem; and the Jordan River, where Christ was baptized and where the group renewed their own baptismal promises.

Pell remembers praying quietly in the darkened Gethsemane church, with the young people spread around him, in the place where tradition has Jesus suffering the agony in the garden. "Mass at the shepherds' field in Bethlehem, like a barren moonscape, unfriendly and uninviting. Unlike the royal babies in the Persian empire, Jesus was not born to the purple!" he remembers. His favorite memory was of the choir lads leading informal hymn singing, "Were You There When They Crucified My Lord?" around the Cross in the basilica at Golgotha, site of the crucifixion.

> For 20 or 30 minutes the group sang as we passed the Cross and waited to enter the Tomb. It was a golden moment. The group sang again at the Cenacle, the traditional venue for the Last Supper, while we had a beautiful solo, deep down in the jail room under Caiaphas' house, where Jesus might have spent time before his crucifixion. . . .

It is interesting to ponder why the good God chose such a hot, difficult spot as the homeland for his Chosen People. And a small nation surrounded by larger, more advanced and powerful neighbours, who were often at war. Perhaps to try to teach us the lesson that growth and survival come from God, not from our efforts.[1]

Many of the Melbourne pilgrims who traveled overseas with Pell were tertiary students. Others took leave from their jobs; a few were married couples (one woman was six months pregnant with her second child); and quite a few were still at school. At age fourteen, twins Brendan and Brad Rowswell, both altar servers from Beaumaris in Melbourne, were the youngest in the group: "Highlights of the Holy Land for both of us, we agreed, were the wailing wall of the temple, the Church of the Nativity, and finally both the spiritual experience and watching the Archbishop come down a waterslide."

The waterslide was in a park beside the Sea of Galilee, where Jesus so often walked with his disciples. In searing hot weather it was a welcome sight for everyone, including the Archbishop, who did not hesitate to follow his disciples in tumbling down. Father Mark Withoos, ordained a priest by Pell in July 1999 after studies at Corpus Christi College, Melbourne, and Propaganda Fide, was one of the priests on the trip. He remembers Pell being very open to the young people and them warming to him: "He's very fatherly."

In Rome, the Melbourne pilgrims stayed in parishes about twenty-five miles outside Rome at Ostia and Vitinia. Pell, an

[1] Reminiscences from pilgrimage drawn from *Testimonies to the Glory of God: World Youth Day Pilgrimage AD2000*, ed. Helen Hedigan (Melbourne: Buxton Printers, 2000).

old hand in Rome, said the city had never seen anything like the two million young people who crammed in for World Youth Day with Pope John Paul II.

> The police chief put it nicely on TV—"From what magic box did these happy young people come?" Droves of them swarmed all over Rome, usually walking in groups, chatting, laughing and singing; greeting one another across ancient enmities and language barriers. There were no arrests; remarkable patience and good humour in the heat; no drugs.
>
> On the Circus Maximus, where Christians were martyred, hundreds of priests heard confessions every day, and platoons of young helpers prepared their peers to confess properly. Hundreds of thousands went to confession, the sacrament of reconciliation. Certainly, most of the Melbourne pilgrims did. Four hundred thousand attended the Stations of the Cross at the Colosseum. Nearly every registered pilgrim queued up patiently in Saint Peter's Square to go through the Holy Door, past Peter enthroned (on a statue near the main altar) and around his tomb. Some waited for over an hour in the heat and were doused and cooled with freezing water when the authorities put the fire hoses on them. Many groups put on street concerts, watched by hundreds at a time.

It could probably only have happened in Rome, but August 15, the feast of our Lady's Assumption into heaven, was traditionally a public holiday, and in spite of two million visitors in town, the authorities decided to stick to the usual public holiday timetable—which basically meant almost no transport. Marc Florio, the director of Catholic youth ministry in Melbourne, and about forty other young people found themselves stranded at night in the center of Rome, unable to return to their billet in a church hall in a parish twenty-five miles outside the city. They did the only thing they could and phoned the Archbishop where he was staying at a clergy house near the Piazza Navona. "The Archbishop opened the doors, and 30 or 40 of us slept around the apartment on the floor, under the tables, on the couches." Marc said the young people on the trip found the Archbishop "blokey, warm, down to earth and not up there in an ivory tower".

Archbishop Pell, Archbishop Desmond Connell of Dublin, and Cardinal Cassidy of the Pontifical Council for Christian Unity provided three sessions of religious instruction for the Australian pilgrims. Father Paul Stuart, the director of vocations, took many of the Melbourne group on a guided tour of Rome, with Father Stuart celebrating Mass in the crypt of Saint Peter's Basilica, followed by breakfast in a café along the Via Conciliazione, where just a few hours later more than one million people would crowd in to see the Pope officially open World Youth Day in Saint Peter's Square.

Seeing the Pope, even amidst a crowd of a million in Saint Peter's or two million at Tor Vegata University on the outskirts of the city, was the highlight of the week in Rome for most of the pilgrims. That was in spite of the over twelve-mile walk to Tor Vegata in 104°F heat to see Pope John Paul II arrive in a white helicopter for a vigil evening of prayer and rejoicing, followed by fireworks and a giant outdoor "sleepover". The Pope returned the following morning for Mass to complete the World Youth Day. "To you boys and girls who will be adults in the next century is entrusted the Book of Life . . . the wellspring of life and hope for the third millennium", he told them. "May it become your most precious treasure: in the careful study and generous acceptance of the Word of the Lord, you will find the nourishment and strength for your daily life, you will find motivation for tireless commitment to the building of a civilization of love."[2]

Toward the end of Pell's time as Archbishop of Melbourne, one of his more controversial moves was his inviting the Opus Dei (Work of God) organization to work in the archdiocese. Opus Dei, founded in 1928 by Spanish priest Monsignor Josemaría Escrivá, is a predominantly lay Catholic organization that has grown phenomenally both in membership and in property and resources in seventy-five years. Opus Dei has eighty thousand members worldwide. Of these, two thousand are priests. Among the lay members, Opus Dei has different categories of membership. "Numerary" members, while they are usually university students or well-paid professionals in the secular workforce, live a celibate life consecrated to prayer, asceticism, and service. Supernumerary members are free to marry but also dedicate themselves to prayer and service.

Pope John Paul II strongly approves of Opus Dei. In 1982, he strengthened its hand by making it the Church's only *personal prelature*—meaning that administratively, it answers, not to local bishops, but to its own bishop and head. On October 6, 2002, the Pope canonized Escrivá, just twenty-seven years after his death. In Australia, Opus Dei has about 450 members, including thirteen priests. The majority of members, about 350, are married supernumeraries. It began working in Sydney in 1963, and it has centers there, and in Parramatta, Broken Bay, Melbourne, and Hobart, and also conducts occasional activities such as lectures, retreats, and special Masses, with the approval of the local bishops, in

[2] Vatican website.

Brisbane, Perth, Newcastle, and Canberra, where there are no Opus Dei centers.

Opus Dei's basic work is to foster holiness and commitment to the Church among lay people using ordinary daily work as a means of sanctification. The organization's spokesman in Australia, Doctor Amin Abboud, a medical doctor and university lecturer in medical ethics in Sydney, said Opus Dei was about helping its lay members to "discover and take on the demands of their baptismal vocation in the specific place they occupy in the world". On this point, Doctor Abboud quotes Saint Josemaría Escrivá: "Great holiness consists in carrying out the little duties of each moment with love of God." Opus Dei, he said, encouraged prayer and sacrifice among members in order to sustain their efforts to sanctify their ordinary occupations. The main responsibility of the priests of Opus Dei is to attend to the spiritual needs of the members.

The first that many Melbourne Catholics, including many priests, knew of Opus Dei's entry into the archdiocese was an article in the Sunday *Age* on April 1, 2001, which said Pell had invited Opus Dei to supply a priest to run Saint Mary's Star of the Sea parish in West Melbourne. The vast parish church, one of the largest in Australia that is not a cathedral, is in dire need of restoration but has vast potential to be restored. Unlike other Opus Dei priests who work mainly with lay members of the organization, the pastor of West Melbourne provides for the pastoral needs of the parish and is answerable to the Archbishop for that work.

As the *Age* reported the story:

Opus Dei has only recently gained a presence in Melbourne. Under the previous archbishop, Frank Little, Opus Dei was unable to get a foothold in the archdiocese. During his reign, Archbishop Little canvassed the opinion of priests on whether the group should operate in Melbourne. The senate of priests, the chief advisory body to the bishops in the archdiocese, voted a resounding no. Father Christopher Prowse, a spokesman for the Catholic archdiocese of Melbourne, said he was unaware of a similar vote taking place during Dr Pell's reign. He said archbishops were not compelled to follow the senate of priests' recommendations.

In fact, before Pell invited Opus Dei a vote was taken among the consulters and the senate of priests, with majority approval for the invitation in both groups. The *Age* article also disclosed that Opus Dei was to open a Au$2.2 million center in Carlton in June called the Drummond Study Centre (close to the Catholic "precinct"), offering spiritual development and personalized tutorials to male tertiary students. It would also house two Opus Dei priests and male members of the group who are professionals and students.

Many were far from happy with Pell's invitation to Opus Dei. Even parish priests regarded as "conservative"—men who agree with Pell on 99 percent of other matters—expressed serious reservations about the group, sometimes based on personal experience of people they had known, including close relatives, who had been involved with Opus Dei. Several such priests also mentioned, perhaps not surprisingly, that the organization deflects the time, talents, and money of its members away from ordinary parish activities.

For all its considerable strengths, Opus Dei arouses intense controversy. In the United States, former members of the organization who have left and told their stories to bodies like ODAN (Opus Dei Awareness Network) describe a pattern of aggressive and manipulative recruitment techniques, such as alienating impressionable university students from their parents and families "who don't understand", and "love bombing" followed by careful staging of a "vocational crisis" at vulnerable moments in potential recruits' lives. These former members claim that they committed themselves to live the "spirit of Opus Dei" without fully knowing or understanding what that entails.

Former numeraries have also described the structure and discipline of Opus Dei as overly rigid and controlling, requiring them to hand over their full paychecks to the organization and live on the "pocket money" given back to them; to read only what they are told (generally, works by Escrivá); to allow their private mail to be read; to confess weekly (preferably to an Opus Dei priest); and to practice corporal mortification including flagellation weekly and wearing a "cilice" (spiked chain) around their thighs for two hours most days. While such practices may seem extreme or even dangerous by today's standards, they harken back to the asceticism commonly practiced by religious orders up until the last forty or fifty years.

Of far greater concern to some observers of Opus Dei are issues such as whether those joining as numeraries are doing so on the basis of informed consent, or whether they are sucked in too quickly, then subtly pressured to stay in a process akin to "manufacturing" vocations. Asked if Opus Dei would adopt a "hands off" policy in terms of recruiting in the West Melbourne Parish, its spokesman said: "I don't quite understand the question. The parish priest in West Melbourne will encourage vocations to priesthood, religious life, and all other vocations that are approved by the Catholic Church."

Speaking from personal experience, Abboud said he encountered Opus Dei as a student. "I can only say that my freedom was respected and nurtured. Nevertheless, I was also challenged to take my faith seriously, being confronted with the reality of the commitments of the Christian life. I am grateful for that encouragement, even though at times I found it challenged my comfort zone." He said that anyone joining Opus Dei was aware of what the commitments entailed.

> In the first year and a half after requesting admission to Opus Dei, all the aspects of the vocation, the spiritual commitments and ascetical life, are explained in full detail. This explanatory phase must be completed before anyone can become incorporated into the Prelature. They are free to decide not to become incorporated at any stage. For the first five years after the initial eighteen months no definitive commitment is made, allowing everyone a chance to grow deeper in their commitment or if they feel it is not for them or they are unsuitable to continue, they are free to leave Opus Dei. Because of the nature of the vocation to Opus Dei any decision to join which was not totally free and responsible would make no sense and would indicate the person should not be in Opus Dei.

Former members of Opus Dei have said that they were strongly discouraged from leaving, to the point that they were told they were risking their souls. In response to that concern, Abboud said:

> A vocation is a call from God. It is always best to respond to that call. In difficult times, everyone is encouraged and helped to respond to that call. If, after a time of reflection, a person does not want to continue in Opus Dei, they are always free to leave. Opus Dei, and I can bear testimony personally, continues to help those persons spiritually and humanly.
>
> My experience has been that those that leave Opus Dei continue to treasure their relationship with Opus Dei and

have as their closest friends people in Opus Dei. I can think
of a number of cases as I write these lines. Occasionally, in
my experience a very small minority, some have negative
feelings. This is saddening and every effort is made to overcome it. Sometimes marriages that have not worked out may
produce bitter resentment. It is part of the pain and confusion
that follows failed relationships.

George Pell acknowledges that Opus Dei is "not everyone's cup of tea" but makes no apologies for its entry into
Melbourne during his time as archbishop. "I invited them,
I thought they were a good thing, they're heading in the
right direction", he said. Pell is well aware of the criticisms
of Opus Dei, including those of former members, and "absolutely rejects" any suggestion that numerary members have
joined Opus Dei with anything less than full, informed consent. He does not share the Opus Dei asceticism, but neither
does he hold it against them and believes that their Spanish
flavor should be welcomed and tolerated within the broad
Church in Australia, not shunned.

"I have never had a complaint about Opus Dei", Pell says.
He finds Opus Dei members "very strict, very disciplined
but friendly and certainly not aggressive". He praises their
loyalty to the Church's teachings and the Pope and their deep
and sincere spirituality. Pell agrees with those who see Opus
Dei as taking up, in modern times and in a different way,
the role that Ignatius Loyola formed the Jesuits to fulfill in
the sixteenth century—that of an elite, self-disciplined, and
self-sacrificing "spiritual army", fiercely loyal to the papacy.

He agrees with the stand taken by the late Cardinal Basil
Hume of Westminster, who banned Opus Dei from recruiting members under the age of eighteen. "If I thought they
were bullying young people, I would stop it, yes", he said.

Many of Pell's friends and foes, both lay people and

priests, remain suspicious of Opus Dei. However, given the organization's current strength in the Church, Pell's approach in working with them at least brings them farther out into the open in archdiocesan work (such as running a parish in Melbourne) and draws on their talents to assist mainstream Church work.

The article about Opus Dei's move into Melbourne appeared at a time of heightened media interest in the Catholic Church. Just a few days earlier, on Monday March 26, 2001, the Apostolic Nuncio in Canberra, Archbishop Francesco Canalini, had made an announcement unprecedented in the history of the Church in Australia: "His Holiness Pope John Paul II has accepted the Resignation of His Eminence Edward Bede Clancy for reasons of age and has appointed as Archbishop of Sydney His Grace Most Reverend George Pell, until now Archbishop of Melbourne. The news will be made public in Rome on Monday, 26 March, 2001 at 12 noon, Rome time."

The promotion of the seventh Archbishop of Melbourne to be the eighth Archbishop of Sydney surprised many of Pell's supporters and opponents. On ABC radio, former Human Rights Commissioner Chris Sidoti, told *AM*: "The church in Sydney is headed back to the Middle Ages." The normally talkative ABC religious affairs commentator and former priest Paul Collins said: "I'm speechless."

Letters and faxes of support arrived at Pell's office and home by the hundred, and talk-back radio lines in both Sydney and Melbourne ran hot. The retired Archbishop of Hobart, Eric D'Arcy, admits he was stunned because he regarded Melbourne, a larger Archdiocese than Sydney, as a more important job. Numerically, it is. The Archdiocese of Melbourne, with one million Catholics, has 232 parishes compared with Sydney's 137 parishes. Sydney, however, is the oldest and most senior archdiocese in Australia, with its archbishops traditionally elevated, within a few years of their appointment, to the Church's College of Cardinals. Because George Pell was only fifty-five when he was appointed Archbishop of Melbourne, Catholics reasonably expected that he would lead their archdiocese for two decades—unless he was promoted to Rome as head of a Vatican Congregation such as Education or Evangelization of Peoples. Rumors of an imminent appointment to both positions circulated in Melbourne before he was announced as the new Archbishop of Sydney.

Writing in the *Age* newspaper, long-time Vatican watcher Desmond O'Grady made a shrewd observation on the appointment.

> George Pell was almost certainly hand-picked by Pope John Paul II for the job of Catholic Archbishop of Sydney. The reasons the controversial cleric was chosen, however, may be more complex than has so far been acknowledged.
>
> Pell fits the model for new church leaders that the Pope has been applying to key appointments. And conservatism is not the prerequisite for promotion. The most important quality he seems to seek is strength of personality. . . .
>
> The Vatican wants leaders who will make their presence felt in and beyond their sees. Many of the appointees are conservative—but not all of them. But the point about all of them is that, while you may disagree with what they say, you know they are there. The Vatican believes Catholics generally are far less alienated from the church's thinking than its middle management and the media convey. This assumption seems to derive partly from the reception John Paul receives on his overseas trips, particularly to the United States.
>
> These assumptions suggest the appointment of bishops

who are vigorous and forceful, traditionalist but populist, often conservative as regards doctrine and discipline, but not necessarily so on social issues.

Pell's appointment must also be seen against the background of Vatican concern about the Church in Australia—concern that came to a head in November 1998. The Vatican, responding to complaints from local conservative Catholics that the Church in Australia was not reflecting Vatican policy, took the bishops to task when they came to Rome for the Synod of Oceania.

The bishops clarified some misconceptions, but the Vatican remains concerned about the low proportion of Massgoers and vocations, about the transmission of the faith, and the survival and Catholic character of institutions such as schools and hospitals. Evidently it believes Pell is the best hope for finding a solution to these problems.

On the day after the announcement, Pell spent a full day in Sydney with Cardinal Clancy, holding a media conference and giving interviews. Marc Florio, director of the Catholic youth ministry in Melbourne, recalls that Pell had a prearranged meeting with young people in North Melbourne for that night: "He was the number one news item for that day, and everyone wanted time with him. Yet despite all this, the Archbishop rushed back to Melbourne for his 7:00 P.M. meeting with young people. He looked exhausted, yet he enthusiastically and energetically participated in the meeting. The fact that he did not cancel the meeting (which he could easily have done and all those present would have totally understood) certainly demonstrated his commitment to young people."

Tributes—and more than a few tears—flowed around the Melbourne archdiocese as the Archbishop was bade farewell by his friends and flock at a special Mass in Saint Patrick's Cathedral and a variety of social gatherings. Youth worker Ana Snjaric spoke for the young people of the archdiocese at their farewell party for Pell:

> No matter how busy he was he always seemed to make time for us; whether it was for youth leader dinners, joining us quietly in prayer at the Holy Hour on Thursdays or playing pool with the cathedral choir boys. None of it went unnoticed.
>
> Many people talk about the youth of today but few actually do something to help young people and encourage them to love and actively participate in the Church. He helped us to be the best we can be. Archbishop Pell is an exception.

Father Peter Hanson, director of the Mary of the Cross Centre, wrote in *Kairos*, the Melbourne Catholic journal, of the families who had been assisted since the center opened the previous October. "Two hundred families whose lives had been turned upside down by the tragedy of drug and alcohol abuse now had somewhere to turn. And for that, they principally have Archbishop Pell to thank."

Pell thanked his priests for their faith, leadership, and service at the annual Mass of the Oils (where the oils to be used during the coming year for Baptism, Confirmation, Ordination, and Anointing) are blessed in the cathedral, with a large number of priests in attendance. "God has chosen us, gratuitously (I am sometimes tempted to think, personally, perhaps a little bit capriciously), to be his ambassadors, to act as his representatives especially through the sacraments. We must never forget the mystical, supernatural dimension of our priestly identity and work, which is nourished by our lives of action, liturgically and in service, but especially by our regular personal prayer."

He also urged the priests to maintain unity. "The maintenance of the public unity and mutual respect of the clergy is the first external defence of this spiritual treasure and that public unity should never be breached in any circumstances."

Under the circumstances, that comment was especially pointed. Just eleven days earlier, in the media frenzy generated by Pell's promotion to Sydney in early 2001, the *Age* published a story on March 31 by Ray Cassin and Ian Munro, claiming that the Vatican II generation of priests (men in their fifties) speak derisively

> of a group of conservative younger priests they call the "Spice Girls", who, they say, have been loyal Pell supporters and have acquired considerable influence in the archdiocese. Asked what the term means, most will reply with an embarrassed "no comment". Others are coyly suggestive: "The 'Spice Girls'? They're the group who prance around George when he's at the altar in Saint Patrick's." But some say it bluntly: "They're a bevy of younger clergy who are strongly supportive of George Pell." They're gay—I'm speaking about orientation, not practice—and they are very focused on elaborate ritual and dressing up in clerical garb, in a way that has not hitherto been typical among Australian Catholic priests. The priests who complain about the "Spice Girls" insist that they are not motivated by homophobia. They say their objection is to what they see as the group's undue influence in the Melbourne archdiocese, and they claim that the number of gays in the clergy is now disproportionately high.

It is not unusual for strong public figures to be the subject of unsubstantiated rumors and snide innuendos, and Pell is no exception. The troublemakers behind such rumors often hide from scrutiny behind a cloak of anonymity, and so it was, and is, with the priest or priests who gave the "Spice

Girls" story to the *Age*, who, it should be pointed out, is not necessarily the one who coined the label in the first place.

In another era, this catty wisecrack, with no substantiating evidence, might have produced an uncomfortable laugh or two and been quickly forgotten by everyone but the one who thought it up. Priests' nicknames for each other are nothing new—in preparing this book I heard about or encountered "Weed", "Monsignor Grunge", "Precious", and "Smoky Pete" to name just a few. While the "Spice Girls" wisecrack might have started out as an in-club joke, the public leaking of the moniker, however, in a tense climate, after years of devastating revelations about clerical pedophilia, millions of dollars in payouts, and the priesthood's reputation in tatters, was always going to cause havoc. It is hard to conclude anything other than that it was spiteful, malicious, and cruelly orchestrated to wreak maximum damage to the reputations of those it was aimed at, which is probably why the perpetrator has never put his hand up. In the following months, the matter was picked up on by various pro-gay websites with claims that "progressive" gay priests "worked very hard in their parishes", suggesting the information stemmed from that wing of the Church. But in the poisonous atmosphere that the original "Spice Girls" article engendered, it is impossible to be sure. The full extent of the damage, which turned out to be devastating for the Church, would not become obvious until August 2002, when part of the original *Age* article was expanded on the Internet, in almost identical rhetorical terms, only with far more serious accusations added on, attributed to "many Melbourne priests".

Initially, along with a lot of angst, the "Spice Girls" crack produced some light banter among some of Pell's younger priest friends as they teased each other about who was Posh, Baby, Scary, and so on—and who qualified as "Old Spice".

Generally, however, most priests, including those not involved, were incensed and shocked at what they regarded as
a cowardly attack from a fellow priest on his colleagues. A
couple of those apparently targeted were deeply hurt. At a
priests' meeting shortly afterward Pell was "as passionate as
I've ever heard him", according to Professor Anthony Fisher
from the John Paul II Institute.

Fisher, who doubted very much that he was one of those
being targeted (but as they were not named nobody actually
knew for sure), was impressed by one of the younger priests
who spoke at the meeting. "He wouldn't have been regarded
as one of the 'Spice Girls', but he felt his whole generation
had been attacked by fellow priests." Fisher said that the
solemn Mass in Melbourne, said every Sunday by the Archbishop, was an important weekly occasion, and if younger
priests were free to concelebrate it was a positive sign that
they wanted to be there. In fact, very few priests concelebrated on most Sundays at the cathedral because they were
busy in their parishes. The "Spice Girl" slur, Fisher argued,
was akin to an "abortion" mentality among some middle-
aged priests in regard to younger priests in the Church. Despite years of a "contraceptive" mentality in regard to vocations, where little was done to encourage new recruits,
young men had begun coming forward again, only to be tar-
nished with the "Spice Girls" brush. "Some of the priests
want no children, no new generation. I think this thing with
the 'Spice Girls' is about abortion. We've actually got the
vocations, we've got the young priests, now we want to run
them out, to get rid of them."

The matter flared again on the *Sunday* program in a profile of Pell just before he took up office in Sydney, about
a month after the initial article. He made his anger clear:
"I thought it was most insulting and most misleading and

a gratuitous slur. I totally reject those anonymous sorts of comments." Melbourne Catholic Mary Helen Woods, traditionally a Pell supporter and the daughter of his old friend B. A. Santamaria, was interviewed on the program about the Archbishop and made many positive comments. She, too, was asked about the "Spice Girls" on the program and said:

> George being a sort of charismatic figure has a close circle of good friends amongst the clergy and amongst the young seminarians, and they are, you know, if you like, ardent friends and they tend to be, if you like, quite a close little circle and they're quite high church. They love their ceremonies and they love their incense and they love the dressing up and if they want to describe that inner circle as the 'Spice Girls' I can sort of see where the comment is coming from. I don't see it as a sexual thing at all. I just see it as, if you like, a power thing. People are attracted to a powerful bloke. They tend to be a bit girlie about it. And I don't mean gay, I mean girlie.

The supreme irony of pointing the finger at Pell and his friends in regards to "bells and smells" is that many of his friends, including Fisher and Peter Elliott, an internationally respected author on liturgy, have often quipped that "George doesn't have a liturgical bone in his body" and sometimes has trouble remembering where to stand, where to put his hands, and many of the other complex rubrics of Catholic liturgy. "Just like Pope John Paul II, it doesn't interest him", Fisher says.

By comparison with some of the elaborate, solemn High Masses in overseas churches such as Saint Peter's in Rome and Brompton Oratory in London, the 11:00 A.M. High Mass at Saint Patrick's can seem a little simple and flat, which suggests that the perpetrator of the "Spice Girls" label has seen little of the universal Church and is hampered by a limited, parochial vision. While an effort was (and is) made with the singing and liturgy in general at Saint Patrick's, the participants during Pell's time as archbishop appeared dignified and prayerful, certainly not "prancing". They wore the standard garb of any priest saying Mass—white alb over black trousers and shirt, with a chasuble in the liturgical color of the day over the alb. Unlike in some overseas Churches that celebrate more elaborate high Masses, birettas and maniples were not worn.

Sensitive to the comments sometimes made about elaborate "bells and smells" liturgies appearing camp, Pell says that early in his episcopacy, he instructed the cathedral liturgists to simplify the trimmings at the High Mass, which they did. It seems extraordinary that an archbishop needed to have such concerns in the first place, but the damage done anonymously by an ordained priest, apparently with decades of experience, in giving the "Spice Girls" story is a telling insight into the difficulties of leading the Church at such a time.

At the Archbishop's Easter Sunday High Mass at Saint Patrick's Cathedral, his last Sunday Mass presiding at Saint Patrick's, protesters from the *Queer* group staged a farewell of their own outside the cathedral grounds, hanging nooses on the fence palings and chanting for Pell to "go to hell" as he greeted Easter Sunday churchgoers after Melbourne's main Catholic Easter Mass. Pell stood on the cathedral steps with his back to the rally as he exchanged Easter greetings with members of the congregation, who at one point competed with the demonstrators with three cheers for the Archbishop.

George Pell bade farewell to Melbourne's one million Catholics in a "thank you" letter in *Kairos*, in which he identified the faith practice of the young and middle-aged as the Church's greatest pastoral challenges. "I am more convinced than ever of the beauty and usefulness of the first rite of penance, perhaps because of my weekly stint in the box at the cathedral," he wrote. "The pilgrimage to the Holy Land and Rome for the World Youth Day last year brought me encouragement and inspiration, as did the number and quality of the Melbourne seminarians and young priests. There are many good memories."

For his Mass of thanksgiving at Saint Patrick's Cathedral on the evening of April 24, Pell chose the same scriptural passages that had been read at his Mass of reception at the Exhibition Building five years earlier, when he never dreamed he would become the Archbishop of Sydney.

"God writes straight in crooked lines", he told the congregation. "There is a lesson here for all of us; to use whatever time we have, because we can never be sure how much time remains to us. *Carpe diem*—seize the day. We must seize our opportunities for prayer and for action, rather than relying on good intentions to be implemented tomorrow!"

Whatever other mistakes he might have made as Archbishop, Pell said, he had not erred in placing Christ at the center of his efforts and preaching; not another good man, a prophet, martyr, and poet, although he is all these things; but Christ, the God-man, our Redeemer and Savior. "There have even been one or two voices in the Catholic community who would reduce Christ to the most perfect human. These have to be resisted, and I am sure they will continue to be resisted, because they destroy the special claims of Christianity. Our Lord would not be our Redeemer, but another brave hero, like many thousands of other men and women. If Christ is not risen, Paul wrote, then our religion is in vain; we are dupes, unfortunate, mistaken do-gooders."

Referring to a passage he admired by G. K. Chesterton

in his 1908 book *Orthodoxy*, Pell concurred with the English convert that orthodoxy never takes the tame course or accepts the conventions. It is always easy, he said, to let the age have its head; the difficult thing is to keep one's own.

To have fallen into any one of the traps of error and exaggeration would have been simple, obvious, and tame, he said. Avoiding such traps as Archbishop of Melbourne, had been, to quote Chesterton's eloquence, "one whirling adventure; and in my vision the heavenly chariot flies— thundering through the ages,—the dull heresies sprawling and prostrate, the wild truth reeling but erect."

Chapter 15

Archbishop of Sydney

The Gospel reading at George Pell's solemn Mass and liturgical reception as Archbishop of Sydney on May 10, 2001, was not the scriptural passage generally chosen for such occasions. It was Saint John's story of the woman taken in adultery, whose accusers were told by Christ that he who was without sin should cast the first stone. One by one the accusers slunk away, until only the woman and Christ were left, and He did not condemn her, but told her to go and sin no more.

In the days leading up to the Mass, much of the media coverage of the Archbishop's promotion had centered on how Sydney, with its exaggerated reputation for brashness, hedonism, and a strong gay culture, would respond to the new archbishop. "In contrast with these scriptural perspectives, one or two local writers seem to suggest that sin is a recent Sydney invention", Pell remarked in his inaugural sermon. " 'Sin City' or 'Tinsel Town' has a contemporary local resonance! However, human weakness also flourishes in other parts of Australia, and the beautiful passage from Saint John's Gospel reminds us that human perfidy is as old as the Garden of Eden."

The Gospel story, he said, represented a "supreme teaching moment highlighting the delicate balance between Our

Lord's justice in not condoning the sin and his mercy in for-
giving the sinner." God would always wipe the slate clean
for genuine sorrow and amendment, even for the men determined to execute the woman.

As in Melbourne, Pell intended to make the recruitment
and nurturing of vocations to the priesthood a key priority. "Without priests our parishes will wither and die", he
said. "These stark realities should not be hidden from young
Catholics, from young parents. A priestless parish is a contradiction in terms, because there is no parish without the
sacraments, without baptism, Eucharist, reconciliation. We
should pray tonight that in the years ahead a sufficient number of young men will be on a wavelength that enables them
to hear Christ's call to the priesthood, to join those gallant
priests expending themselves in faithful service and prayer
in the Archdiocese and elsewhere."

Many Sydney Catholics had had their first detailed look at
their new Archbishop the Sunday after his liturgical reception, when reporter John Lyons presented a detailed profile
on Channel Nine's *Sunday* program. Lyons put a number of
descriptions of Pell to the Archbishop for his reactions:

LYONS: A bully Bishop.

PELL: I think that's misleading and insulting, and there's
no evidence to justify it whatsoever.

LYONS: A right-wing fundamentalist.

PELL: I describe myself as radical centre. I'm very committed to the use of reason. I believe in some fundamentals,
but that's quite different from being a fundamentalist.

LYONS: A homophobe.

PELL: No, I reject that completely. In the Archdiocese of Melbourne I've regularly spoken with many homosexuals. We have two hospices for HIV victims. I've visited both of those regularly. I'm certainly no homophobe.

LYONS: A careerist.

PELL: No, not in the slightest.

LYONS: The Pope's man in Australia.

PELL: I hope so.

LYONS: A misogynist.

PELL: No, that's insulting. As a matter of fact the person who most recently made that claim had to withdraw the claim that she'd alleged . . . I'd made about women's ordination. No, I'm certainly not a misogynist.

LYONS: She withdrew under threat of legal action, did she?

PELL: She did, yes. Because I think a fair comment is fair comment, but if people are purveying lies, I think they should be challenged.

How could the only man ever to hold the reins of both the Melbourne and Sydney archdioceses, who many predict will go on to head a Roman congregation as a cardinal prefect in the future, be anything other than an ambitious careerist? In the secular world, ambition is a virtue rather than a vice, but Pell is adamant that he has never had any ambitions to rise through the clerical ranks and says he was "extremely surprised" to be asked to become Archbishop of Sydney.

Pell acknowledges that people sometimes speculate that he took the public positions he did during the late 1980s and early 1990s in an effort to distinguish himself from the other bishops in a carefully orchestrated plan to secure promotion. "The overwhelming probability would be exactly the opposite", he says. "Moreover, my basic perspectives are in fundamental continuity with my teaching and writings at Aquinas and as seminary rector."

But did not those points of difference set him apart just at a time when the Church was changing under the influence of Pope John Paul II?

"It wasn't changing here in Australia at the time", Pell says now.

Surely it was clear that it would, given the trend in the United States at the time and the appointment of strong pro-Roman prelates like Cardinal John O'Connor in New York?

"I didn't think in those terms", Pell says. "I worried that the Church in Australia was slipping from bad to worse, and that was the basis of my decisions to point out a few things."

Pell is fully cognizant of the daily struggle of priests in dioceses who continue to defend the fullness of Church teaching and refuse to sell out in the face of pressures to trivialize Catholic teaching or reduce the Christian message to a bland, lowest-common-denominator level in the pursuit of short-term popularity and peace at any price. He had been prepared, if asked, to spend his working life as a parish priest in rural Victoria or as a Church academic and enjoy it.

Apart from the central city area around Saint Mary's Cathedral and the North Sydney area where the Caritas offices were, Pell was not familiar with most of Sydney, especially its suburbs and parishes. He generally visits two or more parishes in the city a week, sometimes for Confirmations and sometimes for two-day midweek visitations, where he speaks to different parish groups and schoolchildren, followed by a return visit for the Saturday evening vigil Mass. In recent years, some Australian Catholic dioceses have moved to confirm children at a young age, before their First Communion at age eight, viewing the sacraments of Baptism and Confirmation as sacraments of initiation, culminating in the reception of Holy Communion. Pell understands that theory, but in practice he regards it as a pastoral disaster. He strongly prefers delaying Confirmation until the final year of primary school, or even into secondary school, when candidates are better able to grasp the significance of the sacrament. The detailed instruction given at that time is designed to boost the candidates' faith for the years ahead. As an auxiliary bishop, Pell always made time to meet and instruct Confirmation classes before conferring the sacrament. As an archbishop, this was much more difficult.

As he did in Melbourne, Pell celebrates High Mass most Sunday mornings in his cathedral, except for when he is visiting a parish on Sunday mornings. He also says the evening youth Mass at the cathedral once a month. On weekdays, if he is not visiting a parish or school for Mass, he offers the Sacrifice alone in his private chapel, on the first floor of the cathedral presbytery. This building, erected during Cardinal Clancy's reign, looks like a neo-gothic showpiece: its highly polished downstairs reception rooms more stylish than homey. Some people would feel they were living in a goldfish bowl, with large mirrored windows looking to the cathedral surrounds.

Pell's rooms upstairs are less lavish but more comfortable. They are dominated by the bookshelves holding his vast, well-thumbed library (around three thousand volumes and growing), which covers theology, philosophy, literature, history, and numerous other subjects. Other shelves house the escapist, detective stories Pell enjoys. He has read most of Agatha Christie and P. D. James and all of Frederick Forsythe and John Le Carré. His other favorites include Brian Moore, an Irishman who emigrated to Canada, the English Catholic novelist Piers Paul Read, Alan Furst's books set around the start of World War II, Australia's Christopher Koch, and poet Les Murray. His perennial favorite poets are Wilfred Owen, killed in action at age twenty-five shortly before the 1918 Armistice, and Australia's James McAuley.

The Archbishop's eclectic art collection ranges from Rembrandt prints and an ink drawing of our Lady penned by a German soldier during the siege of Stalingrad to more modern Australian paintings and prints. He has the print from Sidney Nolan's Ned Kelly series he bought after returning to Australia in the early 1970s, watercolors by Milada Kessling, a Polish-Australian artist, landscapes by Max Wilks and Patrick Carroll, and a magnificent replica of the Vladimir *Madonna* by the Polish-Australian artist, Andrew Molczyk. One wall of Pell's private chapel is dominated by a striking print of John Coburn's *Fifth Day of Creation* (one of a tapestry series that is Australia's gift to the Kennedy Center in Washington).

Piled up around the rooms are the theological, philosophical, and social commentary journals he reads avidly, including the *Spectator*, the *New York Review of Books*, *Times Literary Supplement*, the *Tablet*, *First Things*, *Origins*, *Homiletic and Pastoral Review*, *Quadrant*, *Annals*, and *Australian Catholic Record*.

George Weigel, senior fellow at Washington's Ethics and Public Policy Center and Pope John Paul II's biographer, has been impressed over the years by the breadth of Pell's reading and study. "Go into his sitting room, and you'll find files of every important opinion journal in the English-speaking world", Weigel says. "He's far more attuned to what's really going on in the world of ideas than many of his critics, who tend only to read each other's articles and books. George Pell is in close touch with everybody's thought."

The one trapping missing from his desk is a computer. "I'm still at the stage of the quill", Pell says. Margaret, his sister, tells how he took a brand new laptop to the beach one year, before any software had been installed, turned it on and was disappointed when the Internet was not there. And Peter Elliott, who shared Pell's Melbourne house for a time, claims he never did master the remote controls for the television and video.

Though lacking in computer skills, Pell wields his pen with dexterity, turning out complex sermons, speeches, and newspaper columns at a rapid pace, often after settling down to read and write for a few hours late into the night after an evening out. Despite years of early rising in the seminary and for early Masses, Pell by nature is a night-owl rather than an early-bird. "If he's going to be grumpy, it's in the morning", one of his former cathedral staff in Melbourne remembered. "If he had an early appointment and came out to the car with his hair still wet, you shut up and didn't turn the music up too loudly on the way."

Pell's the first to admit he "doesn't suffer fools easily" and can be impatient under pressure, but those who deal with him frequently and those meeting him for the first time invariably find him warm, courteous, and good company. In private, he's as articulate and opinionated as he is in public, and while the language is a little more frank and colorful than he would use in public, he rarely resorts to swearing. "He's always been very stable, very secure", his childhood friend Father Michael Mason observes. "He's also very loyal at keeping up with his friends and keeping in touch." Years after leaving Swan Hill, for instance, friends in the parish were amazed and touched when he made the long trek back for the funeral of a parishioner he had known well. He also turns up to support old friends on important occasions in Ballarat. Those who know him well say he is extraordinarily generous both to charities like Caritas and to others in need and remarkably unattached to money, although he likes to be surrounded by good furniture, art, and books. When his family sold their Torquay beach house in Victoria, he gave most of his share away. His family say he puts a lot of thought and imagination into choosing Christmas presents for them.

While Pell is seen as the leader of the traditionalist wing of the Church, he is friendlier with many priests and lay people on the Church's liberal wing and in the center than most of his more conservative friends, who, he admits, generally take Church politics far more seriously than he does. After his installation in Melbourne, Pell had a group of his most loyal priest friends to dinner at his house in Gellibrand Street, Kew, to celebrate his elevation. One of the younger priests who was there was struck by the Archbishop's lack of rancor toward those who had given him and his friends a hard time previously: "It was clear that those of us who were there were looking forward to important changes in the diocese, but George also said we could afford to be magnanimous to other priests, and he was." Several priests and family members said he cannot bear the rather Celtic tendency of keeping up long-running grudges and resentments. "If he's got something to say, he'll say it, probably in the forceful, colourful language of the pub he grew up in, and then forget it", one old friend said. "In other ways he can be very Irish, a bundle of contradictions. You sometimes get the feeling that the left hand doesn't know what the right hand is doing."

Pell can cook, but he has not since he became a bishop, preferring to return friends' hospitality by taking them out for dinner, where he enjoys relaxing with a glass of wine and the odd after-dinner cigar—the only time he smokes. While generally gregarious, Pell's family and friends who holiday with him say it is hard to get a word out of him at breakfast, when he disappears behind the daily newspapers, which he reads cover to cover. He is naturally fascinated with politics, international news, sport, and the arts, but he also looks through the life-style and popular culture sections to be aware of what his flock, including teenagers, are interested in. He is probably better informed about pop music, most of which he dislikes, than most parents whose children are fans of singers like Eminem, whom Pell has taken to task in print for singing of "killing women, nuns and gays, carving them up like cantaloupes". Eminem's "turgid incoherence", Pell argues, "is a return to barbarism, grossly offensive and pornographic, with not a flicker of intelligent vulgarity or salacious charm", causing a profound coarsening of sensibilities among his young fans. He goes so far as to believe that governments have scope for tight, clear legislation to curb the worst expressions of hate, including any found in the entertainment industry.

In his first few months in Sydney, one of Pell's most important addresses was his speech to the Quadrant Dinner in August. To the surprise of the audience, who were mostly devoted economic rationalists, he began with a look backward to a time when, he said, the family in Australia enjoyed a privileged place in law and in social and economic policy: "Nothing epitomised this more than the 1907 landmark judgment of Henry Bourne Higgins, President of the newly established Commonwealth Court of Conciliation and Arbitration, in the case that established the basic wage, to support a working man, his dependent wife and three children 'in frugal comfort' ", Pell said. As it became more difficult for families to maintain their standard of living on one income, feminism and new opportunities for women in the workforce came to the rescue, he noted, enabling families to maintain and often improve their standard of living, at least initially, although for many poorer families today even two incomes are not enough, and parents find they have to seek a "third income"—part-time work at nights or at the weekend to make ends meet. "This sort of thing is not always good for workers—at whatever level of responsibility, although some love it—and it is certainly not good for families or for children waiting for their parents to come home."

While many in the room took this opening, and his subsequent answers to questions, as an attack on free-market economics, Pell insisted he was not being nostalgic for the basic wage and centralized systems of the past but was focusing on the problems of the present and future: "I am not saying that the collapse of the family was the consequence of some sort of unholy alliance between feminists and radical free-marketeers. It is only when we become a little bit like Marxists and insist that if only we can get the economics right everything else will look after itself that the blindness of the market becomes a problem."

Despite the number of divorcees in the room, and in the general community, Pell then briefly floated the notion of a tax on parents who divorce as a means of helping to defray the costs to the general community. Politicians, lawyers, and commentators roundly condemned the notion as impractical and unfair. Even Pell himself admitted a few months later, in an address to the Pontifical Council for the Family in Rome, that it would probably prove impossible to implement given the difficulties in establishing who was the guilty party in each marriage breakdown. The media fracas over the divorce tax idea overshadowed all of Pell's other points in his Quadrant speech, which drew on the latest available research on family issues—most of which supports the Church's basic position that to preserve social stability it makes good sense to buttress the stability of the family.

Pell said:

> In Australia, 46 percent of marriages end in divorce. The impact on both parents and children is significant, with rates of mortality and illness much higher than in families which stick together. Children of divorced families are more prone to poor results at school and to depression and low self-esteem. One of the most important recent studies of the effects of divorce on children reported that 90 percent of children react to divorce with strong feelings of fear, anxiety and abandonment. The old slogan that divorce is better for both parents and children than staying in an unhappy marriage no longer has credibility.

He was also able to use independent research to debunk the notion of "trial marriages" as a means of preventing separation and divorce by pointing out ABS figures showing that divorce is actually twice as likely for people who cohabited before marriage compared with those who did not. "Cohabitation before marriage has increased from 23 percent of couples in 1979 to 69 percent in 1999", he said. "My fear is that we are setting ourselves up for a vicious circle where family breakdown is perpetuated by behaviours which make it all the more likely."

Pell said that, "without criticising any individual or making judgements about people's situations or experiences", it was time to accept that divorce and births out of wedlock come with high social costs. Social policy should address the underlying causes and, if possible, reverse the trends with what he called "a preferential option" for the family in law and in social and economic policy. He agreed with the suggestion by Barry Maley at the Centre for Independent Studies for reintroducing fault as an element in determining the custody of children and property settlements. "I do not see why marriage should be the only contract people can walk away from without penalty", Pell said. "The weakness of the family is now at the point where it is beginning to undermine the strength of the state. The state needs children just as much as any couple living in a village in India. As falling fertility rates in the West make very clear, we need to start re-thinking this attitude if we want enough people around when we are old to care for us, pay taxes to support us, and if necessary, go to war to defend us." Pell supports the right of all women, including mothers, to undertake paid work outside the home and to receive equal remuneration for that work along with subsidized child care. However, he also points to surveys that repeatedly show that many mothers of young children work, not for fulfillment, but out of economic necessity and would prefer to spend more of their children's early years with them at home.

Pell pushed the envelope even farther, arguing that government policy settings are not enough to reverse the decline of the family and that religion has a role to play: "True and effective love of one's children requires sacrifice, making a gift of oneself to others, and it is this sacrificial love that maximises the chance of an encounter with the transcendent. We may not realise it yet, but the great and now rather dated experiment in radical secularism has failed, and the failure of the family is one of the most important manifestations. It is time for a radical change of outlook, and we need it to come soon for our own good." In other words, individuals and families ignore the spiritual or religious side of life at their own peril.

With a daily schedule akin to that of a cabinet minister or private sector CEO and a position and outspokenness that see him enmeshed frequently in controversies, Pell admits that he can sometimes find it difficult to step back and switch his concentration to his own prayer life, which is something he makes time to do every single day, regardless of the demands of the schedule. Prayer, he admits, can be "a very considerable relief" from the pressures of work and controversies. In addition to Mass, the Archbishop's daily prayer includes the breviary and meditation. While many Catholics have their favorite saints to whom they pray regularly, Pell prays "almost exclusively to Christ". "That's just the way it's evolved with me", he said. He also has a strong devotion to our Lady and says the rosary several times a week—often during one of his frequent walks through the Botanic Gardens to Mrs. Macquarie's Chair or along the surrounding streets. On other days, he swims at an indoor pool or, on days off in summer, surfs at a beach to the north of Sydney where he has a condo. Golf is a favorite pastime of many priests, but not Pell. He says it would take up too much time, and after playing a variety of sports well he's not keen on the idea of dabbling at the edges and playing the game badly. He would love to be able to ski but never managed to accept the invitations of families to go with them.

Shortly after Pell arrived in Sydney, Jeni Cooper, the editor of Australia's most successful newspaper, the *Sunday Telegraph* (circulation of seven hundred thousand plus, readership of two million plus), offered him a weekly column. More than seventy columns later, the Archbishop has covered religious and general topics from stem cells, euthanasia, saints and the Pope to movies, Harry Potter, and sport. His first column was about Sydney:

When I was leaving Melbourne for Sydney, people warned me I was coming to a very different place. I always asked what these differences were and murmured that I was not going to Afghanistan. Central Sydney reminds me of New York; the crowds, the bustle, the tall buildings, and the conviction of Sydneysiders that theirs is the premier city. And so it is. . . . Most people in Sydney are not shy. Students will often say hello to me; even three skateboarders from the square came up to shake my hand. . . .

"Sin City" is secularist spin. There are fewer unbelievers in Sydney and more Christians. Melbourne is a place where Catholics and unbelievers flourish.

The Sydney-Melbourne rivalry is long standing. To the dismay of their respective champions the cities have much in common. Sydney and Melbourne Catholic parishes are indistinguishable, and even the clerical stories overlap, with only the names of bishops changed. I love both cities, but I now call Sydney home.

Somewhat to the Archbishop's amusement and chagrin, the column that has drawn the most responses to date—hundreds of them—was a pre-Christmas column in 2001 about Harry Potter, the world's best-selling children's character ever. While some Protestants and Catholics objected to the book's positive portrayal of witchcraft, the Archbishop enjoyed it and said so, putting many parents' minds at rest and infuriating a few others. Those who criticized the book claimed it made witchcraft and the occult attractive to young children. Pell disagreed: "To my mind there is not much danger of this, because the world of fantasy is so extreme, such a clever and unusual stimulation of the imagination. It is clearly unreal; interesting and totally peculiar."

He read the first book, bought a sequel for his nieces, and saw the film. "I like a good different escapist read, which has to be well written, to take me into other worlds," he wrote in his column.

Would Harry's magic work with me too? I still read a lot; all sorts of things. I probably owe this gift to a young Christian Brother, my teacher in grade five, who launched us into the many kingdoms of fiction. Being able to read easily is the key to all knowledge, and we have to be grateful to any new author who can entice millions of young readers into this adventure and expand their imaginations. . . .

Harry Potter is an eleven-year-old wizard, whose parents were killed in the struggle against evil. When he goes to Hogwarts, the boarding school for witchcraft, this struggle is resumed. . . .

Often when we read a book beforehand, we don't like the characters in the film version, but most viewers seem to have liked the way Harry and his friends Ron and Hermione (the film taught me how this name was pronounced) were cast. So too with the adults.

The headmaster Dumbledore, a venerable patriarch, the deputy Minerva McGonagall (what a great name), the giant Hagrid, the nasty teacher Snape are all well-known English character types, populating an unusual Gothic school building set in an exotic countryside.

More importantly the book (and the film, which differs slightly) are full of good moral teaching just like traditional fairy stories. Harry learns that his parents were killed by the evil Lord Voldemort, and the story tells how he and his two friends continue this fight, conquer their fears, and put themselves at risk for one another as loyal friends.

I happen to believe that it is important for all us, and children, to learn that good and evil are real spiritual forces, that each of us has to commit himself against evil. Voldemort lied to Harry that there is no good or evil, only power, that his parents were cowards; and in a final violent physical struggle Harry triumphed and good prevailed. All of us, and especially the young, need to be reminded good is more powerful and will have the last word.

When Harry was obsessed by the image of his dead parents, his headmaster explained there was neither knowledge nor truth in that apparition. But there is a good dose of moral truth in Harry Potter, book and film. And it is a great yarn.

In his Christmas column, Pell did not miss the chance to hammer home a few truths:

> Ours is not a safe secular Christmas, a kindly festival of gifts and goodwill for the children, which temporarily creates a dream world, where problems and sickness and strife are put to one side. We believe that the Christ Child grew up to be a great man, teacher and healer, who redeemed us; set us on the path which brings human fulfilment.
>
> Seventy percent of Australians are Christians, and there is very little anti-Christian sentiment. All groups are accorded religious freedom. It is therefore a great pity that so few Christians choose to use Christian symbols for their Christmas decorations. I am not against giving, much less receiving gifts. Indeed to give is deeply Christian. I am not even opposed to Father Christmas, although I think he only became popular about the 1920s, after a Coca-Cola advertising campaign. I can understand non-Christians using only holly and reindeers. But why do Christians avoid the crib with Mary and the Christ Child in their business advertising? In the Philippines you would never think Santa was the main person at Christmas; Mary and Jesus have central billing there.

For the first time in a quarter of a century, Pell holidayed at a different place in January 2002, leaving behind Torquay west of Melbourne for the New South Wales central coast. During the break, Pell also kept an eye on one of his abiding priorities for the Archdiocese of Sydney—the renovation of the chapel of the Good Shepherd Seminary at Homebush. Unlike the tension and acrimony surrounding his changes to the Melbourne seminary a few years earlier, the similar reforms in Sydney went smoothly and amicably. Even before Pell's appointment to Sydney, the seminary rector, Father Michael Foster, had indicated that after six years he was ready to move on at the end of 2001. Foster left the seminary with nine first-year students—considered a healthy intake these days. Pell appointed Sydney-born and educated Father Julian Porteous, formerly pastor of Dulwich Hill, to the position of rector, effective in January 2002. Porteous is also Sydney's vocations director. Before his official starting date, Porteous, at Pell's initiative, oversaw an extensive renovation of the seminary chapel.

Nothing illustrates the competing and contradictory visions in today's Catholic Church better than its "before" and "after" images. Before the renovation, the chapel was bare in the extreme—no sanctuary, no fixed altar, no fixed crucifix, no stations of the cross, no statues, and the tabernacle unadorned and tucked away in an alcove to the side. Decoration was minimal—a painted icon of the Blessed Virgin Mary and two colored windows with swirling, abstract patterns, one blue, one red. Porteous says the red one was possibly for Christ, the blue one possibly for His Mother, but it was impossible to be certain. The old chapel had a wooden table-like altar in the center, a movable lectern, and seats for the students placed around the "table" in a horseshoe arrangement, with no fixed kneelers but rather mats to be put down as needed.

Under Porteous' supervision, the chapel was transformed by Sydney architect John O'Brien and Opus Dei priest Father Victor Martinez, a trained architect who also holds a doctorate in theology and who has experience designing chapels. The basic vision for the renovations, however, was that of Pell, who insisted on a traditional sanctuary, a fixed, solid altar (made from Sydney sandstone and granite), a life-size crucifix, a fixed lectern, a tabernacle given pride of place in the center of the sanctuary, a statue of our Lady, and four stained-glass windows depicting Saints Peter and John, Mother Mary MacKillop, and Mother Teresa.

At the end of 2002, the Good Shepherd Seminary had thirty-four students, and twenty-five of these were in first and second years. Half the students are training for the Archdiocese of Sydney, and the remainder for other New South Wales dioceses and for Adelaide, which closed its seminary down due to lack of numbers in the latter years of Archbishop Leonard Faulkner's reign as probably Australia's most liberal archbishop.

Porteous said that the twenty-five younger students, and those who are showing strong interest to follow them in 2003 and 2004, belong to a "post-postmodern" generation of devout young Catholics who are largely untouched by the post-Vatican II struggles in the Church. Pope John Paul II, the rector said, is the only Pope they have known. And his vitality and initiatives like World Youth Day have given them a solid vision of life and a sense of the significance of the Catholic Church in the world. The Pope encouraged them to seek out a place and identity in the Church, which they found attractive, solid, and stable. "These students have come to a point of conviction about the Church and see that it has an important message", he said. Most are in their early twenties when they enter and have worked in a variety of previous occupations—builder, gem merchant, engineer, and teacher, among others. The devotional piety and orthodoxy of some of the younger students impressed and surprised some older Sydney priests more accustomed to the liberal approach of the 1960s.

Like Pell in Corpus Christi in 1985, Porteous introduced "a few small changes" to the Good Shepherd Seminary from the start of 2002. While he did so on the specific instructions of Pell, he fully agrees with the program the Archbishop set out, and they are of one mind on the key issues of seminary training. On weekdays, Sydney seminarians get up at 6:00 A.M. and say the morning prayers of the Divine Office, followed by half an hour's meditation before a communal Mass at 7:30 A.M. After breakfast, they begin classes and come together again at 5:00 P.M. for evening prayer and again at 9:15 P.M. for night prayer. The evening rosary is optional but is well attended. Saturday is the day off, with morning Mass optional, but the students are expected to return to the seminary in the evening (under previous regimes they were allowed to spend Saturday nights away). The Sunday Mass is at 9:30 A.M., and on Sunday evening the Blessed Sacrament is exposed for an hour for adoration, followed by Benediction and the Divine Office. Students traditionally cook Sunday lunch themselves, experimenting with different ethnic cuisines or the dishes of their cultural traditions—five of the current thirty-four students are from Vietnamese families. Within the seminary, Father Peter Dwyer is in charge of first-year formation, which involves a solid spiritual grounding, a study of the Scriptures and their place alongside tradition in the Church, and a detailed study of the *Catechism of the Catholic Church*.

Porteous admits that some of the older students found the new regime restrictive, but he and the Archbishop are convinced it provides the most solid foundation for future priests. The seminary is built for around fifty students, and

Porteous is confident it will need to expand in future if present trends continue.

At the beginning of the 2002 school year, a small number of Catholic primary schools in Sydney began using the Melbourne religious education textbooks on a trial basis. The trials proved successful, and the series was reprinted and adapted for use across Sydney, with local photographs replacing some of those of Melbourne churches. Father John Walter, pastor of Riverwood in Sydney's south, said the year-three children and teachers in his school were enjoying using the books. "I think any move in line with the request of the Holy Father for more solid education in faith for primary-school children is to be encouraged", Walter said. The books could also find their way into the archdiocese's widespread program of religious education for Catholic children in State schools.

In April 2002, Australia's Catholic bishops as a group were in the glare of the national spotlight when the High Court ruled on their application, backed by the federal government, to prevent single women, including lesbians, from accessing *in vitro* fertilization technology. Opposing the application, which dated back to October 2000, were the Human Rights and Equal Opportunities Commission and the Women's Electoral Lobby.

The test case centered on the long-standing efforts of a Catholic Melbourne woman, Leesa Meldrum, to conceive a child by way of the technology. Meldrum, who had failed to conceive in an earlier heterosexual relationship and was diagnosed infertile, had devoted ten years and Au$40,000 in medical expenses to her quest to have a baby. "I want a baby more than life itself", Meldrum told the news media at one point. "I would go to any length to have a baby. I guess I have gone to every length."

In July 2000, the Federal Court had upheld as a right Meldrum's access to the public IVF program, thereby forcing a change in State law in Victoria, which had previously restricted single women from using the technology, thereby prompting the more determined women to travel across the border to Albury in New South Wales for treatment. It was then the bishops appealed to the High Court, which ruled seven-nil to reject their bid and awarded costs against the Church.

Legal commentators gave the bishops' case little, if any, chance of success, although their advice from a variety of senior legal practitioners was that it was worth pursuing. Pell supported the Church's application and continues to defend it. Early in the IVF/single women debate he made his views clearly known when he declared: "We are on the verge of creating a whole new generation of stolen children." Prime Minister John Howard echoed this distress, insisting on "the fundamental right of a child within our society to have the reasonable expectation, other things being equal, of the care and affection of both a mother and a father".

To some it seemed the Catholic bishops were singling out a *small proportion* of IVF applications for opposition when the Church's moral teaching that all human lives be equally respected suggested that a far graver issue—the manufacture of human embryos, many of which are frozen for years, then destroyed—was at stake with IVF technology in general. Life begins at the moment of conception, and this fact is central to the Church's opposition to all violations of the dignity of human embryos, including abortion, experimentation, and the harvesting of cells or organs.

Yet in the High Court battle, the Church appeared to be directing her resources and wrath at a very small number of women wishing to access the technology, while leaving the bigger picture alone.

Pell does not see the issue that way. The bishops' prime

concern, he says, was defending the traditional family and
the ideal of heterosexual marriage from yet another form
of undermining. "A child has the right to a normal sort of
family life."

Pell denied that he, as an unmarried male, was romanti-
cizing the benefits of traditional heterosexual marriage. He
said his pastoral experience with ordinary families had shown
him time and again the unhappiness and consequences, especially for children, that often stemmed from the breakdown
of the traditional family.

In an interview with *Religion and Liberty*, the magazine of
the United States think tank the Acton Institute, around the
time of the High Court ruling, Pell elaborated on the difficulties Church leaders face when they address important
public policy issues:

> The Catholic bishops and many other Christian leaders have
> recently spoken out on the question of refugees attempting
> to enter Australia. The political and cultural Left has uni-
> versally welcomed this intervention, whereas some of those
> on the Right have told us that the church should stay out of
> politics.
>
> On the other hand, we are currently awaiting a decision
> from our High Court [the equivalent of the United States
> Supreme Court] on an appeal lodged by the Catholic bish-
> ops. This appeal challenges a court decision striking down
> a state law restricting access to assisted reproductive tech-
> nology to married and de facto couples and giving access to
> single women and lesbians. Broadly speaking, the bishops'
> intervention in this matter has been supported by the political
> and cultural Right, while those on the Left have told us to
> stay out of politics.
>
> My view is that very few people are consistent in saying
> that the church should stay out of politics, because there will
> always be an occasion where they will welcome the clergy's

support on one issue or another. If, as church leaders, we believe that there are occasions where our contributions to the moral debate are necessary, we have to accept that almost every time we speak on whatever issue it may be someone, somewhere, will tell us to stay out of politics.

At the same time, Church leaders should assess carefully whether an intervention is necessary and appropriate, and they should frame their comments in terms of principle rather than politics. "It is sometimes difficult to know when to speak and when to keep silent", Pell admitted. In the Catholic tradition, he said, priests and bishops are not permitted to hold public office, and, as a matter of practical prudence and professional integrity, they should refrain from using their positions to advance the political interests of any party, except in extreme situations. "We encourage lay people to be actively involved in their communities, and practical party politics is their business, not the business of the clergy", Pell said. "We live in democratic societies, and Christians and Christian churches have the right to be heard, like everyone else."

Contrary to some people's expectations, the Catholic Church is not an enemy of the market, he told *Religion and Liberty*. A great deal depends on what is meant by a free-market economy. "If we mean 'an economic system which recognizes the fundamental and positive role of businesses, the market, private property, and the resulting responsibility for the means of production, as well as human creativity in the economic sector', then the church supports the free market", he said. "But if we mean 'a system in which freedom in the economic sector is not circumscribed within a strong juridical framework which places it at the service of human freedom in its totality, and which sees it as a

particular aspect of that freedom, the core of which is religious and ethical', then the church opposes it.''

The Church could do better, he suggested, in encouraging business people to consider their role in the wider society.

> As willingness to join groups with formal membership struc-
> tures declines, regular forums with different audiences on
> particular moral challenges in business might be one useful
> contribution. There are many fine Christians who are senior
> and successful business leaders, and their witness and exam-
> ple to their colleagues are invaluable. But I think we could
> do more to develop the idea of business as a vocation and to
> deepen business people's understanding of the importance of
> their work not just for themselves and their families but for
> society as a whole. Business people could be more aware of
> the moral imperatives that drive and restrict their activities.

In Pell's first fifteen months in Sydney, his progress getting around to all of Sydney's 137 parishes and the city's
Catholic schools was hampered by spending significant periods working overseas, mainly in Rome. His first trip to
Rome as Archbishop of Sydney was in 2001, to receive a
new pallium from Pope John Paul II, on June 29, the feast
day of Saints Peter and Paul. Popes have been conferring
the pallium on bishops since the sixth century at least, and
it is now given to archbishops of major cities to symbolize
Catholic unity around the pope. As Pell explained to his
Sunday Telegraph readers, the white wool used in the pallia
comes from lambs blessed in Rome on the feast of Saint
Agnes (January 21), who are cared for by Benedictine nuns
in Trastevere (a Roman suburb little changed in centuries
in the ancient Jewish quarter). The pallia are blessed by the
pope and placed overnight on the eve of the feast on the
tomb of Saint Peter in Saint Peter's Basilica. "In 1997 I had

received a pallium as Archbishop of Melbourne, and one unusual tradition is that this will not be used again until my death, when it will be placed under my head in my coffin", Pell wrote in his column.

During the ceremony, the archbishops, from thirty-six cities as far afield as Washington, Delhi, and Acapulco, promised allegiance to the Pope. Their promises were read by Denis Hart, the new Archbishop of Melbourne, because he was the last archbishop appointed before the ceremony. Having two archbishops receiving the pallium on the same day was an Australian first. Rome was fine, clear, and hot for the entire week—except for the half hour during the open air Mass in Saint Peter's Square, when fierce thunder rolled across the sky and rain bucketed down. "A squeal ran through the crowd", Pell recalled.

We were drenched. Umbrellas arrived late, and as the Mass continued I spent fifteen minutes huddled under one in the papal colours with the Archbishop of Florence.

By coincidence June 29 was also the day when Doctor Peter Jensen, the new Anglican Archbishop of Sydney, was consecrated. I prayed during our ceremony and beforehand when I visited Peter's tomb, under Bernini's spectacular 'Baldacchino' that God might bless him and his Archdiocese. The original Saint Peter's was built by Constantine, the first Christian emperor in the fourth century, over Peter's traditional burial place. Today you can walk through this ancient Roman cemetery, first excavated during the Second World War.

It is always a moving experience to concelebrate and pray with the Pope, bishops, priests and people from many different cultures, often leading lives more difficult than ours. It reminds us that we have only a small, brief part in an immense and age-old tradition of worship and service centred on Jesus Christ.

This was true on this occasion too, but it is harder to pray when you are sopping wet. With the red dye from our outer vestments staining the white albs, one had to work harder for reverence and recollection. But life is like this. Christ was born in a stable and crucified on a rubbish tip. I am sure he would have needed a sense of humour.

From Rome, Pell paid a brief visit to the Polish city of Cracow, where Pope John Paul II was once priest and bishop, to look in on a three-week seminar on Christians in a free society, organized each year for ten years by a Polish Dominican priest, Father Marcei Zieba, formerly a lay leader of Solidarity. Two of Pell's American friends, George Weigel and former Lutheran-turned Catholic priest Father Richard Neuhaus, a prolific author and editor of the New York-based monthly journal of religion and social commentary *First Things*, also attended, and they went out to dinner in a city they found much changed—for the better.

"I first visited in 1990 soon after the fall of communism and the city was drab and polluted", he told *Sunday Telegraph* readers.

> Poland has done better than any other ex-communist State, and it is wonderful to see brightly dressed children, restored buildings, and the debates, bustle and colour of a free society. However, unemployment remains at fifteen percent and the challenge of agrarian reform still lies ahead. . . .
>
> Poland, like Ireland, has the strongest Catholic life in the Western world. Contrary to some fears, in the twelve years since liberation there has been no pattern of radical secularisation. I stayed in the monastery of the Dominican priests, founded about 1224, which is now a vibrant centre for students from the Jagiellonian University. The Sunday evening Mass I attended was packed with youngsters. It was not al-

ways like this; in the 1970s only five percent of students from some faculties worshipped regularly.

Pell was back in Rome in October 2001 as one of 250 bishops attending a synod on the role of bishops with Pope John Paul II. Pell spoke about the duty of bishops to teach about good and evil, heaven and hell, the afterlife and genuine Christian hope:

> One could say that there is considerable silence and some confusion on such Christian hope especially as it touches the last things, death and judgement, heaven and hell. Limbo seems to have disappeared, purgatory has slipped into limbo, hell is left unmentioned, except perhaps for terrorists and infamous criminals, while heaven is the final and universal human right: or perhaps just a consoling myth. . . . Christian teaching on the resurrection of the body and the establishment of a new heaven and earth, the heavenly Jerusalem, are a vindication of the values of ordinary decent living, while the final judgement, the separation of the good from evil, marks the establishment of universal justice not found in this life.

According to the international Catholic magazine *National Catholic Reporter* (NCR), one of the topics debated was *subsidiarity* and its application to the role of bishop. Subsidiarity is the social teaching of the Church that in the political and economic sphere a higher body should not assume on behalf of a lower body functions that the lower body is able to perform for itself. There is a faction in the Church that argues for the break-up of papal authority over faith, morals, and Church discipline on the basis of subsidiarity, as if questions concerning these matters could be properly answered by a majority vote in any given diocese. In an interview with

NCR, Pell said this notion was "radically incompatible with
the hierarchical and communitarian nature of the Church".

The synod's theme was *The Bishop: Servant of the Gospel of
Jesus Christ for the Hope of the World.* Among other issues, the
synod looked at: the theological status of national bishops'
conferences; whether bishops are presenting the fullness of
Catholic teaching in language people can understand; are
they practicing what they preach; is their service real and
consistent; and is there a need for formal training for bishops. Pope John Paul II, while physically ailing, told the bishops "I'm OK above the shoulders." The Pope attended all
of the synod's general sessions and had each bishop to lunch
during the month. Pell found him in sparkling form when
he attended on the twenty-third anniversary of the Pope's
election, where the guests sang "Happy Birthday" to the
Pope in Italian and "For He's a Jolly Good Fellow" in English.

As Pell wrote in his *Sunday Telegraph* column, the synod

> met in the shadow of the September 11 attacks, and while
> the war commenced in Afghanistan on October 11 our usual
> morning prayer, mostly Old Testament psalms sung to the
> ancient Gregorian chant, was dedicated to the theme of peace
> and justice, and we prayed the rosary together in the after-
> noon for the same purpose. I was also taken by the terribly
> difficult situation of some bishops. Three million Sudanese
> have died in the last 20 years in the continuing war there. In
> some African countries 30–40 percent of people are infected
> with HIV.

Like many Australians, Pell had first learned of the September 11 tragedy the following morning, from the newspapers. Stumbling down to breakfast after saying some morning prayers, he noticed the headlines, and his first thought

was that it was a spoof or an advertisement. That afternoon, he led a Mass in Saint Mary's Cathedral to pray for those killed and injured and their families, and the following day he led a packed service for schoolchildren in the cathedral. "Religious people pray when there is trouble, even when the trouble is not, strictly speaking, their own", he told the children.

> Prayer gives us strength and patience in tribulations. We ask God to convert the spiritual energy generated by our prayers to give strength and consolation to the family and friends of the victims. And we pray that those who died will be purged, cleansed of the effects of their sins, even the misguided zealots who caused these catastrophes.
>
> We have all suffered a brutal shock, but the shock probably has been greatest for you, our young people, too young to remember even Vietnam, let alone World War Two. This should be a terrible lesson for you that evil and violence don't belong only in nasty, escapist adventure films, but sometimes erupt in spectacular and destructive real life situations. We pray not to be put to the test in extreme situations. We practise in small ways to do good so we can answer the big challenges.

He warned the children against singling out the local Islamic community for blame.

> All of us will have to take more care that this catastrophe overseas does not worsen our pressure points here in Australia. We do have some racial and religious tensions; not bitter and deep by world standards, but trends to be reversed. Hostility towards aborigines; violence and threats of violence against Jewish synagogues; Moslems, even their children, insulted and threatened; violence from race-based gangs, and propaganda hostile to our traditions of public tolerance and

diversity. We need to pull together; without exception. It is unjust to scapegoat the local Islamic community: they too reject these murders.

The October synod of bishops in Rome elected Pell to its follow-up working party preparing the final report, a task that took him back to Rome several times in 2002. He also made a special week-long visit in January to join Pope John Paul as one of the speakers at the Opus Dei conference in honor of the centenary of the birth of Josemaría Escrivá.

In March 2002, following publication of the third Latin edition of the Roman Missal as the official standard for the liturgy, the next step was to make vernacular language editions available, including English. To this end, on April 20, Pope John Paul II established a new body, known as the Vox Clara (clear voice) Committee "to assist and advise the Congregation for Divine Worship and the Discipline of the Sacraments in fulfilling its responsibilities with regard to the English translations of liturgical texts". The twelve members of Vox Clara include bishops and cardinals from the United States, Canada, England, Ireland, Ghana, India, and the Philippines. The Congregation for Divine Worship and Discipline of the Sacraments appointed Pell as chairman. It was a sign of confidence in his leadership in what had become a delicate and controversial area of Church activity.

The committee was established because the Pope and the former prefect of the Congregation for Divine Worship and Discipline of the Sacraments Cardinal Jorge Medina Estevez were dissatisfied with some of the previous work undertaken by the official body charged with producing uniform translations of liturgical texts—the International Commission on English in the Liturgy (ICEL). The use of politically correct, "inclusive" language and poor translations, which altered the meanings of liturgical ceremonies subtly but in important ways, were among the problems identified. The Vox Clara Committee's brief was to help ensure that the Latin was translated as accurately and as authentically as possible, according to the principles set out in the Vatican document *Liturgiam Authenticam*, issued a few days later with the endorsement of John Paul II on April 25, 2001. It specified: "The greatest prudence and attention are required in the preparation of liturgical books marked by sound doctrine, which are exact in wording [and] free from all ideological influence."

While it hardly seems unreasonable for the Pope and his curial cardinals to ensure that the English translation of the Mass was as authentic and accurate as possible, *Liturgiam Authenticam* produced squeals of protest from, among others, influential liturgists in the Australian Church. The response of one of the former members of ICEL, Father Thomas Elich, the head of liturgy in the Brisbane archdiocese, is indicative of the depth and bitterness of the split in the Catholic Church in Australia over such fundamental issues as the wording of the Mass. Despite its papal endorsement, Elich branded *Liturgiam Authenticam*, "a betrayal" and argued that it is "not entirely a surprise" in light of earlier responses from Rome on other liturgical matters.

In the June 2001 issue of *Liturgy News*, the Brisbane archdiocese's liturgical magazine, which is widely read across Australia, Elich was critical of the *Liturgiam Authenticam*'s emphasis on words and expressions that "differ from usual and everyday speech" in order better to convey "heavenly realities". He was especially concerned that "inclusive language is dismissed as an inauthentic development", adding:

"If we use in liturgy language which reflects an unjust world view or the sinful structures of a culture, then the liturgy will be compromised." *Liturgiam Authenticam*, he said: "betrays the hard-won devolvement of responsibility for liturgical translation to bishops' conferences", with the Holy See reserving "to itself the right to prepare translations into any language and to approve them for liturgical use". He concluded: "Taking these various elements as a whole, one cannot escape the conclusion that the collegiality and local responsibility for liturgical translation have been seriously compromised by this document."

Collegiality, or the shared authority of all the bishops in communion with the pope, was a central teaching of the Second Vatican Council and one that Pell wholeheartedly approves. While ICEL retains responsibility for the translations, it is being reconstituted and reorganized, and for the moment its work will be overseen by the Vox Clara Committee, whose task is to advise the Congregation on English translations. As that group comprises bishops from all over the world, this approach can hardly be seen as a stroke by Rome against collegiality; rather, it is a sign that after thirty years, the Vatican's patience with ICEL was finally exhausted. In a scathing rebuke to ICEL in 1999, Cardinal Medina Estevez wrote: "In its present form [ICEL] is not in a position to render to the bishops, to the Holy See and to the English-speaking faithful an adequate level of service." He pointed out that "ICEL texts often did not follow the original Latin closely enough; the process for developing, copyrighting and approving translations did not give bishops enough room for making changes and suggestions; and ICEL was writing its own material, not just translating Vatican-approved Latin texts." Such concerns, he said, had been made clear to ICEL "for a number of years now", including "concerns regarding an undue autonomy that has been observed in the translations prepared by ICEL".

The Vox Clara Committee defined its role as serving "as an instrument of consultation to assist the Congregation for Divine Worship and the Discipline of the Sacraments in its work for English-language translations of liturgical texts and to enhance and strengthen effective cooperation with the Conferences of Bishops." Pell, as chairman, wholeheartedly backs the Pope's insistence that the vernacular translations of the official Latin texts be precise, theologically faithful, as well as beautiful.

What intrigues some Mass-goers about this row is whether Pell and his episcopal colleagues will take the next logical step and assert their authority to ensure that priests stick to the official text of the Mass and other liturgical celebrations. Catholics in some parts of Australia are accustomed to priests: using their own words even for the most solemn parts of the Mass, including the Eucharistic Prayer; leaving out the Creed or substituting a different one that talks about the environment and the Church's weaknesses instead of "the one holy catholic and apostolic Church"; substituting different biblical passages or non-scriptural readings for the scriptural readings of the day; and the regular omission of significant sections of the Mass, such as the preparation of the gifts for the Consecration.

Like Cardinal Ratzinger, Pell sees some merit in the tradition of the priest facing east or its spiritual equivalent, the tabernacle, during certain parts of the Mass. He says that facing the people throughout the liturgy can put too much emphasis on the priest himself at the expense of concentrating on God. However, both facing 'east' and facing the people are licit options. The main thing, then, is to set an example to his priests by following the rubrics when saying Mass and celebrating all the sacraments.

By late May 2002, Pell was looking at home in his new city and was turning his attention to the appointment of a third auxiliary bishop for Sydney. His predecessor, Cardinal Clancy, had had three auxiliaries, but one of them, Bishop Peter Ingham, had been promoted to his own diocese, Wollongong, in July 2001 shortly after Pell arrived in the city.

A year after his appointment, Pell was beginning to know Sydney and its parishes, and his reputation internationally was growing through his work for the synod of bishops and the Vox Clara Committee. He was also in demand as a speaker at international conferences and had engagements booked for later in the year in Rome, New Zealand, and Washington, D.C. Close friends had never seen him looking as relaxed and healthy, compared with his period in Melbourne, when he had sometimes looked tired and pale. In Sydney, he exuded the self-assurance of someone thoroughly enjoying a very fulfilling job. Some people even thought he had toned down his more controversial statements a little. When asked about this, he quipped: "It might just be that I'm behaving." Even his appointment of an Opus Dei priest and experienced university chaplain, Father John Flader, to head Catholic adult education in Sydney drew a generally positive reaction, with many seeing merit in his bringing Opus Dei more into the mainstream life of the archdiocese. Asked if he would object to Flader or others encouraging vocations to Opus Dei, Pell said he would not, provided those involved were over the age of eighteen. "But I'd far rather they went to the seminary to become priests", he said.

Although Saint Mary's Cathedral and Pell himself had been caricatured on a float or two in the Sydney Gay Mardi

Gras in February, Pell's expected clash with the city's powerful gay lobby did not eventuate in his first year. The first Rainbow Sash demonstration in Sydney took place in Saint Mary's Cathedral on Pentecost Sunday, May 19, 2002, with Pell refusing Communion to a small group of sash wearers, including Michael Kelly, who had traveled up from Melbourne. After the Mass, Pell addressed the congregation, reiterating his earlier statements that the Catholic Church had no authority to give those staging such a protest Communion. He drew plenty of smiles when he recycled one of American anti-gay campaigner Anita Bryant's lines "God made Adam and Eve, not Adam and Steve", adding that "important consequences flow from that." He went on: "Our Judeo-Christian religious tradition allows men and women sexual expression within the bounds of family life, a sexuality which is life-giving. Homosexual acts are contrary to the natural law, they close the sexual act to the gift of life. The protesters must realise that the Church's teaching on this matter cannot, will not, change. I deeply regret that such people, who profess the Catholic faith, would choose to mount an ideological demonstration during Mass. This is inappropriate."

American members of the Rainbow Sash movement, who were reportedly given Communion while wearing the sash in churches in New York, Rochester, Chicago, and Minneapolis on the same day, branded Pell's stance "antagonistic" and "ridiculous". "The impression [in America] is that Pell is 25 to 30 years behind the rest of the world", Brian McNeill, a member of the Minneapolis Rainbow Sash told the *Sydney Star Observer*, Sydney's gay newspaper. McNeill said that American Catholics had not heard such language from Church leaders in decades: "The bishops here are too smart to say that kind of thing because they know just how antagonistic and insulting that is to a lot of people—not just to gay people, to society."

Rainbow Sash spokesman Michael Kelly complained that Pell's response to the protesters, "I can't help you", was made in "a tone of rebuke. There was no sense of warmth, understanding, or compassion in the way he handled the issue." The movement, he said, is considering appealing to the papal nuncio. "It is an extremely serious sanction in Church life and is very rarely imposed. Therefore, finding that there are other cardinals and archbishops taking a different approach in America is somewhat confusing, and we are considering taking the issue to the highest authority in the Church", Kelly told the *Star Observer*.

Despite extensive media coverage, the protesters were not the center of attention at the cathedral that Sunday. Pell confirmed several dozen adults who had recently entered the Church and released a major statement on Christian hope, written after lengthy consultations with 250 high school seniors and graduates from Sydney.

"Nearly everyone, even the irreligious, at different times is aware of the power of the Spiritual, of the Mystery behind everyday existence, of the power and majesty of the invisible God", he wrote.

Some of the young people, Pell reported, felt that human beings are most open to God "when we are at our lowest ebb", while others pointed out that "we can hope to encounter God, too, in the emptiness of success. Something is missing, because, to quote Saint Augustine, 'our hearts are never at rest until they rest in God.' " It was Christian hope, he said, that gives us courage to participate in the eternal struggle between good and evil, confident of final victory.

Preaching on Christian hope on that sunny late autumn Sunday, Pell had no idea that a few days later he himself would face the beginnings of an ordeal that would test his own inner strength and hope to their utmost limits and remind him very sharply of the idea that Christ gives His heaviest crosses to His dearest friends. He could not have imagined that by the time spring came to Sydney just a few months later, his name would be spread across the world, from Iceland to South America, from the BBC in London to national newspapers in Japan, as the archbishop who had stood aside awaiting the results of an inquiry into allegations that he had sexually abused a twelve-year-old boy forty-one years before.

Chapter 16

Darkening Days

In 1996 in Melbourne George Pell established a process to handle sex abuse complaints against clergy, and the national process, Towards Healing, was adopted by the rest of the Church in Australia a few months later. Scores of tragic cases of abuse and heartless, irresponsible cover-ups by Church authorities, most of them now dead or retired, came to light. The processes, flawed as many victims, victims' families, and support groups believe them to be, were at least there and provided help for victims. They also prevented the wholesale meltdown of Church credibility seen elsewhere, especially in the United States, where bishops buried their heads in the sand for years longer than their Australian counterparts. This year, 2002, proved to be a crisis year for the United States Church, with stiffer jail terms for offenders and higher court-awarded compensation payouts for victims than anywhere else. In Boston alone, the Church set aside US$18 million for victims of just one priest, John Geoghan, accused of molesting 130 children over thirty years. This case sparked a crisis that saw another three hundred civil law suits filed in sixteen states, and 250 Catholic priests out of 46,000 stepped aside from public ministry from January to October. Some estimates suggest the Church will pay out well over US$1 billion before the crisis is resolved. The most senior United States bishops were summoned to the Vatican and ordered to devise a system to handle the problem.

From the Pope's native Poland to Hong Kong, Ireland to South Africa, it would be hard to find a diocese untouched by this issue. Nor is the problem confined to the Catholic Church. In early 2001, in the lead-up to the Queen's Golden Jubilee Australian tour, Governor-General Peter Hollingworth was under intense pressure to resign over his handling of such matters during his time as Anglican Archbishop of Brisbane. In mid-2003 Doctor Hollingworth resigned. Smaller churches, too, have occasionally come under the spotlight for a problem that afflicts some members of not only the clergy but also the service professions, such as health- and child-care providers. Figures collected by the Australian Institute of Health and Welfare present a shameful picture of the problem across society as a whole.[1] In 2000/2001, the number of child-abuse cases investigated and substantiated across all states and territories was 27,367. This figure covers sexual, physical, and emotional abuse and neglect, with sexual abuse comprising 13.8 percent of the total. The true figure is far higher, as many such crimes go unreported for years and are sometimes never reported. While biological parents, as well as step-parents, de facto step-parents, siblings, and other relatives are overwhelmingly the main perpetrators, the revelation that some priests, brothers, and nuns, who have dedicated their lives to God, are guilty of this crime has deservedly drawn headline treatment in the media.

While girls in general are more vulnerable to abuse than boys, it is boys who are more likely to fall victim to pedophile Catholic priests, a fact that has caused numerous

[1] See www.aihw.gov.au.

Catholic commentators to suggest that homosexuals should be kept out of seminaries, arguing that all-male seminaries are not a good environment for homosexuals and, further, that while homosexual priests are a minority, they have been convicted of far more pedophilia offenses than heterosexual priests. In March 2002, Pope John Paul II's spokesman Joaquin Navarro-Valls told the *New York Times* that "People with these inclinations [homosexuality] just cannot be ordained . . . you cannot be in this field." Pell says he "broadly agrees" with Navarro-Valls, although he qualified this by saying that one or two exceptions could make very worthwhile priests. Seminaries around the world have stepped up the psycho-sexual screening of potential candidates in light of the present crisis.

In the past decade, more than one hundred Catholic priests and brothers have been dealt with by Australian courts for child sex abuse or have died during the legal process. Several Internet sites list these and several hundred other religious offenders, including Protestant ministers, teachers in religious schools of all denominations, and church workers of all denominations. One of the most comprehensive overviews is a document known as *Hypocrites*, a painstaking collection of data researched and collated by the sex industry lobby group the Eros Foundation. The Foundation is demanding a major inquiry, such as a Royal Commission, into the issue of clerical sex abuse. "As a profession, the priesthood has lost its direction and has become a real danger to the community", the Foundation argues on its website. "The scale of this travesty is so great that only the highest level enquiry will get to the bottom of it."

Many of the cases make gruesome reading, with perpetrators setting a pattern of sinister, calculated behavior, preying upon and seducing child after child, mainly boys but sometimes girls as well, in dozens of parishes, moved on frequently by Church authorities after complaints and rumors arose about their behavior.

The crisis has given enemies of the Church powerful ammunition, and some have seized the opportunity to try to bring down an organization they want to see destroyed. For example, the Australian church offenders register, a lengthy Internet list of clerical sex abuse offenders and their crimes, is operated under the name of *Antichrist*. It prominently displays a quote from Émile Zola: "Civilisation will not attain to its perfection until the last stone from the last church falls on the last priest." Although the overwhelming majority of sex abuse happens within families, the site argues: "Forget Osama bin Laden, Saddam Hussein and the renegade Muslims. Our real terrorists live much closer to home. They're in our churches, in our schools, in our community centres —and up our kids' backsides! They're called Christians. For humanity's sake, pray that they are stopped!"

The site has links to Broken Rites, the Eros Foundation, and Melbourne's Haunted Bookshop, among others, and mentions the Church of Satan. Founded on April 30, 1966, by Anton Szandor LaVey, the Church of Satan defines itself as "the first above-ground organization in history openly dedicated to the acceptance of Man's true nature—that of a carnal beast, living in a cosmos which is permeated and motivated by the Dark Force which we call Satan."

The backlog of unresolved abuse allegations, many of them involving numerous complainants, was so chronic and so enormous when Pell took over Melbourne that he pressed ahead with the Independent Commission run by Peter O'Callaghan, Q.C., rather than waiting to join the national Towards Healing process established later. Broken Rites spokeswoman, Chris McIsaacs, a Catholic who feels more aligned to the liberal wing of the Church than to her traditional side, is highly critical of how all Church authorities have handled the sex-abuse issue. However, she believes the Melbourne system set up by Pell, with counseling, investigation, and compensation carried out by independent lay people, is "the best of a bad lot". "At least in Melbourne you know whom you are going to see and who is going to assess a claim for compensation", she said. Under the scheme, twenty-two priests were barred from ministry in six years and more than 120 people compensated.

~

On Thursday, May 30, 2002, George Pell called an extraordinary press conference as a preemptive strike against allegations set to be aired three days later on Channel Nine's *60 Minutes* program. He issued a statutory declaration and a statement denying that in 1993, while Auxiliary Bishop of Melbourne under Sir Frank Little, he had attempted to conceal the sexual abuse of a young man by the name of David Ridsdale by his uncle, Father Gerald Ridsdale, by offering the victim financial assistance in return for his silence.

"The allegation I attempted to silence a victim or cover up allegations is unfounded and untrue and is anathema to me", Pell told the assembled, startled journalists at Saint Mary's Cathedral. "I emphatically and totally deny the allegation that I made any attempt to buy David's silence. It was also alleged that I offered to buy David a house or a car. The allegations that I made any such attempts or offers are not only unfounded but also implausible."

Many observers agreed that Pell was wise to get in first before the airing of the *60 Minutes* program, although the banner headlines the day after his press conference in Sydney's high-circulation *Daily Telegraph*, "Sex Scandal Engulfs Pell", was a taste of what was to come for the following fortnight.

On Sunday evening, the heavily promoted story went to air, with *60 Minutes* reporter Richard Carleton's opening: "It's hard to imagine a graver charge. It's against one of the most powerful men in Australia, the man who is now the Catholic Archbishop of Sydney. Now, the accusation is simply this—that ten years ago, Doctor George Pell attempted to bribe a distressed young man who had been sexually assaulted by a priest, and that Doctor Pell did this to cover up a potential scandal to protect his church."

The young man making the allegation had grown up in Pell's hometown, Ballarat, and was the nephew of Father Gerald Ridsdale, a now-defrocked, disgraced Catholic priest currently serving a lengthy jail term for a string of pedophile crimes (see pages 90–91). According to the program, Ridsdale began assaulting David when the boy was eleven, and the abuse lasted until he was fifteen and involved masturbation, kissing, and oral sex. "Sick as it may sound, the abuse would sometimes occur when the priest was driving the altar boy to the next town to say Mass", Carleton reported.

David Ridsdale claimed that George Pell was one of the few individuals he had trusted as a young man, and he phoned him in early 1993 to tell him of his ordeal and to ask for help: "I was getting so confused and so psychologically agitated and depressed and angry I had to deal with this issue. And I believed at the time that he was the best way for me to go." Ridsdale claimed that Pell took control of the conversation and said: "I want to know what it will take to keep you quiet." The *60 Minutes* interview then proceeded:

RICHARD CARLETON: Are there any doubts in your mind that those were the specific words that he used?

DAVID RIDSDALE: "I want to know what it will take to keep you quiet." None at all. Not those last two phrases, no. . . . That one phone conversation is the reason that I then went to the police and so on and everything that happened afterwards.

Ridsdale's sister Bernie backed up her brother, insisting that David had rung her later that day and related how he had made a phone call to George Pell and that "George had asked him what it would take for it to go away, to make it go away." Another of David's sisters, Trish, concurred: "David told me that after he had told George about the abuse, George asked him what it would take to keep him silent. In fact, David's words to me were, 'The bastard tried to offer me a bribe.'" That same day, the program reported, David Ridsdale phoned the police to report his uncle, who, unbeknownst to David, was already being investigated. A day later, the priest was charged over the sexual assault of David and a number of others. In 1997, the Bishop of Ballarat, Ronald Mulkearns, resigned amid accusations that, as head of Ballarat diocese, he had covered up Ridsdale's offenses.

When Father Ridsdale walked into court in May 1993, George Pell walked beside him—an image played repeatedly on television over the past nine years. Was this a piece of foolish, misplaced loyalty to a former colleague that sent the wrong message to victims of men like Ridsdale and to the shocked public in general? Or was it a magnanimous gesture by a man big enough to be there with "one of the least of my brothers" at his lowest point, when the entire Church and the public shunned him? Should the bishop have entered the court with the victims rather than the accused? In June 2002, in the media storm that ensued after David Ridsdale's claims, Pell conceded that walking the priest to court, something he did with "considerable reluctance" at the request of Ridsdale's lawyers, was a mistake. "I did so in priestly solidarity. This was a mistake as it misled people about my basic sympathies for the victims, borne out by all my subsequent work to root out this evil."

In an early interview for this book, months before the *60 Minutes* program, Pell said that at Ridsdale's first trial, the priest's defense lawyer had asked him to give evidence in court for his client. "He urged me, explaining it could help Ridsdale avoid being sent to jail", Pell said. However, the lawyer later withdrew the request.

> This was because I said: "If I appear in court I would say, 'I'm not commenting in any shape or form on the truth or otherwise of the accusations against Ridsdale.'" And secondly, Ridsdale has done immense damage to the victims, to himself, and to the Church. All I would say is that there was another side to Ridsdale too; he did good things.
>
> I said if I appeared in court, I would insist on saying those three things, and they didn't ask me to appear. Also, at that stage, I had no idea of the extent or the gravity of the offences; I knew they were bad enough, but I knew none of the details of the cases. I never knew then just what an enormous range of offences was involved.

Pell repeated this in his statutory declaration a few days before the *60 Minutes* program went to air. In that declaration, Pell agreed he had received a telephone call from David Ridsdale about his uncle Gerald. However, Pell not only denied offering any kind of financial incentive for David

to keep quiet, but suggested that this would have been implausible, impossible, and pointless at that time.

> First, at the time that I received the call from David, allega-
> tions of misconduct against Gerald Ridsdale, including com-
> plaints from the victims other than David, were already in
> the public domain and were already, to my knowledge, the
> subject of police action [Pell wrote in the declaration]. Sec-
> ondly, David has had various opportunities over the years to
> make these allegations to me had he wished to, but he has not
> done so. Shortly after I became Archbishop of Melbourne
> in 1996, I attended a public meeting with over 200 people
> including victims of sexual abuse, their families and friends.
> I recall that either David or his brother was at that meet-
> ing and, towards the end of the meeting, spoke publicly in
> support of the initiatives that I had announced to respond to
> sexual abuse within the Archdiocese, and urged those present
> to give "George's" procedures a "fair go". In addition, as
> an auxiliary bishop of the Melbourne Archdiocese, I had no
> authority or capacity to purchase an item such as a house
> or car for any other person. Further, I made no requests to
> either the then-Archbishop of Melbourne or Bishop of Bal-
> larat for the provision of any financial assistance for David.

In his declaration, Pell said David Ridsdale's father, Barry
Ridsdale, is a carpenter who had done a considerable amount
of work over the years at Aquinas Campus in Ballarat. Pell
recalled seeing the family regularly at Mass in Ballarat before
he left the city in 1984.

> Although I do not recall the precise date of the telephone
> call, I recall that it was while I was an Auxiliary Bishop of
> Melbourne and that it was around the time of police action
> against Gerald Ridsdale [Pell said]. To the best of my recol-
> lection the call took place early in 1993. When I received the

phone call, I was aware that allegations of criminal conduct were being made against Ridsdale, that they involved offences against a number of children and that the allegations included offences against members of Ridsdale's family. I had no reason to believe Ridsdale was innocent of the allegations. . . . I recall that when David Ridsdale rang me, he told me that he had been abused by his uncle. He also told me of financial difficulties that he, his wife and children were experiencing. I felt sorry for David and would have been keen to help him if I could. However, there was no basis upon which I could have provided him with any significant financial assistance. I did not provide, or offer to provide, David or his family with any financial assistance.

In my telephone conversation with David, there was no mention made of David going to the police. I did not consider his call or the conversation to be threatening in any way. David did not make any threats and did not swear at me.

Pell said that until he viewed the footage shown to him by *60 Minutes* on May 25, 2002, he was unaware of David Ridsdale ever having spoken a cross word about him.

"I recall that I also had a telephone discussion with David's wife slightly later. It was a friendly conversation, but did not involve any offer by me to provide any help whatsoever."

In claiming that Pell and Father Gerald Ridsdale had "been at school together, seminary together and, as young priests, they'd shared a house", the *60 Minutes* report gave the impression of some closeness between the two. Gerald Ridsdale, born in 1934, is seven years older than Pell. They seldom encountered each other at Saint Patrick's College, Ballarat, and they were never in a seminary at the same time. They overlapped in the Ballarat East presbytery for twelve months in the early 1970s, not out of choice, but because they were assigned to it, along with at least two other priests. Ridsdale was forty at the time, and Pell thirty-three.

Pell has never attempted to conceal this. In the interview for this book months before the *60 Minutes* controversy broke, Pell said: "I didn't dislike him. In retrospect, you'd say he was tense and he had a somewhat unusual personality, as events more than amply demonstrated, but it never for one moment entered my head that he had problems of this order." That was hardly surprising, given the secretive nature of Ridsdale's predilections. After all, many people never realize for years on end that their spouse is cheating, or worse, abusing children—their own or other people's. A former priest of the Ballarat diocese, who also spent a year under the same roof as Ridsdale—in Warrnambool—said that he too had no idea of his colleague's behavior.

Off air, Pell insisted that he had been "ambushed" by *60 Minutes*. When the program approached him initially in late April, he said "no" but reconsidered after two producers met with him on May 23. Former editor of the *Australian* and Catholic commentator Frank Devine wrote in *Quadrant* magazine in September 2002 that Pell had been told the interview would be about pedophile cover-up scandals in the United States, their effects on the Australian church, and the ground-breaking system Pell had introduced in Melbourne for dealing with offenders and assisting victims.

"Pell's private secretary also made a record of the meeting", Devine added. "His account has Pell asking who else would be interviewed on the programme and being told that he was the only one. Later Pell repeated his enquiry: Who else would be involved? [Executive Producer] John West-acott responded that there would be nobody else, the pro-

gramme would be a 'stand alone interview' with the archbishop."

On Melbourne radio, Westacott said Pell had been told
that the interview would be about sexual problems in the
Catholic Church of Australia, past, present, and future, and
if the Archbishop thought he was ambushed then they differed very widely on the definition of ambush.

Westacott also told *The Courier-Mail* that *60 Minutes* did
not pay Ridsdale anything for his story, although a Channel
Nine spokesman confirmed the channel did fly him out to
Australia to be interviewed, which was cheaper than sending a crew to Great Britain. While it was not broadcast on
air, Nine's website also carried a pointer to David Ridsdale's
own background, in which he admitted confessing to the
abuse of a twelve-year-old boy himself, something for which
he said he was heartily ashamed and had turned himself in
to police.

Despite the fact the story triggered days of page-one headlines and acres of feature articles, the central claim was not
new. It had first emerged in a now-defunct gay publication,
Outrage, in Melbourne in 1997 as part of a longer piece
on Father Gerald Ridsdale, written by journalist Clive Sim-
mons. According to that article, David Ridsdale telephoned
Operation Paradox, a Victoria police telephone line for reporting sex abuse, in 1992, to ask police to investigate his
uncle's activities in the Victorian town of Edenhope.

At the height of the crisis, Pell met with his priests at
Saint Mary's Presbytery. "He spoke well but he's bleeding
inside", one priest who admires him said. "If nothing else,
this has underlined for him the power of the false accusation." In the current climate, a false accusation is something
many priests fear.

Nine MSN conducted two Internet polls on the crisis, which drew a larger than usual response. The results were:

JUNE 3: Is an inquiry into Catholic Church sex abuse claims needed?

YES   22,194 (84%)

NO   4,195 (16%)

JUNE 4: Should Sydney Archbishop George Pell resign?

YES   20,454 (47%)

NO   22,916 (53%)

The Archbishop's fellow *Sunday Telegraph* columnist in Sydney, Leo Schofield, could not resist a sharp dig at Pell, whom he branded "Melbourne's gift to Sydney". Schofield wrote what a lot of Pell critics said privately:

> Consider two media images of His Grace. In one he is telling a group of Catholic gays, the rainbow-sash people, "I can't help you." In the second, the good prelate is seen accompanying Father Gerald Ridsdale, a self-confessed paedophile, to court "in priestly solidarity".
>
> Ridsdale is a criminal. The only crime of the group of gay Catholic men and women was to peaceably approach the altar for communion.

Some attention also focused on Pell's media adviser, Peter Mahon, chief executive of Royce Communications, who was pictured sitting next to Pell at one of his press conferences—a rare mistake, made in haste, in what has been a long-term and successful association since early in Pell's days in Melbourne. Pell has undoubtedly been helped by Mahon

to get his message across, and he has succeeded like no other
Australian archbishop and few other international Church
figures (such as Pope John Paul II and the late Cardinals John
O'Connor of New York and Basil Hume of Westminster)
in taking advantage of the secular media to put the Catholic
message in the forefront of public debate. For that, Mahon
deserves a share of credit. At the height of the David Ridsdale controversy, the *Australian*'s "Media" liftout reported
on Mahon's role as an adviser to Pell and that of Mike Smith
in helping Governor-General Peter Hollingworth deal with
the fall-out from child-sex scandals from his time as Anglican
Archbishop of Brisbane. In the article, Liberal Party public relations adviser Ian Kortlang observed: "Pell has clearly
been media-trained to within an inch of his life. He's very
good at it. In fact, he's too confident of his ability." However, when the heat's on, confidence and experience in handling the spotlight invariably beat nervous timidity.

Pell cancelled a working visit to Papua New Guinea to
deal with the matter, and the *Sunday Telegraph* gave him extra space to tell his side of the story on June 16. He began
by recounting a recent question he had been asked—What
would Jesus say to those who put the image of the Church
before the welfare of abuse victims? The Church response
to sexual abuse must always have justice and compassion
for the victim as first priority, he replied, and the image of
the Church must always rank much lower than the needs of
the people—especially the victims and their families. Loyal
Catholics, he acknowledged, grieve for the victims and the
crimes committed and the "disastrous mistakes by Church
leaders in dealing with them". Outsiders who do not know
the Church have their darkest fears strengthened by the scandals, he said.

As for David Ridsdale, the Archbishop reiterated his sympathy for the abuse he had suffered but denied his central allegation. "His memories of what was said and offered and when and why he went to the police vary enormously", Pell wrote.

> His memory has played him false.
>
> At different times he has accused me of offering him money, or a house and car. More recently he said in a *Sydney Morning Herald* interview "I did not accuse Pell of offering me anything."
>
> As an Assistant Bishop in Melbourne I had no authority for the Ballarat diocese and no capacity to buy a house or car for anyone. I now know that David has admitted going to the police before 3/2/1993. Recently he conceded that he went anonymously in 1987 or 1988 and in interviews given in 1995 and 1997 he claimed he contacted the Victoria Police "Operation Paradox" in 1992.
>
> I had no reason when he telephoned me or at any other time to try to stop him going to the police because by early February I knew the offender was being questioned by the police, had heard rumours that family members and others had been violated and had no reason to believe the offender innocent. The allegation of attempted bribery for David's silence is both mistaken and implausible. It did not happen.

Much of the controversy after the *60 Minutes* program centered on the rather confusing issue of whether or not the compensation payments made through the Melbourne scheme, and also some made through Towards Healing, were "hush money". Pell stumbled over the issue on *60 Minutes* and later, after media revelations about confidentiality clauses imposed on some victims who went through the Towards Healing process in New South Wales, reviewed the processes with the help of his friend John McCarthy, Q.C., a prominent Sydney barrister.

On June 9, McCarthy, the president of the Saint Thomas More Society, a guild of Catholic lawyers, told the press he had "received many messages of concern relating to clauses in deeds of release for victims of clerical sex abuse" that "seem to be the standard non-disclosure clauses in damage settlements". These clauses, McCarthy said, seemed to be "completely at variance with what Church leaders, including Archbishop Pell, believed was happening under the Church's current process, Towards Healing, for those who had been victims".

McCarthy stated: "For all Catholic dioceses in New South Wales the victims' care programme Towards Healing has been in operation for some years. Since 2000 the programme's charter in Clause 41.4 states: 'No complainant shall be required to give an undertaking which imposes upon them an obligation of silence concerning the circumstances which led them to make a complaint, as a condition of an agreement with the Church authority.' " McCarthy said that after making inquiries, he had found that Clause 41.4 had not been appropriately implemented in deeds of release for settlements with victims. "Customary confidentiality clauses have been maintained", he said. "Sister Angela Ryan claimed in today's paper that these are contrary to the spirit of Towards Healing. I emphatically state that it is contrary to the express directives and that our bishops as much as victims have been afflicted by conduct which has gone unnoticed and unauthorised. Regrettably it appears there are professionals who should have had more regard to the scheme's directives."

McCarthy said that Pell had authorized him to state that

in regards to the Archdiocese of Sydney (for he cannot speak for other dioceses or religious orders), that in all cases where Clause 41.4 has been breached, such cases will be reviewed and any victims relieved of any obligation of silence that may have been mistakenly imposed.

A week later, Pell asserted in the *Sunday Telegraph* that: "There has never been a confidentiality clause in the Melbourne 'release' document for victims. The compensation procedures are designed to allow victims to avoid legal confrontation and legal costs."

However, he agreed with McCarthy that "elsewhere in Australia the picture is more confusing as the confidentiality clauses used everywhere in out-of-court settlements have often been applied."

In December 2000, he said, the Australian Catholic bishops following the Towards Healing protocols agreed that there should not be an obligation of silence, imposed by the Church, on the circumstances around the complaint. "There has been uncertainty and inconsistency in implementing this policy."

In his *Sunday Telegraph* article, Pell also rejected firmly allegations that a compensation offer to a young woman (featured on *60 Minutes* with her parents) from the Melbourne Church solicitors was "hush money" to keep the incident quiet. "At that stage the priest perpetrator had been tried, convicted and was in prison", he said. "There was huge publicity."

There was, because John Kevin O'Donnell, at seventy-eight, was the oldest Victorian to be sent to jail. O'Donnell, a Jekyll-and-Hyde character who made friends with children and bought them milkshakes and hamburgers, had pleaded guilty to abusing two girls and ten boys over a protracted, evil career from 1946 to 1977 in several parishes including Chelsea, Seymour, Dandenong, Hastings, and Oakleigh.

The girl's mother, however, was understandably bitter and angry, and some of that was and is directed at Pell, despite the fact that Archbishop Little was still in charge when O'Donnell went to jail. Interviewed for this book, the woman said she and her family had been regular Massgoers until they found out about the abuse. She said she and her husband had expected more understanding and warmth from Pell when they met him privately at the presbytery at Oakleigh after he became Archbishop. "He was arrogant and a bully", she claimed.

What did she mean by that, exactly? "He wasn't on our side, we'd say something and he'd say 'That happened before my time.' " The woman said the three met in a cramped room. Space was so tight that she and her husband had had to sit up straight, while Pell, who is six feet three inches, had crossed his long legs and one of his feet was near her knee, the woman said, although not touching it. "I looked at him and said, 'Will you move your foot' and he had to uncross his legs and sit up straight like we were. He looked really cut, genuinely upset."

Pell remembers the encounter clearly. "This was a really difficult interview", he says. "Nothing I said helped the situation."

In his *Sunday Telegraph* article, Pell said that the family in question did not accept the compensation offer made to them "and subsequently explained that their objection was to the amount of Au$50,000, more than to any nonexistent confidentiality clause. The compensation procedures continued after my meeting with the parents, and the family continues to receive significant counselling and other support paid by Carelink, the Melbourne archdiocese agency."

The *60 Minutes* controversy had died down by the time
Pell left for Mexico with one hundred young people from
Sydney. They were the advance party en route to World
Youth Day in Toronto, Canada, where another two hundred young people from Sydney joined them. Pell and the
young people were impressed by the crowds visiting the
shrine of Our Lady of Guadalupe, which dates from 1531,
ten years after the Spanish conquest. At that time, as Pell
explained,

> Mary appeared to a young Indian convert, Juan Diego, and
> left a miraculous image of herself as a young Indian woman
> on his cloak to convince a properly sceptical bishop.
>
> More than fifteen million pilgrims now visit this shrine
> every year, so that it ranks second only to the Vatican as
> a Christian pilgrimage centre. The local rulers, the Aztecs,
> were a highly developed civilization in many aspects; trade,
> mathematics, astronomy. But it was an incredibly cruel soci-
> ety, regularly practising human sacrifice, including child sac-
> rifice, sometimes with thousands of victims. . . . Mary told
> Juan Diego that she loved his people and would protect them.
> They converted in millions to follow her God and her only
> Son Jesus.

In Toronto, the people from Sydney, aged from sixteen to thirty-five, joined up with another one thousand
from around Australia, 250,000 from around the world, and
550,000 North Americans for Mass with Pope John Paul II,
aged eighty-two. The Pope looked frail and ill compared
with the dynamic energy he had projected two decades earlier. If anything, Pell found that the Pope, persevering in his
teaching and travel in spite of his infirmities, had an even
more powerful effect on the young people than before. "A
new generation of young people probably loves him more
than their elder brothers and sisters did in his heyday", he

said. "Suffering and perseverance also give powerful witness, especially to those who believe in redemption through the Cross."

Pell himself made world headlines in Canada when a Canadian newspaper, the *Globe and Mail*, picked up on one of the catechesis sessions he gave to five hundred young people in a suburban Canadian parish as part of World Youth Day. Michael Valpy, the paper's religion and ethics reporter, wrote:

> Archbishop Pell taught his listeners about a Jesus who promises punishment for those who stray from the church's teachings on premarital sex, abortion and euthanasia—as well as on social justice and looking after the poor.
>
> He taught them: "It's important for you to defend Catholic tradition as coming to us from Christ and the apostles." He taught them: "The function of the Pope is to protect that tradition, to say, 'This belongs to Catholic tradition and this doesn't.'" He taught them: "We are not free to decide for ourselves what is right and wrong. Our conscience can be wrong."

What he taught them, Valpy commented, was "everything that growing numbers of liberal progressive Catholics, mainly in the West, are rebelling against—from papal authoritarianism to the church's rejection of [artificial] birth control and the ordination of women. Several theologians have called the increasingly fractious dissent a silent schism, a reference to the millions who have left the church because they can't accept its teachings." The Archbishop received a standing ovation from his audience. World Youth Day is not just a sunny gathering for a couple of hundred thousand kids to sing and join hands and let their spirits soar. It is also a time for promulgating the official teachings of the Church and encouraging fidelity to the pope and those bishops who are of one mind with him. As Archbishop Pell told the international Catholic newspaper *Tablet* earlier this year, "Liberalism has run its course and has nothing to offer the Church."

Valpy commented: "As Archbishop George Pell of Sydney told 500 young Roman Catholics yesterday that abortion is a worse moral scandal than priests sexually abusing young people, it became clear why the church is heading in two different directions." Valpy said Pell made the comparison between abortion and priestly sex abuse in response to a question from a Kentucky man, Greg Rickert, who wanted to know what Catholics should say when someone asks them about the sex scandal currently afflicting the Church in the United States. Pell replied that the truth of the scandal had to be faced. There were two levels, he said, the abuse itself and the sometimes inadequate way the Church authorities dealt with it. But there were other scandals that received little coverage.

Valpy wrote: "I asked the archbishop afterward what he meant by saying abortion is a worse moral scandal. 'Because it's always a destruction of human life', he said. Then he said: 'I'm not in any way attempting to downplay abuse. I'm saying there's been a lot of attention on sexual abuse, but not on other things. That's all I'm trying to say.'"

Valpy concluded his article with a reference to Australian author Thomas Keneally, who "wrote a *New Yorker* article a couple of months ago saying he had left the church because of priests such as Archbishop Pell. 'I have long since abandoned any expectation that the institutional church will begin to listen to its people', Mr. Keneally wrote. 'With such men in charge [as Archbishop Pell], men who wield their authority as an instrument of exclusion, I cannot return to the generous mystery of my boyhood faith.'"

The story was given widespread airtime and newspaper coverage in Australia, to the extent that one media crew staked out the Sydney airport to photograph and speak to Pell as he arrived at the crack of dawn after an all-night flight across the Pacific. Later that day, he issued a statement insisting that he was not in anyway downplaying the seriousness of sexual abuse.

> There are many terrible wrongs that people can suffer, often with life-long consequences. But Christian teaching is at one with the law and secular ethics in holding that the supreme wrong that can be done to a person is the taking of his life. This claim does not make any other evils less evil. This was the context in which my remarks were made and in which they should be understood. . . . Sexual abuse is evil, but there are other serious evils in society as well. Where innocent or vulnerable people are hurt, honesty and compassion are essential. The Church has accepted the challenge to respond in this way to sexual abuse. It is important that our community should do the same on the issue of abortion.

Pell acknowledges that many in society do not share the Catholic Church's view on the issue of abortion, "but for Christians abortion represents the destruction of innocent human life". The sharp division between the view of the majority of Catholics and many others was underlined in September when Pell was voted the "worst of the worst" at the annual Ernie Awards for sexist remarks in Sydney. Around four hundred women joined NSW upper house president Meredith Burgmann at the tenth awards ceremony, where the audience votes for the winners on the loudness of their "boos".

According to AAP, Pell earned the Gold Ernie from a field of seven category winners. He also took out the clerical category award, the Fred, "from a distinguished line-up that included Governor-General Peter Hollingworth" and was singled out for his comments on abortion in Canada.

To commentators like the Pope's biographer George Weigel, the fact that Pell attracts such criticisms simply means that he is doing his job in a way that "confounds the hoary media script, which is that orthodoxy is dour, uncompassionate, uninteresting, etc. Doctor Pell proves by his preaching and his life that orthodoxy is far more interesting than the alternatives—and a lot less stifling than secularism, which builds a world without windows or doors." Weigel regards Pell as "one of the great signs of hope for the Church in the twenty-first century" with the capacity to "invite others to join in that great adventure of orthodoxy".

A few hours after flying in from Canada, Pell was working at his desk in Polding House, Pitt Street. He resumed his program of parish visitations, Confirmation ceremonies, meetings, and speeches, including one at the unveiling of a painting of one of his favorite saints, Edith Stein (a Jewish scholar and Catholic convert who became a Carmelite nun and was put to death by the Nazis at Auschwitz), Masses in other parishes, and a lunchtime visit to Saint Ignatius College, Riverview, to mix with the students. On Sunday afternoon, August 11, with the House of Representatives due to debate the federal government's embryonic stem cells legislation, Pell addressed a crowd of 1,300 people in Sydney at a rally against the use of human embryos for such a purpose. He and other speakers, including Professor William Hurlbut, a medical doctor from Stanford University and a member of the United States President's Bioethics Council, spoke in favor of the use of adult stem cells, which, they argued, were showing more research promise.

In mid-August, Pell spoke in favor of paid maternity leave at a conference on "Working Time, Families, Communities" for the Australian Centre for Industrial Relations Research and Training at the University of Sydney. (His comments at that gathering in favor of maternity leave drew national media coverage.) He was scheduled to preside over Adoration of the Blessed Sacrament at 9:00 P.M. on Friday, August 23, followed by Benediction at 11:30 P.M. at the Chapel of the Resurrection, City Road, Chippendale, an occasion that would underline the importance Pell attaches to this form of devotion.

But, it was Pell's Auxiliary Bishop Irish-born David Cremin, then seventy-two, who led the devotions at Chippendale, because on Tuesday afternoon, August 20, Pell stood aside from his duties as Archbishop of Sydney in a fight to prove his innocence of an allegation that he had sexually molested a boy forty-one years before.

Chapter 17

"The age of the martyrs is not yet dead"

At 5:30 P.M. on Tuesday, August 20, 2002, George Pell stood outside Saint Mary's Cathedral Presbytery and in fading light read out a statement.

> Certain allegations have been made about my conduct when I was a seminarian over 40 years ago. The allegations against me are lies and I deny them totally and utterly. The alleged events never happened. I repeat, emphatically, that the allegations are false. An independent inquiry to investigate these allegations has been set up by Archbishop Philip Wilson, Acting Co-Chairman of the National Committee for Professional Standards, which supervises the Church's "Towards Healing" protocols. The inquiry will be conducted, I understand, by a retired Victorian Supreme Court judge. I will, of course, co-operate with this independent inquiry in every way possible—frankly, openly, and unreservedly. For the good of the Church and to preserve the dignity of the office of Archbishop, I will take leave from today as Archbishop of Sydney until the inquiry is completed. I repeat that the allegations are lies and that I am determined to refute them. I welcome the inquiry and a chance to clear my name, recognising that I am not above civil and Church law.
>
> I have taken a leading role in condemning and exposing sexual abuse within the Catholic Church in Australia. Six years ago in Melbourne I set up Australia's first independent

commission to inquire into sexual abuse by members of the Catholic clergy. To allege that I am now personally implicated in this evil is a smear of the most vindictive kind. I truly wish I could say more right now. However, it is important that I do not say anything that could be seen to prejudice the inquiry. Therefore, I am unable to make further comment.

He then headed upstairs to his private chapel.

Every major morning newspaper in Australia led with the story the next morning, filling in some of the detail missing from Pell's statement. The complainant alleged, it was reported, that at a holiday camp for underprivileged children on Phillip Island in 1961, he was molested at age twelve by a seminarian known as "Big George". The story dominated television and radio news all over the country and received prominent coverage in the mainstream media internationally. Retired Victorian Supreme Court Judge Alec Southwell, Q.C., who is not a Catholic, was appointed to conduct the inquiry, which after several changes of dates, occurred in early October.

The complainant could not be named for legal reasons. What little was known of him was that he was about eight years younger than Pell himself—fifty-three—and that he had children and grandchildren. In the 1980s he featured in the report of Royal Commissioner Francis Xavier Costigan, Q.C., who was inquiring into the activities of the Federated Ship Painters and Dockers Union. Among other matters, the report mentions a Supreme Court writ issued against the complainant for unpaid taxes, interest, and costs of more than Au$110,000. The report also details involvement in SP (starting price) bookmaking, a system of illegal gambling on horse races, which he used to augment his wages while employed at a Melbourne dockyard. He even gave his occupation as "bookmaker" when applying for a credit card.

The transcript of the Commission shows the complainant

repeatedly refusing to answer questions, branding the Royal Commission "a farce", talking back to the Commissioner, and accusing him of "squandering taxpayers' money" when he, the complainant, claimed to be "virtually paying your wages". As Andrew Bolt wrote in the *Herald Sun*, "The royal commission also grilled Mr. X about a surprise visit he paid to a nervous witness who was in the middle of giving evidence in which it was hoped he would name names. Mr. X refused to explain why he dropped in on the witness —a man he'd never met before—at his Sydney hotel after flying up from Melbourne."

More than a decade later, records from the Victorian Court of Appeal showed that in the mid-1990s the complainant against Pell appealed against a sentence of forty-five months in jail imposed on him the previous year, when he had pleaded guilty to two counts of trafficking in amphetamines and one count of trafficking in cannabis. Three judges dismissed the appeal unanimously. "On the plea, the applicant admitted 39 previous convictions from eighteen court appearances, and most of these convictions related to street and alcohol-induced offences", Court of Appeal Judge P. Winneke recorded in his judgment.

The judgment also mentioned the man's "recent service to the deprived areas" of Melbourne where he lived, as well as "impressive evidence of the applicant's long fight against alcoholism" and what was described on his application as "his resurrection as a worthy citizen". However, the original sentencing judge, Judge Winneke, had "remarked upon the inconsistency between the community service rendered by the applicant and the peddling of noxious and harmful drugs which are calculated to cause misery within the same community that the applicant was serving. As His Honour correctly noted, the applicant's trafficking was not motivated by any need to sustain a habit of his own but was done purely for the purposes of profit."

Material placed before the sentencing judge by the Director of Public Prosecutions described the man as being "part of a network of operators trading in illicit drugs, largely in the western suburbs of Melbourne" caught as a result of an intensive police campaign using telephone intercepts and listening devices. Judge Winneke ruled that the sentencing judge had been "entitled to find" that the amounts of the drugs "were substantial and involved pounds rather than grams or ounces. It would appear that the applicant was trading on a wholesale level and was also dealing from time to time across state boundaries."

Co-chairman of the Church's National Committee for Professional Standards (NCPS) Brother Michael Hill and members of Broken Rites condemned the leaking of the complainant's criminal history to the media.

It is clear that a number of Catholic figures in Sydney and Melbourne knew about the complaint for weeks before Pell was told. The complainant first approached the Church's sex-abuse complaints authority, the National Committee on Professional Standards, in June—just over a week after David Ridsdale's appearance on *60 Minutes*, alleging that Pell had tried to bribe him to keep quiet. The complainant was interviewed in Melbourne by Sister Angela Ryan, NCPS's executive director, who forwarded the details to NCPS co-chairman Bishop Geoffrey Robinson— one of Pell's two auxiliary bishops in Sydney. Both urged the complainant, repeatedly, to go to the police, but he refused to do so.

The NCPS's other co-chairman, Brother Michael Hill, was overseas in July and first became aware of the complaint in mid-August. Hill said it had been "awful, really awful" for senior members of NCPS to know about the complaint and have to withhold the information from Archbishop Pell. The fact that Robinson was Pell's auxiliary bishop had been "another horrific complication", Hill said. Hill said the NCPS heads were unable to inform Pell "because until you are sure the complainant is not going to the police and you get a definite complaint your hands are tied". He said that maintaining confidentiality, even from the person accused, was standard practice while those taking details of the complaint were urging the complainant to go to the police. This was because in some cases, telling the alleged perpetrator about the matter could mean repercussions that "bounce back on whoever was making the complaint".

One of the key mysteries about the complaint is who posted details of it on the Sydney Independent Media Centre website August 7, a fortnight before Pell stood aside. Publication on the web was followed swiftly by the posting and faxing of copies to selected journalists, lobby groups, and victim support groups around Australia. The detailed account of the allegation was published under the by-line "Xavier O'Byrne, Parramatta". The material suggests that the author either had detailed contact with the complainant or someone he had confided in or someone with access to the NCPS process.

According to "Xavier O'Byrne", Bishop Robinson "decided that the church could not investigate this complaint under its sex-abuse protocol [the 1996 document entitled Towards Healing] because Pell was an archbishop." The website article continued:

> The complainant was left with the impression that the church was not eager to act on this complaint. The complainant still believed that his complaint needed to be investigated by someone. But, if not by the church, who then? The complainant was considering taking his complaint to an investiga-

tive journalist of a leading newspaper, so that the journalist could make the necessary inquiries that the church had failed to do. As soon as the National Committee for Professional Standards heard about this intention, they decided—urgently —to initiate a church investigation after all, although (said Robinson) a church investigation would not have any teeth because Pell is too big.

The alleged instances of indecent touching by the man the complainant refers to as "Big George" make appalling reading. Since the material was posted before any inquiry was launched, let alone anyone prosecuted and found guilty, the web article appears to have been intended to do serious damage to Pell. Such an attack on the reputation of any citizen would be a grave matter. Against an archbishop whose preaching on issues of faith and morals had made him a well-known public figure, the potential damage to his reputation and good name, should any of the mud stick, could be catastrophic.

Pell's solicitor, Richard Leder, of Corrs Chambers Westgarth in Melbourne, wrote two letters to the Adelaide-based operators of the Internet site, which were also posted. "The assertions in the article are scurrilous and without foundation", the first letter said. "Archbishop Pell rejects the allegations entirely. The article is highly defamatory of the Archbishop. You would, no doubt, be well aware of our client's standing in the community and the strong stand that he has taken against sexual abuse within the Catholic Church. The damage that our client will suffer as a result of the publication of the article is incalculable. We are instructed to demand that the article be removed from your website immediately." The second letter said that Pell had "received further advice that as well as giving rise to a civil defamation action, the article also constitutes a criminal libel".

At this point, it is impossible to determine what links, if

any, exist between the anonymous complainant and "Xavier O'Byrne's" Internet article. The complainant's solicitor, Peter Ward of Galbally and O'Bryan in Melbourne, said he was "quite confident" his client had nothing to do with the Internet item. Ward said he had a professional, rather than personal, relationship with the man and did not know whether he owned or could operate a computer, but doubted very much if he would seek to draw attention to the case, even with his name protected.

Galbally and O'Bryan agreed to represent the complainant for nothing after they found out that Towards Healing would not pick up the legal costs. Nor did the Church pay Pell's legal costs. Ward, a practicing Catholic, said he was astonished by that but decided to continue to work for the complainant to ensure he got a fair hearing. "Pell probably wouldn't agree but I think we did him the greatest favour [in representing the client for nothing] by giving him the chance to clear his name", Ward said. He said the ethics of his profession meant he would prepare the strongest and most thorough case possible for his client to ensure he received a fair hearing. Ward has also represented the complainant in other matters.

As a Catholic, Ward had no qualms about lining up against an archbishop, although he said he admired Pell for speaking out the way he did when he was Archbishop of Melbourne. "He was conservative and that upset a number of people, but you knew where you stood with him", Ward said. "He was an excellent spokesman for the Church."

Peter Ward said it was "no secret" that South Melbourne parish pastor Father Bob Maguire knew the complainant. "By that I mean he assisted him, told him where to go."

Father Maguire, well known in Melbourne's inner suburbs for his hands-on, practical help to drug addicts, street children, and gamblers, was, initially, in no mood to talk to me, venting his spleen over the telephone about Archbishop Denis Hart and his administration of the archdiocese. "And now you're torturing me with questions", Maguire said. He referred to an on-going row with Hart over funding for the range of welfare projects run from South Melbourne, for which, he points out, he has been awarded the Order of Australia. Maguire described himself as both orthodox and orthopractic (practicing the faith at street level). Was Maguire close friends with the complainant? He refused to speak publicly about the matter until the man was named. "We don't know who he is, officially."

Did he agree with Father Gerry Diamond's article defending Pell?

"My brother in Brisbane sent it to me; it was a cleric's delight", Maguire said.

Did he agree with it, though?

"Some people are running off at the mouth talking about a saint and an icon. George is all right as a human being."

So he liked Pell, then?

"He gave us dough. He also said he'd back anyone who was doing things."

Did he respect Pell's background running Caritas, the Church's aid agency?

"Any fool can run things. It's about being hands on and getting your feet wet."

Diamond, the pastor of Glenhuntly in Melbourne, was one of the first priests into print to speak up publicly for Pell, branding the allegation against him as "preposterous", given the kind of seminarian Pell was in 1961. "The routine of the seminary was designed to foster growth in faith and in moral virtue", Diamond wrote. "This was facilitated by daily Mass, meditation, spiritual reading and daily examination of conscience as well as by weekly confession and

spiritual conferences." As a seminarian, Pell was serious and
self-disciplined and, in 1962, was chosen by the Jesuit rector
of the college as rhetoricians' prefect to guide the first-year
students in their growth in self-discipline. He also was noted
for his prowess on the sporting field and in debating. At the
end of each academic year, seminarians were reminded of
their responsibilities during the holidays and of the need to
continue their daily spiritual life. They also were specifically
called upon to watch for and not place themselves in imprudent situations that could serve as "occasions of sin". At
times, during the summer holidays, students assisted with
camps run at Phillip Island, camps that were intended to
enable boys, especially from deprived areas of Melbourne,
to spend a week at the beach, which otherwise would not
have been possible. These camps were supervised strictly
and consisted mostly of team games. The accusation appears to be totally groundless and reflects behavior totally
out of character with the one anonymously accused.

Diamond's description of the strictness and discipline of
seminary life in the 1960s was echoed in some pulpits around
Australia by other priests from the same era, who said students as serious and dedicated as Pell did not commit the
kind of offenses alleged. Another Melbourne priest disagreed
with Diamond's analysis of the times: "There was so much
testosterone around that it's a wonder they weren't all at it."

The night of the announcement, Prime Minister John
Howard defended Pell strongly as a person of honor: "I believe completely George Pell's denial", he said. "I rang him
this evening and spoke to him. They are, of course, very
serious allegations, and he's done the right thing to have the
allegations fully investigated." Howard said someone in his
position had to make personal judgments from time to time
about people. "You either believe somebody or you don't."

A few hours later on the ABC's *Lateline* program, Patrick Power, the Auxiliary Bishop of Canberra, one of Pell's staunchest ideological opponents within the bishops' conference, was more circumspect. Asked by compere Tony Jones if he would be prepared to say the same thing as the Prime Minister, Power replied: "I think I would say that given that there is going to be an inquiry, I think it is best to leave it to the inquiry to make those judgements, rather than to try and pre-judge or pre-empt what Judge Southwell will come up with."

John Howard, Power said, was "in the situation that any friend of Archbishop Pell would be in. Namely, that they would see him as a person of great integrity and in that sense express their support for him in this difficult situation. I think, as I say, he's come to the defence of a good friend of his, and I think many of Archbishop Pell's other friends would take a similar stance."

Asked whether the accusation would damage Pell's chances of being promoted to the rank of cardinal in future, Power surprised many Catholics, accustomed to previous archbishops of Sydney being promoted to the ranks of cardinal, when he said: "Could I say that all the presumption that he was ever going to be a cardinal, I think, is simply presumption. I don't think that that ever necessarily followed in any case."

To the annoyance of some rusted-on Labor-voting Sydney Catholics, Opposition Leader Simon Crean accused the Prime Minister of making a "serious misjudgment" in supporting Pell so strongly and claimed that support could send the wrong message to victims of child abuse. Crean said the Prime Minister could say someone was innocent until proven guilty, but "he has gone further", declaring innocence "on the basis of a conversation with one side", he said. The day after Pell's announcement, the issue flared in federal

parliament with Mark Latham, who is now Australia's Oppo-
sition Leader, taking a verbal swipe at Workplace Relations
Minister Tony Abbott (a former seminarian and a friend of
Pell's) in Parliament: "It's a bad day for seminarians."[1]

In Brisbane, popular Labor Premier Peter Beattie, an experienced lawyer, praised Pell for stepping down with dignity
and told the Queensland Parliament that people who made
false claims should feel the full force of the law and that his
government was considering upgrading criminal defamation
to an indictable offense. In a plea for a level of censorship
that newspapers and the electronic media would regard as
dangerous, civil libertarian and prominent Brisbane lawyer
Terry O'Gorman went farther, arguing that people accused
of sexual abuse should not be identified unless they have
been found guilty, to avoid reputations being irretrievably
damaged. Sexual abuse allegations, he said, were "very easy
to make and very hard to defend". That much is true, but
with Internet open publishing sites making a mockery of
existing defamation laws, it would be hard to justify further
crackdowns on the mainstream media, which are already
heavily restricted by defamation laws.

Speaking from London, David Ridsdale, who had accused
Pell of trying to buy his silence about the abuse he suffered
at the hands of his uncle, urged the complainant to go to
the police to have the matter dealt with properly. Ridsdale
also said that, while "there are plenty of reasons why I do
not believe that George Pell should be a spiritual leader",
he also held a deep respect for the right of people to the
presumption of innocence until they were proven guilty.[2]

While researching this book I interviewed a Melbourne

---

[1] Dennis Shanahan, Political Editor, *Australian*, August 22, 2002, p. 2.
[2] *Australian*, August 21, 2002, p. 4.

man who is supporting the man who claims he was abused by Pell. This friend portrays the complainant as a "deeply sensitive, wounded man, who was never looking for money or publicity or to embarrass Pell publicly, but rather is a reformed character who has left behind his life of crime and wanted a quiet, private meeting with Archbishop Pell and a 'rapprochement', after which they'd each go their separate ways." The man likens the complainant to a hypersensitive little boy, outwardly tough, who was frightened by a "large spider" when young and has carried irrational fears and aversions ever since.

According to this supporter, the complainant never wanted to damage Pell's career, but, rather, he was acting out of a sense of personal injustice and out of a sense that Pell was too hard on people over issues like premarital sex, abortion, and homosexuality: "He simply wanted to make the point that Pell isn't above everybody else—remember George that thou art but a man, a human being flawed like other men." According to this friend, and other associates as well, the complainant said he first noticed George Pell on television in the late 1990s and recognized him from the long-ago camp.

In the *Age* newspaper on Saturday, August 24, Martin Daly also reported that the complainant had not been after publicity, quoting him as saying: "I did not think it would even make the Melbourne papers. That [publicity] was not what I wanted. George Pell made it public, not me." But Pell had little option after the Internet posting and believed that going public was the only thing to do.

Daly reported that the man "feels vilified by the Catholic Church and its sources who allegedly revealed to the media his criminal history". He also quoted a friend of the alleged victim, who asked not to be named. "He [the alleged victim] is very angry. Our intention was for reconciliation and healing for both parties", he said. "But what has happened is as far away from that as you could possibly imagine. We are in shock. He does not deserve to feel this bad a second time around. It is not what we expected. This all flies in the face of the spirit of Towards Healing. This is Goliath talking down to David."

"The alleged victim took the first step on 2 May 2000, in the process that this week forced George Pell to stand aside", Daly reported.

> Broken Rites, the Melbourne-based organisation for victims of church abuse, said he had telephoned them. He alleged he had been abused at a Phillip Island camp for altar boys by George Pell, who was a student priest at the time. Bernard Barrett, of Broken Rites, said: "He gave his first name. But we did not press him. We told him to call us back when he wanted." The alleged victim called again on 8 June this year and repeated his claims. He rang back a few days later, saying that, on the advice of his parish priest, he had contacted Angela Ryan, the Melbourne-based executive director of the NCPS, which supervises the church's Towards Healing process. Sister Ryan interviewed the man in June and sent him a copy of his statement, which he returned with corrections to parts that were not in sequence. Sister Ryan, the Sydney-based chairman of the NCPS, Geoffrey Robinson, and Broken Rites, all advised the man to contact police. "But I estimate 90 percent of them [complainants] still go through the church process, rather than the police," Mr Barrett said.

Daly said that the complainant wrote to Bishop Robinson on July 17, expressing concern about the lack of progress in his case and threatening to take his case to the media unless something was done. On July 20, Daly said, Bishop Robinson wrote to the man offering a process of inquiry.

"He also promised that if the complaint was proven, the accused person would be confronted with the findings, 'and the difficulties of his situation would be pointed out to him as forcefully as possible' ", Daly wrote. "The man agreed to the inquiry offered by the bishop."

The *Age* report claimed that the complainant did not want publicity but wanted the matter dealt with by the Church. As Daly reported, the allegations were leaked to an Adelaide website, the *Age* submitted a series of questions to Pell on the night of Monday, August 20, and on Tuesday Pell stood down.

Pell's announcement came shortly after Archbishop Wilson of Adelaide, the acting co-chair of the NCPS, announced publicly that there would be an inquiry.

The breaking of the story triggered an avalanche of well over a thousand letters, cards, emails, and telephone good wishes for Pell, which poured in for weeks from around the world, including a personal message of support from Pope John Paul II sent via a senior Vatican cardinal. Sydney's senior auxiliary bishop, David Cremin, was appointed to oversee the archdiocese during Pell's leave. For several weeks, Cremin was the only bishop functioning in an archdiocese that has long had an archbishop and three auxiliaries. Apart from Pell's leave, Bishop Robinson was ill and took holidays, and the third vacancy had not been filled.

Not surprisingly, those who suffered the most anger and grief about the allegations were Pell's family. At the height of despair one day, one close relative admitted: "Coping with a death would be easier." The weekend after his announcement, Pell headed off to his beach-side unit with his sister, Margaret, and their cousin from Melbourne, for four days. He walked on the beach but rarely went out otherwise, and he said Mass every day. Back in Sydney, one of his close friends spotted him walking around the cathedral presbytery grounds early one morning praying the rosary with an intensity not seen before. When Pell ventured outside the grounds for walks, people in the street were invariably friendly and wished him well.

Among dozens of letters to the editor published at the time was one in the *Australian* newspaper by Brian Haill, President of the Australian AIDS Fund, Inc., who told of Pell's kindness to AIDS patients.

Haill wrote:

> Those of us who are able to, have an obligation to bring other matters into the light that might have gone unreported and that throw into relief goodness and character that might otherwise be denied in a general rush to judgment. To some, any demonstrated gesture of concern for gay people is itself an indictment, especially by a churchman. Archbishop Pell took up some rare opportunities, as the Catholic Archbishop of Melbourne, to step into this shadowy world even while his harshest critics damned him as being unsympathetic to the plight of homosexuals. The Archbishop quietly visited many of the men and women with HIV/AIDS that my organisation cared for across the years in our supported accommodation facilities of San Michel and Rosehaven in Melbourne. He brought gifts and laughter and offered himself openly to intense questioning at each of these meetings.
>
> The metropolitan media never knew of this side of him, but these meetings revealed a deeply compassionate side to a really caring pastor. For those reaching to throw stones, take care—this is a good man. Justice too must be served. But let there not be a rush to judgment beforehand.

From the time of his announcement, George Pell made himself incommunicado to journalists, which, among other things, brought an abrupt end to interviews for this biography. Pell's anonymous accuser also kept his head down. His Melbourne solicitor, Peter Ward, said the man was very distrustful of strangers and would not be interviewed by someone he did not know. Nor would he answer questions put to him in writing, Ward said.

The crisis caused Pell to cancel three important speaking engagements—one to a think tank in the United States, one at a conference on the family in New Zealand, and the other a lecture in Rome to 120 new bishops, where he had been scheduled to join other leading Church figures, including Cardinal Christoph Schönborn, Archbishop of Vienna, Cardinal Joseph Ratzinger, Cardinal Alfonso López Trujillo, president of the Pontifical Council for the Family, and Cardinal Walter Kasper, president of the Pontifical Council for Promoting Christian Unity, in offering pointers to the newcomers.

In Australia, Pell's leadership was sorely missed by Catholics. The week he stood aside, debate in the House of Representatives indicated that the government's legislation permitting embryonic stem cell research on unwanted, frozen embryos was likely to pass easily on a conscience vote. That same week, also in Canberra, the ACT Legislative Assembly voted by a majority of one to become the first Australian state or territory to remove abortion from the criminal code. When news broke in Western Australia some time later that professional tests had been unable to find a rational, scientific explanation for the apparent weeping of rose-scented tears by a Madonna statue, thousands of worshippers converged on a suburban church—many out of curiosity, many with a sense that the tears were a message from above, reflecting current events in Australia.

In the *Age* newspaper Bishop Power seized upon the crisis to push his own agenda for change in the Church. In an article published on August 29, he argued:

> On several occasions since 1996, I have spoken about my hopes for the future of the church. It would be a more human, humbler, less clerical, more open church, a more inclusive (and therefore more Catholic) church, a church that finds unity within diversity, that embraces the whole of its tradition and truly reflects the person and teaching of Jesus. . . . A church that has been overly triumphal, hierarchical and dominated from the top, has been brought to its knees. Yet it is from such a lowly position that Catholicism can again become a truly servant church, modelling the person of its founder.

Power then argued that

> an examination of compulsory celibacy is one element of the reform needed in the light of present abuse problems. More important is consideration of the issue in view of the diminishing numbers of priests and those offering themselves for the priesthood. Many good potential candidates for the priesthood are deterred by the fact that they must also accept celibacy as part of a "package deal". There are, too, many good men who have left active ministry, married and are now debarred from exercising a priestly ministry. All this is happening at a time when more and more is being demanded of remaining priests in terms of providing pastoral care and a sacramental ministry to their people.

His advocacy of a rethink of Church teaching on homosexuality underlined just how far apart he and those who agree with him are from those who support Pell's views:

> A few years ago when I was approached in Canberra by a group of Rainbow Sash people, I did not give them Holy

Communion, but I did accede to their request for greater understanding, dialogue and readiness to question the church's approach to homosexuality. I said honestly that I believed it necessary for the church to revisit its teaching not just on homosexuality but on sexuality in general. Clearly, that is even more important today and it is imperative that any reformulation of its teaching must call upon the wisdom and experience of all the faithful, not just be handed down from 'on high'. Such teaching must also emphasise the relational aspect of sex and the harmony between sexuality and spirituality.

An opportunist taking advantage of Pell's temporary indisposition or a reformist visionary? The reactions of Catholics to Power's pronouncements differed sharply, reflecting the long-running, deep divisions within the Church. While some hailed him as the voice of the future, others, including senior Catholic figures overseas, were livid, and the outburst undoubtedly prompted letters to Vatican authorities. While many Catholics in dioceses increasingly short of priests believed that Power was talking sense, others pointed out that it is the more traditional, stricter seminaries, like Melbourne, Sydney, and many in the United States, that are flourishing and that those with liberal agendas are emptying out or even closing. Also, countries like Holland that had experimented with the kind of lay-led Church many of Power's supporters wanted had found Catholicism melting into irrelevance.

While Pell stayed out of sight, many of his friends and foes were only too willing to be interviewed, although only a few would speak on the record. One or two of the complainant's friends and associates were also cooperative. Some of the claims made by people on both sides were impossible to check, although they were indicative of the passionate feelings the issue provoked. One usually reliable source even claimed that embittered families of victims of a convicted Melbourne pedophile priest had put a private investigator on Pell's tail for a time hoping to discover something that could be used against him. Little of interest was uncovered, the source said, and the information, such as it was, was passed to an organization opposed to the Church.

Several people sympathetic to the complainant and who also appeared to be fully informed about details of the case made it clear that they disliked Pell and traditional Catholic teachings on sexuality. They said that had Pell been a Uniting Church minister, a Jewish rabbi, or anybody else but an outspoken Catholic archbishop, the matter would never have arisen. Why not? Was this some kind of New-Age sectarianism taking hold? Did this mean that the complaint was partially motivated by some kind of ideological conflict with Pell? No, but exposing what the complainant and his supporters regarded as "hypocrisy" was a factor, one of his friends closely associated with the Church claimed. This man, who said he believed the complainant "97 percent", also said he believed the incident had been a one-off "flash in the pan" and that Pell did not deserve to lose his career but should "tone down the holier-than-thou rhetoric". This man was being either naïve or disingenuous in the extreme. In the current climate of concern around the world over clerical sex abuse, it is utterly fanciful to suggest that any bishop convicted of such an offense could hold his position. Another man closely associated with a sex-abuse victims' support group said Pell had set himself up "to be taken down a peg" by speaking loud and long about "no sex before marriage" and making "other statements that don't gel or that are out of kilter with people".

All the members of victim-support groups interviewed stressed that the complainant deserved to have his story heard. So why did he not come forward earlier? Why did he not pursue his right to have his day in court, report the matter to police, and work through the legal system? It is impossible to ask him, but one woman with years of experience assisting sex-abuse victims said she believed he was "hedging his bets" by pursuing several avenues—he was in contact with Broken Rites and his parish priest and had kept the *Age* newspaper in the background as well.

Not surprisingly, several of Pell's friends, including people with children, leapt to his defense, insisting that "he just wouldn't have it in him" to abuse—or even hurt—a child. Parents who know him well say he has encouraged their children to excel and to practice the faith and that he has played sport with children, listened to them, read to them, taught them, recommended books for them, and helped them all of his adult life without even a suggestion of scandal. "I've watched him with my child; he's open, warm, and really loves children, and they love him, they respond to his goodness", one mother said. Another friend thought it ridiculous even to suggest that Pell had gay tendencies as it was well-known among his circle that had he not been a priest he would have liked to have married and to have had children, whom he loves. In one of the first interviews for this biography, late in 2001, Pell said that he favored the retention of mandatory celibacy for clergy. He also said that he had found the hardest part of keeping that vow had not been living without sex but "living without the love and close companionship of a wife and children".

Hard-headed supporters of Pell, both in Australia and overseas, especially in America, do not underestimate the ferocity of the hatred some of his opponents hold for him and bishops like him. Such people fear that after the allegations by this complainant are settled, others could materialize on the Internet or elsewhere as part of a calculated process to render his position untenable and intimidate less brave Church leaders into compromising, or remaining silent, on the harder aspects of Church teaching.

So has Australia really become so secular, so insular that Church leaders whose views contradict the prevailing social mores cannot go about their work without derision, harassment, or worse? The loud "boos" at the Ernie awards for Pell's anti-abortion statements must give people who care deeply about such matters pause for thought about what has, by degrees of encroaching secular humanism, become socially acceptable and what is not. Certainly, as social trends stand at present, the Church faces a long, uphill battle for her ideas on marriage, family, and society to gain widespread credence, especially while the Church struggles to put her own badly shaken house in order. In September, Archbishop Jozef Zycinski, fifty-four, of Lublin, Poland, an archdiocese with 190 seminarians, visited Australia. Zycinski praised Prime Minister Howard for supporting Pell, but he rather startlingly compared modern-day Australia's attitude to the Church to that of the Communists who formerly ran Poland.

"Under the communist system we used to repeat the joke that to become innocent, one has to prove that one is innocent. Because the basic principle was that everyone is guilty", he said. "But I am afraid that in a free, civil Australian society, what was a joke in Poland is a reality here."[3]

At the first interview for this biography, on November 10, 2001—federal election day—I asked Pell why some people saw him as such a divisive figure: "I think one of the functions of a bishop is to try and ensure that the fullness of the

---

[3] James Murray, *Australian*, September 24, 2002.

Catholic faith is taught. It has been a temptation for twenty or more years to try to improve the situation of the Church by going silent on some aspects or underplaying other challenges." The Church, he said that day, was not a sociological institution, "or a shop selling a variety of merchandise, and if some brands aren't selling we just cancel that brand. I believe that we're basically about something that is supernatural, revelations from the Son of God. Some of his teachings were hard and provocative, but they have been proved to bring life in the long run even in human terms, and we don't have any warrant or authority to change them."

One of the prices to be paid for leadership, he recognized in a slightly later interview, on the eve of his thirty-fifth anniversary of ordination, was "opposition from people who conscientiously feared that you were mistaken in what you stand for." People were more prepared to ride with that sort of thing, he said,

> if they suspect that you're a complete dope or you're harming your own cause or you're quite ineffective. It can become a bit more irritating if in fact they fear that you're making progress. Now the other thing is, and I will be careful how I say this because not everybody who opposes me by any means falls into this category, but I do feel that if you're going to bat for what is good and for the faith, you might be opposed by what euphemistically might be described as evil. I think that once in a while there has been a dimension of that in the opposition team.

In the lead-up to the inquiry into the allegations by the anonymous former painter and docker, the dean of Saint Patrick's Cathedral, Melbourne, Father Gerard Dowling, reminded radio listeners on September 8, 2002, and *Kairos* readers in print that one of the hardest aspects of Jesus' final hours was the false accusations directed at him. He was sentenced to death on trumped-up charges, with false statements sworn against him. Those who heard or read the rector's words drew comfort from them as they prayed and waited in the expectation that Pell would be cleared. Father Dowling said:

> As a priest in today's society, I am only too well aware that I could be falsely accused. The same can be said of my brother priests and quite obviously of one of those who bears the added responsibility of being a bishop in this critical climate. To make this claim is not to put any of us above reproach, nor beyond the requirements of justice, if we have failed. Nevertheless, it does put the spotlight on the inherent vulnerability of anyone who is game enough to take up Jesus' cross and follow him, be that as a lay person, a religious, deacon, priest or bishop. . . . The age of the martyrs is not dead.

As Pell prepared to face the Southwell inquiry, his supporters in Australia and around the world prayed that the episode would be put quickly behind him and that he would resume his duties with the same fearless vigor as before. The Sydney archdiocesan website invited all people "to pray for the Archbishop and his accuser, that the truth will prevail and that justice be done". At sixty-one, he was just beginning what should be his most productive decade in the Church, the decade when senior clerics generally make their strongest marks. Like anyone on the wrong side of middle age, Pell occasionally thinks about death and dying, but it does not bother him. When it happens, he says, he would want his friends and flock to thank God for his life as well as pray for his soul, that he be loosed from his sins in purgatory and enter heaven.

~

Pell's birth date, June 8, 1941, was Trinity Sunday. June 8 in the Catholic calendar is also the feast of Saint Medard, a late fifth/sixth-century French bishop whose story bears a passing resemblance to Pell's. From all accounts Medard was a pious youth and an excellent scholar, and after he became a priest he encouraged young people of that time to study and take an interest in spiritual matters. He is also the patron saint for, among other things, toothaches and brewers. George Pell, a publican's son who missed a lot of school when very young due to a growth under his chin, possibly caused by the filling of a baby tooth, also showed early signs of being a good scholar as well as a sportsman. While he had no interest in being a priest until his final year at school, one of his former teachers remembers he was prayerful and involved in sodalities (prayer groups) at school.

The career that followed has been by any standard extraordinary. By the time Pell was aware of his calling to the priesthood, his reputation as a leader was well established. He was school captain, had played in the 1st XVIII for four years, was active in cadets and a leading debater. At Corpus Christi Seminary, those leadership qualities impressed the Jesuit fathers sufficiently for them to place him in charge of the first-year students as prefect when he was just three years older. As Pell was to find again and again in life, leadership had its prices. In Rome at the time of the Second Vatican Council, when he and his fellow students put together a magazine that captured the spirit of those tumultuous times, the universal Church broadened his horizons. For four years, Pell was in his element in Oxford—studying the early Church Fathers in depth, working as a priest in local churches and at the university chaplaincy, and making new, lifelong friends.

A country curacy in Swan Hill, an initial shock to the

system, was, in hindsight "the best thing that ever happened to me", he concedes. Of his many roles in the Church since then, his eleven years as director of Aquinas College, Ballarat, somehow seem closest to his heart—it was a job he says he would have been happy to stay in indefinitely. His next position, rector of Corpus Christi Seminary, was undoubtedly one of the toughest jobs in the Church at that time. So was sorting out Caritas, as an auxiliary bishop, at a time it was under scrutiny after allegations of some donations finding their way to Communist causes in the Philippines.

In 1996, promotion to the job of Archbishop of Melbourne brought prestige, power, overwhelming responsibility, and the difficult task of tackling the mounting problem of clerical sex abuse. Pope John Paul II's view of how Pell performed in Melbourne was shown when he promoted him to Sydney after five years.

After a productive first year in Australia's senior archdiocese, a year in which his status in the universal Church grew through his chairmanship in Rome of the Vox Clara Committee and the synod of bishops steering committee, Pell hit a type of adversity no senior cleric before him in Australia has had to face.

Those who know him well and who admire his handling of a succession of difficult jobs in the Church have no doubt that he has the strength of character and purpose to come through the ordeal stronger than before for having endured it. Not a man to wear his heart on his sleeve or give in to excessive displays of emotion, it will undoubtedly shake him, however, more than anyone, even those closest to him, will ever see.

Despite his formidable intellect and extraordinary wide reading, those who know Pell well say that he is remarkably free of guile and is inclined to think the best of individuals, giving them the benefit of the doubt, even when they are diametrically opposed to him. "What you see is what you get with George, and he expects others to be the same", several people commented to me during the writing of this book.

As Pell so often acknowledges, Christ and His teachings are at the heart of all of his work—not just Christ the prophet, the martyr, the perfect Man, but Christ as God, the Divine Redeemer and Savior. In addressing the most pressing problems of contemporary society Pell challenges his fellow Australians, among the most secular people in the world, to look for a solid foundation in religious and moral belief to give their lives the meaning they seek so desperately. Or, as one of Pell's favorite saints—Augustine—wrote sixteen hundred years ago: "Thou hast made us for Thyself, O Lord, and our hearts will never rest until they rest in Thee."

A few of the archbishops who came before Pell, like Brisbane's James Duhig and Melbourne's Daniel Mannix, were Australian Church giants whose biographies are long, absorbing tomes. Pell, the Ballarat boy who was a reluctant starter for the priesthood, is the first man for decades with the vision, substance, and energy to fill their shoes. His story has a long, long, way to go, and the next few chapters of his life, whether set in Sydney, or elsewhere, are likely to be just as significant for Catholicism as the story so far.

Chapter 18

Cleared

George Pell and the former painter and docker who accused him of sexual abuse that had allegedly taken place more than forty years before had one direct exchange during the inquiry into the allegation. The two came face to face outside the first-floor boardroom of the Rydges Hotel in Exhibition Street, Melbourne. "Day of reckoning, George", those nearby heard the complainant say. Pell looked his accuser directly in the eye. "Yes, it is", he replied. The day of reckoning was Monday, October 14, 2002, the feast day of the Roman martyr Saint Callistus, when former Victorian Supreme Court Judge Alec Southwell, Q.C., released his report dismissing the complaint. He went as far as the terms of reference allowed him to go in exonerating Pell.

"In the end, and notwithstanding that impression of the complainant [that he was speaking honestly], bearing in mind the forensic difficulties of the defence occasioned by the very long delay, some valid criticism of the complainant's credibility, the lack of corroborative evidence and the sworn denial of the respondent, I find I am not satisfied that the 'complaint has been established', to quote the words of the principal term of reference", Southwell reported. He described the investigation, which heard evidence for five days, from September 30 to October 4, as similar to "a royal commission or statutory board of inquiry".

Southwell said: "I accept as correct . . . that the complainant, when giving evidence of molesting, gave the impression that he was speaking honestly from an actual recollection. However, the respondent [Pell] also gave me the impression that he was speaking the truth."

The report was released two days after the bombings of two Bali nightclubs, which killed almost two hundred people and maimed many others—including many Australians. Pell said the lunchtime Mass that Monday in Saint Mary's Cathedral for victims of the Bali attack. His appearance at the altar, dressed in green vestments, was the first many of the congregation knew of his exoneration.

Soon afterward, he released a statement:

I am grateful to God that this ordeal is over and that the enquiry has exonerated me of all allegations. The Honourable A. J. Southwell, Q.C., was appointed to determine, under specific Terms of Reference, whether or not the complaint was established. In his findings released today the Commissioner has gone as far as the Terms of Reference allowed him to go in exonerating me.

When a person is under extreme pressure, personal values may crumble. However my Catholic convictions sustained me during those dark weeks. I found a great strength in regular prayer and in reflecting on the great Christian teachings about suffering, death and resurrection. My confidence that God loves us all without exception, and that He asks of us justice, truth and a compassion which bears no one ill will, was never shaken. In addition, I was immensely consoled by the love, support and loyalty of family and friends.

As you are well aware I submitted myself to the rigorous scrutiny of this five-day enquiry, which produced 561 pages of transcript. It heard from fifteen witnesses and considered statements from another seventeen witnesses. I have faxed to Archbishop Philip Wilson, co-chair with Brother Michael Hill of the Towards Healing process and co-appointer of the enquiry, my consent to the public release of the full transcript of the enquiry and all the exhibits.

I am deeply grateful to all those who supported me in many different ways: my family and friends, my defence team, the Catholic community, lay people, bishops, priests and religious, and Christians of all other denominations, people of other religions, people of no religion and, in a particular way, people who explained to me that, although they differed from me in matters of religion, morality or social life, they wished to offer me their support.

I have just celebrated Mass for all those caught up in the tragedy of Bali, and look forward to being in the office tomorrow, resuming my work of spreading the Catholic faith and celebrating Mass on Sundays, as usual, at Saint Mary's Cathedral.

But would any of the mud stick, one of the journalists asked at his press conference afterward. "There's no mud to stick", Pell said, "I've been exonerated." He had no criticism of the inquiry but was disappointed there were "a lot of leaks". "I had nothing to do with them", he said. "I don't know who did." The complainant's solicitor, Peter Ward of Galbally and O'Bryan in Melbourne, said his client also had no complaints. "He reckons he got a fair hearing", Ward said. "We are delighted with the hearing. We have been vindicated." Ward accepted that Southwell had found in the Archbishop's favor, but pointed to the paragraph where the judge said the complainant gave the impression that he was speaking honestly. However, Pell said: "What is important is that the judge did not find that the accounts the complainant gave were truthful and substantially accurate. He did not accept that."

Pell said he bore his accuser no ill will and said that "after a little interval of time" he had been able to pray for him and continued to do so. He said he would be happy to meet the complainant if the man so wished. "I think I'd say, well, this is a great mystery to me. These things didn't happen. How it's developed like this, I just don't know." Pell said it was "a bit of a mystery" whether the complainant's accusations were "the product of a delusion or a violation by somebody else or lies or a combination of all three". Asked if he was considering legal action for defamation, Pell said: "Well, I've never sued anybody. Bishops don't normally sue. I'm aware in the United States that, as people falsely accused, some of their ministers of religion have sued for defamation. I wouldn't rule it out forever and a day as a general principle, but it's not part of my thinking at the moment." Asked should there be changes to a situation where people could make anonymous allegations against public figures and remain anonymous when the charges were not substantiated, Pell said: "I think that's one of the factors we should be looking at." Rejecting suggestions that the inquiry was not transparent, Pell pointed out that he did not set it up and that it was closed in order to protect the complainant's anonymity. Had the complainant gone to the police, he said, and "in the unlikely event that it had got to court", proceedings would have been open. So intent was the complainant on preserving that anonymity that he swung a punch at a Melbourne *Herald Sun* photographer who tried to photograph him.

Pell criticized the conveners of the Church's Towards Healing process, noting it was "remarkable" that it took two months from the time the complaint was lodged with them until he was informed of it. "I think I would've anticipated that I would've been informed earlier than that. That'll be one of a number of things that I'll be discussing with those who are in charge of Towards Healing." Asked if the delay had harmed his case, he replied: "It certainly didn't help it." In an extraordinary twist, one of the main targets of that criticism is a man who should be one of the archbishop's closest associates, Sydney's Auxiliary Bishop Geoffrey Robinson, the Sydney-based chairman of the Church's National Committee for Professional Standards (NCPS). Feeling among many Catholics, including priests, is running strongly against Robinson and Sister Angela Ryan of the NCPS Melbourne office, who first took down details from the complainant on June 11, 2002. The Archbishop knew nothing of the matter until August 8, when he was told by his lawyer, Richard Leder, that defamatory claims had been posted anonymously on a website. However, Ryan did keep Robinson in the loop, and the bishop dealt extensively with the complainant for most of two months.

Robinson had been on holiday recovering from health problems. One Sydney priest quipped: "He needed some warmer weather after having pneumonia—but the heat in Sydney was getting too hot for him." In the days following October 14, Robinson did not return calls from journalists about the matter, and Ryan said it was not appropriate for her to comment.

Sydney traditionally has three auxiliary bishops. For more than a year, the archdiocese had had only two—Robinson and Bishop David Cremin, then seventy-two, who ran the archdiocese single-handedly in Pell's absence. Appointing a third auxiliary was undoubtedly high on Pell's "to do" list.

As for the complainant, what he stood to lose after the verdict was . . . nothing at all. His good name was unaffected, and his legal team, unlike the Archbishop's, acted for nothing after the Church made it clear she was not paying the legal fees for either party. In contrast, Pell had everything to lose—his reputation, his position as head of Australia's most senior Catholic archdiocese, and a probable cardinal's hat in the future. Australia's Catholics stood to lose their strongest leader in fifty years. As Southwell noted: "Although this is not a criminal proceeding requiring proof beyond reasonable doubt, I must bear in mind that serious allegations are involved and that an adverse finding would in all probability have grave, indeed devastating, consequences for the respondent." Southwell said that early in the hearing it became apparent there was considerable doubt whether the alleged molestation took place at a camp in 1961 or 1962. While the complainant's recollection was that he attended only one camp, "between schools" in 1961, church records show he definitely attended the 1962 camp. To ensure that the merits of the complaint could be properly investigated, Southwell had the terms of reference amended so the matter related to "1961 or 1962". As to motive, Southwell said extensive inquiries made on behalf of Pell had unearthed "no evidence of any other matter or incident which might have aroused spite or malice on the part of the complainant towards either the respondent or the church".

Ward said it was clear that the complainant had been vindicated against suggestions he was acting out of some vindictive motive. "The fifteen-page report is a well-compiled, well-weighted document", Ward said. Southwell said the complainant's credibility was subjected to a forceful attack during the hearings but that his record was "notable more for alcohol and violence than dishonesty".

However, [Southwell continued], there is sufficient evidence
of dishonesty to demonstrate that the complainant's evidence
must be scrutinised with special care. It would be difficult
to be satisfied about his version against that of the respondent unless some support were to be found in the evidence
of other witnesses, or in circumstantial evidence. . . . The
complainant has been before the court on many occasions,
resulting in 39 convictions from about twenty court appearances. Most of the convictions were for drunk-driving and
assault, between 1969 and 1975, but there were also three
convictions for SP betting; two fines for contempt, a jail sentence in 1995 for three counts of trafficking amphetamines.
The complainant had also evaded taxation.

Ward admitted that the complainant was responsible for
one of the leaks from the inquiry—that of Pell's opening
statement, reported in the *Age* in Melbourne by Martin Daly.
Ward agreed that he had spoken to Daly in the foyer of the
hotel during the inquiry, "but that doesn't mean I was leaking to him; I wasn't".

Ward complained about the leaking of part of a transcript
of the inquiry to Andrew Bolt, leading columnist with another Melbourne newspaper, the *Herald Sun*. That section
of the transcript detailed evidence given to the inquiry by
the complainant about his relationship with the former state
historian of Victoria, Doctor Bernard Barrett, who works
with the lobby group for victims of clerical sex abuse, Broken Rites. According to the published transcript the complainant told the inquiry: "We were in a coffee shop and
he had a really loud voice, Bernard Barrett. And they just
seemed about their own agenda a little bit. He was talking
about victim impact statements and how much money I was
going to get". But the complainant made it clear he was not
after money. In response to this, Barrett told the inquiry

he had only explained the maximum amount the Church might pay.

The complainant also told the inquiry: "I was crook on Barrett because I thought, still think, that Barrett leaked this." Before the inquiry, Barrett hotly denied leaking the matter to a website and repeated that denial after the release of the judge's report. It seems whoever did post the information on the Web and circulated it to various journalists and organizations was intent on inflicting maximum harm on Pell.

At his press conference, Pell said he was looking forward to resuming work and regaining his equilibrium. During his month in exile, Pell said Mass and read the breviary every day as usual and took comfort from doing so, but, not surprisingly, he found meditation difficult. Instead, he worked his way slowly through the Gospel of Saint Matthew. He returned to full duties on Tuesday, October 15, the feast of Saint Teresa of Avila, whose famous quotations include this: "We always find that those who walked closest to Christ were those who had to bear the greatest trials."

In February 2003, Archbishop Pell led a concelebrated Mass in the chapel of the Good Shepherd Seminary for the opening of the seminary year. The Sydney seminary had twenty-one new students in all—seven studying for the Sydney archdiocese, seven for the regional and country dioceses of New South Wales, and another seven belonging to the recently opened Neocatechumenal Way seminary in Sydney, who study alongside the Good Shepherd students and who are destined to work as priests throughout Australia and Oceania. Also present were nine second-year students, plus

a smaller number in the senior years. The size of the first-
year class had not been seen anywhere else in Australia for
at least twenty years.

To George Pell, the promising turnaround in vocations in
Sydney was evidence that "God writes straight in crooked
lines." After all, it came about immediately after the worst
year for publicity the Church had ever seen.

Unlike a few of his colleagues in the Australian episcopal
conference, who appear to want to create a lay-led Church,
Pell acknowledges that the need for more priests is "probably the single greatest need of the Church in the next twenty-
five years." On that score, he is optimistic:

> Vocations have always been somewhat scarce. The priest-
> hood is a great life and not a refuge for those who cannot
> make it in the wider world. It holds many consolations, at-
> tracts great support from many people, and provides many
> opportunities for service and leadership in faith.
>
> We know the Holy Spirit will continue to flow where He
> wills, but one constant in all Catholic history is the need for
> priests, for vocations to the ministerial priesthood. Our Lord
> himself appointed the Twelve, called forth the shepherds, the
> fishers of men. Saint Paul underlined the importance of am-
> bassadors for Christ. Without priests our parishes will wither
> and die. The call of Christ to young men to be priests is a
> call to a great adventure.

Later in 2003, Doctor Pell appointed two new auxiliary
bishops who share his understanding of the importance of
nurturing vocations to the priesthood. One was Bishop Julian Porteous, rector of the Good Shepherd Seminary—one
of the more successful men in such a position in Australia for
decades. The other new bishop was Doctor Anthony Fisher,
O.P., the director and a former professor of bioethics and

moral theology at the John Paul II Institute for Marriage and Family in Melbourne, which under his leadership was flourishing with 150 students.

After a rough go the preceding year, the archdiocese seemed stronger than ever.

Chapter 19

Raising God's Profile

News of George Pell's promotion to the College of Cardinals broke in Australia on Sunday evening, September 28, 2003, moments after Pope John Paul II read his name and twenty-nine others from his balcony to the crowd gathered in Saint Peter's Square for the Angelus. A thirty-first cardinal was created *in pectore*.

The consistory was set for October 21, which caught many by surprise. With only three months to go in the year and a heavy schedule ahead of the Holy Father, with the beatification of Mother Teresa and his own Silver Jubilee celebrations, many were expecting a February consistory.

The announcement threw Rome's already busy ecclesiastical tailors into a frenzy as orders poured in by telephone and fax from the thirty cardinals from twenty-two countries for the distinctive crimson red robes they would need in time for the big day. "Usually we have at least two months' notice, but this time the Pope caught cardinals and tailors off-guard", said Gabriele Masserotti Benvenuti, one of the partners at Barbiconi, a tailor shop that has been serving the Vatican for more than two hundred years.

George Pell's statement was short and to the point:

It is a signal honour to be appointed a Cardinal of the Catholic Church. The ancient College of Cardinals reflects the

400

unity and universality of the Catholic Church, both wonderful blessings.

As Archbishop of Sydney, my appointment also recognises
the contribution of the Catholic community to Australian
life. I will continue working to maintain and deepen this
tradition of service.

Like Pell, most of the new cardinals were serving as archbishops of major episcopal sees; they came from all corners of the Church: the United States (Justin Rigali of
Philadelphia), Canada (Marc Ouellet, P.S.S., of Quebec),
Italy, Scotland, Mexico, India, Brazil, Guatemala, Spain,
Nigeria, France, Sudan, Ghana, Croatia, Vietnam, and Hungary. Four of the new cardinals were priests rather than bishops—from Switzerland, Belgium, Poland, and the Czech
Republic—whom the Pope honored for outstanding service. As George Pell said: 'I'm sure that my story today is
repeated amongst the overwhelming majority of the thirty-
one new cardinals. That is, local boys, people who worked
as priests and bishops from right around the world and who
are now called to this office.'

Some of the group were colorful characters. Cardinal
Tomas Spidlik, S.J., for instance, was born in the Czech
Republic in 1919, a year before Pope John Paul II, and like
the Holy Father endured forced labor under the Nazis. He
was ordained in 1949 and later taught Czech and Russian
at a secondary school and lectured in Rome. For more than
half a century from 1951, he worked with Vatican Radio,
preparing the homilies in Czech—an invaluable service for
Czech Catholics who suffered for decades under Communism. He has also led retreats for the Holy Father and the
Curia.

On the weekend his appointment as a cardinal was announced, George Pell's office desk in the cathedral presbytery was weighed down with even more books and

scholarly journals than usual as he wrote out by hand a major paper he would give the following Saturday to the symposium on "Catholic Moral Teaching in the Pontificate of John Paul II" at Philadelphia's Saint Charles Borromeo Seminary. Like most skilled writers, Pell focuses best with a looming deadline and often settles down to write in the evening after a long working day. Largely overlooked in the excitement of his promotion to cardinal, the Philadelphia paper is one of his best pieces of writing, drawing upon the wisdom he has gained in his many battles for the Church.

Pell began the speech with Pope John Paul II's observation in his 1993 encyclical *Veritatis Splendor* (The splendor of truth) that the Church was facing a genuine crisis touching the very foundations of moral theology. "He explained that this crisis was no longer a matter of limited and occasional dissent but of an overall and systematic calling into question of traditional moral doctrine", Pell told the Symposium. "In this year in which we celebrate the twenty-fifth anniversary of the election of the Holy Father and the tenth anniversary of *Veritatis Splendor* it is a moot point whether the crisis has lessened or deepened, or indeed whether the situation remains basically as it was. Rome has spoken, but in the English-speaking world there is no evidence that the matter has been successfully concluded."

Indeed, traditional moral doctrine is under widespread attack in ways that were unimaginable to most people when Pope John Paul II was elected as the Vicar of Christ a quarter of a century ago. While "gay rights", de facto relationships, abortion, and high divorce rates were already important parts of the social landscape in 1978, the head-long rush toward legally binding "gay marriages", the impact of ever more sophisticated reproductive technology, as well as the practice of partial-birth abortion were still a long time in the future. Other realities of twenty-first-century life, such as the inexorable push toward human cloning and genetic engineering, were unimagined by most.

Much of Pell's Philadelphia speech centered on two topics central to these issues—the role of conscience and the Christian understanding of human rights. "I believe in both conscience and human rights, but I believe the doctrine of the primacy of conscience is incompatible not only with the Christian concept of human rights, but with any concept of human rights", he said.

The speech represented a major development and clarification of issues that had clearly been on Pell's mind for several years. While archbishop of Melbourne in 1999, Pell had caused a stir in the Australian media among some liberal Catholic commentators when he addressed a secular Sydney think tank, the Centre for Independent Studies, and argued that the so-called primacy of conscience doctrine within the Catholic Church be "quietly ditched".

In May 2003, addressing Catalyst for Renewal, a group that promotes discussion and conversation about various aspects of theology and Church life, Pell revisited the issue: "In the past I have been in trouble for stating that the so-called doctrine of the primacy of conscience should be quietly dropped. I would like to reconsider my position here and now state that I believe that this misleading doctrine of the primacy of conscience should be publicly rejected." Citing chapter 3 of the first letter of Saint John, which spells out the link between conscience and the commandments, Pell said that "Christians have no entitlement to define sins out of existence, to deny or ignore fundamental teachings of faith, by claiming that their consciences [which can sometimes be mistaken through their own fault] are free."

In Philadelphia he spelled out more fully why the issue is so critical both to the Church and to the future of humanity. The world had changed, he pointed out, since 1968, when

Humanae Vitae first sparked dissent. In 1968 the arguments for individual judgment or private conscience centered on a then-new means of contraception. "Today what remains in dispute are the grounds for moral argumentation itself within the Catholic and indeed Christian tradition, and the controverted areas now include every area of sexual practice, and many issues which touch human life."

The current debates on marriage and family life are unlike anything seen in the past, he said. At no period in Church history had such a range of moral teachings been rejected while at the same time the rejecters continued to insist on remaining within the Church, aspiring to change Church teaching. And never had so many been able to do this without effective retribution. "To my knowledge no bishop has taken up the recommendation of the Holy Father in *Veritatis Splendor* to take away the title 'Catholic' from Catholic institutions which are deviating significantly from sound moral doctrine."

In 1968, Pell said, many in the Church were optimistic that the progressive reforms of the Second Vatican Council would soon bring wonderful fruits and that dialogue with the world would be one of the means for this. *Humanae Vitae*, however, corrected this inflated optimism. The collapse of the Church, for example, in Holland and French-speaking Canada then lay in the future, as did the exodus of many priests and religious and the radical decline in vocations to the priesthood and religious life in many parts of the Church. "Today we are much better aware of the consequences of the acid rain of modernity on our Catholic communities, of our minority status as serious Christians everywhere in the English-speaking world, and of the damaging power of the neo-pagan world of communications."

As Pell observed, Pope John Paul II had proven himself

an immensely more powerful counterpoint to the prevailing secular and pagan influences than Pope Paul VI had in the 1960s and 1970s. Fated to lead the Church at an intensely difficult time, Paul VI will not rank with Leo the Great or Gregory the Great, Pell said, but John Paul II will, and one major reason for this will be his moral teaching, especially his encyclicals *Veritatis Splendor* and *Evangelium Vitae* (The gospel of life, 1995). Sections 54–64 of *Veritatis Splendor*, Pell said, "are the best short piece written on conscience since Cardinal Newman's *Letter to the Duke of Norfolk* in 1875. It is a sophisticated and accessible piece of work, quoting section 16 of the Second Vatican Council's pastoral constitution *Gaudium et Spes* (The Church in the modern world) about the voice of conscience always summoning us to love good and avoid evil."

The so-called "doctrine of the primacy of conscience", Pell argued, was being used increasingly in Catholic circles "to justify what we would like to do rather than to discover what God wants us to do". The word of God—truth—has primacy, and a person should use his conscience to discern the truth.

"Individual conscience cannot confer the right to reject or distort New Testament morality as affirmed or developed by the Church", he said. Even Kant, Pell contended, would be appalled by contemporary liberalism, given his acceptance of objective morality. Advocates of the primacy of conscience, he said, often quote Saint Thomas Aquinas, who wrote that a man admonished by his conscience, even when it is erroneous, must follow it. "The supporters of primacy of conscience do not go on to explain, as Aquinas does and John Paul II has done over a life-time of writing, that the binding force of conscience, even mistaken conscience, comes from the person's belief that the conscientious decision is in accord with the law of God," Pell said. "I also believe that a person following Aquinas' advice might not only err in an objective sense, but could be guilty for his mistaken views."

Pell's point about Aquinas was especially close to home, in light of comments made early in 2002 by a priest of his Sydney archdiocese, Father Michael Whelan, the head of Sydney's adult education center, the Aquinas Academy, and executive director of Catalyst for Renewal, the group Pell had addressed just a few months earlier in Sydney. In a highly critical review of this biography published in *The Tablet* in London, Father Whelan remarked of Pell: "In view of the archbishop's distinguished association with Australia's Aquinas College, it might have been useful to explore the tensions between Aquinas's views on conscience and his own."

In Philadelphia, Pell also laid bare the erroneous notion that primacy of conscience advocates have Cardinal John Henry Newman on their side. The passage often cited to support this argument is Newman's famous declaration at the end of his *Letter to the Duke of Norfolk*: "Certainly, if I am obliged to bring religion into after-dinner toasts (which indeed does not seem quite the thing) I shall drink—to the Pope, if you please—still, to Conscience first, and to the Pope afterwards." In that letter, Pell explained, Newman was concerned about Ultramontane claims of extreme infallibilists and was facetiously explaining that if the Pope told the English bishops to order their priests to work for teetotalism or to hold a lottery in each mission, they would not be obliged to do so. There was no doubt, Pell said, that Newman's understanding of conscience was very specifically Christocentric, within the Catholic tradition:

> Conscience is not a long-sighted selfishness, nor a desire to be consistent with oneself; but it is a messenger from Him,

who, both in nature and in grace, speaks to us behind a veil, and teaches and rules us by His representatives. Conscience is the aboriginal Vicar of Christ, a prophet in its informations, a monarch in its peremptoriness, a priest in its blessings and anathemas, and even though the eternal priesthood throughout the Church should cease to be, in it the sacerdotal principle would remain and would have a sway.

He went further: "I do not even favour the substitution of the primacy of informed conscience, because it is also possible that with good will and conscientious study a devout Catholic could fail to recognise some moral truth and act upon this failure. It is truth, or the word of God, which has primacy, and we have to use our personal capacity to reason practically, that is, exercise our conscience, to try to recognise these particular truths."

Of course discovering truth has been made difficult by the spirit of the age, which denies its existence. As to Pilate's derisive question to our Lord, "What is truth?", Pell noted that Nietzsche regarded it as the only insight of any value in the entire New Testament. And in the modern Western world, which Nietzsche did so much to bring about, Pilate's question is increasingly thrown in the face of the Church, sometimes searchingly, but more often than not with cynicism and condescension. This incident in the Passion reflects our own situation too, where power sits in judgment on truth and finds it worthy only of condemnation. In the current world, Pell said, the arguments against truth take the form of a cascade designed to ensure that it is ruled out of consideration one way or another: there is no such thing as truth; or if there is, we cannot know it with certainty; or if we can, we cannot agree about it. "Our purported inability to know and live the truth places only one demand before us, that we be tolerant of the views of others. But in the absence of any genuine knowledge about what is intrinsically good or right, tolerance becomes merely one value among many, of equal dignity in fact with intolerance."

The denial of God's truth, Pell argued, makes an enduring concept of justice that genuinely serves human life and love impossible. He said:

> The practical meaning of this can be seen in the contradiction the Holy Father identifies between a growing awareness of human rights and a repudiation of the fundamental rights of some of the most vulnerable members of the human family. We are so familiar with talk of the "right" to an abortion that it can be difficult for us to recall what a shocking and absurd debasement of the language of rights this is. And now, as medical science continually pushes back the age at which premature babies can be saved, including babies who have survived abortion, abortion activists are beginning to insist that abortion is not just the "right" to terminate a pregnancy, but the "right" to "the extinction of the foetus".

In the wider world, Pell noted, many areas of sexual conduct and activities such as contraception, abortion, euthanasia, the number of children were "free go" areas of personal choice, where one opinion was held to be as good as another. What few limits public opinion did place this world of easy options was often coterminous with notions of "political correctness".

The Cardinal then switched his attention from society back to the Church's own role in standing up for truth and noted that even in the Catholic world, the category of mortal or death-bearing sin was now "an endangered species because the unthinking presumption is that everyone is honestly doing his or her 'own thing'".

Using terminology long forgotten by most Australian Catholics over fifty years of age and perhaps never before heard by most of those younger than fifty, Pell said the idea of "culpable moral blindness" was now discussed as infrequently as the pains of hell. "Once upon a time it was pastorally useful, sometimes necessary to explain the possibility of invincible ignorance among those who differed from us, because of the temptation to presume bad faith in opponents. Now for many, tolerance is the first and most important Commandment. Now it is necessary and important for us to argue for the possibility of culpable ignorance, indeed the possibility of culpable ignorance that usually has been built up through years of sin and is psychologically invincible, short of a miracle."

The insights Pell provided in Philadelphia were a shock to the system of many Australian Catholics educated in the 1970s and later, who have grown up in a Church that tended to emphasize ecumenism and particular areas of social justice to the exclusion of all else. For most of the past thirty years, many if not most Catholic secondary school students in Australia heard nothing about the binding truths of Catholic moral teaching. At times, the twists on ecumenism and social justice even undermined those truths. For example, social justice classes on anti-discrimination and the need for fair legislation often left the impression that one type of life-style or relationship was as good as another, that Catholics could argue the case for "reproductive rights", including abortion. At worst, abortion was seen as "sad" rather than "wrong". Strong words like "wrong" were reserved for "social sins" like intolerance, and the rare student who did try to argue for a more traditional Catholic understanding was patronized as "narrowminded" or "fundamentalist". In the same way, the intrinsically good practice of ecumenism became confused in many young people's minds with the idea that all the churches were equally good. This was regardless of their stance on moral issues or even more

important questions like the divinity of Christ or transubstantiation, which were rarely discussed in the classroom.

Exacerbating all of this ignorance was the telling, public
silence of most Australian bishops throughout the 1970s and
1980s on moral and other issues, which is why, when Pell
emerged as the auxiliary bishop of Melbourne in the late
1980s and demonstrated a willingness to defend Catholicism, he attracted the attention both of the media and of
Catholics around the country. Several other bishops, no-
tably Archbishop Barry Hickey in Perth and Pell's auxiliary
in Sydney, Doctor Anthony Fisher, have followed the same
path, but most of their colleagues still go about their work
with little or no public profile even within the Catholic media or their own dioceses.

The tendency in Australia has been for those bishops and
priests who do speak out to make the public argument for
Catholic moral claims and social teaching on the basis of reason, without much reference to God. Over the years Pell
has largely relied on this approach himself. Often he has
done so for a very good reason, and one that will remain
valid for decades to come. In the secular media, where Pell
has fought many of his battles, it is easier to gain traction
against propositions such as heroin injection rooms, the use
of condoms, and the unfettered access to reproductive technology by using prudential arguments rather than by citing
the will of God. In a nation of twenty million people with
an abortion rate of more than eighty thousand a year, the
bishops have tried to use arguments that will gain airtime
and be listened to by the young women tempted to undergo
such a procedure.

The prudential arguments against many of the practices
opposed by the Church—such as the social costs of encouraging the birth of fatherless children through reproductive

technology, the dangers to addicts and others of injecting rooms, the imperfections of condoms, the threat to the elderly of the encroaching acceptance of euthanasia, the side effects of artificial birth control, and the breast cancer link to abortion—are sound. This is no surprise, as there can never be a contradiction between truth and reason. At the same time, by October 2003, Pell had clearly decided that such an approach had its limitations. "Relying on this approach too much can be a mistake", he said in Philadelphia. "I think we should follow the example of Saint Thomas More and Saint Catherine of Siena and others—including the Pope— and make God a central part of the case we make to the world."

This refreshing and unusual admission from an officer on Christ's front lines should give many of Pell's episcopal colleagues around the world food for thought. It is sound advice, going straight to the heart of the Church—Christ himself. It also demonstrates the urgent need for the Church's most senior bishops to have the intellect and skill to make a convincing case in media that generally lack understanding of Catholic teaching and are sometimes hostile to the Church. Pell himself writes both about God and current issues in Australia's biggest-selling tabloid newspaper, *The Sunday Telegraph*, read by around two million people every week—a tenth of Australia's entire population. The column is so effective that in a cut-throat media world where column inches are at a premium, it has been running for more than two and a half years, attracting plenty of feedback, both positive and negative.

In one recent column Pell posed the question:

Is it important to know the difference between right and wrong? Nearly every Australian would say yes. To know that God exists? Probably most Australians would agree. To know that God loves us? The number would be smaller, but still substantial.

Is it important to know that Jesus Christ is divine and the only Son of God? I don't know how many Australians would answer yes, and some who believe it wouldn't be sure what difference it made. Some claim that there is no point in giving answers to questions nobody is asking. This seems reasonable, but there can be situations where questions should be asked, even when there is silence.

He then went on to discuss Australia's uneasy silence about abortion, equating it with the many years few people questioned slavery or the ill treatment of Australia's Aborigines. In another recent column, he warned that the ubiquitous New Age movement had "no God capable of hearing our prayers, much less capable of answering them".

The warmth of Mother Earth, so prominent in the New Age, removes the threat of judgment by the Father-God of Judaism and Christianity, he said. "But it also removes all possibility of justice and redress in the next life for those who have suffered."

In his Philadelphia speech, Pell acknowledged the enormous social pressure on the Church to mind her own spiritual and religious business and to leave the question of which values the community should adopt to those who can consider it in an "unbiased" or secular way. "This is not a position that the Church can ever accept", Pell said. In *Veritatis Splendor*, the Pope cites the Code of Canon Law to make this abundantly clear, declaring that "the Church has the right always and everywhere to proclaim moral principles, even in respect of the social order, and to make judgements about any human matter in so far as this is required by fundamental human rights or the salvation of souls."

Language such as "the salvation of souls" Pell admitted

in Philadelphia, is not much in vogue in Australia and this is "something we should rectify". As a prelude to discussion the "salvation of souls" in the wider community, the Australian bishops could give a lead in encouraging priests and Catholic teachers to reacquaint Catholics in the pews and at the school desk with the concept (or introduce them to it for the first time). Some priests, of course, have never lost sight of that concept and dedicate their entire working lives to it, but others seem preoccupied with other concerns.

If Catholic truth is to be restored to its rightful place among Catholics and eventually the wider community, there is also clearly a pressing need for professionally trained Catholic psychotherapists to assist the faithful in dealing with their personal problems and overcome the wounds that fate and unfortunate childhood experiences have dealt many of them. These days, people with psychological and emotional problems are encouraged to seek help, and rightly so, but if the therapist, however well meaning and competent, does not share or understand Catholic moral teaching, the patient may not embrace the very teachings which could help them on the road to recovery. With leadership from the top, more Catholic universities could provide such courses. And as Pell himself has observed in the past, in an age when counseling and therapy are commonplace, individual Confession should also be encouraged as a forum with much to offer.

The current international emphasis on human rights offers the Church an important opportunity to claw back some ground for an authentic understanding of the person, human freedom, and the common good, Pell said. This is especially so at a time when the secular understanding of rights is beginning to collapse under the weight of its own contradictions.

Just as people have the right in a democracy to choose

their religion, Pell pointed out, so too some Catholics feel they should be able to choose the type of morality they follow and remain "good" Catholics. "Unless all kinds of implicit Christian assumptions are made explicit, the claim to the primacy of individual conscience easily becomes in our cultural context the same as a claim to personal moral autonomy."

The Church, Pell said, should never concede that secularism is the only basis for public discourse. The Holy Father is right to claim that "the Christian faith gave form [to Europe], and some of its fundamental values in turn inspired the democratic ideal and the human rights of European modernity."

At home in Australia, Pell's promotion to cardinal drew warm congratulations from many people in public life, from Prime Minister John Howard down, with Howard, a Protestant, praising him as "a great intellectual, a person of great determination and strength". New South Wales Premier Bob Carr put on a civic reception for the Cardinal, and thousands of letters, faxes, and emails streamed into his office and presbytery from around the world.

Among the well-wishers there was one notable and prominent exception. Claiming he did not want to be a "party pooper", Auxiliary Bishop of Canberra Patrick Power said publicly that the appointment "further shows the Church to be representing many elements that I think are not doing the church very much good at the moment". He went on: "Many of the values that I think are dear to Australian Catholics, such as the dignity of the human person, the primacy of conscience, the theology of communion, the need for dialogue in our Church, reading the signs of our times, I don't think that they're values that are particularly clearly enunciated by Archbishop Pell."

Perhaps Bishop Power forgot that loyalty is another value Australians hold dear, and many ordinary Catholics in the pews were shocked and outraged, recognizing that the dignity of the human person, from the moment of conception to natural death, had been a constant strength of Pell's work and that of the Pope. Many priests and bishops were furious about Power's comments, too, with a number of priests speaking out publicly and at least one writing an angry letter to the apostolic nuncio in Canberra. In Rome, a senior Vatican cardinal in charge of a major congregation said he had never heard of such a public reaction by one bishop to another's promotion anywhere else in the world. Pressed by journalists to respond, Pell, ever the team player and reluctant to sink the boot into a brother bishop, opted for diplomacy:

> The Catholic Church is not a small sect. There are a billion Catholics throughout the world and obviously there are different schools of theology. I hope I preach Christ. I certainly try to explain that the Christian teachings are true and beautiful and useful for people in this life and the next. I'm a loyal son of the Second Vatican Council. I don't run around making up teachings. I've got no mandate from the Church to correct or improve Christ's teachings, but I've got to try to understand them more deeply and explain them.

Pell also promised to continue to speak out on issues such as the Australian government's hard-line stance in detaining asylum-seekers from abroad in detention centers. "I've said many times I think the policy of the government is too hard and too tough", he said. "But I also recognise the reality of Australian public opinion, the constraints on the Government, but it's certainly not our finest hour."

Writing of Cardinal Pell's promotion, Bishop Anthony Fisher, O.P., said: "The word cardinal comes from the Latin *cardinalis*, meaning hinge. It means someone in a pivotal position; a leader 'outstanding in doctrine, morals, piety and prudence in action' according to the canonical job description. When the Pope appoints a Cardinal, he sets the bar high on the kind of leader God requires and we deserve."

Fisher's touch of wry humor put Pell's critics into perspective: "The usual suspects were rounded up to make the usual tut-tut noises. Some pretended surprise. Others thought it typical of a church going the wrong way. But they agreed on this: church or state, our leaders should agree with us. They should follow the polls and lead from behind. Otherwise they are out of step with the community."

Asked by journalists about his chances of being elected Pope, Pell, who enjoys the odd flutter on the horses, answered as only an Australian could. "We've got the Melbourne Cup in a month or so . . . and a little bit of form on the country course doesn't signify you should be a major challenger for the Melbourne Cup." The Cup, which every year brings Australia to a grinding halt for several minutes as even kindergarten children watch on television, is one of the world's leading horse races, always held on the first Tuesday in November and contested by horses from the world's most successful racing stables.

The Cardinal's good humor was not lost on one sharp Melbourne journalist, who noted that in 1861 Archer was walked all the way from Nowra in country New South Wales to Melbourne's Flemington racecourse, a journey of several hundred miles, to win the first Melbourne Cup. In 1869 a 200-to-1 long shot called The Monk came second, and in 1996, the Cup was won by a horse called Saintly.

Long shots indeed . . .

Chapter 20

Witnessing Christ in Crimson

The bells of Saint Peter's Basilica began ringing out across the Eternal City at 10:10 A.M. on Tuesday, October 21, 2003, and shortly afterward, thirty new cardinals walked into the square for the ninth consistory of the extraordinary pontificate of John Paul II. Each cardinal was accompanied by a priest, and walking beside George Pell that morning was his cousin Monsignor Henry Nolan from Ballarat, who had also accompanied him when he entered the seminary forty-three years earlier. Monsignor Nolan was the eldest of the twenty-seven cousins on Pell's mother's side of the family, and several others had made the long journey to Rome as well. Pell's sister, Margaret, was there and his brother, David, with wife, Judy, and Pell's nieces, Sarah, Rebecca, and Georgina, and his nephew, Nicholas. They were happy to see that the pectoral cross Pell was wearing was the one they had had made for him when he became a bishop in 1987. The ruby at the center of the cross and the diamonds at the four points were from his mother's engagement and eternity rings. The day before, Margaret had bought her brother a set of cuff links when they found that the white shirt made to go under the red soutane needed them.

As Pell told readers of his weekly column in *The Sunday Telegraph*:

The Pope created thirty new cardinals, twenty-six of us bishops along with four priests from twenty-two nations. The ceremony was celebrated outside in Saint Peter's Square in beautiful sunny weather, cooled by a slight breeze. This was welcome, as five layers of clothes and vestments make it easy to build up a head of steam. On Tuesday there was no Eucharist as the Pope conferred the red hat on each cardinal in a ceremony of music, Scripture readings and prayer. The office of cardinal does not derive from the Scriptures, so there is no ordination ceremony. When the list of names is announced by the Pope, and the red hat is conferred, the Pope's decision becomes effective. The spectacular crimson red vestments are to remind us that the cardinals should be prepared to die in witnessing to Christ's person and teaching, as the early martyrs did in the pagan Roman Empire. Actually the century just concluded produced more Catholic martyrs than any other. Faith and heroism are still flourishing, usually in situations of great adversity.

Despite the vastness of the crowd, the congregation had a sense of real involvement with the ceremony, cheering loudly as the name of each cardinal was read out. Pell's name drew loud cheers, and a startling "Aussie Aussie Aussie, Oi Oi Oi" (a popular sporting cheer) from one scallywag from Down Under. About one hundred of Pell's friends from Australia were there as well as friends he had made over the years who came from Canada, England, Ireland, and the United States. His party included his auxiliary bishop from Sydney, Anthony Fisher, O.P., Archbishop Philip Wilson from Adelaide, South Australia, and priests from Sydney, Melbourne, Ballarat, Brisbane, London, Dublin, and Rome. An additional ninety Australians who saw the ceremony were in Rome on a pilgrimage for Mother Teresa's beatification, led by Archbishop Barry Hickey of Perth, Western Australia.

In the Gospel reading, James and John were wanting to be

the first in the Kingdom, and Jesus was saying that that is not
what it is all about, telling his disciples: "Whoever would
be first among you must be slave of all. For the Son of Man
also came not to be served but to serve, and to give his life
as a ransom for many" (Mk 10:44). As the Pope reminded
the cardinals in his homily, which was read out for him by
Archbishop Leonardo Sandri of the Vatican Secretariat of
State:

> Only after his death, however, would the Apostles under-
> stand the full meaning of these words and, with the help of
> the Spirit, fully accept their demanding logic.
>
> The Redeemer continues to propose this same program
> to those who, through the sacrament of Orders, are most
> closely associated with his mission. He asks them to convert
> to his "logic" that contrasts starkly with that of the world: to
> die to oneself, to become humble, disinterested servants of
> one's brethren, shunning every temptation to make a career
> and to seek personal advancement.
>
> This is undoubtedly a difficult ideal to achieve, but the
> Good Shepherd assures us of his support. We can also rely
> on the protection of Mary, Mother of the Church, and the
> Holy Apostles Peter and Paul, the pillars and foundations of
> the Christian people.
>
> As for me, I once again express my esteem to you and
> accompany you with constant remembrance in prayer. May
> God grant, in the various offices he entrusts to you, that you
> spend your whole life for souls.

Before approaching the Pope one by one to receive their
red birettas and the bulla of office, each of the new cardinals
took an oath of fidelity and obedience in Latin (translated
by the Vatican wire service, Zenit):

> I [name and surname], Cardinal of the Holy Roman Church,
> promise and swear to be faithful henceforth and forever, while

I live, to Christ and his Gospel, being constantly obedient to the Holy Roman Apostolic Church, to Blessed Peter in the person of the Supreme Pontiff John Paul II, and of his canonically elected Successors; to maintain communion with the Catholic Church always, in word and deed; not to reveal to any one what is confided to me in secret, nor to divulge what may bring harm or dishonor to Holy Church; to carry out with great diligence and faithfulness those tasks to which I am called by my service to the Church, in accord with the norms of the law. So help me Almighty God.

The Holy Father, speaking in Latin, personally told the cardinals that the red of the biretta, "symbolizes that you are ready to conduct yourselves with fortitude to the spilling of blood for the spreading of the Christian faith, for peace, and the tranquility of the People of God, and for freedom and the spread of the holy Roman Church."

Vast screens in the square provided close-up footage of each cardinal kneeling before the Pope and receiving both the biretta and the Holy Father's blessing. Later, as the cardinals were embraced by more than one hundred of their fellow cardinals, the Pope appeared to wipe a few tears from his eyes before the crowd bade him farewell with enthusiastic applause, waving and cheering as he was wheeled in his chair from the square.

Cardinal Pell's press conference, held immediately afterward, was packed with journalists from religious and secular publications from Australia, the United States and Britain, and from most Australian television networks. As the journalists waited for the Cardinal to arrive, it was fascinating to listen to the tape of another new cardinal's press conference from the day before—that of Cardinal Keith O'Brien of Saint Andrews and Edinburgh—as he tried to hose down the controversy over reports in Scotland's media that he had called for a debate over the rule of celibacy for priests, suggested a review of the Church's ban on contraception, and said that if 10 percent of priests are "gay" then it is reasonable to assume that 10 percent of priests and bishops are gay.

Pell's press conference had a very different focus. Following Christ comes at a cost, he said, but it brings great benefits.

"One great Protestant theologian said when preaching you should have the Gospel in one hand and a newspaper in the other", he said. "We've got to talk to the needs of people today. We've got to support the communities and form communities, especially with young people, we've got to get young people to bear witness to other young people. That's one of the most potent of all sorts of witnesses for youth."

He identified the erosion of faith, especially among the young, as one of the major challenges facing the Church. He said:

> We have a slow erosion of church practice. In Australia the Catholics are not disassociating from the Church, but there are about 18 percent who worship weekly; we'd like that to be more than that, and as always of course we've got to practise what we preach, and we have to work as well as we can so that the flame of faith will catch, especially in the hearts of young people and younger middle-aged people.
>
> Sometimes young people drift away, at least temporarily. With those drifting away after being Catholic educated, I want them to know what our basic claims are, and I want them to know the basic rationale we give for those claims. I think if we can get that across, it's a better basis for the flame of faith to catch, but it's also a better basis from which people might return after they drift away.

The neo-pagan mix, afflicting every Western society including Australia, had to be resisted. Asked what he meant by the neo-pagan mix, Pell said: "Very easy, slack rules on sexuality, suggestion that the question of God is irrelevant, very little regard for marriage and the family, very little regard for clear moral teachings, the suggestion we can all paint the moral picture any way we like. This is the sort of mix that is breeding a lot of unhappiness in the Western world, and in other places."

Asked about ecumenism and the on-going crisis in the Anglican Church over the appointment of an openly gay bishop in the United States, he said:

> Obviously it has significant consequences, but whatever the way that crisis develops, co-operation with the Anglican Church, dialogue and common prayer must continue. One of the great gains of the Second Vatican Council is the Catholic insistence on the importance of ecumenism.
>
> I think, too, the difficulties in the Anglican Church or churches highlight the usefulness of the primacy of Peter; because we have a focus of unity in the successor of Peter, and one of the great attributes of the papacy is that it is able to act when there isn't a clear consensus.

In relation to his role as chairman of the Vox Clara Committee advising the Congregation for Divine Worship and Discipline of the Sacraments on the English translations of the liturgy, Pell said it was important for the translations to be faithful to original Latin and that they be beautiful translations. "The language will be, you might say, slightly more sacral, not everyday language, but given the significance of what we're enacting, especially in the Mass, in the Eucharist, it's my ambition to see beautiful and faithful translations of the Roman Missal, and I hoped we'll have a translation of the Roman Missal closer to two years rather than three or four or five."

As to his personal feelings, Pell admitted that it had been hard to take in all the details of the ceremony in the square.

"I listened attentively, but I was slightly distracted." It had all been touched by a "hint of sadness" with the obvious decline in the Holy Father's health. It would be wonderful he said, if the next pope was "like the present Holy Father".

And did he take any personal pride in all of this, he was asked? "I hope I don't allow myself too much pride, but I'm certainly very pleased and grateful to be a cardinal of the Holy Roman Church."

That afternoon, as gentle rain began to fall, each of the new "princes" spent two hours greeting visitors and imparting blessings to them. Pell was one of those positioned in the Paul VI audience hall. Others were seated in even greater splendor in the Vatican palaces. Afterward, Pell joined about 150 friends for a reception in his honor hosted jointly by his friend from Sydney barrister John McCarthy, Q.C., and the Knights of the Holy Sepulcher, a Catholic chivalry order dating back to the first Crusades.

The reception was held at the Order's Roman headquarters on the Via della Conciliazione, an ancient fifteenth-century palace of Pope Julius II when he was Cardinal Giuliano della Rovere. The palace was built by Julius' ancestors between 1480 and 1490. After Julius' pontificate, it was occupied at one stage by Jesuits and was known as the Palazzo dei Penitenzieri, as they were the penitentiaries (or confessors) at nearby Saint Peter's. After the Lateran treaty with Mussolini in 1929, the full glory of the palace was revealed as other buildings around the area were demolished to create the Via della Conciliazione linking Saint Peter's Square to the Tiber. The palace contains a small, richly decorated chapel and elegant reception rooms with ornate ceilings and impressive works of religious art.

Rome's severe summer drought, in which many trees had been lost, broke with a vengeance the following morning,

Wednesday, October 22, and the concelebrated Mass scheduled for Saint Peter's Square was shifted to the papal altar inside the basilica, beneath Michelangelo's dome and the bronze canopy of Bernini's baldacchino. Cardinal Joseph Ratzinger, Prefect for the Congregation for the Doctrine of the Faith and Dean of the College of Cardinals, was the principal celebrant, with Pope John Paul II, resplendent in gold vestments reading some of the prayers and presenting each cardinal with a gold ring bearing an image of the crucifixion. The Pope's sermon, read out for him, encouraged the new cardinals: "If at times one is overcome by fear and discouragement, may the consoling promise of the divine Master be of comfort: 'In the world you have tribulation; but be of good cheer, I have overcome the world!'"

Despite his struggles to breathe and speak, the Pope read the Latin formula before presenting the rings. "Receive the ring, sign of dignity, of pastoral zeal, and of a firmer communion with the See of Peter. Receive the ring from the hand of Peter and be conscious that in loving the Prince of the Apostles your love for the Church is reinforced."

The Holy Father amazed those with a view of the altar by kneeling during the Eucharistic Prayer and other parts of the Mass. The thirty cardinals, in cream vestments with gold trim, concelebrated the Mass.

That evening, Pell hosted a dinner for his family and friends at Rome's Orazio restaurant, with the Cardinal taking a delight in organizing the seating plan himself, mixing up his extraordinary range of friends from around the world in a way that made for a stimulating, happy evening.

"Having the family and a lot of my friends and priests there made it a really lovely week", Pell said later. "It was a wonderful time. One friend says a little bit like heaven.

We were praying and feasting and seeing new things and enjoying one another's company, it was great."

On Thursday morning, the Cardinal was able to present his three nieces and nephew to the Holy Father. Like all who met the Holy Father, the youngsters were impressed by his warmth and gentleness. "I just felt like hugging him", one of Pell's nieces told her aunt, Margaret Pell. "May your time in the City of the Apostles confirm you in faith, hope and love", the Pope said at the audience.

Pell himself was lucky to make it to the papal audience. Early that morning, he and around a dozen priests in his party had concelebrated an early Mass at one of his favorite places in Rome, the fourth-century church of Saint Clement, built on top of two buildings dating back to the Roman republic before the time of Christ, one of them a temple to the pagan goddess Mithra.

"There is a tremendous feeling of history in Rome", Pell said at the Mass. "The history of Europeans in Australia is so brief, we very much appreciate being in such a holy place, a sacred site where people have prayed for more than 1500 years."

The church has been cared for by Irish Dominicans since 1667 and actually comprises three Catholic churches built on top of one another dating from different eras; it was first mentioned by Saint Jerome in his writings in 392. It is named after Saint Clement, Christianity's fourth pope (88 to 97), who, according to legend, was banished from Rome to the Crimean mines, where he converted so many soldiers and fellow prisoners that the exasperated Roman authorities tied an anchor to his neck and threw him into the Black Sea.

After Mass, Pell and his party explored the church until it was time for him to return to Cardinal Francis Stafford's residence in Trastevere to dress for the papal audience. A torrential rainstorm, however, meant finding a taxi was harder than walking on water, so the Dominicans' gardener set off with the Cardinal in his car, only to stop with a flat tire, which had to be repaired. Pell was drenched and arrived at Cardinal Stafford's only just in time to change and make it to the audience. Lay pilgrims who have despaired of Roman transport in the rain can only chuckle that it happens to high-ranking princes of the Church as well.

After six exhausting, exhilarating days in Rome, Pell flew to Lebanon en route home. "This land has been a centre of civilization from well before the time of Christ", he told readers of his *Sunday Telegraph* column.

> Here the alphabet was invented, a simple development with immense consequences linking symbols to sounds, which made literature accessible to people generally. . . .
>
> Many Lebanese of different religious traditions have migrated to Australia since the 19th century, making a wonderful contribution. More recently they have come here to bring up their children in peace, especially after the Lebanese civil war, where local factions and eventually foreign armies fought one another, killing about 150,000 people between 1975–1990. More than one million Lebanese left the country during this time.

"Lebanon", he said, "is the only Arab democracy, where all citizens have civil rights and the leadership positions are shared between the different religious groups. There is a cautious optimism about the future, a determination to maintain and deepen the traditions of tolerance." Pell was welcomed by President Emile Lahood, the Maronite Catholic bishops, the leader of the Shiite Muslims, Sheik Kabalaan, and the leader of the Sunni Muslims, Mufti Rasheed Kabbani.

The Maronite Catholics in Lebanon have been in a minority situation for almost fifteen hundred years, and Pell, always fascinated by history, wanted to see the small chapel and residence where the Maronite patriarchs had to live in the Valley of Saints for 450 years until about 1850. He found there is still no road leading to the historic center, and he joined other pilgrims in walking the last half mile. The simple, poor buildings still standing were an "eloquent testimony to an unconquerable faith".

Back home in Australia, Pell spent a busy fortnight in his archdiocese before heading back to Rome (a twenty-hour plus plane journey from Sydney) for a week of meetings. This was his third long-haul international trip since the beginning of October, and Pell's friends can only admire his stamina. "It seems as though Pell is doing two jobs, his work in Sydney and fulfilling his obligations in Rome to the various bodies and committees on which he serves", one man observed late in 2003. That is not unusual for a cardinal, but what makes it so demanding for an Australian cardinal is the twenty-hour-plus plane journey from Australia to Europe. After the consistory, Pell was appointed to two more Vatican bodies—the Pontifical Council for Justice and Peace and the Presidential Council of the Pontifical Council for the Family. It is a full life, not for the faint-hearted.

On his last Roman trip for 2003, Pell visited, for the first time, his titular church in the Archdiocese of Rome —Santa Maria Domenica Mazzarello, a new church built along modern lines in 1997 in an outlying Roman parish created in 1982. The Church is dedicated to the Salesian saint Maria Domenica Mazzarello, canonized by Pope Pius XII in 1951 for her work, along with Saint John Bosco, of founding the Salesian nuns known as the Daughters of Mary Help of Christians. The order is one of the largest of women religious in the world, with fifteen thousand members in eighty-seven countries—including more than five thousand in North and South America. Our Lady Help of Christians, by coincidence, is patroness of Australia.

Pell returned to Australia in time for the Australian Bishops' Conference bi-annual meeting, which gave approval for Sydney to bid for the 2007 World Youth Day, an event that would be likely to eclipse even the 2000 Olympics in terms of visitor numbers. Sydney's natural beauty and mild winter climate lends itself to such an event. Back at home, Pell was celebrating at least four Masses a week, often more, in different Sydney parishes, visiting several schools, and celebrating Mass for many different groups from the Chinese community to the Italian Charismatic Renewal to the wider Italian community to mark fifty years of service by the Scalabrinian order in Australia. Also in early December he conferred the Sacrament of Confirmation according to the Tridentine Rite at the Maternal Heart Chaplaincy at Lewisham, conducted by the Fraternity of Saint Peter, and joined Catholics at Saint Ambrose Church, Concord West, for First Saturday devotions. This schedule of getting out and about in his archdiocese is one way Pell puts into practice what he said at his Roman press conference after becoming a cardinal: "I think as a bishop, it's my task to encourage those movements or parishes or people where there is life and vitality."

It was also his task, he said that day, to be "vigilant to see that the teachings of Christ are presented accurately and comprehensively, especially to our young people".

In some parts of Australia not under Pell's jurisdiction, or that of his many like-minded episcopal colleagues, it is harder to think of an issue that causes ordinary Catholic parents as much angst as the poor, sometimes harmful catechetics taught in Catholic schools. Catholic parents in many parts of the world know the sinking feeling of loss when their son or daughter comes home from their Catholic school with the teacher's latest innovation, such as substituting "In the name of the Creator, the Redeemer, and the Sanctifier" for the sign of the cross or replacing God the Father with Father-Mother.

Lest North American readers think that the battle for truth is won in Australia with Pell at the helm as cardinal, it is not. It is well on the way to being fought and fought hard in Sydney, Melbourne, Perth, and a number of smaller dioceses, but it has not even begun in other parts of the country where the local ordinaries resent receiving "rude letters" from mothers about way-out religious practices in certain schools.

After a hard year in 2002, George Pell had an outstanding year in 2003. But for all the glory of the consistory in Rome, it was a smaller, quieter event late in the year that will ultimately touch many more lives and, possibly, save many more souls.

On December 4, Pell's old friend from Oxford days Monsignor Peter Elliott traveled north to Sydney from Melbourne for the launch of the *To Know, Worship and Love* series in Sydney. The series was Pell's idea when he was Archbishop of Melbourne, and Elliott oversaw the project, which has now grown to eleven books ranging from early childhood to tenth grade, with two more to be added.

In 2004, Catholic schoolchildren, not only in Sydney and Melbourne, but also in the provincial New South Wales dioceses of Armidale, Lismore, and Wollongong will be learning from the colorful, well-produced textbooks. And in parts of Australia less fortunate, some families have ordered sets to help their children at home.

The children are encouraged to learn and understand four

points Pell himself insisted be printed on the back of each individual book:

> We believe in one God, Father, Son and Holy Spirit who loves us.
> We believe in one Redeemer, Jesus Christ, only Son of God, born of the Virgin Mary, and who died and rose from the dead to save us.
> We believe in the Catholic Church, the Body of Christ, where we are led in service and worship by the Pope and Bishops.
> We believe that Jesus, Our Lord, calls us to repent and believe; that is, to choose faith not doubt, love not hate, good not evil, and eternal life in heaven not hell.

In leading tens of thousands of Catholic children every year to grasp these important tenets of the faith while still at school, Pell is fulfilling the vision of his hero Pope John Paul II, who urges Church leaders to "live as witnesses to a hope that never disappoints and as missionaries of a life that conquers death."

APPENDICES

Appendix 1

An Unscientific Postscript on Catholicism in an Age of Science

Archbishop George Pell

I. Science and the Changing Value of Human Life

Three great women made the headlines last year. Blessed Teresa of Calcutta died having poured out her life in low-tech care for the most needy and abandoned of our planet. Princess Diana of Wales died at the hands of more sophisticated science, that of high speed glamor and glitz, the motor-car and flash photography. And Dolly the Sheep was born.

Dolly got less coverage in the newspapers and magazines than the other two ladies, and much of it was undoubtedly hype and hysteria. But it also reflected the growing realization that we are at the beginning of a biomedical revolution more significant than industrialization, nuclear power or the computer. Recent advances mean we are fast acquiring the power to modify and control not only the world around us, the world which humanity must inhabit, but also humanity itself, the when and how and what of people's lives and deaths and much in between. Some of these means are

Address to the 1998 Conference of the Fellowship of Catholic Scholars, Denver, September 26, 1998.

433

already in use or at hand; others will be in the near future. All this presents some very exciting new opportunities and some very difficult new challenges for the Catholic Church and for Western society, which is marked by a very adult science sadly all too often hitched to a rather childish ethic and spirituality.

The cloned sheep was not the first headline-grabber to hail from Edinburgh in Scotland. From there came the proposal a few years ago that brain-dead women might be utilized as surrogate mothers (they used the word "incubators") for others who could not carry their own children or did not want to do so (pre-natal nannies). The next creative proposal from technologists in that city was that eggs of aborted girls might be used for IVF programs, so that the dead unborn children would be the genetic mothers of children created for other people. Perhaps Scots scientists should stick to perfecting malt whiskeys.

The Scots wanted to use their cloning technique to create some special animals for medical research; but meanwhile Australian IVF scientists have been cloning cattle (by a different method) for big profits on the open market. Both assured us that human cloning was not on their drawing board. But the world was far from confident. After all, Australia's leading cattle cloner, Alan Trounson, is also that country's leading human IVF technician. At his hands and those of others like him, perhaps 100,000 test-tube babies were born around the world since 1978. Children for the infertile sounds great, at least until you learn a little more about the intrinsic immorality of the processes used, the risks to those involved, the thousands of embryos killed in the past few years or left in limbo in frozen storage. But what about artificial insemination and surrogacy for "gay" couples; pregnancies for octogenarians; taking sperm from recently deceased men so the widow can have a child; men carrying babies; cloned human beings used for spare parts; animal-human hybrids; genetic tests for unborn children's sex, coloring, likely shape, longevity, athletic and other physical potential; more genetic tests (and perhaps abortion) for unborn children's part-genetic behavioral dispositions such as schizophrenia, substance dependency, depression, aggressiveness, homosexuality, religiosity. . . .

At the other end, we may soon be able to extend life to 120 years or so for those who want to live for much longer here on earth; or offer a quick medical injection for those who are sick of it. Until then we can help people live healthier lives, in greater comfort, though at some considerable cost. Further improvements can be expected, not only in life-extension and health-improvement, but in medically-delivered "quality of life", such as cures of chronic conditions such as arthritis, sight and hearing problems, and various changes to body shape, color, texture and so on. Cindy Jackson, who runs London's thriving "Cosmetic Surgery Network", recently made headlines by writing up the nine years, thirty-seven operations, and hundreds of thousands of dollars she has so far spent on having herself surgically remade in the image of the Barbie Doll. And the big field for the future will be the scientific control of human capacities such as strength, agility, reflexes, emotion, memory, imagination, desire, libido, aggression, thought, choice, speech and action. Heroin, anabolic steroids, Prozac, these are only the tip of the pharmacological iceberg of the future. The possibilities in bioscience are tremendous!

Yet as Pope John Paul has noted: "The development of science and technology, this splendid testimony of the human capacity for understanding and for perseverance, does not free humanity from the obligation to ask the ultimate religious questions. Rather, it spurs us on to face the most painful and decisive of struggles, those of the heart and of the moral conscience."[1]

In a series of encyclicals culminating in the apostolic letter *Tertio Millennio Adveniente* Pope John Paul II has challenged the Church and humanity, on the eve of a new millennium, to take stock of where we are going: like the prophets of old crying out to Israel "look at how you treat the widows, the orphans, the refugees", like Our Lord asking "how did you treat the least of these my brethren . . . hungry, thirsty, naked, lonely", like Leo XIII proposing in *Rerum Novarum* that how workers are treated is the test of our whole economies, so *John Paul now points to abortion, euthanasia and the reproductive technologies—how we treat the youngest and the oldest, the most vulnerable of people—as the litmus test for our civilization at this turning point in our history.*

> Humanity today offers us a truly alarming spectacle, if we consider not only how extensively attacks on life are spreading but also their unheard-of numerical proportion, and the fact that they receive wide-spread and powerful support. . . . The twentieth century will have been an era of massive attacks on life, an endless series of wars and a continual taking of innocent human life. . . . On the eve of the Third Millennium, the challenge facing us is an arduous one: only the concerted efforts of all those who believe in the value of life can prevent a setback of unforeseeable consequences for civilization.[2]

Greeting *Evangelium Vitae* enthusiastically, Paul Johnson in *The Spectator* agreed with the Pope as to what is ultimately at issue: "Crueler things were done [during the totalitarian

[1] *Veritatis Splendor*, 1.3.
[2] *Evangelium Vitae*, 17, 91.

twentieth century], on a larger scale, and with more devilish refinement, than ever before in the sad story of mankind. . . . Still, the totalitarian century is behind us." He then continues, "But it is already evident what we shall have to fear. In our own century, we allowed vicious men to play with the state, and paid the penalty of 150 million done to death by state violence. In the 21st century, the risk is that we will allow men—and women too—to play with human life itself."[3]

Johnson agrees with John Paul that there is much more at stake here in the great controversies over biotechnology than is commonly appreciated: in one of the most memorable phrases of his pontificate, the Pope declares that humanity at the turn of the millennium is in the midst of a dramatic conflict between the "culture of death" and the "culture of life".[4] And he pulls no punches as to its causes, both outside and inside the Church: a wrong notion of freedom, the "eclipse of the sense of God", a radical undervaluing of human life, all contributing to "a social and cultural climate dominated by secularism".[5] This practical atheism has its impact upon science as elsewhere:

> Once all reference to God has been removed, it is not surprising that the meaning of everything else becomes profoundly distorted. Nature itself, from being *mater*, is now reduced to being *matter*, and is subjected to every kind of manipulation. This is the direction in which a certain technical and scientific way of thinking, prevalent in present-day culture, appears to be leading when it rejects the very idea that there is a truth of creation which must be acknowledged, or a plan of God for life which must be respected. . . . By living *as if*

[3] *The Spectator*, April 4, 1995, p. 22.
[4] *Evangelium Vitae*, 50.
[5] Ibid., 21.

God did not exist, man not only loses sight of the mystery of God, but also of the mystery of the world and the mystery of his own being.[6]

Amidst his critique of the hidden violence in supposedly peaceful modern societies, the Pope acknowledges the contribution of science, where there is so much that is "positive for the unborn, the suffering and those in an acute or terminal stage of sickness".[7] Science also allows couples to exercise responsible parenthood through advances in natural family planning.[8] And various agencies are making the benefits of advanced medicine available in the developing countries; a considerable blessing.

On the other hand, in a society in which violence against the youngest and oldest is increasingly condoned, the wonderful "new prospects opened up by scientific and technological progress" are turned into "new forms of attacks on the dignity of the human being".[9] Far from supporting the weak, scientific research in fertility and embryology becomes "almost exclusively preoccupied with developing products which are ever more simple and effective in suppressing life".[10]

The various *techniques of artificial reproduction,* which would seem to be at the service of life and are frequently used with this intention, actually open the door to new threats against life. Apart from the fact that they are morally unacceptable, since they separate procreation from the fully human context of the conjugal act, these techniques . . . expose hu-

[6] Ibid., 22–23.
[7] Ibid., 26.
[8] Ibid., 97.
[9] Ibid., 4.
[10] Ibid., 13.

man embryos to very great risks of death . . . , embryos are over-produced . . . and [subsequently] destroyed or used for research which, under the pretext of scientific or medical progress, in fact reduces human life to the level of simple "biological material" to be freely disposed of.

So prenatal testing, instead of being for diagnosis and treatment, all too often becomes a tool for "eugenic abortion", and handicapped babies even after birth are increasingly at risk. "In this way, we revert to a state of barbarism which one hoped had been left behind forever."[11]

Christ's Gospel of Life proposes an alternative to this reversion to neo-paganism. "Human life, as a gift of God, is sacred and inviolable. The meaning of life is found in giving and receiving love, and in this light human sexuality and procreation reach their true and full significance. Love also gives meaning to suffering and death; despite the mystery which surrounds them, they can become saving events. *Respect for life requires that science and technology should always be at the service of man and his integral development.*"[12]

Science needs more than big grants, big labs, big kudos: as its power and potential for both good and ill grow exponentially every minute, it more desperately than ever needs moral wisdom and democratic constraints. If we are to be improved and remade by science, Barbie should not be the model.

II. The Eclipse of the Sense of God

The scientific developments I have outlined make quite clear that this human remaking is not to be constrained to the

---

[11] Ibid., 14.
[12] Ibid., 81.

realm of the body. The aspiration seems to be for the *total* remaking of man, to alter not only the individual's personality and character but—if such a thing were possible—his soul. We have noted that prenatal testing and abortion are already used eugenically to prevent the birth of children who are in any minor way "defective"; bearers of the genes for diseases such as diabetes or cystic fibrosis. Professor James Watson, one of the scientists who discovered DNA, recently argued for the extension of this approach if we ever discover a gene for homosexuality. What if scientists could manage to isolate a gene which gives rise to the troublesome human need for meaning, or the gene that accounts for our yearning for God? Eugenics is now poised to move to an altogether more sophisticated level, no longer mopping up nature's mistakes by abortion, but preventing their emergence by modifying and remaking human nature.

Today none of this is farfetched. One critical consideration is that the remaking of man has not emerged incidentally to the general direction taken by contemporary science, but now constitutes one of its major objectives. We are so used to this that many do not appreciate the novelty of the development. There are factors beyond the advance of science which are also at work to facilitate this reshaping. The absence of legislation, or government disinterest, together with the eclipse of God and diminished respect for any normative version of human nature all mean that for some, or many, scientists, the major constraint on human biological experimentation is the fear of catastrophic unforeseen consequences.

We all know of Nietzsche's infamous declaration that "God is dead." In making this claim Nietzsche is sometimes linked to Dostoyevsky, who in his major novels argued that if there is no God, "then everything is permitted."

For both writers, but especially for Nietzsche, the more important dimension of this argument is not so much what it becomes possible to *do* in the wake of the death of God, as what it becomes possible to *think* and *desire*. In Nietzsche's view, Christian revelation, with its insistence on a higher and greater reality beyond the reality of human life constrains the possibilities of human existence, not least by constraining what it is possible to imagine ourselves doing. For example: attempting to fertilize human ova with the spermatozoa of a rat, or an orangutan, continues to be "unthinkable" in an important sense to faithful Christians—and to many other people. These are not ideas that would normally or spontaneously occur to us, and if and when they did occur, they are not ideas that we would entertain with anything other than horror. But when the sense of God has been eclipsed, this very gradually ceases to be the case. What was once morally repugnant becomes scientifically interesting. The horizon which revelation once placed around existence falls away, leaving man surrounded by "the roar of the boundless". This risks bringing catastrophe and terrible human suffering. But for Nietzsche and those like him, the death of God means a new and exhilarating freedom—to think and do what it was not possible to think and do before.

This wrong and ultimately unsustainable notion of freedom continues to have a powerful appeal for many moderns. We see it clearly in the notion common to many of our disenchanted young people that a rich and fulfilled life is one where the individual has *experienced* as much as possible, irrespective of the nature of those experiences and the harm they may do physically, morally and spiritually. But it is among intellectuals and scientists in our society that Nietzsche's concept of freedom has also been most influential, even when Nietzsche's authorship is not recognized. The hostility of a significant group of intellectuals and scientists towards orthodox Christianity, perhaps particularly in the United States, flows in part from the steadfast way in which the Church has resisted this spurious notion of freedom and insisted that science and all scholarly endeavor must be subordinated to the service of authentically human values. But I also suspect that the roots of the animosity between the new class elites and the Church go even deeper than this.

Writing in 1971, when Communist oppression still flourished in Europe and the U.S.S.R., George Steiner remarked on "the brain-hammering strangeness of the monotheistic idea".[13] The concept of the Mosaic God is a unique fact in human history, without parallel in any time or place. It combines an injunction to almost impossible transcendence with a system of moral demands unequaled in history. On the one hand,

> brain and conscience are commanded to vest belief, obedience, love in an abstraction purer, more inaccessible to ordinary sense than is the highest of mathematics.[14]

In addition to this, there is the moral demand of monotheism. As Steiner says,

> Because the words are so familiar, yet too great for ready use, we tend to forget or merely conventionalize the extremity of their call. Only he who loses his life, in the fullest sense of sacrificial self-denial, shall find life. The kingdom is for the naked, for those who have willingly stripped themselves of every belonging, of every sheltering egoism. There is no salvation in the middle places.[15]

[13] George Steiner, *In Bluebeard's Castle* (London, 1971), p. 36.
[14] Ibid.
[15] Ibid., p. 39.

It is Steiner's controversial and daring contention that Western man, recognizing the supreme value of this idea, but filled with self-reproach from his inability to realize it, turned on the original bearers of the message of the Covenant—the Jews—in a way which ultimately culminated in the Holocaust.[16] "The summons to perfection" which monotheism "sought to impose on the current and currency of Western life" enforced "ideals [and] norms of conduct out of all natural grasp". Impossible to realize they nevertheless weighed heavily on individual lives, building up in the subconscious deep loathings and murderous resentments. "The mechanism is simple but primordial":

> *We hate most those who hold out to us a goal, an ideal, a visionary promise which, even though we have stretched our muscles to the utmost, we cannot reach, which slips, again and again, just out of the range of our racked fingers—yet, and this is crucial, which remains profoundly desirable, which we cannot reject because we fully acknowledge its supreme value.*[17]

This provocative analysis might help explain the compulsive hostility among new class elites towards the orthodox monotheistic religions which refuse to compromise the hard teachings. I certainly believe it helps explain the systematic attempt of the Communists to eradicate Christianity. In a different way it also enables us to identify some of the psychological sources of the opposition and personal hostility to the arguments for design in molecular biology, explained so lucidly to us yesterday by Dr. Michael Behe. As Sir Hans Kornberg, a distinguished British biologist, remarked at a seminar in Boston this week, "For scientists teleology is like a lady of ill repute. No one wants to be seen with her in

[16] Ibid., pp. 38–42.
[17] Ibid., p. 41.

public, but many use her by night." Even in the age of science, where the sense of God has been eclipsed or weakened for many Westerners, the claims of monotheistic revelation continue to trouble and annoy those who would wish to be free of its demands, to escape successfully from their guilt. Our task in this situation must be to keep the reality and central importance of the one true God in the public mind, in spite of the constant hostile pressure among the elites and the cheerful and careless agnosticism of others. Many of our own young Catholics will need to be given good reasons for believing in God's existence and shown this love in our practice. In doing all this, we must recognize that we cannot hope for easy approval. But if science and technology are to serve human life rather than dominate it, we have no choice. The mistaken individualistic notion of freedom so influential in our age must be opposed by authentic freedom linked to truth and producing real human service. Science and society will benefit from this in the long run, although the working out of these tensions over the generations will be a fascinating struggle, with the *Brave New World* of Aldous Huxley seeming a likelier immediate destination than the grim constraints of George Orwell's *1984*.

III. What Is to Be Done?

A pamphlet of Lenin in 1902 was entitled *What Is to Be Done?* This remains the crucial question, although mapping the territory and analyzing the situation are essential prerequisites for action, and I still wish to say a few words about the crucial group in this discussion, i.e., Generation X, those born between 1963 and 1980 and their children.

They take for granted the fact that they live in a scientific-technological world and find it difficult to imagine living without the advantages of such a world. They would be dimly aware that 95 percent of all scientists in human history are now living (still a small minority of the generation), but little vexed by the origins of the universe, the neurochemistry of consciousness, genetic planning of the species or the nature of matter, much less by any moral or theological problems attendant on such scientific work. In fact most have never been involved in a church, or even a Sunday school (this is certainly true in Australia; perhaps less true in the United States); they have watched five thousand hours of television by the age of five. Many have suffered from the divorce of their parents and are reluctant to make lifelong commitments, while inclined to delay child-bearing. Feminism is no longer a burning issue, because male and female equality is taken for granted and it is assumed that women should be church ministers. At least in Australia, motherhood has replaced homosexuality as a topic that should not be discussed. The educated among Generation X are also seriously tempted by post-modernism; inclined, like us, to the easier short-term solutions, to relativism, to avoiding the examination of grand themes on the meaning of life. Some of course insist that there are no such truths.

The overwhelming majority of Generation X still identify themselves as Christian; a bigger majority are monotheists. In times of public crises many turn to the Christian churches. Interestingly enough, the irreligious minority does not like to be described as neo-pagan (which it certainly is), probably because it senses that majority opinion is opposed to paganism.

A preliminary conclusion is that it will take much wise

and persevering effort and more than a touch of luck and grace to enlist majority support among Generations X and X + 1 to oppose the Culture of Death on abortion and euthanasia, although the struggle to defend heterosexual marriage should be less difficult. In the democracies, religious leadership to inform public opinion and legislative struggle and political activity will be needed to constrain the more grotesque forms of experimentation touching humans (with some hope of success), and we should be able to achieve continuing majority belief in the One True God, provided we realize that this, and more particularly the Divinity of Christ within the Catholic community, will be severely contested.

A couple of small personal reminiscences will help explain my approach in listing my recommendations.

My work as a priest and then a bishop has meant that I have traveled a lot by air, both within Australia and internationally. I always travel in uniform, dressed as a priest, because it pays to advertise. During long flights most in the next seat do not want to talk much, but there are some exceptions. One was an Australian businessman who seemed prosperous, was certainly confident and wanted to talk, indeed philosophize. He had some land he thought the Church might be interested to buy, etc., etc. He then explained that the secret of success in life and in business was to identify what are the few key issues, and find the right answers to these few. If these right solutions are found, generally the multifarious secondary problems fall into place.

My second reminiscence draws on many years as a junior school football coach, which I thoroughly enjoyed. Experience taught me that when the game started to flow against my young team, many players became rattled, did strange things like attempting the most basic procedures. The only way to play against strong opposition was to remember and follow our basic ground rules. When those were in place, then we could afford to be more adventurous: we did not always win, but we generally used our strengths to the best advantage.

Church people can often be more like my young football players than my business acquaintance. They can forget the fundamental point that our success and failure can only be judged in Christ Our Lord's terms.

My first recommendation is about ways and means; to encourage every variety of Catholic teacher to do two things: to use all available technology and so reach out beyond the Catholic community, as well as instructing committed and cultural Catholics. It has often been remarked that the Protestant Reformation would have been impossible without the invention of printing. Luther was a master publicist. It was the Lutherans who first invented catechisms, while the Catholics were hampered by their use of Latin, and by poor and infrequent popular teaching.

We were behind the play then technologically, but risk having learned that lesson too well by too much reliance now on printed media (books and Catholic newspapers) and speaking only to the Catholic community, in an age of radio, television, videos and the Internet, and many interested, uncommitted outsiders.

In the Western world there will continue to be an exodus from faith, or at least from regular practice. But if we face outwards in our parishes and agencies through service, and use technology and the secular media to explain our morals and our faith (something the Holy Father does so outstandingly), there should be a balancing stream of converts and returnees, many of them damaged by contemporary society and others, while very successful in the eyes of the world, still personally empty and dissatisfied.

The regular practice of religion now parallels the patterns of employment across generations since the Industrial Revolution. Once generations of men in the one family had the same type of job. With the rise of prosperity, migration and social mobility, many sons held jobs different from their fathers, but often for a lifetime. Now many women and men have a variety of jobs in one lifetime, and too many have no jobs or long periods of unemployment. Being a committed Catholic will be more like this, with many committed parents seeing their children drift from practice, and individuals shifting position across their lifetime; all of this because of the steady flow of news and views hostile to Christian belief and practice, and because of the weakened sense of tradition in the West. This is another reason to reach beyond the churchgoers.

As a digression, I am inclined to think that in this age of fast, scientifically induced change, we should make an explicit and regular appeal, counter-cultural as it is, to tradition, "the democracy of the dead", pointing out the advantages of knowing where we come from and of knowing the wisdom that has sustained men and women for millennia. I believe there is a religious market for tradition, especially among the young!

Whatever of tradition, when I preach each Sunday in my cathedral I reach some hundreds of believers, who need encouragement and information. With articles or interviews or a few paragraphs in a secular newspaper, or even some minutes on television or the radio, we reach tens or hundreds of thousands. Recently an elderly priest writer in Sydney launched his own website on the Internet, accompanied by good press in our national newspapers. He claimed 32,000 hits in the first thirty-six hours, and 50,000 hits by the end of the first week![18]

Second-level consequences also follow from the involvement of Catholic teachers in public debate and discussion on issues important to us or society. Churchgoers are generally heartened by these signs of life, and Catholic youngsters are reminded of our claims, of where they should belong.

Such activity also focuses on where the basic tension should be, i.e., between the Church and the world, and not between Catholics. Public differences among Catholics are sometimes necessary in these times of division; but they are unfortunate, never more than a second best.

Last year a coalition of all the Christian leaders in my state of Victoria objected to the exhibition in our government-financed state art gallery of a blasphemous photo of a crucifix in urine. As Catholic Archbishop I also lodged a legal objection in our Supreme Court. Predictably we lost the law case, but unexpectedly the entire show, consisting almost entirely of pornography and blasphemy, was closed down and withdrawn.

The moral of the story for present purposes is that I received overwhelming Catholic support, public prayers for our campaign in a Jewish synagogue, and letters of endorsement from the Moslem community and from some religious congregations not usually listed among my public admirers.

More idiosyncratically my second recommendation in this age of science is to insist that priests are thoroughly formed, not just in sound Catholic doctrine, but more importantly in the practice of prayer and an understanding and love of Christian spirituality. We need God-centered priests.

[18] Website address is: www.costello.au.com.

In this Vatican II age of the laity such a high priority for priests might be politically incorrect, even hazardous. But Our Lord himself was quite explicit about the need for fishers of men, for shepherds and for workers in the harvest (although this final reference is capable of wider meanings).

As the pressures against full Catholic living continue from outside and within the Catholic community, we shall continue to need a network of local leaders who know that the central external challenge is against God; who cannot be knocked off balance into believing the threats are elsewhere, much less inveigled into believing the answers to our problems will be found by "improving" [softening up] Christ's teachings.

Regular prayer is necessary for this steadiness as well as a clear head, accurate knowledge of the tradition and personal and intellectual self-confidence. To achieve this every priest needs a sound formation in philosophy, with Thomism as a significant constituent, and a goodly number of years in an updated version of the Tridentine seminary, which was the greatest gift to the Church from that long, difficult but profoundly important Council that promoted the Counter-Reformation.

Whatever the gains and losses might be in the future in the Catholic universities and universities more generally; whatever the consequences of the convulsive changes in religious life, decline, disappearance and vigorous new life (often in canonically hybrid communities), the parish network has to survive. And its leaders have to be prepared for the bleakest winter as well as for the springtime.

Many other things might be said, particularly on the difficulties of a community who finds its truth in a two-thousand-year-old apostolic tradition; whose Redeemer and

Founder lived at the beginning of our era. All this in an age geared to the future, to progress and innovation.

But enough is enough.

A final word about the importance of maintaining Catholic self-confidence, a worthy sense of identity as the human framework for the flame of faith, for personal conversion.

IV. Conclusion

We should not be daunted by our situation, remembering the Christ we follow and the saints, martyrs and writers of two millennia who fire our imagination. As G. K. Chesterton reminded us, "It was no flock of sheep the Christian shepherd was leading, but a herd of bulls and tigers, of terrible ideals and devouring doctrines."[19] May the good God preserve an increasing number of us from the tyranny of personal consciences shaped by metaphysical muddle, fear of public opinion and an all too easy hedonism.

May the same good God preserve more and more of us from the pathetic illusions that religious vitality can be repurchased without duty, discipline and explicit faith; that our guilts can be banished without repentance and God's forgiveness.

The only way forward is to embrace the love, the steel and the romance of orthodoxy. With the grace of God, prayer, learning and hard work, it is not beyond our capacity to have "the equilibrium of a man behind wildly rushing horses, seeming to stoop this way and to sway that way, yet in every attitude having the grace of statuary and the accuracy of

[19] G. K. Chesterton, *Orthodoxy* (1908; reprint, New York, 1990), p. 100.

arithmetic".[20] We must never forget the orthodox Church was never respectable, never took the tame course.

Let me conclude with the famous and inspiring passage from Chesterton's *Orthodoxy*.

> *To have fallen into any of those open traps of error and exaggeration which fashion after fashion and sect after sect set along the historic path of Christendom—that would indeed have been simple. It is always simple to fall; there are an infinity of angles at which one falls, only one at which one stands. To have fallen into any one of the fads from Gnosticism to Christian Science would have indeed have been obvious and tame. But to have avoided them all has been one whirling adventure; and in my vision the heavenly chariot flies thundering through the ages, the dull heresies sprawling and prostrate, the wild truth reeling and erect,[21]*

even and especially in an age of science.

---

[20] Ibid., pp. 100–101.
[21] Ibid., p. 101.

Appendix 2

From Vatican II to Today

George Pell, Archbishop of Sydney

I am grateful to the Secretary and Committee of the Catalyst for Renewal for the invitation to speak to you. It is generally useful for Catholics to talk together about the work of Christ and the Church which is so dear to us all. Quite a few people suggested to me that I should not talk here because they wondered whether your agenda was the same as groups such as "We Are Church" in Austria or "Call to Action" in the United States, which are clearly contrary to essential elements of the Catholic and Apostolic tradition. I am not sure if the Catalyst for Renewal has spelt out what doctrines of faith and morals that it accepts or rejects, but I felt there was such good will and openness in the committee that came to invite me to this gathering that I was justified in speaking to you. It also seemed to me that my robust reputation for defending the faith would protect me from any misunderstandings that I was going soft on essential doctrines.

The Second Vatican Council was the largest restructuring

Address to Catalyst for Renewal's Bishops Forum, Saint Mary's Cathedral, Sydney, May 30, 2003.

in Catholic history for at least four hundred years, since the Council of Trent (1545–1563) responded to the challenge of Luther and the Protestant Reformation. Indeed there are not too many useful parallels even in the fifteen hundred years before the Council of Trent.

Vatican II was also followed by a dramatic downsizing in some Western countries, such as Holland and French-speaking Canada, a collapse of faith and practice which was also unequalled for hundreds of years; in fact the immediate parallels are the aftermath of the French Revolution of 1789 or the exodus into Protestantism in the sixteenth century.

The Second Vatican Council was a momentous event in Church life, changing Catholic life in Australia irreversibly. None of us would want to go back completely to Catholic life as it was before the Second Vatican Council. Its reforms in many cases are now taken for granted, and young Catholics often imagine that life in the Church was always like this. In fact the Second Vatican Council would probably rank in their subconscious, if not their unconscious, with the Council of Trent. The Council was also followed in Australia by all sorts of unplanned and unanticipated events. On the negative side these include the departure of many priests and religious, the collapse in vocations, the decline in churchgoing and the spread of doctrinal and moral confusion. Many positive developments were planned (and I will touch on those later) and achieved, but a couple of unplanned positive developments are the rise of the charismatic movements and the growth of the so-called New Movements such as the Emmanuel Community or the Neocatechumenal Way.

1962–1965: The Years of the Second Vatican Council

The Bishop of Ballarat, Dr. James Patrick O'Collins, sent me to study theology in Rome in September 1963. Therefore I was not in Rome for the funeral of Pope John XXIII nor for the enthronement of Pope Paul VI. Obviously too I missed the first session of the Council, but I was there as a student for the last three sessions, being present in Saint Peter's Square for the closing ceremony and being smuggled in on one day to help the clerical assistants during an actual session of the Council.

Many of the Australian bishops had thought that the Council would be over in a few months, after adopting a few house-keeping measures. There was almost no public pressure in Australia beforehand for a great reforming council, and this was true of Catholic opinion throughout most of the world and certainly the English-speaking world.

The Council was an exciting time. Pope John XXIII in his opening address had spoken against the prophets of doom and of the need to express the ancient truths in new ways. During the first session some of schemata prepared by the Roman Curia were rejected. There was a mounting enthusiasm for change, fanned by effective use of secular and religious press. There was then a large group of significant and important theologians, most of them from Northern or Central Europe. Such names include Hans Küng, Edward Schillebeeckx, Karl and Hugo Rahner, Yves Congar, Henri de Lubac, Jean Daniélou. The last three were to become cardinals, and the first two were eventually censured by the Church. One of the later books about the Second Vatican Council was headed *The Rhine Flows into the Tiber*.

Naïve young students like myself expected a new Pentecost. Catholic confidence was high with the first Catholic president of the United States, John F. Kennedy (we knew nothing then about his personal weaknesses), and the leaders of France and West Germany, General De Gaulle and Konrad Adenauer, were both practising Catholics. The Cuban crisis had been successfully surmounted. Vietnam had not

yet been lost, and student unrest and rebellion would not cul-
minate until the student revolutions of 1968, which nearly
brought down the French Government. De Gaulle remained
in power only with the help of the Communists.

This optimism quickly turned sour. Pope Paul VI's 1968
ruling, which reaffirmed the traditional Church opposition
to artificial contraception, provoked massive public dissent,
whose consequences we are still experiencing. Ironically
Pope Paul's affirmation of the unitive and procreative goals
of marriage set the scene for Pope John Paul II's theology
of the body which speaks so powerfully to young adults
today. Incidentally most of the students from Australia and
New Zealand who were studying with me in Rome for the
priesthood, a highly talented group of men, either chose
not to be ordained or left the priesthood after ordination.
The percentage who still remained would probably be less
than 10 percent. For some of my friends an enthusiasm for
reform turned into a radical dissatisfaction with the status
quo, a disdain for the past and a sense of superiority towards
those old-fashioned people attached to older ways. It was the
first indication to me that the way forward might not be as
straightforward or pleasant as I had expected.

The Achievements of Vatican II

The achievements of Vatican II are of course contained in
the Conciliar Decrees, inspired by the two basic motifs of
(1) a return to the sources, i.e., Scripture and Tradition,
ressourcement, and (2) *aggiornamento*, an Italian word meaning to bring things up to date.

For the first time a Council spoke about the role of the
Church in the world and urged all Catholics to dialogue, not
anathematize developments around them, and urged them

to engage with the world rather than to retire into a ghetto. In retrospect this now seems to reflect an excessive optimism and overconfidence. Practising Christians are everywhere in a minority, and in the English-speaking world baptised Catholics are also in a minority. We are regularly swamped and battered by the consumer society in which we live.

One of the most important developments to follow from the Council was the development of the Catholic participation in ecumenism, a social benefit in Australia as well as something that is doctrinally essential for the different followers of Jesus Christ. Friendship and co-operation are far preferable to the hatred and violence of, e.g., Northern Ireland. The Council also urged regular dialogue and good relations with the other great religious traditions, an approach which is now under new pressures with the rise of Islamic fundamentalism. The Declaration on Religious Liberty, which espoused the view that the State cannot compel people to follow Catholic truth, which recognises people's civic rights to choose the truth as they see it, was also a significant development. The consequences of this civic doctrine are also now being wrestled with within Church life.

The most immediate consequence to follow from the Council was the introduction of the celebration of the sacraments in the vernacular languages, rather than Latin, something the Council itself never decreed and which Pope John XXIII did not foresee.

Often the major achievement of the Council is described as the doctrine of the collegiality of bishops, the explicit recognition that as successors of the apostles bishops share leadership of the universal Church, with and under the Pope, the successor of Saint Peter. The Council immensely strengthened the position of the bishops and had the consequence of internationalising the Roman Curia. Nearly all the cardinals leading the Roman Curia now have many years of pastoral experience in their home dioceses. Unfortunately there was not a corresponding development in the theology of the ministerial priesthood.

Another important but under-noted development was the espousal of the role of the laity, of the rights and responsibilities that follow from Baptism. This was first apparent in the order of chapters in *Lumen Gentium*, the constitution on the nature of the Church where the dignity and role of all the baptised was discussed before that of the clergy. Here the Council has been followed by wonderful but perhaps unexpected fruits, and not only in the parish councils and school boards which are now commonplace.

There is no doubt that this was a reforming Council, but the Council preferred to use the term renewal *Ecclesia Renovanda* rather than the term reformation used by Luther. Perhaps in the light of our present troubles an even better title would be *Ecclesia Semper Purificanda* that is a Church always in need of purification.

Where Are We Now?

It is now more than forty years since the start of the Second Vatican Council. The number of Catholics in Australia is still increasing, with a rise of 202,000 between the 1996–2001 censuses. There are increasing demands on nearly all Catholic agencies. Catholic school numbers are rising as is the number of facilities for care of the aged, while hospitals continue strongly. The Catholic Centacare agencies still make an enormous contribution to healing in our society. As a bishop I am one of the few privileged people who regularly visit many of our different parishes and institutions.

Very few if any of our Catholic parishes are dead or dying. In many places they are strong and vibrant communities, which figure very rarely in the public media. Vocations to the priesthood are now almost adequate in some of the major Catholic archdioceses, although in other places numbers continue to be low. Unfortunately many religious orders are dying, their demise welcomed by some of their members. I am told that one or two orders have already formally decided to take no more novices. Although many religious are retired, members, young and old, still contribute magnificent service to the community. This has to be replaced in some way if the Church's contribution to the Australian community is not to be radically reduced. The new lay movements which flourish in some countries overseas have not had equal growth here, but we have some vigorous youth groups, and increasing numbers have gone to the World Youth Day and experienced either genuine conversions or a strengthening of existing faith. Approximately 17 percent of Catholics still worship at Sunday Mass, a number which has fallen from approximately 50-plus percent forty or fifty years ago. We still have formidable strengths in many areas, quite unmatched in all the other mainline Christian Churches. Many of our Catholic ethnic communities remain particularly strong.

Catholic liberalism seems to be dying, and there are only small pockets of Catholic radicals. It is hard to find a Catholic dissident under fifty years of age. There are a few people in Australia who speak loudly of "loyal dissent", a new category which has been introduced into the conversation since the Council. When does loyal dissent become unacceptable disloyalty?

Catholicism teaches that Christ is the Son of God who came to redeem and save us and explain to us the secrets of this life and the next. His teaching has a unique authority. We regard it as divinely revealed rather than simply the work of human intelligence.

For any religion which claims to be divinely revealed there are two burning questions: (1) What is the essential core of belief and practice that must be preserved in any restructuring and updating? (2) What is necessary for continuing or increasing spiritual vitality? These questions are different, and the answers are not entirely the same.

The nub of the difficulty is identifying where the legitimate diversity in nonessentials begins after the unity which is necessary in essentials. At every level of course there should be charity.

From the first days of Christianity a hierarchy of truths has been recognised with fundamental truths enshrined in either the baptismal promises or in the creeds said at Mass, e.g., the Apostles' Creed, the Nicene Creed.

The category of loyal dissent now means that many want to stay as full communicant members of the Catholic Church while rejecting specific doctrines of faith and morals that nearly everyone would have regarded as essential in the past. Examples from my own limited experience of such doctrines include the denial of the divinity of Christ, claims that abortion and euthanasia can be legitimate, that homosexual activity and pre-marital sexual activity generally should also get a tick. Other possibilities which are urged are the reception of Communion after divorce and remarriage, and women priests. Yet a further category would touch on the issues of artificial contraception and married clergy.

Why and how have we arrived at this situation? George Weigel, the author of the best biography of Pope John Paul II, claims that theologians today learnt from the fate of Charles

Davis, who left the Catholic Church round about Christmas time 1966 over important doctrinal differences. He disappeared from public view, being mentioned publicly only at his death some years ago. Weigel suggests that dissident theologians have learnt from this and believe they can get much more publicity for their views while remaining in the Catholic Church. There is no doubt that many, perhaps all of them, want to reform the Church in major areas, to make it more "acceptable", to bring it closer to the spirit of the age. And one of the enabling mechanisms for this has been the appeal to primacy of conscience.

Conscience

I believe strongly in the importance of individual conscience. It is indispensable. I have already endorsed the Second Vatican Council document on Freedom of Religion. In the past I have been in trouble for stating that the so-called doctrine of the primacy of conscience should be quietly dropped. I would like to reconsider my position here and now state that I believe that this misleading doctrine of the primacy of conscience should be publicly rejected.

Let me tell you a story. At a cocktail party one evening a fairly prominent figure in Australian public life told me that he was not a Christian because he could no longer believe in the divinity of Christ. I replied that I agreed that he could not be a Catholic while rejecting the divinity of Christ, but it could be possible for him to call himself a Christian, if he accepted many of Christ's teachings about God and on morality. "No", he said, "I do not accept the divinity of Christ, and therefore I am not a Christian. But I do believe in God and I am not frightened to meet my Maker after death."

This was a man of integrity. He had reached a wrong conclusion, but there was every indication that he had come to this decision honestly and honourably. I admired his integrity. He acknowledged that he stood under the truth, that he would answer to God, and that he had to take the consequences of his position regarding membership of the Catholic Church. This was an appropriate exercise of individual conscience, even though, as I mentioned, the conclusion was mistaken.

In chapter 3 of the first letter of Saint John, read at Mass some weeks ago, Saint John spells out the link between conscience and the commandments, between freedom and truth. He explained that the way to love God is to follow his commandments. This is basic. Christians have no entitlement to define sins out of existence, to deny or ignore fundamental teachings of faith, by claiming that their consciences are free or that they believe in the primacy of conscience. There is no substitute for personal sincerity, and we honour striving for the truth. But our consciences can be mistaken, sometimes mistaken through our own fault. And in any event we have to take the public consequences for our positions. It will not help me in a court of law to claim that I did not realise I was driving on the right hand side of the road!

It is somewhat misleading also to claim that our conscience is free. Free for what? We do not boast that we are free to tell lies, although usually lies do not put people in gaol. Neither do we boast that we are free to read our watch in any way we like, to get the time wrong intentionally. So too with conscience. Conscience is at the service of truth; it stands under God's word. Conscience has no primacy. Truth has primacy. The Word of God has primacy. When basic Catholic and Christian doctrines are explicitly and sometimes publicly denied, basic questions of personal integrity then have to be answered. I believe that the mischievous doctrine of the primacy of conscience has been used to undermine the Church, used to justify many un-Catholic teachings, ranging as I mentioned from denying the divinity of Christ to legitimising abortion and euthanasia.

The so-called primacy of conscience offers no useful way forward in our current dilemmas.

What Is to Be Done?

I was born during the Second World War. I can remember as a youngster my mother explaining to me what a shock it was when the British base at Singapore fell to the Japanese, probably the greatest defeat in British military history. The Japanese came down the Malayan peninsula while most of the big British guns faced out to sea.

A similar thing happened with the old Chinese empire. For hundreds of years they were concerned about the approach of enemies from the west and the north. Hence the Great Wall of China. In the nineteenth century Europeans invaded from the East, they came in from the sea.

Those Christians who believe that the fortunes of Christianity can be revived by conforming basic teachings of faith and morals more closely with the spirit of the age are like the British and Chinese of old; their defences are facing in the wrong direction. Similarly those within the Christian Churches, liberals or radicals, who are struggling to eliminate many important Christian moral teachings are damaging fellow Christians; something like friendly fire in a war. There can be no retreat from the basics of the Apostolic tradition of faith and morals, although we must continue to penetrate it more deeply in dialogue with the modern world and with new and developing insights from a variety of modern and ancient disciplines like philosophy, medicine, and psychology.

For many this is counter-intuitive. However it is interesting to chart the areas where there is Christian vitality today, especially among young people. This is overwhelmingly where the fullness of the Christian tradition is taught, where the call to conversion is taught, the call to repentance and belief following the person and teachings of Jesus Christ. This is already true in Australia.

Undoubtedly the major challenge is with young people and with middle-aged people. Many of those have not been adequately introduced to the basics of the Catholic tradition. In fact a contemporary temptation is to rely on someone else to be teaching the basics so that in fact these rudimentary truths are not explained strongly and clearly at all. Such basics include: (1) the teaching that the one true God —Father, Son, and Spirit—loves us, especially when we are in trouble; (2) that Jesus Christ the only Son of God redeemed and saved us through his teaching, suffering, death, and resurrection; (3) that there is one true Church led by the Pope and the bishops, although we work happily with our sister Churches such as the Orthodox and with the other Christian denominations; and (4) that Christ calls us to follow him. In other words Catholicism is primarily a religion concerned about worship, service, and right personal conduct. On too many occasions the principal energy of some Catholics has been diverted into other areas; for example, nationalism, being successful, keeping the organisation running efficiently, concern for social justice or ecology or life issues or feminism. It is not too difficult for the primary religious call to be misplaced.

It might also be an appropriate time to say a few words on the sexual scandals that have beset the Catholic Church. Their gravity cannot be ignored or underestimated, but I believe that these abuses and crimes (and the way they have been dealt with) are symptoms of malaise and confusion, evidence of personal sin and evil rather than evidence of widespread corruption. We must continue to face up to the truth and deal justly with complaints. We should also acknowledge that only a small minority are offenders. Clear moral standards are a help to everyone in avoiding sin and to superiors in enforcing discipline. People, religious and irreligious, are correct to insist that we practise what we preach. It is not clear to me that mandatory celibacy is a major cause of paedophilia, most of which occurs in family situations. But bishops and religious superiors must continue to be vigilant against all misdemeanours, especially with children but also with adults.

Another important issue is women in the Church: The position of women in the Church continues to be vexed, even though most Catholic church-going women in Australia are not opposed to Church teaching against women priests.[1] There is some anecdotal evidence that religious practice is as unpopular among young Australian Catholic women as it is among young men,[2] a finding (if confirmed) which would be unprecedented in sociology. However we shall see continuing change here as the Western birth rate continues to fall and population numbers decrease radically in Europe.

As in the Roman Empire, the Catholic Church will have new opportunities to give leadership on the emancipation

---

[1] *Woman and Man: One in Christ Jesus: Report on the Participation of Women in the Catholic Church in Australia* (HarperCollinsReligious, 1999), p. 145, table 5.9.

[2] Catholic Church Life Survey 1996 (CCLS96).

of women from the constraints of a permissive and anti-child society, protecting women who choose not to enter employment and encouraging flexible working hours so that mothers with children can continue in the work force.

Conclusion

Undoubtedly the best-known exponent of the Vatican II exhortation to dialogue with the worlds of popular culture and contemporary thought is Pope John Paul II. In many areas, from philosophy through his great moral encyclicals to the theology of the body, he has broken new ground and changed the parameters. It is quaint to see a few commentators repeating positions fashionable in the 1970s and imagining that these continue at the centre of discussion and development.

Some talk also as though a change in the balance of power between the Roman centre and individual dioceses or bishops' conferences would radically enhance the preaching of the gospel and the number of personal conversions. This would be as effective as the Chinese stationing most of their troops in Sichuan to protect their Eastern seaboard.

Modern communications and travel have changed the way the Roman Curia and the Catholic world interact. These changes will continue. I even have a cautious optimism that some such changes could benefit Catholic life. My opposition to the suggestion that the political notion of subsidiarity, built on the premise that all power comes from the people, can be usefully applied to Church life does not betoken an opposition to gradual development, provided the special role of the successor of Saint Peter is preserved. Even baptismal power comes from God, and the priestly authority to teach, sanctify, and govern comes from ordination, the

From Vatican II to Today 467

sacrament of orders, not from majority opinion, especially
when most of these are not regular worshippers.

The Church always needs purification (*semper purificanda*),
especially through prayer and penance. All suffering, including the humiliation of public scandals, can be used as occasions for learning and improvement, for doing better, much
better.

Some Catholics, even senior students in Catholic schools,
might not believe in the divinity of Christ, the special status of the sacraments, the Real Presence, the authority of
the Pope. They might accept the legitimacy of abortion, euthanasia, and every form of adult sexual activity. In many
cases we are powerless to prevent this. But they should not be
so mistaken to imagine these are legitimate Catholic teachings. Clear Catholic teaching is needed.

In working to protect the core of the Catholic tradition
of faith and morals, the tradition bequeathed to us from
Christ and the apostles, one is not playing at cowboys and
Indians or cops and robbers. Whatever our position, these
are substantive issues, worthy of discussion and debate.

Over two thousand years the Catholic Church has weath-
ered persecutions, storms and trials, enemies from within
and outside. Secularism will prove a more enduring challenge than Communism, and the lethal influences on Catholic life, the acid rain, are coming from the society around us.

In the nineteenth century the philosopher Nietzsche
claimed that the newspaper had replaced daily prayer. Later
TV replaced the newspaper, and now the Internet is replacing TV! Last century G. K. Chesterton wrote that man has
always lost his way, but modern man has lost his address.

The Western world is more and more preoccupied with
self, extolling personal autonomy, obsessed with self-reali-
sation. People are urged to turn inwards, to confront the

emptiness with clichés from the New Age or the sophistication of Eastern religions.

Catholicism strikes out in a different direction. The Vatican II constitution on the Church in the World (par. 22) insists that the human mystery is intelligible only in the light of Christ. "Through Christ and in Christ, the riddles of sorrow and death grow meaningful. Apart from his gospel they overwhelm us." Christ and the Catholic tradition call us to faith, hope, and love, to an eternity of happiness won through Christ's death and Resurrection. The Church reminds us of the necessity of community, of the moral law, natural and revealed; reminds us too that we need to worship and pray regularly.

Membership in the Catholic Church is a wonderful honour. We belong to a proud community of worship and service; flawed and sinful certainly, always in need of purification, but a tradition of truth, beauty, and unselfish love.

This is why the Catholic Church has survived and continues to prosper, even in Australia.

Acknowledgments

Thank you to Father Joseph Fessio, S.J., founder of Ignatius Press in San Francisco, for publishing the American edition of this biography. For years, the many diverse publications from Ignatius Press have informed and inspired readers Down Under and strengthened their faith in Christ and his teachings more than Father Fessio or his team could ever know.

Thank you to my editor, Vivian Dudro. Her patience and editing talents helped translate a few idiosyncratic Australianisms into the kind of English that will hopefully be understood on the other side of the Pacific. Only once was I rendered speechless—when she asked me the meaning of "bloody dill". I was tempted to inform her it meant "drongo", "jackass", or "as thick as two short planks" but settled instead for polite clarity with "not too bright". No wonder the Aussie slang dictionary grows thicker every year! Art director, Roxanne Mei Lum, and others who work with or for Ignatius Press have been helpful as well. After years as a journalist in the secular media, I only hope a little of the truly Catholic spirit of the people who make up Ignatius Press rubbed off on me.

Sincere thanks to Cardinal George Pell for being generous with his time, providing access to his written work, and answering questions so candidly and thoughtfully. It is important to place on record that while Cardinal Pell's recollections are central to the writing of this book, it is an unauthorized biography in the sense that he did not control what I wrote, including what was covered, or who was interviewed.

A special thank you to Margaret Pell for opening her heart and her treasure trove of photographs and memorabilia and for an unforgettable visit to the Pells' old family home and other places in Ballarat. Thank you, also, to David Pell for being so approachable and for providing several of the photographs used.

I am most grateful to Archbishop Denis Hart, Monsignor Peter Elliott, and Father Gerry Diamond for invaluable reminiscences stretching back to the 1960s and to Father Michael Mason, C.Ss.R., whose friendship with George Pell dates back more than half a century to their Ballarat schooldays. Bishop Anthony Fisher and philosopher Doctor Hayden Ramsay provided fascinating insights into George Pell's five years as Archbishop of Melbourne. In Sydney, Cardinal Pell's loyal and dedicated staff, Doctor Michael Casey and Josie Tesoriero, were wonderfully obliging and professionally helpful throughout this lengthy project, and I thank them both sincerely.

Thank you, also, to the following who made time to answer questions about particular aspects of George Pell's life to date and/or to help with valuable research materials: Archbishops Sir Frank Little and Eric D'Arcy; Fathers Vincent Bywater, S.J., Paul Connell, Peter Cross, Sam Dimittina, Martin Dixon, Brian Harrison, Peter Joseph, Bob Maguire, Frank O'Loughlin, Charles Portelli, Julian Porteous, Greg Pritchard, Leo Saleeba, James Staunton, Michael Tate, Edward Yarnold, S.J., John Walter, and Mark Withoos; Doctor

Amin Abboud; Paul Bongiorno; Marc Florio, Gerard Henderson, Michael Gilchrist, Nola Jenkins, Michael Kelly, Professor John Molony, James Power, Clare Ryan, Ana Snjaric, Rob Stove, Professor Claudio Veliz, Peter Westmore, and some helpful parishioners at Swan Hill, especially Claire Betts, Margaret Jirik, and Audrey Walsh.

Lance DeVine provided a fascinating guided tour at Propaganda Fide, Rome, as did Mark Waddington at Saint Patrick's College, Ballarat. Priest, author, and musician Peter Brock not only published his own highly readable recollections of Propaganda Fide, *Home Rome Home*, at a perfect time to provide a valuable source for material about Propaganda in the 1960s, but he lent me his treasured copies of *Loquitur*, containing George Pell's first forays into journalism as a student in Rome.

While the idea of writing this book first occurred to me while listening to Cardinal Pell preach at B. A. Santamaria's funeral in March 1998, Bob Santamaria and I had several lengthy conversations about Catholicism in general and George Pell in particular in 1996 and early 1997. What I learned from these was particularly useful when it came to putting together chapter 9, "Preparing for the Second Spring".

In 1999, Professor George Weigel set a new standard for papal biographies with *Witness to Hope*, the definitive biography of Pope John Paul II. I am honored to have his foreword at the front of this work.

Most of all, loving thanks to the one person who was there in Sydney at the first interview at Saint Mary's Cathedral presbytery on federal election day, November 10, 2001, and who trekked countless times through Brisbane, Sydney, and Tullamarine airports on Friday and Sunday nights, endured the Ballarat/Bendigo/Swan Hill/Melbourne drive with good grace and a few good books, trouped around Rome, Oxford, and the Cotswolds, and fixed the computer whenever I was in trouble. Jacinta gives me the heart that makes it all worthwhile and, like me, enjoyed getting to know George Pell.

TESS LIVINGSTONE
All Seasons, Brisbane
Our Lady Help of Christians
Patron Saint of Australia
May 24, 2004

Index

Readers from around the world are invited
to email their comments to the author on
pellbiog@hotmail.com